BENJAMIN FRANKLIN

Philosopher & Man

ALSO BY ALFRED OWEN ALDRIDGE

Man of Reason: The Life of Thomas Paine
Benjamin Franklin and His French Contemporaries
Jonathan Edwards

FRENCH EMBLEMATIC PORTRAIT OF FRANKLIN
At last Diogenes has found a *Man!*

BENJAMIN FRANKLIN

Philosopher & Man

BY

ALFRED OWEN ALDRIDGE

Philadelphia & New York

J. B. LIPPINCOTT COMPANY

TO ADRIANA

CONTENTS

CONTENTS

A Foreword

THE concept of the "many-sided" Franklin has existed from the time of the earliest books about him, but nearly all biographers have neglected his human side in favor of the heroic. This panegyrical discreetness has prevailed despite the frank exposure of his frailties in the writings of John Adams and other contemporary observers. The present biography is designed to bring up to date all essential aspects of the story of Franklin's life while emphasizing the man himself.

Since James Parton's celebrated nineteenth-century two-volume biography, which probably never will be entirely superseded, only two biographers have added materially to our concrete knowledge of Franklin—Verner W. Crane and Carl Van Doren. Crane's work, not intended as a full-scale study, gives an admirable sketch of Franklin's political career, particularly in his years as a colonial agent. Van Doren's comprehensive survey treats solidly and thoroughly Franklin's achievement in every area but conceals his lustiness, his acknowledged vanity, and his occasional callousness toward fellow human beings.

Franklin's contemporaries were understandably awed by his eminent political and scientific accomplishments. When they portrayed him on canvas and in stone, they gave his physiognomy a distinction and dignity which he did not possess in nature. In the same way, every modern biographer has overlooked or tempered certain human frailties in order to emphasize Franklin's role as a philosopher or statesman. He represented the nobility of nature, not perfection.

Although the present biography avoids the excess sweetness of previous interpretations, it is in no sense a *chronique scandaleuse* or an exercise in debunking. My object is not to draw attention to feet of clay. Indeed Franklin's type of enlightened *joie de vivre* is more to be admired than condemned.

My purpose is to reveal Franklin as a man first; as a universal genius second. I am actually going back to the method approved by some of Franklin's contemporaries, who deliberately "set aside the dignity and grandeur" of the subject to "shew nothing more than the man."

   In attempting to synthesize all that is known about Franklin's life and character, I am, of course, indebted to the research and discoveries of a long line of biographers, historians, editors, antiquarians and critics. My own previous publications on Franklin have been devoted primarily to identifying hitherto unknown periodical pieces and in tracing intellectual sources. In the following pages I have, to some degree, pursued a similar method of relating Franklin's ideas to his historical milieu. But I have subordinated specialized bibliographical and critical concerns to the more rewarding task of examining a complete personality—of relating the human qualities of a superbly talented man to the crowded panorama of his achievements.

                                                       A. O. A.

1. A Start in Life

WHEN Franklin's French contemporaries wished to sum up the elements of his greatness, they placed under his portrait the single word VIR, Latin for *man*. They respected his achievements as a scientist, economist, diplomat and man of letters but admired his human qualities even more.

Franklin was not a great man primarily because he invented the lightning rod, edited *Poor Richard's Almanack,* or persuaded the French court to ally itself with the new United States. If Franklin was "the greatest American of them all," it was because his personality shone out beyond his achievements. He had an intense interest in all phases of life, particularly in science and human relationships, because he found amusement in them. Franklin's "equable disposition or happy constitution" together with his insatiable emotional and intellectual curiosity brought about his success in practical affairs and earned him the respect of his peers.

In his day-to-day existence, Franklin sought to extract the utmost drop of physical and intellectual experience. Like Poor Richard he cared "not so much to live long as to live well." And although unquestionably a genius in an age of universal knowledge, Franklin believed that "he that lives well is learned enough." He never forgot his proletarian origins and responded to most situations with the impulses of the common man. In terms of a proverb he adapted from Bishop Berkeley, he wrote with the learned but pronounced with the vulgar.

Most of Franklin's family were not learned or even well educated. His mother, sister, wife—all spelled by ear and formed halting sentences with great difficulty. Yet Franklin wrote to them—as well as to children and various youngsters whom he adopted as intellectual protégés—with an affectionate relish which he never felt in his relations with heads of governments and societies of scholars.

[3]

Nearly all of what we know about Franklin's early life is drawn from his autobiography, an amazingly frank revelation of many of his most intimate feelings and activities, including some of his major "errata." But even though, like every other autobiography, it naturally presents the subject in the light in which the author wishes to be viewed, reflecting the portrait which he hopes to be handed down to posterity, the autobiography also indirectly reveals aspects of Franklin's mind which he may not have been cognizant of himself.

By and large agreeing with Dr. Johnson that a biographer should pass over incidents producing vulgar greatness and stress domestic details, Franklin brought together in his memoirs the simple affairs of his daily life, his humble concerns and intimate thoughts. These are the matters which he considered most important, and these are the aspects which will be stressed in the present biography.

Franklin was dedicated to the principle that man's whole life should be rational in the eighteenth-century sense of methodical, disciplined and ordered. In his autobiography he presents some of his rational systems: of making money, of attaining virtue, of keeping fit, and even of worshipping God. He tried to impose a discipline upon himself in each of these areas, but at the same time his emotions frequently led him to violate his rules. He was conscious of some of these failures—completely unaware of others. In theory he wanted to be a moral superman; in practice he succeeded in being a plain human being.

While still a boy Franklin adopted his earliest system to regulate life according to reason: a strict vegetarian regime. In his autobiography he attributes his decision to reading Thomas Tryon's *The Way to Health, Long Life and Happiness,* a book which prints scores of meat recipes even though advising against their use, but he told his French friends he reached it through reading Plutarch's *On the Custom of Eating Flesh.* Franklin adhered to his resolution until one day the odor of sizzling fish toppled the system: he remembered seeing small fish taken out of the stomach of larger ones and concluded, "If you eat one another, I don't see why we mayn't eat you." Later recognizing his sophistry, he commented wryly, "So convenient a thing it is to be a *reasonable Creature,* since it enables one to find or make a Reason for everything one has a mind to do."

Born into a large family, untroubled by theories of over-population, Franklin throughout his life strongly approved of maximum procreation and close family ties. As there was scarcely a subject of any kind within his purview which he did not find interesting, he always had "a pleasure in obtaining any little anecdotes" of his ancestors. He even sought and obtained exact accounts of every person of his family as far back as 1555, "when it was established in England." On one of his trips to England he took his son on an expedition to Northamptonshire to search the parish register of Ecton, where he learned that he was "the youngest son of the youngest son for five generations back." Always intrigued by coincidences or examples of design in nature, Benjamin fancied a similarity in character and career between himself and his uncle Thomas, who had died in 1702, just four years to the day before Benjamin's birthday, 6 January 1706.* Had it been on the very same day, "one might have supposed a transmigration," for Uncle Thomas had been a scrivener, "a considerable man in the county affairs" and a "chief mover of all public-spirited undertakings for the county or town of Northampton."

Another of Franklin's uncles, the Benjamin for whom he was named, came to America in 1715 and lived to a great age. "He was very pious, a great attender of sermons of the best preach-ers," which he took down in his own system of shorthand and later offered to bestow upon the young Benjamin. Zealous Protestants since the early days of the Reformation, all members of the Franklin family adhered to the Church of England until the end of the reign of Charles II, when Franklin's Uncle Benjamin and his father Josiah renounced the family tradition to become nonconformists. Because conventicles or associations for independent worship had been forbidden by law, Franklin's

---

* Dates before 1752, when Great Britain and the colonies adopted the Gregorian calendar, are given Old Style; those from 1752 on, New Style. Cf. Franklin's 69th birthday, 17 January, 1775, p. 244.

father emigrated to New England in 1683. He sired three children in England and four more in America before the death of his wife. His second spouse, Benjamin's mother, gave birth to ten more.

Franklin, born in Boston, was "the youngest son, and the youngest child but two." One of the most vivid memories of his childhood was sitting at his father's table when thirteen children were present. His mother was Abiah Folger, daughter of "one of the first settlers of New England." Both sides of his family, therefore, had a respectable history and solid material stock in society. But since the economic substance of the family was based upon continuing labor, daily work was considered as vital as property. The family made candles and soap, and Franklin blew soap bubbles. Equally important with work in the family tradition was a sense of independence—of respect for the dignity of the individual and his rights, particularly in religion. Franklin's father and uncle had imbibed the stern piety of Puritanism, and this more than any other influence conditioned the Boston household. Out of this background grew Franklin's common-sense materialism, his intellectual and political independence, and his pleasure in children and family relationships. In religion, however, he reacted against his environment rather than inclining toward it, discarding his father's strict Calvinism in favor of a broad toleration. As a child, bored by the tedious family devotions which he was forced to attend, he learned geography by studying during his father's interminable prayers four large wall maps which hung in the parlor. And one day when his father was salting down a barrel of herring to serve during the winter months, Franklin asked, "Why not ask the blessing now over the whole barrel to save the trouble of doing it at each meal?"

In his old age, Franklin remembered hearing Increase Mather preach and retained impressions of Cotton Mather in the vigor of his usefulness. One may reasonably assume that Mather Byles, Increase Mather's grandson, was one of Franklin's childhood playmates. Byles, only one year younger than Franklin and like him an incorrigible punster, probably swapped funny stories with his friend. As adults, Franklin and Byles did each other favors, and Franklin testified to their having been acquainted for many years.

Shortly after Franklin's sixth birthday, his father bought a house at the corner of Union and Hanover Streets. "It was Indeed a Lowly Dweling," his sister Jane later recalled, "but we were fed Plentifully, made comfortable with Fire and cloathing, had sildom any contention among us, but all was Harmony: especially between the Heads—and they were Universally Respected, & the most of the Famely in good Reputation."

Franklin's sober father had the power of observing human conduct and character, a trait which Franklin inherited and used to advantage in his political career. He remembered his father's shrewd observation that those who loved one another at a distance, particularly relatives, frequently quarreled when they came together. Franklin saw concrete proof in his father's association with his uncle Benjamin: the two brothers wrote extremely affectionate letters, when living apart, but generated disputes and misunderstandings when they came together in the same house.

Franklin particularly commended his father's "sound Understanding and solid Judgment in prudential Matters." At table the elder Franklin customarily led the conversation to some useful topic which might improve the minds of his children, turning their attention to "what was good, just, and prudent in the conduct of life." Conversely, they were taught to pay little attention to the food on the table, a circumstance which may explain why Franklin in later life was indifferent to a refined cuisine.

In his autobiography Franklin says practically nothing at all about his mother except that she had an excellent constitution and suckled all her children. In his old age he confided to the eminent French physician Cabanis that he owed much of his natural good sense to her sound judgment and steady calm. She tolerantly accepted his eccentric vegetarian diet, and when his friends enquired what had brought it about she calmly replied, "a mad philosopher," but added, "There is no great harm—this will give him the habit of self-control; he will learn that everything is possible with a strong will." She also encouraged him in active sports, allowing him in particular to indulge his fondness for swimming. In our day, Franklin would certainly have earned a high-school letter. He anticipated by two centuries the devices of modern frogmen. While still a boy he made two oval palettes for his wrists, "each about ten inches long and six broad, with a hole for the thumb," and fitted similar sandallike contrivances to his feet. These made him skim through the water at increased speed. He also used a kite to propel him across a mile-wide pond while he floated on his back, an early example of his technical ingenuity. Swimming remained one of Franklin's favorite diversions. Later in London he gave professional lessons, and in his old age he passed on the art to his grandson, going back and forth across the River Seine in Paris.

Childhood for Franklin was a normal, active period in which his natural curiosity and exuberance led him to gradually increasing awareness of the wonders of animal life and the complexities of human relations. Even though Boston had no zoo, Franklin sometimes had the chance to see exotic animals. A good-natured merchant once paid twopence a head for Franklin and his schoolfellows to see two moose which had been brought to the city as a great rarity. And, like many other boys, Franklin kept pigeons at home and experimentally learned mating and nesting habits.

The young Franklin was so susceptible to the bright uniforms of soldiers and other trappings of military splendor that, in his fourth year, his uncle Benjamin felt it necessary to admonish him gently in verse with the warning that war is a dangerous trade. Franklin sometimes formed his own moral precepts as an aftermath to painful experience. One holiday at the age of seven when his pockets were filled with halfpence, he became so fascinated with the sound of another boy's penny whistle that he paid out all his money for it and returned triumphantly home. When the older children, taunting him for his folly, convinced him that he had given four times as much as the whistle was worth, Franklin cried with vexation. The indelible impression which this incident made—he was still talking about it in his seventies—indicates a deeply ingrained fear of being cheated, which was responsible in some measure for his business success.

According to his own account, Franklin always took the helm when he went sailing with other boys—and he sometimes led them into scrapes. One he remembered because it exhibited a precocious spirit of public service, although misdirected. Wanting a dry foothold in a salt marsh where he and his band used to fish for minnows, Franklin noticed a heap of stones which had been piled up for constructing a house; he engaged his playmates to move them to the marsh and reassemble them as a wharf. Franklin's father rebuked him for this feat of organization on the grounds that "nothing was useful which was not honest."

Franklin earned his leadership as much through his powerful fists as through his dominant personality. As a "boxing boy," he followed the tradition that "even after an adversary said he had enough," it was allowed "to give him a rising blow."

Because Franklin learned to read almost as soon as he could talk, his father enrolled him in the grammar or Latin school in his eighth year, intending him "as the Tithe of his Sons, to the Service of the Church." Franklin entered as middle pupil in the first-year class, advanced to head pupil, and in less than a year was promoted to the second class in order to move with it into the third class in the following year. But Franklin's father abruptly withdrew him, having decided that ministerial rewards were too small to justify the expense of a college education. For about a year Benjamin was sent to a writing and arithmetic school, where he easily acquired a fair hand but failed in figures. Then at the age of ten he was put to work in his father's business, manufacturing soap and candles, a trade which he heartily disliked.

When his father realized that this aversion was too ingrained to be overcome, he feared that Benjamin's hankering for the sea might lead him to run away. He began taking him for informative walks by tradesmen's shops and yards so that he might observe which trade the boy seemed inclined to. From these walks Franklin acquired a pleasure in seeing workmen of all trades handle their tools, and he picked up the knack of using some of them himself. After a brief and unsatisfactory trial with a cutler, Franklin at the age of twelve reluctantly signed indentures as an apprentice to his brother James, who had just returned from England with a printer's press. Although only gradually reconciling himself to the sacrifice of his career at sea, Franklin soon realized that the printing trade brought with it one great advantage: access to good books.

He embarked upon his serious reading with *Pilgrim's Progress* and progressed to Plutarch's *Lives.* At the same period he read a poor translation of Pascal's *Les Lettres Provinciales,* a work to which he returned with delight on repeated occasions. He also read Bacon's essays and, like everyone else in New England, the Bible. But unlike most Bostonians, Franklin was particularly attracted by the Book of Proverbs, which he prized for its excellent lessons applicable to daily life, expressed in pithy and energetic phrases. Thus as a boy Franklin acquired his taste for formulating generalizations about human conduct in apt, precise maxims. Later he would be introduced to the work of La Rochefoucauld, who had brought the art to the highest development it has ever reached, and before long Franklin would himself produce the greatest collection of proverb literature in the western hemisphere.

Franklin read his way methodically through his father's library, which consisted chiefly of polemic divinity, and paradoxically hereby adopted the deism which became the predominating philosophy of his life. The books against deism which he read at the age of fifteen turned out to have just the contrary effect to that intended, for the deistical arguments appeared to Franklin stronger than the refutations. After the weak antidote he soon progressed to the strong physic, Shaftesbury's *Characteristics,* the deists' Bible, after which his scepticism became irrevocably entrenched.

Although Franklin's father failed in inculcating the principles of orthodox Christianity, he had more success in molding his son's literary style. As early as his seventh year, Franklin had begun to write verses—good enough to inspire his Uncle Benjamin to indite a poetic tribute to the child in "Hanging-sleeves" who could "Read, Write, and Rhime Like Men." Five years later Franklin turned out some commonplace jingles on a maritime disaster and on a notorious pirate. Although "wretched stuff, in the Grub-street ballad style," Franklin's brother saw the commercial possibilities of the poems, printed them, and sent the boy with awakened vanity to hawk them about town. His father stepped in before this juvenile infatuation with the Muse could develop into serious dedication; he ridiculed the halting verses—giving his son a volume of Pope to read for contrast—and pointed out the close connection between poetry and starvation. Franklin henceforth retained his affection for verse making but never again took his poetic efforts seriously.

In prose, however, Franklin's efforts were more salutary. His writing became not only a principal instrument for his advancement, as he says in his autobiography, but probably the most efficient tool at his service in every intellectual and political activity in which he engaged. Here again the elder Franklin exercised a wholesome control. Benjamin had been engaged in a dispute with another bookish lad over a subject considered radical at the time, "the propriety of educating the female sex in learning." They put their arguments in written form, passing them back and forth. Prophetical of the tutorial role he was to assume in later teacup seminars with several feminine protégées, Franklin took the affirmative side. His father, happening to find Franklin's papers, subjected them to a rigid stylistic analysis, pointing out that they were superior in punctuation and spelling—an advantage derived from working in the printing shop—but they were deficient "in elegance of expression, in method, and in perspicuity." To attain these qualities, Franklin, like nearly every aspiring writer in the classical English tradition, thereupon gave his days and nights to Addison. But he followed a system more ingenious than would have occurred to Dr. Johnson. Setting down a number of paragraph headings, he would try to reconstruct an entire *Spectator* essay after allowing several days to elapse. Realizing that a lack of vocabulary was a primary deficiency which might have been obviated had he continued as a poet, he turned whole essays into verse and then after several days back again into prose. In this endeavor his rationalism succeeded—he developed the lucid style which made him the first great writer in American literature. For Franklin the indispensable characteristics of good writing were clarity, precision and smoothness. These he exemplified in his own works—all of which combine purity with vigor, classical ease with colloquial strength. In gratitude for the help which Addison's writings had afforded him, he later declared that they had "contributed more to the improvement of the minds of the British nation, and polishing their manners, than those of any other English pen whatever" (*Poor Richard* for 1748).

After perfecting his style, Franklin considered himself ready for original composition and aspired to see himself in print. His brother had established a newspaper in 1721, the *New England Courant,* the fourth in America, where he printed local literary materials as well as news from Europe. Having reason to suppose that his own compositions would be rejected with disdain, Franklin wrote under a pseudonym, Silence Dogood, and left his papers at night under the door of the printing shop. More than a pseudonym, Silence Dogood was a completely developed personality conceived in the vein of Isaac Bickerstaff and Sir Roger de Coverley. Ostensibly the widow of a New England minister, this vital literary character combined a love of virtue and political liberty with "a natural Inclination to observe and reprove the Faults of others." Franklin had the "exquisite Pleasure" of hearing his essay warmly commended by his brother and the coterie of local wits who gathered in the printing shop. In speculating on the identity of the author, they named only those reputed for learning and imagination. Franklin's brother immediately printed the piece along with a request for more contributions from the same pen. Franklin gleefully obliged, delivering in the same manner thirteen other papers, ranging from a burlesque of Harvard divinity students to an imitation of Alexander Pope's satirical receipt to make an epic poem. At sixteen Franklin had more than justified his uncle's prediction of a precocious literary career.

When Franklin finally avowed his paternity of Silence, his brother offered him only grudging congratulations, fearing that this success would add to Franklin's vanity and assurance. James and Benjamin were probably too much alike to be good business associates. James considered their relationship to be that of master to apprentice, whereas Benjamin wanted it to be that of brother to brother. When their frequent disputes were taken to their father, he usually sided with Benjamin. The elder brother, considering this a mark of favoritism, naturally became even more exasperated, and the master and apprentice drew further apart.

A stroke of luck suddenly paved the way for Franklin's release from his brother's service. James in an issue of the *Courant* had affronted the government of Massachusetts by suggesting that it had been dilatory in its obligations to defend the coast against pirates. The General Court in retaliation ordered the printer to be imprisoned for the rest of the legislative session. Franklin thereupon took over nominal management of the *Courant,* a development which afforded him an opportunity to wriggle out of his indentures, of which he promptly took advantage, even though he resented the high-handed behavior of the government toward his brother. James was finally released, but on the condition that he submit his paper to censorship. As an expedient to keep the *Courant* in existence and still preserve his own interest in it, James continued printing it under the name of Benjamin Franklin. And to make the arrangement pass inspection, he signed Franklin's papers of indenture with a full discharge (a document to be shown in public) —and in secret they executed new papers of indenture under the original terms.

The paper continued under Benjamin's name for several months, but Franklin eventually rose up against his brother's control and declared his independence. In his autobiography Franklin alleges that his brother frequently lost his temper and beat him and attributes his own "aversion to arbitrary power" to his brother's "harsh and tyrannical treatment." He was undoubtedly extremely sensitive, and on those occasions when his father did not take his part he suffered acutely, imagining that the entire world had combined against him. But brother James may not have been quite as tyrannical as Franklin imagined, and the precocious apprentice, flushed with his literary triumphs to the point of arrogance, may have been a difficult worker to contend with. Franklin later admitted that he had not been quite fair in taking advantage of his brother's inability to enforce the secret indentures and called his sly extrication from them one of the "first errata" of his life.

James saw to it that his brother was blacklisted by all the Boston printers. In the meanwhile Franklin's exuberance and disputatiousness had acquired for him the reputation of a political firebrand, and good people singled him out in horror as an "infidel or atheist." This time his father unequivocally supported James, and Franklin determined to violate his articles of indenture by flight. Realizing that a shipmaster would never take aboard a runaway apprentice, he fabricated a plausible story: he was leaving town to avoid marrying a girl whom he had made pregnant. As he later recognized, he fled as a fugitive and, like Parson Adams and Tom Jones, had the world before him with no other guide than good fortune or his good sense, which had not yet been cultivated by experience.

Arriving in New York and finding no printing work available, Franklin set off for Philadelphia on a journey filled with discomfort and fatigue. On the first stage, by water to Amboy, a furious squall blew up, during which Franklin saved a drunken Dutchman from drowning. All hands aboard remained soaked to the skin during "30 Hours on the Water, without Victuals, or any Drink but a Bottle of filthy Rum." The next stage of the journey—on foot to Burlington—took nearly three days of weary trudging. But Franklin's luck turned on the evening of his arrival when a boatload of travelers offered him a ride to Philadelphia. Since there was no wind, they were forced to row the entire eighteen miles, Franklin taking the oars with the rest. City lighting in those days was not as the light of the sun, and at midnight the argonauts were not certain whether they had reached Philadelphia or rowed past it. They landed on the banks of a creek, therefore, and, making a fire of some old fence rails to keep warm from the October night, waited until daylight, when they discovered they were almost within sight of the city. A short row brought them to Market Street wharf early the next morning, a Sunday.

Although Franklin's entire funds consisted of a Dutch dollar and a shilling and the others considered his rowing ample recompense for his passage, he insisted on paying them the shilling. He remarked in his autobiography that a man is "sometimes more generous when he has but a little Money than when he has plenty, perhaps thro' Fear of being thought to have but little." This example of Franklin's early generosity or vanity shows that even as a youth his celebrated frugality existed more in word than in deed.

In retrospect, Franklin felt that he had made a ludicrous showing on his first appearance in Philadelphia, tired, hungry, clad in work clothes, a change of linen protruding through his stuffed pockets. He immediately looked for a bakery, the most reliable source of cheap and substantial food. Prices and shapes were different from those in Boston, and when Franklin asked for threepenny worth of bread, he was given three enormous rolls. Placing one under each arm and eating the third, he marched up Market Street, passing in front of the house of his future wife, Deborah Read, who smiled at his awkward appearance. Returning to the river for drinking water, he gave his two remaining rolls to a woman and child from the boat—certainly an example of disinterested altruism.

Franklin next fell in with a stream of Sunday morning worshippers and followed them to the Quaker meetinghouse. He entered and promptly fell asleep. After the service he found an inn, where he went to bed for the rest of the day. The next morning he discovered that there were two printers in town, neither one very well qualified for the trade. Both gave him part-time work, and he found lodgings at the home of John Read, father of the girl who had smiled at him as he passed with his arms full of bread. Later, when his chest of clean clothes arrived by sea, and he began to accumulate money in his pockets, she began to imagine him as a potential husband.

Franklin's prestige and his self-esteem rose together when the governor of the province, Sir William Keith, sought him out with many compliments at the printing shop, took him to drink wine at a tavern, and there made the flattering proposal that, if he would set up his own business, the governor could send his way the official printing of the colonies of Pennsylvania and Delaware. It is hard to believe that such an important personage as the governor would have thus concerned himself with a lad of seventeen—the explanation is found in the unique position of the printing craft in colonial Philadelphia. It was one of the few mechanized trades and was at the same time closely affiliated with the arts, which were not then in a flourishing state in the colonies. Also the administration depended upon local printers for the supplying of currency, legal forms, notices and other documents. Since Franklin with his Boston experience greatly excelled either of his employers in knowledge and ability, the governor had reason enough to notice him. Also, the governor was engaged in a political struggle with the colonial proprietors, and a new printer could be very useful.

Sir William drafted a letter to Franklin's father, praising the young printer and painting a glowing picture of the advantages he would find in Philadelphia as proprietor of his own shop. While waiting for a suitable vessel to take him with this letter to seek his father's help in Boston, Franklin dined occasionally with the governor and kept the project of starting his own business a strict secret from his employer—behavior more politic than honorable. In April 1724, Franklin set sail, pretending to his employer that he was merely going to see his friends. His family, which had received no news whatsoever about him during the seven months of his absence, welcomed him joyfully—all except his brother James. Franklin added insult to injury by visiting the printing shop to show off the opulence he had acquired by violating his contract—a watch, a pocketful of silver, and a suit much better than he ever wore when being clothed by his brother. After treating the journeymen to his "raree-show," Franklin ostentatiously gave them money for drink. His brother, feeling that he had been injured before his workmen, turned his back on Franklin, and even their mother failed to win him to a reconciliation.

On this trip Franklin visited the famous preacher and

scholar, Cotton Mather, who received the precocious youth in his library. On the way out, the minister warned his guest about a low beam in the passageway by saying hastily, "Stoop, stoop!" But Franklin, immersed in the conversation, misunderstood and hit his head. Mather thereupon remarked, "You are young, and have the world before you; STOOP as you go through it, and you will miss many hard thumps." In his old age, when telling this story, Franklin remarked that this sound advice beaten into his head had frequently been of use to him, but at the time in his relations with his brother he certainly carried his head as high as he could.

Franklin's canny father categorically refused to set up an eighteen-year-old in an expensive and complicated business but promised to reconsider the matter when his aggressive son should come of age. Doubting the governor's good faith or his good sense, he nevertheless wrote a polite letter of thanks for his interest in his son's future. Franklin took ship back to Philadelphia, the vessel en route narrowly missing a crisis with a sunken rock and Franklin a crisis with two friendly strumpets.

When the boat made a routine call at Newport, Rhode Island, Franklin visited another brother, John, fifteen years his senior, who had always treated him with great affection. One of John's friends, named Samuel Vernon, asked Franklin to collect some money for him in Pennsylvania and hold it on call. Franklin obligingly carried out the request but almost immediately used part of the money for his own needs. "Breaking into this money of Vernon's" he later considered another major "erratum," and it weighed heavily upon him for years.

After Governor Keith heard of the failure of Franklin's mission, he blandly promised to finance the printing shop himself, inflating the naive youth's grandiose expectations by exhorting him to go immediately to England to purchase type and contract with booksellers to handle their wares in Philadelphia. Franklin, taking these blandishments seriously, resolved to take passage on the next boat, and while waiting for it to sail went back to work for one of his former employers, Samuel Keimer, an eccentric intellectual with many of the traits of today's beatniks.

Given to both religious enthusiasm and delights of the flesh, this "odd Fish" was slovenly to an extreme, wore his beard at full length, and rejoiced in disparaging accepted traditions. Although Franklin considered him somewhat of a knave, there is no record of any transaction in which Keimer got the better of Franklin in sharp practices. Keimer was twenty years older than Franklin, but they associated as equals and contemporaries outside working hours. Franklin indeed adopted almost a patronizing attitude toward his employer. When Keimer wanted him to collaborate in setting up a new religious sect based on Keimer's twin doctrines of observing the Sabbath on the seventh day and leaving his beard unshaved, Franklin agreed on the condition that Keimer, a ravenous gourmand, accept Franklin's doctrine of strict vegetarianism. Their joint religion, which they practised for three months, made no demands on their sexual pleasures, for they at least once entertained women together in Keimer's lodgings.

Franklin also paid more or less serious court to Deborah Read, for whom he had "great respect and affection." But since her mother was in the secret of Franklin's imminent departure and Deborah was two years younger than Franklin's eighteen years, the watchful mother kept the romance from progressing to a compromising stage. When Franklin finally set sail, they "interchanged some promises," and that was all. Governor Keith was too busy to see Franklin during the days before sailing, but Franklin went on board believing that the governor had made provision for him in his official dispatches. On arrival in England, Franklin discovered that the governor had done nothing in his behalf, possessing neither the influence nor financial means to do so. With good intentions and a desire to please, he had deceived the young man as effectively as though he had been a confidence man.

Franklin's printing trade served him, however, when promises had not, for he had no difficulty getting work at one of the city's most important publishers, Palmer's. After he had been there some months, he set the type for the 1725 edition of a well-known deistical treatise, *The Religion of Nature,* by William Wollaston. Feeling dissatisfied with Wollaston's hypothesis of free will and his distinctions between good and evil, Franklin wrote a refutation which he printed at Palmer's under the title *A Dissertation on Liberty and Necessity, Pleasure and Pain.* In it he argued that man is a machine, denied the distinction between virtue and vice, set forth a novel psychological theory that our pain is exactly balanced by our pleasure, and denied the immortality of the soul. Although Franklin seemed to admit the existence and sovereignty of a god, he limited his deity by mechanical operation to such a degree that his god turned into as much of a machine as man.

Franklin's treatise of virtual atheism has close resemblance to a French seventeenth-century tradition of the beast-machine. Franklin probably did not know French well enough at this time to have read Descartes and other exponents of the notion in the original, but he may have heard discussion of the beast machine in London taverns. His treatise extended the concept to human beings a quarter of a century before a notorious discourse by La Mettrie appeared in France entitled *The Man-Machine.*

Franklin's argument runs: "As Man is a Part of this great Machine, the Universe, his regular Acting is requisite to the regular moving of the whole." Regular acting means following a preordained pattern. Since all human actions are part of a vast chain of cause and effect, the moral world has the same flawless regularity and order which exists in the stellar universe. Franklin believed, therefore, that we are much better off as controlled beings than we would be as free agents. The motivating force behind human activity, he attributed to pain—every organism reacting in a perpetual effort to avoid it. Our sensations, Franklin depicted as an alternating cycle of pleasure and pain in equivalent degrees—going from one extreme to the other like the pendulum of a clock.

Franklin designed his pamphlet to shock his readers both in ideas and style. He expected no acclaim, therefore, for his doctrine which brought mankind down to the level of field animals. Franklin's employer found the pamphlet completely abominable and expostulated with him against it. We can see why earlier in Boston and Philadelphia Franklin had been pointed at for being "an infidel or atheist" as well as for his lampooning and libeling. Franklin later considered his pamphlet another "erratum," as we shall see in a subsequent chapter.

Meanwhile, because of his pamphlet, Franklin was taken up by a literary surgeon, a certain Lyons, who introduced him to the cynical philosopher Bernard Mandeville, whose style Franklin had emulated in his pamphlet. Mandeville presided over an alehouse club, where Franklin saw him in his glory, "a most facetious, entertaining companion." The nineteen-year-old Franklin was not held back in any of his London activities by the least sign of diffidence. He had no hesitancy in attacking Wollaston, a divine whose book commanded great respect. Franklin was not even a minister, let alone a theologian. He had merely become accustomed to intimacy with the great: winebibbing with Governor Keith and hobnobbing with Mandeville.

Franklin's first year in the metropolis was a round of visits to theatres, taverns, and any other gay resort he could afford. His inseparable companion was James Ralph, a minor poet later to be satirized by Pope. They had sailed from Philadelphia together, Ralph abandoning a wife and daughter. Since Franklin bore most of the expense of their nocturnal ramblings, he was unable to save for his return passage to Philadelphia. To Deborah he wrote only one letter, and that was to hint that he had no plans to leave London.

Ralph eventually took up with an attractive young milliner and persuaded her to become his mistress. Since she lacked the means to support them both, Ralph went off to the country to work as a schoolmaster, leaving his paramour vaguely under Franklin's care. Because of her liaison with Ralph she had lost most of her customers and was obliged to call frequently upon Franklin for financial aid. Profiting by her dependence, he began seeing her regularly and worked up to some "familiarities," which she not only rebuked and resented but reported immediately to Ralph. The latter took advantage of the situation in his own way by telling Franklin that he had no intention of repaying the money which Franklin had lent him.

Franklin now began to think about acquiring some capital and took a new job in a larger printing shop, Watts's, where he soon rose to become a high-speed compositor. He started out, however, working the press, a job requiring stamina and stalwart muscles. Franklin was a vigorous, husky youth and deliberately chose the arduous presswork in order to satisfy his need for physical exercise. As he abandoned his tavern companions, he tells us in his autobiography, he reverted to health dieting and persuaded many of his co-workers to take hot-water gruel for breakfast instead of beer and cheese.

Perhaps one should not accept without some question Franklin's professions of abstemiousness, for in his old age he confided to James Madison that as "a young man he was much subject to fits of indigestion brought on by indulgence at the table." On the advice of one of his friends, Franklin carried a vial of oil of wormwood around with him as a remedy for overeating and then "went on sinning more freely than ever."

As the novelty of the glitter and excitement of London life began to wear away, he contemplated a voyage over the European continent, to be financed by giving swimming lessons en route. But a benevolent citizen of Philadelphia, Thomas Denham, who had previously befriended him, advised him to return to Philadelphia and offered to give him employment in a store he was about to establish there. Franklin agreed on the spot, for he had grown tired of London. Its hustle and bustle and cosmopolitan atmosphere had appealed to him at first, but he came to associate the metropolis with his mistakes—the moral cynicism he had manifested in his desertion of Deborah, his trifling with Ralph's mistress, and the materialistic philosophy of his pamphlet. Revolting against all this, he sought to attain moral equilibrium through the sober atmosphere of Philadelphia. Possibly he even began to think once more about Deborah, for he later wrote that "the Cords of Love & Friendship" had drawn him back to Pennsylvania. Material prospects could hardly have been decisive, for the annual salary which he had agreed upon with Denham represented less than he could make in London—even though opportunities may have been greater in the new world. And from the point of view of literary prestige, his London pamphlet certainly overmatched his Boston journalism.

Franklin's sojourn in the metropolis may not have brought him a fortune, but it had rewarded him with "some very ingenious acquaintance," allowed him to read considerably, and brought him face to face with the realization that his happiness depended on a relatively stern pattern of moral conduct.

As he began the voyage back to Philadelphia, Franklin glimpsed the coast of France on the left, the town of Dover with "the green hills and chalky cliffs of England" on the right, and voiced the appropriate "Albion, farewell." On the eight-week voyage, he passed the time in playing cards and checkers, a game he delighted in, in observing marine life, and in writing a journal. The most important part of this journal was a four-part plan which Franklin formed for the future conduct of his life. First, because of the weight on his conscience of having appropriated Vernon's money, he determined "to be extremely frugal for some time, till I have paid what I owe." Second, he resolved to speak truth and aim at sincerity; third, to apply himself with industry to any business he might undertake and not be led astray by such schemes as Keith's for rapid riches; and, finally, to speak ill of no man whatsoever, but to praise whenever appropriate. Significantly, Franklin made no reference whatsoever to God. His spiritual awakening was to come later.

Franklin and Denham landed in Philadelphia, 11 October 1726, and immediately opened their store. They lodged and boarded together almost as father and son, an early example of the ease with which Franklin could enter into intimate personal relations. Unfortunately, five months later, just after Franklin's twenty-first birthday, both fell seriously ill. Franklin came close to death, and his kindly benefactor eventually succumbed.

After his recovery Franklin somewhat reluctantly returned to his old trade of printing. Samuel Keimer had assembled a half dozen "raw, cheap hands" to run his business, and he was delighted to have an experienced operator such as Franklin to break them in and put his establishment in order. At first Keimer treated his foreman with respect and civility, but after six months, when his workers had grasped the hang of things, he became disagreeably authoritarian and captious. The breaking point came one day when a commotion outdoors caused Franklin to stick his head out the window to investigate, and Keimer, who happened to be standing below, berated him for slacking. Humiliated in front of his fellow workers, Franklin replied indignantly; they exchanged injuries and counter injuries; and Franklin finally walked out in a huff, sacrificing his right to a quarter's notice. This behavior contrasted sharply with Franklin's state of mind a few months later when he systematically sought to acquire moderation by observing the injunction: "forbear resenting injuries so much as you think they deserve."

On the night of Franklin's explosion, one of the journeymen, Hugh Meredith, a genial ne'er-do-well, came to him with a proposition for setting up a rival printing shop. Meredith's father was to put up the capital, and Franklin was to supply the managerial and mechanical skill. Franklin consented, and before Keimer even knew what was going on, his competitors were established in a house near the market with a press and sparkling new type from London. By this time, Franklin had many friends who exerted themselves to find him customers. Orders came in regularly, in small numbers at first, more in a short time. Franklin rapidly built a thriving business on two principles: industry and quality. On one occasion when Bradford, under contract to the Pennsylvania Assembly, printed an address to the governor in a slipshod unesthetic manner, Franklin and Meredith reprinted it "elegantly and correctly" as an advertising scheme and sent a copy to each member. Soon they became the official printers.

Printing to Franklin was more than a trade or a means of livelihood. He found real pleasure in holding the composing stick, smelling the ink, and bearing down on the press. Greatest of all was the esthetic satisfaction of reading a finished page—beholding the straight columns and perceiving the words without error. Franklin was proud of his craft and proud of his abilities as a superior craftsman. With the first capital he had clear after paying his debts, he ordered a set of small-letter type from

London—and boasted of being the only printer in America to possess it.

In the early days, Franklin often worked past eleven at night setting or distributing type. He worked hard not only so that he could fill the maximum number of orders but also to use his labor as a form of advertising: by making it visible to his neighbors, he increased their respect.

He was proud of the comment of one of them: "The Industry of that Franklin . . . is superior to anything else I ever saw of the kind; I see him still at work when I go home from Club, and he is at Work again before his Neighbors are out of bed." Franklin dressed simply, avoided "places of idle diversion," and gave up sports such as hunting and fishing. To show that he was a plain man, not ashamed of labor, he sometimes trundled paper through the streets on a wheelbarrow.

Soon another of Keimer's employees, George Webb, came to Franklin, asking for work. Franklin, having none available at the moment, indiscreetly confided that he planned very soon to establish a newspaper and might in the future be able to use another hand. At that time there was only one newspaper in Philadelphia, Andrew Bradford's *American Weekly Mercury,* which Franklin considered "a paltry thing, wretchedly manag'd, and no way entertaining." Webb returned to Keimer and blurted out Franklin's project to set up a rival newspaper. Keimer, deciding that the idea was good enough to adopt, issued proposals for a newspaper of his own and published the first number 24 December 1728. Not in the least troubled by modesty, he called his paper *The Universal Instructor in All Arts and Sciences and Pennsylvania Gazette,* the title referring to extracts from an encyclopedia then being published in London, which Keimer reprinted in regular segments, beginning with the letter A. Franklin was justifiably annoyed at Keimer's duplicity and went to work systematically to undermine his paper. Keimer's encyclopedic transcription gave him his first opportunity. Without thought to the consequences, Keimer had reprinted verbatim the article ABORTION (21 January 1729), replete with certain biological details which maidens in the Quaker city were not in the habit of reading. Franklin quickly took advantage of the slip. While waiting to issue his own newspaper, he waged the battle against Keimer in the pages of the *Mercury*. Under the pseudonyms of Martha Careful and Celia Shortface, as spokesmen for modest women of the city, he issued a warning, 28 January 1729, that if Keimer continued his indecent revelation of feminine secrets in taverns and coffee houses, Martha and her sister Molly were "Resolved to run the Hazard of taking him by the Beard . . . and make an Example of him for his Immodesty." In the next week, Franklin began in the *Mercury* a series of sprightly essays, "The Busy-Body," designed to expose by contrast the dull and heavy fare of the *Universal Instructor*. In the third number he depicted the character of Keimer under the guise of Cretico, a "sowre Philosopher" and "cunning States-man, . . . crafty but far from being Wise." According to Franklin, "the cringing, mean, submissive Deportment of thy Dependants [Webb and the other printers] is (like the Worship paid by Indians to the Devil) rather thro' Fear of the Harm thou may'st do to them, than out of Gratitude for the Favours they have receiv'd of thee." Keimer retaliated with more direct personal abuse—the first literary attack ever directed against Franklin. As epigraph, Keimer used a very poor paraphrase of Dryden:

> *He seems to be*
> *Not one but every Ape's Epitome.*

In the same vein, he characterized Franklin as an obscure fellow and poor poet with "Merits as threadbare as his Great Coat, and Scull as thick as his Shoe-Soles."

As Franklin expected, Keimer's newspaper soon went under—either because of its poor printing and dull content or the effect of Franklin's satire in "The Busy-Body." After Keimer's subscription list fell to ninety, he sold out to Franklin for a trifle. Franklin shortened the name of the paper to the *Pennsylvania Gazette* and began, 2 October 1729, a successful publishing career of more than thirty years. Meredith, who was drunk most of the time and a poor workman, sold his share after nine months, leaving Franklin as the sole proprietor as well as editor and feature writer.

2. Wife and Children

IT IS time for a word about Franklin's physique and features, a subject heretofore strangely neglected. Not until Charles Sellers's magnificent discussion of Franklin in art have we had an accurate word picture of his appearance. Franklin's height was an inch or two short of six feet; and his proportions seemed massive, a large head on a large body. Bishop William White was the authority for ascribing to him "a very handsome leg," the reason perhaps for his writing a squib as an old man entitled *The Handsome and Deformed Leg*. As he grew older, he put on more and more weight, until in old age he was fat by the standards of his day. The years also made him stoop, this tendency combined with his stoutness making some observers consider him short. As a young man, he had a crop of dark brown hair, which gradually thinned to a silvery grey semibaldness. His eyes were hazel, his mouth unusually wide but in old age somewhat pursed. The best contemporary description is that of Deborah Logan, remembering him in his sixties:

He was fat, square built, and wore his own hair, thin and gray: but he looked healthy and vigorous. His head was remarkably large in proportion to his figure, and his countenance mild, firm, and expressive. He was friendly and agreeable in conversation, which he suited to his company, appearing to wish to benefit all his hearers.

Although not an Adonis, Franklin was a strong and vigorous man with all the qualities to appeal to women, especially after he overcame the rawness and innocence of youth.

During the period that Franklin was keeping his press going all of the day and most of the night, he gave a thought every now and then to his family back in Boston, particularly to his favorite sister Jane, six years his junior. Six months after his return to Philadelphia, when Jane was approaching her fifteenth birthday, he sent her a spinning wheel as a present with a somewhat pompous letter accompanying it. Hearing that she had become a celebrated beauty, he had been on the verge of sending a tea table but had decided on the more utilitarian gift on the grounds that the character of a good housewife is preferable to that of a pretty gentlewoman. Perhaps Franklin was even then considering the advantages of marriage for himself. He unctuously reminded his sister that "modesty, as it makes the most homely virgin amiable and charming, so the want of it infallibly renders the most perfect beauty disagreeable and odious."

Probably Franklin's brothers and sisters continued to look upon him as headstrong and brash and left him alone to go his own way. In June 1730, he wrote to his elder sister Sarah complaining that for two years he had not received a line from any relation with the exception of his mother and father. A year later Sarah died, and Franklin heard the melancholy news from Jane—along with other woeful tidings that another older sister, Mary, suffered from a breast cancer. Although repudiating the idea of superstition, Franklin reported incidents of cures in Pennsylvania which had been operated by the wearing of a shell of wood on the breast and promised to do his best to procure this treatment for his sister.

In his letter to Sarah in June 1730, Franklin had written, "I am not to be married as you have heard." Three months later he had taken Deborah Read as his wife, and at about the same time he became the father of an illegitimate son.

The story of Franklin's amorous pursuits in this year is the most obscure and intriguing of his whole life. His autobiography gives us some information on his "marriage" but none whatsoever about the antecedents of his natural son, William, for whose benefit the autobiography was purportedly written. The fact of William's illegitimacy has been common knowledge almost from the moment of his birth, but no biographer has been able to name his mother. Some have even speculated that it may have been Deborah before Franklin made an honest woman of her.

Originally Franklin satisfied "that hard-to-be-governed passion" of youth by frequent "intrigues with low women," a solution which he found both hazardous to health and expensive. He first entertained thoughts of taking a wife when the family with whom he shared his house, that of Thomas Godfrey, a surly mathematician, threw an attractive female relation in his way by means of repeated supper invitations. Franklin, finding the lass pleasing, was ready for the match but, since dowries were customary in the period, felt entitled to enough money to pay off his outstanding debts, about one hundred pounds. The family demurred and proceeded to keep the lovers apart, either because they felt that Franklin's financial prospects were not bright or, as he suspected, because they counted on the enforced separation to inflame his ardor and push him to a clandestine marriage with no settlement whatsoever. Franklin's resentment of the Godfreys' niggardly behavior was so great that he severed all relations. But with his mind now inclined toward marriage, he began seeing more of Deborah Read and soon rekindled the spark of romance. The obstacles in the way of a match here, however, were almost insuperable. Ill-fated Deborah, after receiving Franklin's discouraging letter from London, had given up hope of seeing him again and had been persuaded to marry a potter, John Rogers, who soon turned out to be a worthless adventurer already in possession of a wife. Deborah refused to live with him or bear his name, but her continence unfortunately could not nullify the marriage. The rascal fled to the West Indies, where it was rumored that he died, leaving Deborah in the ambiguous state of neither maid nor confirmed widow. She could not prove that the potter had died or that he had married her illegally. What was clear, however, was that he had left many debts in Pennsylvania, which Deborah's next husband might be liable to. Despite all these hazards, Franklin decided that Deborah would make a suitable helpmate and "took her to wife, September 1st, 1730." This means merely that they undertook a common-law relationship since a ceremony was out of the question. Franklin says nothing about a financial settlement, but evidence from legal documents and ledgers still extant indicates that the Reads were a family of considerable substance in the community and that they showed their gratitude to Franklin in a tangible fashion. Four years after the union, Deborah's mother deeded jointly to her son and two daughters and sons-in-law a valuable property on High Street.

It is not clear whether William Franklin was born before or after Franklin began to live with Deborah, but, in view of his attitude toward the expense of pleasure outside of the marriage bed, a prior time is highly likely. The only evidence is a letter from Franklin to his mother, 12 April 1750, in which he describes her grandson as "now 19 Years of Age, a tall proper Youth, and much of a Beau." This would indicate, of course, that William had been born a respectable period after his father's marriage. But it is quite possible that Franklin deliberately concealed two or three years of his son's age to keep from distressing his parents. It has been argued that William's real age must have been considerably more than Franklin represented since William received a commission as ensign in the Pennsylvania militia in 1746, which would have made him only fifteen had he been born in 1731. And even for the eighteenth century this was a tender age for an officer.

One thing is clear. Less than three months before his marriage Franklin had been associated in the public eye with some type of liaison. Otherwise he would not have been obliged to tell his sister that he was "not about to be married as you have heard." Could the rumor have started because of his attentions to the relative of the Godfreys, to Deborah, or to a third woman, perhaps the mother of his child?

Strong reasons to suppose that a third woman was indeed William's mother and that she was one of the low creatures whom Franklin sometimes frequented came to light in 1764 when he was attacked in a scurrilous political pamphlet, *What Is Sauce for a Goose Is Also Sauce for a Gander*. Here William's mother is pictured as an obscure, neglected female with no means of support other than a mere pittance unfeelingly doled out by Franklin. The pamphleteer disclosed that this unfortunate creature had just died and accused Franklin of hurrying her away, without a burial dress, to an unmarked grave.

Franklin's earlier biographers, uncertain whether to take this story of a disreputable and shameful connection as truth or

malicious slander, have generally ignored it. Some have preferred to accept a hypothesis much more flattering to
Franklin—that William's mother was actually Deborah. The
slim evidence on which this theory is based is that William in
letters frequently referred to Deborah as "my mother" and she
addressed him as "my son." This evidence is almost entirely
discounted, however, by the circumstance that the entire Franklin family continually employed all manner of pet names and
affectionate terms without much regard to literal relationships.
Deborah and Benjamin in their letters, for example, addressed
each other as "My dear Child." Some biographers have even
asserted that Franklin had an illegitimate daughter merely
because he used the same salutation in letters to a quite innocent English girl.

The main reason for considering Deborah at all is the
contention that colonial laws against bastardy were more rigidly
applied to the woman than to the man. Deborah, therefore, it is
said, would have been afraid to acknowledge William whereas
Franklin had nothing to lose by doing so. This theory is
nullified by the fact that Franklin's later children, known to be
Deborah's, were both considered legitimate. Since Franklin
went through no legal ceremony in marrying Deborah, there is
no reason why she could not just as well have acknowledged
William.

A contemporary eyewitness account reveals, moreover, that
Deborah showed uncontrolled animosity in William's presence
and used venomous language about him. Daniel Fisher, employed by Franklin as a temporary clerk in 1755, when William
was about twenty-five, reported that Deborah was consumed
with jealousy because she considered that Franklin treated his
son with greater esteem than herself or their daughter Sally.
William at that time neither boarded nor lodged in his father's
house but frequently visited on business, a fact which can be
documented by sources other than Fisher. When William became deputy postmaster during his father's absence in 1753, he
moved the post office from Franklin's house to his own bachelor
residence in Third Street. At confrontations between William
and Deborah, they exchanged no greetings or other words

whatsoever. On one occasion Deborah hissed, as William passed, "Mr. Fisher, there goest the greatest Villain upon Earth." She continued with "Invectives in the foulest terms" Fisher ever heard from a lady. So great was Deborah's antipathy toward William that Fisher became convinced that her violent spirit would never accept his treating William with respect, and on that account he regretfully gave up his position with Franklin. Deborah's extreme aversion toward William fits much better the hypothesis that his mother was a low wench than that she was Deborah herself.

The most convincing evidence to confirm the theory that William's mother was a disreputable woman of the streets has only recently come to light and is here published for the first time. In the year before the publication of *What Is Sauce for a Goose,* one of Franklin's associates, George Roberts, replied to the query of a friend who had heard some unpleasant gossip about William:

'Tis generally known here his Birth is illegitimate and his mother not in good Circumstances, but the Report of her begging Bread in the Streets of this City is without the least foundation in Truth. I understand some small provision is made by him for her, but her being none of the most agreeable Women prevents particular Notice being shown, or the Father and Son acknowledging any Connection with her.

This is a private letter—not a weapon of political warfare—and there is no reason to question its sincerity. When it is considered in conjunction with the evidence previously available, it leads to the conclusion that Franklin's sexual need had led him to an intrigue with a disreputable woman, one perhaps even older than himself, that she had borne him a son which Franklin had been unwilling to trust to her care, that he had declined to maintain any close connection with her but had provided a subsistence allowance until her death.

Franklin's decision to marry Deborah probably had nothing to do with his having an infant son on his hands. He would have had no objection to turning over his child to some sober, responsible family for rearing if he had continued a bachelor.

Franklin found in Deborah someone who could help him in his rising business, who brought with her extensive material aid—dowry or family connections—and who offered a reasonably adequate outlet for his sexual energies.

What manner of woman was Debbie? Her portrait, made as she was just entering middle age, gives the impression of a plump, pasty-faced, and fiendishly respectable *Hausfrau.* She was merely two years younger than her husband, and about the time of her portrait, when Franklin was in England, he was put in mind of her by a large toby jug. He was of course tactful enough to point out the resemblance in affectionate terms: the jug "look'd like a fat jolly Dame, clean and tidy, with a neat blue and white Calico Gown on, good natur'd and lovely."

Two essays in the *Pennsylvania Gazette,* almost certainly by Franklin although not printed in any edition of his works, go into the subject of shrewish wives, one of Franklin's methods no doubt of coping with Deborah's notorious bad temper. One of them (11 January 1733) depicts a character type, Mrs. Saltbox, who "like some other good Housewives, is apt to be a little loud, somewhat sharp with her Tongue, and commonly reputed a Scold." The other essay (5 July 1733) defends the paradox that the conveniences of a scold greatly outweigh the inconveniences. "Women of that Character have generally sound and healthy Constitutions, produce a vigorous Offspring, are active in the Business of the Family, special good Housewives and very careful of their Husbands Interest. As to the Noise attending all this, 'tis but a Trifle when a Man is us'd to it." And Franklin, we may be sure, was used to it.

Someone has said that Franklin himself adopted Poor Richard's advice, "Keep your eyes wide open before marriage, half shut afterwards." And he is supposed to have said: "You can bear with your own Faults and why not a Fault in your Wife?" Also he adapted an Italian proverb for *Poor Richard* for 1734:

> Grief for a dead wife, and a troublesome guest,
> Continues to the threshold, and there is at rest.

Then he added, perhaps out of deference to Deborah:

But I mean such wives as are none of the best.

More than once during Franklin's married life, outsiders wrote to him complaining of some aspect of Deborah's behavior and appealing to him for satisfaction. After they had been living together for fifteen years, James Read, one of Deborah's distant relations, who had gone into business in the house next to Franklin's, got into some kind of altercation with Deborah and asked Franklin to arbitrate. Franklin replied with a good-humored letter, replete with a pun on *in angulo cum puella* (in a corner with a girl) which he had slyly changed to *in angulo puellae* (in the corner of a girl). Read and his wife had stopped their visits to the Franklins because of Deborah. Franklin expressed his fondness for his neighbors but at the same time pointed out that in domestic crises he was powerless to interfere. "Would you," he asked, "submit to the decision of a husband, a cause between you and his wife? Don't you know that all wives are in the right?"

One naturally wonders whether Franklin really loved Deborah or whether he was making the best of a bad bargain. When he took her to wife he undoubtedly, as usual, consulted his "true Interest." Deborah satisfied his sex needs and had the qualities to speed his material advancement. Her widowed mother came to live with the Franklins and brought with her enough property to set up the household in comfort. Deborah helped out in the printing business, keeping books and minding the store. She also manufactured soap and homespun clothes, Franklin at one time being clad from head to foot in wool and linen of her manufacture.

What Franklin expected from marriage can be seen from an anecdote about him which circulated in London. "When he heard people say, 'they were tired of a thing,' merely through a want of proper perseverance, he used to reply, 'Well, do as married people do: *tire* and *begin again.*' "

Franklin at all times regarded Deborah with affection. After twelve years of married life, he composed a song for public performance in appreciation of the qualities of his wife, whom he termed "my plain Country Joan." Partly in protest against conventional drinking songs enumerating the physical charms of mistresses, Franklin excluded all mention of "her Face, her Shape, or her Eyes" in order to extol her virtue alone. And physically Deborah was nothing to brag about anyway. To Franklin it was more important that she served as companion in health, as nurse in sickness, and that she managed his household with thrift and occasionally officiated as a hostess. Her faults through long association and habit became scarcely perceptible.

Within the family, Franklin's song was interpreted as an espousal of the "Matrimonial Interest." One of Franklin's nephews, Benjamin Mecom, having named a daughter after Deborah, expressed his opinion that Franklin's "Writing in praise of his lovely Joan, has made him the Spiritual Father of many . . . Children, born in honest Wedlock." Deborah probably found comfort in this back-handed reference to William Franklin.

During his sixties, Franklin advised a young man who had just entered matrimony: "Treat your Wife always with Respect; it will procure Respect to you, not from her only but from all that observe it. Never use a slighting Expression to her, even in jest, for Slights in Jest, after frequent bandyings, are apt to end in angry earnest." Franklin soon outgrew his wife socially and intellectually, but he followed his precept of always treating her with respect.

After Deborah had been dead for many years, Franklin began to idealize and romanticize. He said to Cabanis in his old age that Deborah "always knew what I did not know, and if something escaped me, I was sure that it was precisely that which she had seized." He told another of his French acquaintances, moreover, that he accustomed himself to being guided in difficult decisions by Deborah's opinions, going on the theory that women have a kind of tact which is much more sure than reason. Once he sang his song about Deborah to his French admirers on their wedding anniversary, almost fifty years after the union.

On 20 October 1732, Deborah provided her husband with

his second son, Francis Folger, so named in honor of the family of Franklin's mother. Almost nothing is known of little Francis except the circumstances of his death and that Franklin adored him. He died of smallpox, 21 November 1736, shortly after his fourth birthday. Smallpox at that period was one of the most frequent causes of mortality, and the efficacy of inoculation was bitterly debated by physicians and laymen. Franklin accepted the practice and had remarked to some of his friends that he intended to have the child inoculated as soon as he should have recovered sufficiently from the "flux," a common childhood ailment. Before regaining strength enough to take the new preventive, Francis caught the smallpox, and the report went round that inoculation had killed him. Franklin, who allowed his spirit of scientific exactitude and civic responsibility to master his grief, reported the true circumstances in the *Gazette*, 30 December 1736, in order that others might not be deterred from protecting their children. In *Poor Richard* for 1737, Franklin included some stoic verses on "The Thracian infant," whose birth, because of the sorrows of life, gives his parents grief and his death joy. It has been widely accepted that the death of Francis Folger inspired Franklin to write this brief poem. Actually it had been printed in *Poor Richard* several days before the death of his son and is not even of Franklin's composition. The verses are copied verbatim from an English collection of epigrams.

Franklin did compose for *Poor Richard* of this year, how-ever, a quotation defending inoculation against popular preju-dice.

> God offer'd to the Jews Salvation
> And 'twas refus'd by half the Nation:
> Thus, (tho' 'tis Life's great Preservation)
> Many oppose *Inoculation*.

The depth of Franklin's grief may be judged by his ordering a posthumous painting of Little Franky, an "artistic treatment usually accorded to high station and great wealth." And on his son's gravestone Franklin placed the inscription: "The DELIGHT of all that knew him." He never completely reconciled himself to the loss. In 1772 he confided to his sister that he still cherished thoughts of his "son Franky, . . . whom I have seldom since seen equal'd in every thing, and whom to this Day I cannot think of without a Sigh." And in the part of his autobiography written in 1788, Franklin revealed that his failure to inoculate Francis still weighed heavily upon him.

Six years after the death of Francis, Deborah gave Franklin another child, a daughter, named after Franklin's older sister Sarah and Deborah's grandmother. Although the new baby eventually became the darling of the household, Franklin seems at first to have been indifferent rather than tender, perhaps because she failed in his eyes to compensate for the loss of Francis. In his autobiography, moreover, Franklin did not even mention Sally, a rather clear indication of a casual attitude toward her. This circumstance is somewhat surprising since she was still living while Franklin was composing his memoirs, and he was very much concerned with the effect of his writing upon posterity.

In his autobiography, Franklin tried to give the impression that he rose in life through constant thrift and frugality—and that it was Deborah who introduced into the household certain luxuries which he grudgingly permitted. He was lucky, he said, to have a partner as disposed as himself to industry and frugality.

She assisted me chearfully in my Business, folding and stitching Pamphlets, tending Shop, purchasing old Linen Rags for the Paper-makers, &c. &c. We kept no idle Servants, our Table was plain and simple, our Furniture of the cheapest. For instance my Breakfast was a long time Bread and Milk, (no Tea) and I ate it out of a twopenny earthen Porringer with a Pewter Spoon.

After this circumstantial recital of his thriftiness, Franklin proceeded to relate how luxury can contaminate a household in defiance of the strongest principle. One morning as he was called to breakfast, he found at his place a china bowl and a silver spoon, which Deborah had bought for him without his knowledge. To Franklin's remonstrance, she had "no other Excuse or Apology to make but that she thought *her* Husband deserved" these luxuries as well as any of her neighbors. This fable would be more convincing if we did not know that at about the same time that Franklin was writing this part of his autobiography, he confided to a young friend, "Frugality is an enriching Virtue; a Virtue I never could acquire in myself; but I was once lucky enough to find it in a Wife, who thereby became a Fortune to me." Nevertheless, some years before this, Franklin accused Deborah of not being "very attentive to Money-matters [even] in your best Days." One hardly knows what to believe.

Franklin practised self-denial by fits and starts. At various times, particularly in his youth, he followed strict diets, some-times for health, more often for thrift; he drank water instead of tea; and he limited his venery to a minimum. At other periods, he drank with his pot companions, composed drinking songs, and frequented compliant ladies. The periods of privation stood out in his mind, and he stressed them in his autobiography ("I spent no time in Taverns, Games, or Frolicks of any kind"). We learn about his periods of normal gratification only indirectly, but they were nonetheless real.

All evidence points to Franklin's increasing indulgence in comforts along with his growing prosperity. In January 1739, he rented a more commodious house four doors nearer the river. By this time his retail business had come to embrace considerably more than the books, paper and printed documents associated with a printshop. In addition to these articles, Franklin sold chocolate, dry goods, clothes and spectacles. A specialty of the shop, and of many other branches of the Franklin family itself, was superfine crown soap. With the glib facility of a modern ad-man, Franklin extolled in the *Gazette* its qualities for cleansing fine fabrics "with Ease and Expedition."

Signs of Franklin's more ample scale of living may be found in the inventory of clothing which an Irish schoolmaster stole from his house in 1739. Among the luxury items in his ward-robe were a silk-lined Sagathee coat, "a fine Holland Shirt ruffled at the Hands and Bosom," and a pair of calfskin shoes. In a later theft in 1750, Deborah lost "a double necklace of gold beads," a long scarlet cloak with a double cape, and a "very remarkable" brocade print gown. In 1753 Franklin ordered from London a bolt of expensive Italian silk to make a suit for Deborah.

As already noted, one must also assume that Franklin's table was not quite as austere as he pretended in his memoirs. In addition to consorting with his pot companions at various clubs, Franklin composed a drinking song in 1745 inculcating the philosophy "there can't be good Living where there is not good Drinking." In later life, he became noted for his conviviality — and more than held his own in an age of heavy alcoholic indulgence.

3. Intellectual Clubman

AFTER setting up for himself in business, almost the first thing Franklin did in his leisure hours was to organize the young men of his economic status into an intellectual and benevolent society called the Junto, which came into being in the fall of 1727. His ostensible model was Cotton Mather, who had organized neighborhood church societies in Boston, but Franklin also took some hints from Addison's fictional Spectator Club and the convivial drinking clubs he had frequented in London. Meetings, held every Friday evening, consisted of debates and the reading of papers. Franklin drew up the rules. He "required that every member in his turn should produce one or more queries on any point of morals, politics, or natural philosophy, to be discussed by the company, and once in three months produce an essay of his own writing on any subject he pleased."

Before reading and discussing papers at the meetings, the members went through a ritual of question and response. By means of twenty-four "Standing Queries" they were expected to review their useful reading, report observations on business trends and opportunities, and indicate methods by which the other members could help them. They were asked, for example:

Hath any body attacked your reputation lately? and what can the Junto do toward securing it?
Is there any man whose friendship you want, and which the Junto, or any of them, can procure for you?
Have you any weighty affair in hand, in which you think the advice of the Junto may be of service?

New members before being admitted were required to answer negatively to the questions "Have you any particular disrespect to any present member?" and "Do you think any person ought to be harmed in his body, name or goods, for mere speculative opinions, or his external way of worship?" They were to answer affirmatively "Do you sincerely declare that you love mankind in general; of what profession or religion soever?" and "Do you love truth for truth's sake, and will you endeavour impartially to find and receive it yourself and communicate it to others?"

Franklin later boasted that the club was "the best school of philosophy, morals and politics" in the colony.

Although the high-minded ritual of the Junto suggests that it was entirely an organ for philosophical inquiry and social benevolence, Franklin's own testimony indicates that he shrewdly designed it as an instrument to help him and his associates to rise in the community. He tells us that every one of the members exerted himself to get business for Franklin's printing shop. And two of the body who were substantial citizens advanced Franklin the money which enabled him to dissolve his partnership with Meredith and become sole proprietor. These were William Coleman, a merchant's clerk, and Robert Grace, "a young gentleman of some fortune." Except for Philip Syng, a silversmith, the other members were of humble origin: three of Franklin's former subordinates at Keimer's, a copier of deeds, a self-taught mathematician (Thomas Godfrey), a surveyor, a shoemaker and a joiner. Franklin insisted that everything about the Junto, including its very existence, be kept secret, a sure way of strengthening the members' methods of mutual assistance. Franklin's apparent reason for secrecy was "to avoid applications of improper persons for admittance." By day the members kept their identity of Leather Apron Men; on Friday evenings only were they intellectual clubmen.

One of the first subjects which the Junto debated was "a cry among the people for more paper money." Franklin took their side against the wealthy inhabitants, who feared the evils of inflation. He had reached his opinion by contrasting the wretched condition of Philadelphia on the first day he saw it with its prosperity on his return from London, attributing the transformation to an emission of currency which had just taken place. Shifting his Junto arguments to a broader arena, he then published an anonymous pamphlet in April 1729, *A Modest Enquiry into the Nature and Necessity of a Paper Currency.*

Franklin followed the same approach to determine colonial economic policy which he had used to arrive at his personal moral standards. In his meditations and Junto discussions, he had devoted himself systematically to ascertaining what he and each rational being should consider "the Knowledge of our *true Interest;* that is, . . . what is best to be done in all the Circumstances of Humane Life, in order to arrive at our main End in View, HAPPINESS." In his economic pamphlet, he devoted himself to "the Knowledge of the true Interest of one's Country."

The sparse currency which existed in Pennsylvania at the time Franklin wrote his pamphlet was issued exclusively in the form of loans on land. Under colonial law, the amount to be loaned was strictly limited, never sufficient for prevailing commerce, and since the notes were gradually redeemed and called in, the currency in circulation was continually on the decline. In his pamphlet Franklin called for a radical increase in the amount of currency, proceeding on the principle, according to his later admirer, Thomas Paine, "If we have not Credit enough to borrow, perhaps we have Credit enough to lend."

Franklin's visual imagery—his knack of presenting abstract concepts in concrete form—enabled him to bring the complexities of colonial finance within the range of the most literal-minded of his readers. In one of his "Busy-Body" essays in the previous month, he had advised seekers of buried treasure and valuable mineral deposits that their most certain method of finding wealth was to abandon their subterranean excavating in favor of digging only plow-deep. Agricultural land was, in Franklin's opinion, uncoined gold. In his economic pamphlet, he described paper money as "coined Land," a brilliant summary of the currency system and a clever appeal for extending it.

In the next year, Franklin delivered to the Junto a discourse *On the Providence of God in the Government of the World.* Although not recognized as such, even in the latest edition of Franklin's works, his discourse was a deliberate refutation of his

London *Dissertation on Liberty and Necessity*. Not only is it plain that the argument of the Junto speech contradicts the *Dissertation,* but he specifically labeled it a refutation in one of his letters to Benjamin Vaughan, his friend and first English editor. For almost the only time in his career, Franklin proclaimed *mea culpa* in public.

He abolished the necessitarian position by simply calling attention to the existence of prayer. God would be a cruel joker if men were allowed to pray and supplicate in a world where everything is ordained; therefore all things must not be ordained. Franklin found equally unsatisfactory the opposite hypothesis—that God leaves everything in the universe to the operation of free agency. This presents the deity as an indifferent spectator or parent who has abandoned his creation. Franklin could find no other solution but "that the Deity sometimes interferes by his particular Providence, and sets aside the events, which would otherwise have been produced in the Course of nature, or by the free agency of men." He exhorted his listeners, therefore, to love and revere the deity "for his Goodness and thank him for his Benefits; . . . adore him for his Wisdom, fear him for his Power, and pray to him for his Favour and Protection." Religion of this kind, he promised, would be "a Powerful Regulator of our Actions, give us Peace and Tranquility within our own Minds, and render us Benevolent, Useful and Beneficial to others."

Franklin also proposed for discussion such questions as "Can a Man arrive at Perfection in this Life, as some Believe; or is it impossible, as others believe?" "Wherein consists the Happiness of a rational Creature?" "Whether Men ought to be denominated Good or Ill Men from their Actions or their Inclinations?" and whether it is worth while for a rational man to forgo the pleasures of eating and drinking for the sake of enjoying a healthy old age.

The old question of whether virtue may be taught Franklin had unequivocally answered in the affirmative. A primary means of instruction he felt was to publicize outstanding benevolent acts. He proposed, therefore, among the Junto questions: "Do you know of any fellow citizen, who has lately done a worthy action, deserving praise and imitation? or who has committed an error proper for us to be warned against and avoid?" He carried over this principle of advocating benevolence to *Poor Richard* for 1749, where he pointed out that we find no pleasure from hearing of perfumes in Arabia, music in China, or exquisite food in Japan. "But the benevolent mind of a virtuous man, is pleas'd, when it is inform'd of good and generous actions, in what part of the world soever they are done."

One day while reading history in 1731, Franklin conceived the grandiose notion of extending the Junto to form an intellectual League of Nations or International Rotary. His reading had brought him to the conclusion that all parties in world events, while presumably intent upon the welfare of a large body, are composed of individuals seeking their narrow self-interest. He reluctantly admitted that only a few individuals act with a view to the good of their country and fewer still with a view to the good of mankind. Franklin proposed to counteract this selfish spirit by uniting virtuous men of all nations into Juntos with an interlocking correspondence—in essence a super Junto or universal party for virtue. Franklin never carried out this ambitious and idealistic project, perhaps because his attention had been diverted to other affairs by the time he acquired the capital necessary to finance his travel to initiate the venture. Also, as he grew older and wealthier, he became more conservative and less confident that anything could be done to change the behavior of the masses of mankind.

We must not conclude that all concerns of the Philadelphia Junto were staid and self-righteous. The meetings were designed to promote conviviality as well as morality. At first they took place in a tavern, and Franklin referred to his fellow members as his intimate pot companions. Once a month on a Sunday afternoon during clement weather, the members crossed the river to engage in bodily exercise.

One may assume that Franklin used the convivial atmosphere of the club as an outlet for his facetious disposition. A great deal of punning went on at Junto meetings, and Franklin, who greatly enjoyed punning, claimed great talents in the art. Although there are no records of any of the jests at the Junto, we have full minutes of a similar society, the Tuesday Club at Annapolis, Maryland, where Franklin once participated in a ribald punning session. He attended a meeting at the home of Dr. Alexander Hamilton, on 22 January 1754, at which the secretary proposed that one of the members who was planning to leave the club, be "from a long standing . . . transmogrified into an honorary member." Jonas Green, editor of the *Annapolis Gazette,* immediately objected: "Why, Mr. Secretary, you would not have us dock the gentleman. I suppose the member, however he may stand now at this juncture, is as long as ever." After much laughter, the president rejoined, "The longstanding members methinks are waggish." Then Franklin, who appears in the minutes under the appellation of Mr. Electro Vitrifico (electric glass-rubber), carried on the jest with the comment, "Longstanding members, I think gentlemen, with submission, are not so properly waggish, because if they stand they cannot wag." Had the minutes of the Junto been as carefully and fully preserved as those of the Tuesday Club, we would undoubtedly have many similar examples of Franklin's ribald wit.

In many ways, Franklin's Junto was a sister organization to the Masons, the Philadelphia branch of which, the St. John's Lodge, was active in 1730. Both organizations inculcated a rationalistic approach to religion and a benevolent attitude toward fellow members and society at large. The Masons, however, incorporated a membership of greater wealth and community influence, both the proprietor and the governor sometimes attending. Franklin joined in February 1731, was made a warden in the next year, and in two more years became Grand Master of Pennsylvania.

In June 1737, Franklin's Masonic associations involved him in a practical joke upon a weak-minded apprentice, which ended tragically for the unfortunate lad and highly embarrassed Franklin in his public career. Daniel Rees, a dim-witted apprentice to a local pharmacist, Dr. Evan Jones, cherished aspirations to join the mystic ranks of the lodge. Jones and other tricksters put the hapless lad through a bogus initiation ceremony, borrowing some of the blasphemous and obscene claptrap of the black mass. Rees was required to take an oath of allegiance to

Satan, to drink a "sacramental" cup, containing a violent purgative, and to kiss the posteriors of one of the pranksters.

A few days later, when Franklin met Jones and some others at a tavern on legal business, Jones gave him an amusing account of the proceedings. Franklin, who always relished a good joke and a good story, admitted that "I laugh'd (and perhaps heartily, as my Manner is) at the *Beginning* of their Relation." But he later maintained that he felt disgust at the cruel and obscene elements of the ceremony and affirmed that, when the young man entered the tavern, he refused to acknowledge the lad's secret signs and greetings. When Rees took his leave, Franklin even followed him outside to warn him of the hoax, but the lad disappeared before he could do so. Franklin was sufficiently amused by the Satanic oath, however, to ask for a copy, which he showed widely to his acquaintances.

In the meantime, Jones offered to initiate Rees into a higher Masonic degree and invited a number of cronies to watch the fun in the cellar of his house. One of the number dressed himself in a cow's hide with horns to impersonate the devil, and Jones held a bowlful of burning brandy to give a ghastly hue to the surroundings. Approaching the candidate, Jones accidentally spilled the brandy, fatally burning the unfortunate apprentice.

Although at the trial of Jones and two others for manslaughter, Franklin gave evidence for the prosecution, and the Masons denied any connection with the episode, Andrew Bradford used the event to attack both Franklin and Masonry by association. The *Mercury*, 14 February 1738, accused Franklin of expressing his approbation of the original blasphemous oath and of subsequently diverting himself by reading it aloud in social gatherings. Franklin naturally felt sensitive over the stigma attached to his name and published a sober defense of his conduct in the *Gazette*, 15 February, alleging that he had merely laughed at the account of the ridiculous signs and ceremonies which had been passed off as Masonic symbols, but that he had protested against the physical abuses which followed.

Accounts of Rees's death and Jones's trial, at which he was

found guilty and burned in the hand, reached the Boston papers and alarmed Franklin's parents, who associated their son's Masonic activities with blasphemous ritual and lurid crimes. Attempting to put their minds at rest, Franklin assured them by letter, 13 April 1738, that the Freemasons are "in general a very harmless sort of People; and have no Principles or Practices that are inconsistent with Religion or good Manners." At the same time Franklin attempted to explain his religious beliefs, which had deviated drastically from the strict Calvinism of his parents. His exposition of virtue and tolerance revealed that his private religion could be reconciled with fraternal activities, but, as we shall see in the next chapter, he needed more than an intellectual system to satisfy his spiritual need.

4. Public and Private Worship

ALTHOUGH Franklin approved of the ritualistic element in Masonic gatherings and used the Junto as a forum for the discussion of religious and ethical problems, he did not consider either secret society as a substitute for worship. Nor was he satisfied with any of the churches then available in Philadelphia—Anglicans, Quakers, Presbyterians and Baptists. Convinced of the error of atheism, he still could not accept the divinity of Christ.

He devised, therefore, in November 1728, a private system of devotion, comprising a highly personal creed and method of worship. This he inscribed in a small notebook, about the size of the prayerbook for which it was a substitute. Some of his doctrines obviously stem from the deistical authors he had read in his teens; others are highly individualistic—and would have occurred only to a mind combining the imagination of genius with the method of an electronic brain. Like many poets, theologians and contemplative laymen in the eighteenth century, Franklin believed in the concept of the great chain of being: the notion that since existence in itself is a great blessing, God's benevolence forced him to create the maximum number of forms of being to share existence with him; as a consequence living forms exist in a continuous unbroken chain, descending from God to the meanest insect (the lowest form of life known in 1728). Man was not considered to be the highest form next to God, but to be ranked somewhere between angels and worms. To this generally accepted philosophical notion, Franklin added a highly unconventional one, which scarcely anyone else in the century dared to suggest: polytheism. As the first of the fundamental principles of his *Articles of Belief and Acts of Religion,* he affirmed:

I believe there is one Supreme, most perfect Being, Author and Father of the Gods themselves. For I believe that Man is not the most perfect Being but One, rather that as there are many Degrees of Beings his Inferiors, so there are many Degrees of Beings superior to him. . . .

I conceive then [Franklin continued] that the INFINITE has created many Beings or Gods, vastly superior to Man, who can better conceive his Perfections than we, and return him a more rational and glorious Praise.

Franklin was not sure whether these inferior gods—including the god of our own planet—are immortal or whether after many ages they die out and are supplanted by others. But he was confident "that each of these is exceeding wise and good, and very powerful; and that Each has made for himself one glorious Sun, attended with a beautiful and admirable System of Planets." Franklin directed his praise and adoration to the particular god, "who is the Author and Owner of our System." Although wise and good, he is still inferior to the "Supremely Perfect," and he has in himself some of the passions he has planted in human beings. Our praise is therefore acceptable to the God of our system, but the main purpose of prayer is to benefit those who offer it. We are led to contemplate the marvels of the planetary system and confirmed in our resolve to lead a useful life.

Primarily for this psychological reason, Franklin added a complete system of adoration and petition, modeled stylistically on the Anglican Book of Common Prayer. But the content of Franklin's manual is entirely deistical. Instead of Scripture readings, Franklin proposed passages from semiscientific theological books on creation and others inculcating moral virtue. Periodically, as he worshipped the god of our planet, whom he addressed as "friend," "father" or "creator," Franklin exercised his imagination by contemplating the sublimity of the universe and strengthened his moral character with the comforting reflection that virtue and happiness are inseparable.

Voltaire once remarked that there are few men into whose heads the insane project does not enter of becoming perfectly virtuous. This notion not only entered Franklin's head but remained there throughout his life. Seven or eight years after devising his private liturgy, Franklin conceived "the bold and arduous Project of arriving at moral Perfection." He "wish'd to live without committing any Fault at any time" and determined to resist all vicious conduct that "either Natural Inclination, Custom, or Company" might lead him into. Convinced that the essence of human behavior is habit, he brought to bear the same method upon his daily pattern of life that he had earlier devised for his devotions. Taking another little notebook, he listed what he considered the thirteen necessary virtues together with a precept to enable him to attain each one. The first virtue was temperance and its accompanying precept "Eat not to Dulness. Drink not to Elevation." The last two were chastity ("Rarely use Venery but for Health or Offspring—Never to Dulness, Weakness, or the Injury of your own or another's Peace or Reputation") and humility ("Imitate Jesus and Socrates"). In his book he ruled vertical columns for each day of the week crossed by horizontal lines for each virtue, so that in the resulting squares he could check infractions whenever they occurred. He systematically devoted a week to each virtue in succession, hoping eventually to eradicate every violation.

On a typical day Franklin rose at five and proposed the morning question: "What good shall I do this day?" Until eight he devoted his time to washing, prayer (address to Powerful Goodness), planning the day's business, and breakfast. From eight to twelve he worked. Then during a two-hour lunch period, he ate, read, and looked over his accounts. From two to six he worked again, and from six until ten he relaxed with supper, music, diversion or conversation. After proposing the evening question, "What good have I done today?" he retired at ten. Franklin's day was nowhere near so arduous as he suggests in the parts of his autobiography devoted to his economic struggle. He worked only eight hours and slept seven.

When we consider this routine and the meticulous planning on which Franklin established his personal, professional and intellectual life, it may seem paradoxical that he should maintain that he found more difficulty with order than any of his other twelve virtues. Despite the obvious controlled method in his thought processes, literary style and scientific investigations, he actually asserted that order cost him painful effort and that in the final analysis he was incorrigible. Without doubt there is a strong element of exaggeration here—reminiscent of John Bunyan's self-accusation of delighting in vice because he rang the church bells and occasionally played games on Sunday. Also we need to make a distinction between method and order. There is no question about the high degree of method in Franklin's life. His difficulties with order occurred in such matters as keeping records and filing papers in the proper places—and this he had not bothered much about because of his excellent memory.

One of Franklin's virtues, closely related to order, was cleanliness ("Tolerate no uncleanliness in body, cloaths, or habitation"), and this gave him very little trouble since he was almost fanatical on the subject. In an era when bathing was very little practised, Franklin designed his own bathtub and during his old age sat in it for hours at a time. He experimented also with "air baths," sitting or lying nude in the fresh air. He objected violently to Keimer's appearance, "slovenly to extream dirtiness," and in his correspondence as well as in his autobiography he revealed his aversion to the dirty fingers and offensive breath of barbers. In his old age the people of Paris particularly noted his fastidiousness for white linen.

In middle age Franklin gave up his practice of daily checking faults in his table, but he still kept it with him constantly—having transferred it in indelible ink to an ivory memorandum book, which enabled him to wipe away the checks after each week. In his seventies Franklin had this notebook with him on his diplomatic mission to France. Cabanis, who saw it there, considered this "precious little book" a sort of "chronological history" of the development of spiritual perfection in Franklin's mind and character.

With the benefit of his daily devotions and weekly Junto gatherings, Franklin did not devote much time to churchgoing but perpetuated his youthful practice of preserving Sunday as his studying day. Since he always held a favorable opinion of the propriety and utility of public worship, however, and since he had been baptized and educated a Presbyterian, he regularly paid his annual subscription for supporting the only minister of that sect in Philadelphia, the Reverend Jedediah Andrews. The latter sometimes visited Franklin as a friend and admonished him to attend his services. Franklin occasionally did so, once for five consecutive Sundays, and had he relished the preaching, he might have attended regularly. But he felt that Andrews's "Discourses were chiefly either polemic Arguments, or Explications of the peculiar Doctrines of our Sect, and were all . . . very dry, uninteresting, and unedifying, since not a single moral Principle was inculcated or enforc'd, their Aim seeming to be rather to make us Presbyterians than good Citizens."

In the middle of the summer of 1734, Franklin amused himself in the pages of the *Gazette* by burlesquing the joyless perspective by which some orthodox theologians viewed the universe. In one number in August, he published a dismal monologue by an English theologian, Joshua Smith, "On the Vanity and Brevity of Human Life." Then for the next issue, he wrote a parody not known to previous writers on Franklin. He effectively used the ribald earthy style which even Puritanical minds seem to have accepted in the eighteenth century.

Comparing the lamentations of the elegant author to the pouting of a little child who wants to eat his cake and have it too, Franklin pressed home his point by vivid parallels:

[Smith:] *All the few days we live are full of Vanity; and our choicest Pleasures sprinkled with bitterness:*
[Franklin:] All the few Cakes we have are puffed up with Yeast, and the nicest Gingerbread is spotted with Flyshits! . . .
[Smith:] *But the longer we live, the shorter is our life; and in the end we become a little lump of clay.*
[Franklin:] And the more we eat, the less is the Piece remaining; and in the end the whole will become Sir-reverence! [eighteenth-century euphemism for a turd].

In place of dismal meditations such as Smith's, Franklin believed in contemplating the joy of life; and in place of sermons on Presbyterian dogma, Franklin wanted the social gospel.

In the month after he printed his burlesque, a new minister

from Ireland arrived in Philadelphia to occupy Andrews's pul-
pit for a few weeks. The newcomer delighted Franklin by
preaching, with a good voice and "apparently extempore,"
sermons inculcating morality, or in theological jargon "good
works." Franklin immediately began attending church regularly, but the orthodox members of the congregation were
horrified. Andrews labeled his brother minister a deist and
Socinian, went around from door to door exhorting the congregation not to attend his sermons, and instituted charges of
heterodoxy in the synod. The new minister, Samuel Hemphill,
was graced with elegant delivery but little in the way of drive or
intellectual powers, and would have capitulated immediately
had not Franklin urged him to stand his ground and face his
accusers in the synod. As an intense ally, Franklin wrote three
pamphlets and a dialogue in the *Gazette* defending Hemphill's
right to preach morality in a Presbyterian church. Although
admitting that dogma had a legitimate function in the service,
Franklin argued that the Philadelphia congregation—composed
entirely of baptized believers—had a greater need of morality.
"Is Virtue, Heresy; and Universal Benevolence False Doctrine,
that any of us should keep away from Meeting because it is
preached there?" Franklin charged moreover that the synod had
no right to exercise thought control over Hemphill. Its authority to interpret Scripture was no more valid than that of the
Pope, whose doctrine of infallibility their ancestors had properly rebelled against. By seeking to impose its will upon Hemphill, Franklin argued, the Synod was behaving in the fashion of
the Inquisition.

In the midst of the hubbub, Hemphill's opponents made
the discovery that his "apparently extempore" sermons had
been plagiarized from English divines. This did not in the least
diminish Franklin's ardor for the cause. In one of his pamphlets,
Franklin reasoned that a minister attends seminary precisely to
attain learning from books, which he naturally then passes on to
his congregation. Accordingly, when Hemphill had occasion to
borrow for his sermons, he had selected the best parts of the best
authors—and should have been complimented for his taste.
Paraphrasing Jonathan Swift's famous apologue from *The*

Battle of the Books, Franklin concluded that Hemphill and his detractors were like the bee and the fly in a garden. The one goes from flower to flower collecting the most delightful honey; "while the other (of a quite different Taste) places her Happiness entirely in Filth, Corruption, and Ordure."

Despite Franklin's rhetoric, the synod suspended Hemphill; and Franklin gave up all interest in the Presbyterian church. In the first of the many public battles he was to wage throughout his life, he had suffered a defeat; but since all his writing had been anonymous, he suffered no personal loss of face.

Both before and after the Hemphill affair, Franklin used the *Gazette* as an organ of concealed deism and open latitudinarianism. In it he published nothing in favor of evangelical Christianity until 1739, when he came in contact with an English evangelist on a triumphant tour of the colonies, George Whitefield, a personality in his own way as vigorous and brilliant as Franklin.

Whitefield, then only twenty-four years old, nine years Franklin's junior, was already a celebrity, the stentorian voice of the Great Awakening. Franklin immediately printed a eulogistic report of Whitefield's preaching in the *Gazette* and published an edition of his sermons and journals. As one of the multitudes who attended his sermons in the open fields, Franklin marveled at

the extraordinary Influence of his Oratory on his Hearers. . . . It was wonderful to see the Change soon made in the Manners of our Inhabitants; from being thoughtless or indifferent about Religion, it seem'd as if all the World were growing Religious, so that one could not walk thro' the Town in an Evening without Hearing Psalms sung in different Families of every Street.

In this atmosphere Franklin gave up all attempts to use the *Gazette* to foster his own religious notions. And in his personal contacts with Whitefield he was diplomatic enough to keep their theological differences in the background. During Whitefield's first visit, the evangelist considered the printer as a backsliding Christian rather than as a deist and wrote comfortingly, "I do not despair of your seeing the reasonableness of Christianity.

Apply to GOD; he is willing to do the divine will, and you shall know it." Somewhat later Franklin allowed his scepticism to manifest itself more openly. Whitefield, having been invited to stay at Franklin's home, replied that if the offer were made for Christ's sake, Franklin would certainly receive his reward. Franklin returned, "Don't let me be mistaken; it was not for Christ's sake, but for your sake."

Franklin nevertheless admired Whitefield's "benevolent Heart," the trait which cemented a bond of friendship between them. Whitefield engaged in as many philanthropic projects as Franklin—the most famous of which was an orphanage in Bethesda, Georgia. Franklin believed in caring for orphans but considered Philadelphia a more logical site. In his autobiography he describes his response to Whitefield's oratory at a meeting which he had attended with the definite determination not to contribute. He had in his pockets some coins of copper, silver and gold. As Whitefield depicted the woeful plight of the orphans, Franklin softened enough to consider giving the coppers. "Another Stroke of his Oratory made me asham'd of that and determin'd me to give the Silver; and he finish'd so admirably, that I empty'd my Pocket wholly into the Collector's Dish, Gold and all." This incident illustrates perhaps the greatest paradox in Franklin's character: an acquisitive, competitive materialism coexisting with a broad humanitarianism.

Franklin was eventually appointed a trustee of the tabernacle, or "New Building," not because of his reputation for religious zeal but because of his freedom from sectarianism. The original plan was to have one trustee of each religious sect. The Moravian member turned out to be very unpopular with the rest, and when he died the others decided not to take another Moravian. In order not to have two of some other sect, they chose Franklin: "merely an honest man, and of no *sect* at all."

5. Busy Projector

BY THE time Whitefield first preached in the "New Building" in November 1740, Franklin had already become
known in Philadelphia as a leader in community enterprises.
His first project of a public nature, that of a subscription
library, had been a direct outgrowth of the Junto. In the early
days of Franklin's club, there was not even a good bookstore in
Pennsylvania, and the only books were those in private hands.
When the Junto changed its meeting place from an alehouse to a
room acquired from Robert Grace, Franklin suggested that the
members pool their books in this room for the common use.
Next Franklin persuaded fifty other Philadelphians, mostly
young tradesmen, to contribute annually to a lending library
called the Library Company. By 1 July 1731 the necessary
subscriptions had been found and Joseph Breintnall elected
secretary. Franklin drew up the plan, rules and articles of
agreement but preferred not to be known as the organizer. At
first in soliciting subscriptions he had encountered reluctant
ears and suspicious eyes, which made him "feel the Impropriety
of presenting one's self as the Proposer of any useful Project that
might be suppos'd to raise one's Reputation in the smallest
degree above that of one's Neighbors." Then he began describing his scheme as that of a *Number of Friends,"* and all
opposition faded. Henceforth, as a steady principle in all of his
benevolent projects, Franklin kept himself in the background,
finding the minor sacrifice of his vanity amply repaid in the
results. After many years of adhering to this policy, he concluded
that if the originator of a project conceals his hand, sooner or
later some vainer person will try to take the credit for it, at
which time some envious third party will pluck "those assum'd
feathers" and restore them to their rightful owner.

To the Library Company and other associations which

developed from it, Franklin attributed the high intellectual level of the average American—common tradesmen and farmers, who were at the time of the Revolution "as intelligent as most Gentlemen from other Countries." Reading had done for America at large, he believed, what the ability to write had done for his private career.

During the two formative years of the Library Company, 1730 and 1731, an epidemic of smallpox beset Pennsylvania and the northern colonies. Franklin wrote and published in the *Gazette* (25 March 1731) an essay on visiting and caring for the sick. In the vein of Addison he pointed out that man has more diseases to combat than any other creature, whether naturally through the effects of intemperance and vice or by divine intervention to give us a greater opportunity of exercising charity, the virtue which most recommends us to the deity. As Thomas Paine was to do many years later, Franklin packed his essay with Scripture quotations to sway the Biblically pervaded Philadelphians, but at the same time he subconsciously revealed his distaste for the dogmatic part of Christianity by observing that the famous good Samaritan was "esteemed no better than an Heretick or an Infidel by the Orthodox of those Times." According to Franklin, "I was SICK and ye VISITED me" is one of the terms of admission to heaven. Since as many people had lost their lives in the epidemic from the lack of suitable care and attendance as from the natural malignity of the disease, Franklin appealed for volunteers to assist among poor families. And lest some of his readers be impervious to considerations of religion and humanity, Franklin added that no kindnesses done by one man to another are so long remembered as those given in time of sickness.

Twenty years later, when Franklin joined in a project to establish a hospital in Philadelphia, he dug this essay out of his files, fitted it with a fresh conclusion, and republished it in the *Gazette*.

In the Junto Franklin also initiated a scheme for policing the streets of Philadelphia at night and instituted a monthly social gathering of able-bodied citizens to discuss fire prevention and fire-fighting. This was the groundwork for the Union

Fire Company, a volunteer fire department organized in 1736.

Following his usual custom of promoting in public the projects he had originally advanced in the Junto, Franklin published essays on fire-fighting in the *Gazette* (December 1733 and February 1735). He also included in his paper an appeal for householders to sprinkle ashes on icy streets (January 1733) and a suggestion that public-spirited men of means use their wealth and influence to set up younger men in business (June 1732). The latter concept became famous when Franklin introduced it in the last of the many wills he drew up throughout his life.

In his autobiography Franklin suggests that his public-spirited activities directly led to his "first promotion"—being chosen clerk of the General Assembly 15 October 1736. The nominal salary was of slight importance, but Franklin valued the post since it offered him the opportunity of securing public printing contracts for his press. He was highly gratified to be reappointed the next year despite the disturbing opposition of a new member, who made a long speech against him in favor of another candidate. Instead of treating the new member as an enemy or conversely paying him servile remarks of respect, Franklin gained his favor by asking to borrow a valuable book and returning it with a note of gratitude in a week. This illustrated, Franklin felt, an old maxim which says, "He that has once done you a Kindness will be more ready to do you another, than he whom you yourself have obliged."

One can see that the years from 1729 to 1736 were busy years for Franklin as a projector as well as a rising businessman. Since his private affairs failed to give his bursting energies their necessary release, he felt an insatiable need for social activity. This gregarious impulse, combined with his benevolent nature, forced him into the public arena. The question arises whether self-interest may have impelled this civic furor as much as benevolence. Certainly Franklin realized that his diplomatically concealed philanthropic leadership would do him no harm. But his desire to prevent suffering and provide more commodious and comfortable living for his fellow citizens was nonetheless genuine. This is amply demonstrated by the continuation of some forms of Franklin's benevolence far beyond the time when he became the possessor of an ample fortune and the object of universal respect. But benevolent as he was himself, Franklin was well aware that all mankind do not respond to appeals to moral sense and the love of virtue. Indeed some of his own compilations of hints for the prosperity of tradesmen seem to strengthen the competitive and self-seeking impulses in man. Because of such works as *The Way to Wealth,* Franklin has been frequently characterized as the archetype of worldly materialism.

To decide exactly where Franklin belongs on the scale between materialism and benevolence has been a difficult problem for critics. Unfortunately one cannot arrive at an answer simply by counting his prudential writings and his altruistic ones to see which group is the more numerous. The second group is far in excess of the former, even though writings such as *The Way to Wealth* have overshadowed the others. The real problem is to know how Franklin himself decided the fundamental moral issue involved—whether man is moved naturally by love for others or by his own interest. In the eighteenth century, Shaftesbury and Hutcheson were considered as authorities for the first opinion; Hobbes and Mandeville for the second.

Recent criticism has tended to stress the philosophic roots of Franklin's humanitarianism, associating it almost exclusively with Shaftesbury's urbane system of esthetic Platonism. This conveniently rescues Franklin from two contradictory groups of nineteenth-century critics: those who stressed and approved the didactic character of Franklin's utilitarian ethics; and those who could see nothing in Franklin but his "scoundrel maxims." Most modern biographers have based their analyses of Franklin's moral philosophy upon two outspokenly Shaftesburian dialogues "Between Philocles and Horatio . . . concerning Virtue and Pleasure," which Franklin published in the *Gazette.* Actually Franklin did not write these essays but merely transposed them from an English periodical, the *London Journal.* But he wrote other essays which amply bear out the Shaftesburian system, particularly a dialogue proving that "a vicious man could not properly be called a man of sense" and a "discourse on self-denial, showing that virtue was not secure till its practice became a habitude." In these essays Franklin was certainly supporting Shaftesbury against the iconoclastic view of Bernard Mandeville, who maintained that human virtue was an illusion and that all conduct is designed to gratify narrow self-interest.

The truth is that Franklin wavered between the altruistic system of Shaftesbury and the selfish system of Hobbes and Mandeville, and he never succeeded in completely resolving the conflict. Although in his formal writings Franklin settled the matter in Shaftesbury's favor, the contrary spirit in his thought is too vital to be ignored. In 1737, Franklin wrote to a friend that the notion of Hobbes "is somewhat nearer the Truth than that which makes the State of Nature a State of Love: But the Truth perhaps lies between both Extreams."

According to Mandeville, pride, the natural faculty by which every mortal overvalues his own qualities, is the ruling passion of all mankind. All behavior is designed to secure our self-interest, but we sometimes pretend to benevolence in order to hear ourselves praised by others. In this sense, "the moral virtues are the political offspring which Flattery begot upon Pride."

In a letter to his friend Jared Eliot, 12 September 1751, Franklin explained our love of praise, "the Sweetest kind of Musick," on the same principles. In a virtual paraphrase of Mandeville he pointed out that when we pretend to be displeased with praise of ourselves, we are hypocrites. "This Hypocrisy, is only a Sacrifice to the Pride of others, or to their Envy." We are making a similar sacrifice when we give up the pleasure of praising ourselves. According to Franklin's theory, since convention denies us the pleasure of self-praise, we seek it in a roundabout way by condemning others. "This Fondness for ourselves, rather than Malevolence to others," Franklin took to be "the general Source of Censure and Backbiting."

Franklin's analysis of the love of praise is essentially an elaboration of a maxim of *Poor Richard* in 1745: "Vanity backbites more than Malice." And this maxim, like two dozen others in *Poor Richard,* is taken directly from the cynical French philosopher La Rochefoucauld, whose collection of maxims represents the *locus classicus* in western literature for the doctrine of self-love. As everybody knows, La Rochefoucauld teaches that all human behavior stems from self-love and interest; but this is not always our best interest—or true interest, as Franklin would say—which is more often an interest of honor or glory.

It is true that one cannot assume that Franklin himself accepted the teaching of any proverb in *Poor Richard* merely because he included it in his collection. Many single proverbs contradict each other and go contrary to opinions which we know Franklin held. Yet from La Rochefoucauld, Franklin took such a large number of maxims that they almost constitute a system of morality. As he had elaborated one of them in his letter to Eliot, he similarly worked into his autobiography another which has a direct bearing upon his skeptical attitude toward motives and impulses. In *Poor Richard* for 1751, Franklin printed from La Rochefoucauld: "The Proud hate Pride—in others." In his autobiography, alluding to his view that we all relish self-praise, he remarked: "I scarce ever heard or saw the introductory Words, *Without Vanity I may say,* &c., but some vain thing immediately follow'd. Most People dislike Vanity in others, whatever Share they have of it themselves."

But even in *Poor Richard* we may find echoes of Shaftesbury:

Hast thou virtue? acquire also the graces and beauties of virtue [April 1738].
You may be more happy than princes, if you will be more virtuous [May 1738].
The noblest question in the world is, *What good may I do in it* [December 1737]?

The latter is a sentiment which Franklin repeated many times, in correspondence as well as in his autobiography. We may assume that he sincerely believed it and acted upon it.

In another maxim Franklin succeeded in balancing the cynical and the benevolent systems:

Love your Neighbour; yet don't pull down your Hedge (April 1754).

Whatever fundamental contradictions exist in these systems existed in Franklin's life as well. In some of his activities he sought his narrow self-interest and took advantage of human weakness in his rivals; but in others—the major part—he was moved entirely by social consciousness or the love of virtue.

But he was always motivated by internal psychological forces rather than by intellectual adherence to Shaftesbury or other benevolent philosophers. His political leadership, for example, grew out of his gift for organizing activities and his love of social intercourse. His later diplomatic career similarly owed more to his equable disposition than to any theoretical system of political behavior. And his own joy in living as well as his universal popularity may be traced to the same source. He believed, as he affirmed, that "Happiness in this Life rather depends on Internals than Externals; and that, besides the natural Effects of Wisdom and Virtue, Vice and Folly, there is such a Thing as being of a happy or an unhappy Constitution."

6. Publisher's Progress

AT THE same time that Franklin was spending his leisure
hours with high-minded speculation on morality and
religion, he had to make a daily living, and he succeeded in
making a good one by concentrating on the quality of his
newspaper.

In his first issue (2 October 1729) Franklin observed that an
editor "ought to be qualified with an extensive Acquaintance
with Languages, a great Easiness and Command of Writing and
Relating Things clearly and intelligibly, and in a few Words; he
should be able to speak of War both by Land and Sea; be well
acquainted with Geography, with the History of the
Time, . . . and the Manners and Customs of all Nations."
Adding that men so qualified were rare in the colonies, he
modestly hoped that his friends would help to compensate for
his own deficiencies.

Franklin in effect required essentially the same qualities for
a journalist which literary critics were demanding of epic poets.
But neither he nor any other colonial editor exhibited extraordinary abilities in writing news stories since the approved
practice consisted in printing most of them verbatim from
English papers. Colonial citizens thirsted for European tidings
but showed only negligible interest in local materials. They
were likely to hear of events in their own area as soon as the
printers did. Since early papers were weeklies, public interest
faded before most items could be published. Traces of Franklin's hand in the *Gazette* may be discerned, however, in humorous touches which he gave to otherwise routine stories. In June
1732, for example, he reported severe thunderstorms in New
York. "The same Day we had some very hard Claps in these
Parts; and 'tis said, that in Bucks County, one Flash came so near
a Lad, as, without hurting him, to melt the Pewter Button off

the Wasteband of his Breeches. 'Tis well nothing else there-abouts, was made of Pewter." On another occasion Franklin reported from Boston (January 1732) that "the LYON, King of Beasts, who had travelled all over North America by Sea and Land, died here in a Tanyard. Like other Kings, his Death was often reported, long before it happened." Franklin was not above making fun of himself in print. With obvious enjoyment of his discomfiture, he or one of his helpers reported (September 1731) that a certain printer

walking carefully in clean Clothes over some Barrels of Tar on Carpenter's Wharff, the head of one of them unluckily gave Way, and let a Leg of him in above the Knee. Whether he was upon the Catch [chasing!] at that time, we cannot say, but 'tis certain he caught a *Tartar*. 'Twas observed he sprung out again right briskly, verifying the common Saying, *As nimble as a Bee in a Tarbarrel.* You must know there are several sorts of *Bees*: 'tis true he was no *Honey Bee,* nor yet a *Humble Bee,* but a *Boo bee* he may be allow'd to be, namely *B.F.*

When ice closed the port of Philadelphia, cutting off European news as well as shipping, Franklin published essays and other literary materials as filler, some extracted from English periodicals and some coming from his own pen. Some are brief nuggets of felicitous humor worthy to rank with the best facetiae in English prose. His most successful sketches constitute a gallery of indigenous "humor" characters: Alice Addertongue, the center of all scandal in the province; Anthony Afterwit, the victim of an extravagant wife; Celia Single, the observer of others' matrimonial difficulties; and Belinda, a husband-hunting maid. The last three form a trilogy on the subject of courtship and marriage. Despite the homespun qualities of these characters, probably patterned on Franklin's acquaintance in Philadelphia, their letters are decidedly Addisonian in flavor.

Franklin used a variety of styles in the *Gazette,* imitating Shaftesbury, Mandeville and Swift as well as Addison. Among others, we may find the ornate rhetorical style, the religious, the argumentative, the informal, the humorous and the scientific. Franklin even devoted an entire essay to presenting his own stylistic principles (2 August 1733). Typically he maintained that no piece can be considered well written which fails to benefit the reader "either by improving his Virtue or his Knowledge." A newspaper performance must be orderly, advancing from the known to the unknown. Also it must be *"smooth, clear* and *short:* For the contrary Qualities are apt to offend, either the Ear, the Understanding, or the Patience." As a practical student of human nature, Franklin observed "the different Ways of Writing and Expression used by the different Sects of Religion" and admitted that "it is improper to use the common Stile, when we address some of these Sects in particular."

In colonial America, the biggest publishing money-maker was the annual almanac. Households which might not possess another book, unless perhaps the Bible, were obliged to buy an almanac; and every printer who was at the same time a good businessman regularly produced at least one, sometimes as many as five. An almanac maker, traditionally called a philomath, appeared to the public either under his own name (Felix Leeds, Titan Leeds, John Jerman) or under a pseudonym (Poor Robin, Abraham Weatherwise). Almost as soon as Franklin had put the *Pennsylvania Gazette* on its feet, he set about to capture some of the almanac market. He prevailed upon Thomas Godfrey, the mathematical member of the Junto, to produce the necessary calculations and published his work under the title of *Pennsylvania Almanack* for the years 1730 and 1731, advertising it in the *Gazette* as "Done on a large Sheet of Demi Paper, after the London manner" (19 January 1731). One of the features of the almanac of Godfrey's principal competitor, Titan Leeds (an unlikely name, but still that of an actual person), had been three mathematical questions. Franklin boasted in the *Gazette* that these *"were solved and answer'd by Godfrey, in less than half an Hour after he saw them."* Godfrey had sent the answers by post to Leeds with three other questions for Leeds to answer in turn, but, according to Franklin, Leeds had pretended not to have received them. To embarrass his competitor, Franklin forthwith published the questions in the Gazette, *"that there may be no Room for further Excuse."* In this year Franklin also brought out John Jerman's *American Almanac.* In the fall of 1732, for reasons unknown, Godfrey and Jerman both engaged Bradford as their printer, and Franklin thereupon put together his own almanac for the next year. This was the world-famous *Poor Richard,* purportedly written by an excessively poor stargazer, Richard Saunders, who was continually berated by a down-to-earth wife, Bridget. In the preface to his first number, Franklin borrowed a joke from Jonathan Swift, who had, several years previously, adopted the pseudonym Isaac Bickerstaff to forecast the death of a notorious astrologer, Partridge. Franklin naturally predicted the death of his chief rival, Titan Leeds. When in his almanac for the following year Leeds called Poor Richard *"a false Predicter, an Ignorant, a conceited Scribler, a Fool, and a Lyar,"* Franklin continued the joke. The new almanac, he blandly replied, must have been the work of a wretched impostor, for "Mr. Leeds was too well bred to use any Man so indecently and so scurrilously, and moreover his Esteem and Affection for me was extraordinary."

In the fall of 1737, when the Partridge jest had run its course and every phase of its humor had been extracted, Franklin transferred his ridicule of Leeds from *Poor Richard* to the *Gazette.* In the issue of 20 October, he printed a burlesque essay, not identified by earlier writers on Franklin, on "those Labours of the Learned, called ALMANACKS." Imitating Pope's "Receipt to make an Epic Poem," Franklin ironically applied the precepts of neoclassical criticism to Leeds's style, "a Sort of Gravity, which keeps a due medium between Dulness and Nonsense, and yet has a mixture of both." Like the approved almanac writer, Leeds was not *"a finish'd Poet, but a Piece of one,* and qualify'd to write, what we vulgarly call Doggerel."

In 1739 the much-persecuted Leeds actually died, and Franklin turned his attention to John Jerman, who had been publishing his almanacs alternately with Franklin and Bradford. In *Poor Richard* for 1740, Franklin predicted that Jerman would be "openly reconciled to the Church of Rome," and in subsequent years, despite Jerman's indignant protests, Franklin gloated over the presumed fulfillment of the prophecy. Franklin used rough and tumble methods to take business away from his rivals, and he had a good time doing it. His hoaxes succeeded, not because anyone took them seriously but because they made his publications lively and amusing.

But the feature which gave Franklin the upper hand over all his competition and turned his almanacs into works of literature was his proverbs, the interlineal sayings which he drew from the wisdom of all ages and transformed into the brisk colloquial style appropriate to the character of a homespun philosopher.

Maxims, proverbs and aphorisms, they represented Franklin's idea of the world's most witty and succinct comments on sex, religion, psychology and professions. The best known are prudential, advocating discretion, thrift and material providence. These were later gathered into *The Way to Wealth.* But almost as many, of a contrary significance, recommend conviviality and hedonistic indulgence. Some are cynical and captious; others idealistic and cheerful.

Proverbs belong to the folk tradition of a people; whereas maxims and aphorisms usually have individual authors. Franklin drew nearly all his sayings of both types from English or European sources, adapting them to his own personality. In the early years he printed mainly proverbs taken from English anthologies such as James Howell's *Lexicon Tetraglotten* and Thomas Fuller's *Gnomologia.* In the later years he drew on collections of maxims and aphorisms as well, showing even more skill in revision than he had with proverbs.

An exhaustive study by Robert Newcomb has provided the sources of two-thirds of all the sayings in *Poor Richard,* including four which previous biographers have considered to be original with Franklin. To illustrate Franklin's method, we shall print these below with their sources:

An empty Bag cannot stand upright [January 1740].
An empty Sack cannot stand upright [*Gnomologia*].

The sleeping Fox catches no Poultry. Up! Up! [September 1743].
The Fox who sleeps in the morning hath not his tongue feathered
　[*Lexicon Tetraglotten*].

Experience keeps a dear school, yet Fools will learn in no other [December 1743].

Experience teacheth fools; and he is a great one that will not learn by it [*Gnomologia*].

Sloth (like Rust) consumes faster than Labour wears: the used Key is always bright [July 1744].

The best Metals lose their Lustre, unless brightened by Use [*Gnomologia*].

Still unidentified and probably Franklin's are:

If you'd have it done, go; if not, send [November 1743].

Three removes is as bad as a fire [*Way to Wealth*].

Franklin had a considerable debt to La Rochefoucauld, from whom he drew twenty-four maxims, including one of his most famous:

To bear other People's Afflictions, every one has Courage enough, and to spare [January 1740].

Despite a common assumption, Franklin took very little from Bacon. His most important sources were Montaigne, Samuel Richardson, Lord Halifax and Francis Quarles.

Until Newcomb's study, mentioned previously, biographers and literary critics universally discussed the manner in which Franklin "put his stamp" on the proverbs he took from "the wisdom of many ages and nations" without knowing the sources from which he took them. Now that most of these sources have been identified, we see that Franklin used a variety of techniques—none of which can be considered as a particular identifying mark. These include making bland phrases more blunt, picturesque or rhythmical; creating a heightened sense of immediacy and directness; establishing a closer rapport with the reader; underscoring the moral; adding introductory phrases or after comments; and, most important, stripping redundant phrasing in a general effort for economy. Much of this compression was dictated by the lack of physical space between the prosaic calendar entries. Despite Franklin's successful stylistic techniques, some of the credit given him by previous authors must be taken away, for many of his most admired sayings he copied completely without changes from single collections such as Fuller's and Howell's.

As Franklin approached the eleventh year of his editorship of the *Pennsylvania Gazette* and the eighth of *Poor Richard,* he began to think of undertaking another form of journalism, a monthly magazine. The first English magazine, the *Gentleman's,* had been born only eight years previously, and twenty imitators had almost immediately come into being. But there was as yet no magazine published in America.

Franklin discussed the possibility of starting one with John Webbe, a lawyer and political writer, who had already contributed a series of articles on government to the *Gazette.* Webbe seemed interested in the venture, and Franklin drew up preliminary articles of agreement. In essence, Franklin was to bear all the expenses and Webbe to do all the writing; Franklin was to get loosely three-fourths of the gross receipts and Webbe one fourth.

Franklin thought he had time to pursue his scheme at leisure but was shocked out of his tranquility when Andrew Bradford advertised, 6 November 1740, the plan of an intended periodical, the *American Magazine, or A Monthly View of the Political State of the British Colonies.* After learning that Webbe was to be its editor, Franklin hurriedly announced his own project, the *General Magazine and Historical Chronicle, for All the British Plantations in America,* and accused Webbe of betraying to Bradford the idea of publishing a magazine. Webbe replied in the *Mercury* that Franklin's accusations were false. He insisted that Franklin had spoken of a magazine in merely general terms and had given no details of any plan. He had agreed to Franklin's proposal of conducting the work on Franklin's assurance that the editing would not require more than three or four days a month, but after he had realized that it would take practically full time and that Franklin's justification for taking three-fourths of the profits was groundless, he considered himself the victim of a fraud. It is hard to say on which side justice lay; Franklin had undeniably been the first to propose the scheme, but as a shrewd businessman he seems to have been willing to exploit Webbe. Probably Franklin had assumed that the editor would fill his pages with material extracted from British books and periodicals (the policy he himself followed in the *General Magazine*) ; whereas Webbe understood that he would be required for the most part to compose original material (his method in the *American Magazine*) . The situation is rather well stated in a couplet based on La Rochefoucauld which Franklin included in *Poor Richard* for 1741, which he was printing about the time of the altercation:

> Quarrels never could last long,
> If on one side only the wrong.

The quarrel continued in the press for several weeks, branching out into two subordinate issues—Franklin's capacities as a writer and his business ethics, both of which, according to Webbe, were deficient. On the first score, Franklin needs no defense; on the second, the situation is again ambiguous.

To understand it we must go back in history several years. Bradford had served as postmaster of Pennsylvania from 1728 until 1737, when Colonel Spotswood, the postmaster general, transferred the office to Franklin because of Bradford's failure to settle his accounts promptly. While Bradford was postmaster, he ordered that the *Mercury* be carried as mail but refused to accept the *Gazette*. Franklin circumvented him by bribing the riders. Eventually Spotswood intervened and ordered Bradford to carry the *Gazette* on the same terms as his own paper. When Franklin took over the postmastership, he allowed the *Mercury* to be carried free, according to his own explanation, in order to avoid imitating Bradford's meanness, but, according to Webbe's analysis, in order to get Bradford into his power and prevent him from criticizing in the *Mercury*. In October 1739, Franklin received an order from Spotswood forbidding him to carry any of Bradford's mail until the latter settled his accounts. Bradford thereupon adopted Franklin's old device of bribing the riders, a practice which Franklin tolerated until Webbe's blast against him, after which he expressly forbade the riders to carry the *Mercury* under any conditions. For this Webbe accused him of unfairly taking advantage of his position. In his own defense Franklin could do nothing but publish Spotswood's letter, which was in a sense irrelevant. In his autobiography, Franklin makes no allusion to this altercation, perhaps because he realized that it was sordid and that his own part in it contributed nothing to his honor.

Bradford and Franklin each tried to stimulate interest in his own magazine by means of newspaper advertisements, and each editor tried to beat his rival to prior publication. Bradford carried the day by publishing his *American Magazine* 13 February 1741, making his the first magazine in the colonies. Franklin published his *General Magazine* three days later. Contrary to modern practice, they were dated for the past month, January. Each editor sought to corner the limited market for himself, Franklin stressing the small-sized type used in the *General Magazine* and Bradford stressing the originality of the articles in the *American*. Bradford proudly affirmed that he would not reprint "any of the Rubbish or Sweepings of Printing-Houses" and justified the higher price of the *American Magazine* (threepence more than Franklin's) by the continued "Study and Application" required for exclusively original materials. Having lost Webbe and not having the time to write seventy-odd pages a month, Franklin was vulnerable on this score. He retaliated by publishing in the *Gazette* (26 February 1741) a doggerel poem in Irish dialect, burlesquing Bradford's claims of originality:

> 'Tis true, my Book is dear; but de Reashon is plain,
> The best Parts of it ish de Work of my own Brain:
> How can odher Men's Writings be wort so much!
> Arra! if you tink so, you're no vherry good Shudge.

Although Franklin had little time for composition, he wrote at least one long article for the *General Magazine,* discovered by the author of this biography and not included in the Franklin *Papers.* His essay *On Paper-Currency, proposing a new Method for fixing its Value,* appeared in the second issue. Here Franklin suggested a means of issuing currency which would at the same time serve as a source of revenue for the state. The colony would emit currency in the amount of 110,000 pounds. Of this specie,

100,000 would be circulated in loans on interest-bearing real estate mortgages; the remaining 10,000 would be invested in commodities and sold at a profit in foreign markets. Many years later, when Franklin was serving as an agent for the colony of Pennsylvania at the English court, he proposed an adaptation of this system as a substitute for the unpopular Stamp Act.

In Bradford's magazine, the most significant piece was a deistical essay incorporating the ingenious reply of an Indian to a Swedish minister, expounding the superiority of natural religion to Christianity. Franklin was so much impressed by this essay, even though published by his competitor, that he used it as the basis for similar later pieces of his own.

Despite the merit of this and other original essays in the *American Magazine,* it lasted for only three issues; Franklin's survived for six. The colonies were not yet ready to support this sort of periodical publication.

In addition to his book-publishing and bookselling activities in Philadelphia, Franklin branched out into other colonies and created the first chain of printing establishments in America. In 1731 he sent one of his workmen to Charleston, South Carolina, as a co-partner to operate a printing press; and ten years later he made a similar arrangement for New York. Two successful newspapers, the *South-Carolina Gazette* and the *New-York Weekly Post-Boy,* grew out of these arrangements. Franklin also established the first German-language newspaper in America in 1732, the *Philadelphische Zeitung,* but it died after only two issues.

Franklin continued to use his press for job work as well as various official documents for the Assembly. In the summer of 1736 he was in the neighboring colony of New Jersey, printing paper money in Burlington. Shortly after Lewis Morris became governor of New Jersey in 1738, a committee of the Assembly implored Franklin's aid in drawing up an answer to one of the governor's messages. They were respectable men of good understanding, but such was the "State of Literature in Jersey" at the time that not one of them was capable of writing a proper answer. Franklin came to their rescue and wrote such an excellent response that the Assembly allowed him to print many of its official papers.

By the summer of 1743, Franklin's publishing empire was in such thriving condition that he was ready to set up a fourth printing house. A London printer, William Strahan, recommended one of his journeymen, and Franklin invited the young man, David Hall, to try the colonies for a year. He had originally intended to employ Hall in a new printing office at Antigua, in the West Indies, but cautiously kept his plans to himself even after the young man arrived. At first Hall was dubious and discontented, Franklin circumspect and reserved. Hall, in spite of an attack of jaundice, nevertheless pitched into his duties with such energy that Franklin warmed to him as an example of the worthy young tradesman he was perennially advising. Instead of sending Hall away to open a new branch in his printing chain, Franklin kept him in Philadelphia and eventually, after making him a partner, confided all the care of the business to his reliable hands. Franklin settled another young man in Antigua in 1748 and, when he died, replaced him with his nephew, Benjamin Mecom.

In the meantime, Franklin by correspondence became closely attached to Strahan, using him as his London agent for the purchase of books, new types and other supplies. Strahan for his part, in June 1745, conceived Franklin "to have a very good heart, as well as to be a man of honour & good sense." In 1749, Franklin asked Strahan to collect some money which the government owed his son, and Franklin performed a similar service for Strahan in Philadelphia, trying to collect money due from James Read, Deborah's distant relative, who carried on a rival book business next door to Franklin. It was Read who, on a trip to London in 1739, had first brought the two printers together by correspondence. In 1748 Strahan appointed Franklin his agent to collect a three-year-old debt of well over one hundred pounds. Just previous to this, Franklin had had a minor falling out with Read on his own account. Read had used his influence in the Assembly to try to wrest the clerkship from Franklin, who had held it since 1736. Franklin strongly resented Read's intrusion and refused to speak to him for some time. Shortly before

Strahan's letter, Read got further into Franklin's bad books by obtaining a judgment against Franklin's old benefactor, Robert Grace, for an insignificant debt of twelve pounds. Read approached Franklin in a haughty, insulting manner and asked him what should be done about his friend Grace. When Franklin replied with aspersions on Read's gratitude and justice, Read walked away. Franklin considered this an appropriate time to bring up the debt to Strahan—on the grounds that "a Consciousness of his ill Behaviour to me and my Friend would pique him to make immediate Payment"—somewhat questionable psychology. Anyway, Franklin wrote a spirited letter acquainting Read that at the moment when he had been speaking in his "lofty Strain" against Grace, Franklin held in his pocket Strahan's paper against him for more than ten times the amount of Grace's debt. Oddly enough, Franklin's strategy worked to a degree. Although Read did not pay up, he gave Franklin an interest-bearing note for the full amount. Acquainting Strahan with these developments, Franklin encouraged him to hope for reasonably swift payment. Read's relatives were wealthy, he explained, and he would keep pressing the issue even though he scarcely ever dunned for himself.

Franklin used to call his own newspaper debts "an Estate in the Clouds," but his various printing enterprises still provided the foundation for his subsequent financial independence.

7. Public Man

AT THE same time that Franklin was using his pen to make his newspaper and almanac appealing to the public and to amuse himself in the process, he was also trying to influence public opinion. Contrary to the unanimous opinion of previous biographers and historians, Franklin used the *Gazette* to advance his own views of political affairs in the colony of Pennsylvania, particularly on the major controversy of the time, whether the proprietary interest or the local interest was to be supreme. Consistently during the first decade of his editorship, Franklin printed political pieces supporting the Assembly and the people of Pennsylvania against the proprietor and the governor. Bradford, editor of the rival *Mercury,* took the other side. Franklin not only limited essays in the *Gazette* to those concurring with his political opinions but deliberately suppressed news favorable to the proprietors.

Franklin attributed the early success of his newspaper in large measure to his defense of local interests, particularly to "some spirited remarks . . . on the dispute then going on between Governor Burnet and the Massachusetts Assembly" which "struck the principal people" and brought them all to be his subscribers.

The conflict in Massachusetts between governor and Assembly was parallel to that in Pennsylvania. Franklin (9 October 1729) warmly commended the citizens of Massachusetts for refusing to submit to the governor in financial measures and concluded with a somewhat complacent observation

Their happy Mother Country will perhaps observe with Pleasure, that tho' her gallant Cocks and matchless Dogs abate their native Fire and Intrepidity when transported to a Foreign Clime (as the common Notion is), yet her sons . . . still retain that ardent Spirit of Liberty, and that undaunted Courage in the Defence of it, which has in every Age so gloriously distinguished BRITONS and ENGLISHMEN from all the Rest of Mankind.

The ideological significance of this comment transcends its political importance. It reflects the notion of biological degeneration made famous by a number of French writers toward the end of the century and widely expressed in England also—the notion that biological species when transported to the new world lose their strength and vitality. Franklin affirmed that even though this may be true of inferior animals, human beings certainly do not deteriorate in the new world. He repeated this defense of America as a salutary habitat on many occasions—particularly in reply to British aspersions just before the Revolution—and in this sense he became the spokesman of the new world against the old.

Immediately after taking over the *Gazette,* Franklin allied himself with the most distinguished political figure in the colony, Andrew Hamilton, the jurist who later gained international eminence as defense attorney in the famous Zenger trial in New York over the freedom of the press. For his consistent defense of local against absentee government and his championship of personal rights, Hamilton has been justly termed the morning star of the American Revolution. Franklin had performed a minor service for Hamilton on his voyage to England, and they became close friends—greatly to Franklin's advantage on several occasions.

In the October election of 1733, Patrick Gordon, governor of Pennsylvania, with the support of Bradford and the *Mercury,* worked to bring about Hamilton's defeat in seeking to retain his post as speaker of the Assembly. Despite Franklin's efforts in the *Gazette,* Hamilton lost, and as an aftermath Franklin and Bradford acrimoniously rehashed the campaign in their papers.

Franklin offered no coverage whatsoever of the famous Zenger trial in the next year, but in November—December 1737 he printed four essays stemming from the trial, defending civil liberties and freedom of the press. In 1735 and 1736 he printed a similar series of essays on the Court of Chancery in Pennsylvania, presenting the view that local rights were guaranteed by the second Pennsylvania charter and that sovereignty was vested in the English Parliament or the colonial Assembly, not in either the proprietor or the governor.

When Franklin took Hall as his partner in 1748, the *Gazette* began to straddle or avoid party issues. Then in 1766, when Franklin dissolved the partnership and withdrew from the *Gazette* altogether, it turned into a proprietary organ.

Franklin's early political independence forecasts his role in the American Revolution. He held a personal conviction of right and wrong, and his spirit would not allow him to remain silent in the face of injustice. A frequently told legend illustrates his moral courage. Some of his friends, alarmed at his vigorous attacks in the *Gazette* upon influential men and favored measures, urged greater moderation. Franklin invited them to dinner the following night, when Deborah served nothing but pudding and water. After the guests had eaten their meager fare, Franklin thanked them for their advice and explained why he would not follow it: "he who can subsist upon saw dust pudding & water, as can Benjamin Franklin, needs not the patronage of any man."

Hamilton was returned to the Assembly in 1734, and it was no doubt in part due to his influence that Franklin was appointed clerk. Franklin's duties were not onerous, but the sessions sometimes seemed interminable. Apart from observing the play of personalities and seeking to understand the motives behind every public utterance (a training which proved invaluable in Franklin's later diplomatic career), he spent his time working out mathematical puzzles and taking notes on the proceedings for his own amusement.

The chief public problem at this time was the defense of the community against the French and their Indian allies. Franklin consistently advocated military preparedness and action—in opposition to the timorous views of the Quakers and the avarice of the proprietors. He never ceased warning that economic necessity impelled the French to invade English possessions. Simple fact showed that from the mouth of the Mississippi to the St. Lawrence, the French had no ports to the sea. Even before becoming clerk of the Assembly, Franklin used the *Gazette* to publicize the imminent danger. In one particularly vigorous piece (6 March 1734), he asked such pertinent questions as whether the French "would not take as much Pride in deflouring *Quaker* girls, as the *English* did in the Nuns of the Town they took in Spain?"

At the outset of his public career, Franklin held an anti-Quaker position—so marked that he was later accused of having proposed "to a very considerable Gentleman in this City [probably William Allen], that they should Unite in Order to demolish the Quakers entirely." By the time this accusation was made, however, he had become pro-Quaker as well as one of the leading opponents of the proprietary party.

In the spring of 1745 the New England colonies organized an expedition to capture Louisburg on the St. Lawrence River. Franklin condemned Governor Thomas of Pennsylvania for pretending to support the expedition in public addresses, gaining thereby the approval of the people of New England, but using his influence in the Assembly to keep Pennsylvania from participating. According to Franklin, Thomas and the Assembly had been "only acting a Farce and playing Tricks to amuse the World."

As the fighting extended southward and Pennsylvania lay in real danger of invasion, Franklin printed a number of pieces in the *Gazette* designed to inculcate the "absolute and obvious necessity of self-defense." He had a personal as well as patriotic motive: because of the war, his book business had declined to almost nothing.

Chief barrier to local defense was the religious scruple of the Quakers against bearing arms, which not only kept them from serving in the militia but hindered the efforts of other citizens in the Assembly. In one of his *Gazettes*, Franklin printed an exegetical essay examining the various New Testament passages which the Quakers regarded as prohibiting them from fighting. The essay asked the Quakers what better reason they could require for lawful warfare than "the Defense of our Country, and the Protection of the Helpless and Innocent."

This was preliminary to a separate tract, *Plain Truth*, pub-

lished 17 November 1747, the piece of writing which effectively
launched Franklin upon a full-time career as a public man.
Since French privateers had been raiding the mainland near
Philadelphia, Franklin had little need to convince his readers of
the likelihood of an enemy invasion. Assuming in his tract the
identity of a tradesman, he berated both the Quakers and the
wealthy element in the city "as People from whom no good
cou'd be expected"—the first because of their conscientious
abhorrence of violence; the second because of their selfishness,
cupidity and resentment. By this artifice Franklin aroused not
only the middle segment of society but most of the others as
well. He argued that the best means of avoiding bloodshed was
to prepare to meet the enemy, "for 'tis a wise and true Saying,
that *One Sword often keeps another in the Scabbard."*

As a practical contribution, Franklin offered to submit a
plan for an Association of military volunteers. He did so within
four days, and within another three days 500 citizens had
enlisted and promised to arm themselves. Eventually more than
a thousand joined the ranks. Since the Assembly persisted in
taking no action whatsoever, the municipal governing body, the
Philadelphia Common Council, gave its support to the Association as the only means of preserving the lives and properties of
the citizens.

Franklin took full charge of almost every phase of the
organization, yet without giving the appearance of imposing his
leadership. Back in 1741 he had published in his *General
Magazine* a manual of arms. Now he sold other manuals as well
as muskets and ammunition. At the first meeting of the Association, 7 December 1747, he read proposals for dividing the city
into districts and the men into companies. The approaches to
the city had to be fortified, and to pay for them Franklin
suggested a lottery. He printed the necessary handbills and
tickets and gave the scheme free publicity in the *Gazette.* While
waiting for new cannons to be shipped from London, the
Council sent Franklin and three other citizens to New York to
borrow some old ones. To keep the Quakers acquiescent, Franklin called in "the Aid of Religion" by proposing a fast day and
drawing up the proclamation when the proposal was approved
by the Council.

The officers of the Philadelphia regiment chose Franklin for colonel, but he declined, following his principle of working behind the scenes. But when the guns were installed in a battery south of the city, he regularly took his turn of duty as a common soldier.

From the first meeting of the Association in November 1747 until the proclaiming of peace in May 1749, Franklin was, in the words of the admiring Quaker, James Logan, "the principal Mover and very Soul of the Whole." Thomas Penn, the proprietor of the colony, however, looked upon Franklin and the Association from a different perspective. An independent armed body within the colony seemed to him to be too much like "a Military Common Wealth" and a threat to his prerogatives. Of Franklin he wrote, "He is a dangerous Man and I should be very Glad he inhabited any other Country, as I believe him of a very uneasy Spirit. However as he is a Sort of Tribune of the People, he must be treated with regard."

Even though Franklin deliberately kept in the background as much as possible, his fellow citizens realized that they owed him their security of life and property. And if *Plain Truth* "bore somewhat hard" on both Quakers and the wealthy, it offended neither group. The citizens showed their gratitude by electing Franklin a member of the Philadelphia Common Council in October 1748. Some of his friends were alarmed that his military activities would alienate the Quakers and that he would consequently lose his influence in the Assembly as well as his clerkship. His neighbor, James Read, who wanted the job for himself, tried to bluff Franklin to step down, pretending that he had inside information that Franklin would be displaced at the next election and advising him to save his honor by resigning. Franklin replied by citing a public man "who made it a rule never to ask for an office, and never to refuse one when offered to him." Franklin made the small addition: "I shall never *ask,* never *refuse,* nor ever *resign* an office."

As soon as the militia had been successfully established, Franklin turned his attention to what he considered the colony's second fundamental need, an institution of higher learning. As early as 1743, Franklin had drawn up a preliminary plan for an

Academy and had tried to interest the Reverend Richard Peters in becoming its head. The latter, an Anglican clergyman of refined tastes, who had come to the colonies after being exposed as a bigamist, demonstrated a sublime indifference to higher education, preferring to devote his talents to the service of the proprietors. In 1749, Franklin revived the academy project among "a Number of active Friends, of whom the Junto furnished a good Part." As usual, he prepared the way for public acceptance by a piece in the *Gazette* (24 August). Here he excused the inhabitants for having devoted themselves in the formative years of the colony to securing the necessities of life but admonished them that the time had now come to cultivate their minds "by the finer arts and sciences." A few weeks afterwards he published a pamphlet *Proposals Relating to the Education of Youth in Pennsylvania,* which he gave away to influential members of the community. True to his policy of concealing his guiding hand in public schemes, he presented the proposals as emanating from a group of "publick-spirited Gentlemen."

Franklin and the attorney-general of Pennsylvania, Tench Francis, together drew up the Constitutions for the Academy, and they and twenty-two other trustees were appointed to serve without compensation. The trustees were to engage a rector and masters and supervise the financial affairs of the school. In addition they were to serve the students as a kind of paternal Junto. In both his Proposals and Constitutions, Franklin required the trustees zealously to unite in a common purpose to aid graduating students, "whether in Business, Offices, Marriages, or any other Thing for their Advantage, preferably to all other Persons whatsoever, even of equal Merit," a kind of nepotism on a broad scale.

Even though writing his proposals at the peak of his experiments with electricity, Franklin allotted to science an extremely minor role. As part of the equipment of the school he proposed merely "some mathematical Instruments, an Apparatus for Experiments in Natural Philosophy, and for Mechanics." Nobody would have expected or accepted more this far back in the eighteenth century. Similarly, in the curriculum, Franklin did not present science as having any great practical value, merely recommending the reading of *"Histories of Nature,"* primarily as a source of delight to the students which would incidentally furnish them material for letters and conversation. The future merchant would be able better to understand his wares; the handworker, to improve his product; and the divine, to adorn his discourses with beautiful comparisons and proofs of divine providence.

Franklin's chief claim to originality was his stress upon English as well as classical languages, and he buttressed his arguments with extensive quotations from Locke and other authorities.

To twentieth-century readers it seems strange that Franklin in his *Proposals* did not portray the new world as a land of unlimited opportunity but pointed out that it had hitherto not furnished the inducements to study which had been offered in the old world. In Europe, he observed, a poor man's son had a chance of rising to eminence in the professions, the church and politics. Franklin wanted to remedy this deficiency by establishing a center of learning in Philadelphia. The new world, he felt, offered one important advantage. "For us, who are now to make a Beginning, 'tis at least as easy to set out right as wrong." Instead of following the old forms of education, he proposed a new era of experiment to suit the new world. Students should be taught "those Things that are likely to be *most useful* and *most ornamental.*" He proposed as subjects of study, writing, mathematics, English, history, geography, and classical and foreign languages.

Swimming he particularly emphasized, not only for the traditional reasons of relaxing body and mind but because it would free the students "from the slavish Terrors" nonswimmers feel "when they are oblig'd to be on the Water even in crossing a Ferry." Apart from their subject matter, Franklin wanted the students to develop "that *Benignity of Mind,* which shows itself in searching for and seizing every Opportunity *to serve* and *to oblige;* and is the Foundation of what is called GOOD BREEDING." This benignity of mind was the keystone of Franklin's own character, the magic ingredient which endeared him to his family, friends and women of all ages, and was the ultimate source of his public popularity. By and large everyone agreed with James Logan's appraisal in 1750, "he is an excellent yet a humble man."

On 1 January 1748, Franklin turned over the running of his printing business to David Hall, resigning himself to moderate circumstances. According to their agreement, Franklin was to furnish his name and the capital investment; Hall to conduct all phases of the business; and they were to have an equal share in the profits. After eighteen years, Hall was to have the option of buying the presses and materials at their value when the contract was drawn.

Franklin retired from active business in part because he hoped to have more time to devote to science and perhaps civic service, but he was mainly interested in taking his ease and traveling. During the relatively tranquil years before and after his decision, he nourished the idea of returning to England to meet Strahan in person. He had no desires whatsoever of amassing a large fortune, considering as absurd the general foible of mankind in pursuing wealth "to no End." He could see no difference between *"dying worth* a great Sum" and of dying in debt for a great sum.

Franklin's first will, which he drew up 22 June 1750, reflects this antimaterialism born of a sense of security. He thanked God for conducting him throughout life "so happily, so free from Sickness, Pain and Trouble, and with such a Competency of this World's Goods as might make a reasonable Mind easy." Franklin attributed his mental health to the moderateness of his passions and to his scheme of virtue which enabled him to control them. For this reason, he felt he had been emancipated from "Ambition, Avarice and Superstition, common Causes of much Uneasiness to Men."

8. Philoprogenitiveness

FRANKLIN'S benignity of mind caused him to extend his
tender emotions beyond the confines of a tightly knit family
group. Respectful of age, tender toward youth, and affectionate
toward women of any age, he warmed toward any human being
who earned his esteem and showed no great partiality toward his
immediate family. Feeling most comfortable in the bosom of a
family, he was not greatly concerned whether the members of
the circle were his blood relations or not.

Toward his parents in Boston, Franklin felt filial gratitude
and respect, touched with a certain admiration of his father's
intellectual powers. Josiah Franklin was a cultivated man, despite his modest social and economic station. He had once
instructed his son with a lively and scientific account of the
heraldry and genealogy of the Franklin family, and Franklin
later adopted some of his father's phraseology for his autobiography. He also acknowledged his father's good sense in criticizing his earliest attempts at verse writing.

Although living at a great distance from his parents, Franklin always remained solicitous of their welfare. When they
complained of physical ailments, he wrote them letters crammed
with physiological detail—on one occasion an elaborate sketch
of treatment for gallstones. During his father's serious illness in
1744, Franklin expressed tender gratitude to his sister Jane for
her care of the invalid. Three years later he sent his mother
money for hiring a carriage so that she might "ride warm to
meetings this winter." As he was entering middle age, he wrote
to his mother that he enjoyed "a tolerable Share of Health" and
that his daily life was agreeable as the years rolled past. Here is
the secret of his universal popularity. People liked him because
he enjoyed life. Looking ahead to his final days, he affirmed that

he would rather have it said of him *"He lived usefully,* than, *He died rich."*

After his brother James died in 1735, Franklin became the virtual head of the Franklin family. The two brothers had been reconciled in 1733 when Franklin revisited Boston and on the way stopped at Newport, where James had established another printing office. At their "very cordial and affectionate" meeting, James, in declining health, received his brother's promise that he would bring up his son, James, Jr., to the printing business. In giving it Franklin made amends for breaking his indenture many years before. When James died in 1735, his son between three and five years of age, Franklin took the boy back to Philadelphia and, before breaking him into the printing trade, sent him to school along with his own son, William.

Like most apprentices, James, Jr., frequently grumbled about the quality of the clothes which his master provided. Shrewdly he doubled his complaints to Deborah when Franklin was out of the way on a trip to Boston in 1746. The indulgent aunt bade him go to a shop and order what he pleased. Franklin later wryly remarked that "the gentleman . . . bought a suit of clothes on my account dearer by one half, than any I ever afforded myself, one suit excepted." He observed that it was the nature of boys to make most fuss about their wardrobe on Sunday morning as a pretext to avoid church, reporting to Jane Mecom, June 1748:

I have brought up four or five myself, and have frequently observed, that if their shoes were bad, they would say nothing of a new pair till Sunday morning, just as the bell rung, when, if you asked them why they did not get ready, the answer was prepared, "I have no shoes," and so of other things, hats and the like; or if they knew of any thing that wanted mending, it was a secret till Sunday morning, and sometimes I believe they would rather tear a little, than be without the excuse.

In considering Franklin's feelings toward his son William, we must be careful not to allow our knowledge of Franklin's coolness when William had attained middle age to color our impression of the period of early childhood. But even though we consider exclusively Franklin's comments before the Revolution, it is impossible to show that he revealed any inordinate pride in his son or derived unusual satisfaction from him. He never voiced any great tenderness for William, as he did for Francis Folger, or exhibited any desire for his continued presence, as he later did for his favorite grandson, Benjamin Franklin Bache. Franklin seems to have been a dutiful father but not particularly attentive or affectionate.

But he was materially as indulgent as any father in the colony. William attended the private school of Theophilus Grew, second mathematician of the Junto, and rode on his own mare. Once the animal strayed away when William was eleven, and Franklin published an advertisement in the *Gazette* under his son's name offering any boys who might bring her back "the Liberty to ride her when they please."

At an early age William developed a lust for adventure. He had hardly turned fifteen when he clamored to join a military expedition against Canada being organized in Pennsylvania. When Franklin refused to give his consent, the lad stole out of the house and tried to ship on board a privateer. The alarmed father had to go on board to retrieve him. After this demonstration of William's determination, Franklin not only relented in regard to the Canada expedition but used his influence to secure his son a commission as ensign in charge of twenty-five men. He also ordered from London a copy of Polybius so that William could learn classical military tactics. The troops marched off to Albany, where they passed the winter of 1746–1747. William became so fond of military life that he would not listen to his family's pleas to come home, but the expedition was called off in the summer before William had a chance to show his mettle. When Franklin made his will in 1750, he allotted William and his daughter Sarah almost equal portions, and he named Deborah and William as joint executors.

Sarah, the only girl in the household, who was born when William was thirteen, came to be somewhat of a pet. For one thing she arrived on the scene when her father had more leisure and fewer worries. When she attained the age of seven, Franklin praised her for "the best Natural Disposition in the World" and told Strahan that "she discovers daily the Seeds and Tokens of Industry, Oeconomy, and in short, of every Female Virtue, which her Parents will endeavour to cultivate."

"Of a most affectionate Temper, and perfectly Dutiful and obliging," Sally endeared herself to her father by her resemblance to his favorite sister Jane—and he expressed to his mother his hopes "that she will prove an ingenious sensible notable and worthy Woman." Already he had enrolled her in dancing school—and two years later he was to order for her from London an elaborate dressing glass. The only anecdote involving the young Sally which has survived concerns the application of Franklin's principle that the individual should persevere at a task until all difficulties are overcome. Once Franklin observed his daughter give up in despair after vainly attempting to make a proper buttonhole. At the moment he said not a word, but on the next day he told her, "Sally, I have made an arrangement with the tailor to have you go to him every day at a fixed hour. He will teach you to make buttonholes."

Franklin admired intellectual women but showed no disappointment that the women of his family achieved no mental distinction. Indeed he probably prized the feminine rather than the sophisticated traits of the women he came in contact with later in life.

As Franklin enjoyed the association with children in a large family, he felt that procreating numerous offspring was a good in itself. This notion, which may be called philoprogenitiveness, was typical of the entire eighteenth century, but no one approached Franklin in the warmth and conviction of endorsing it. The concept was composed of three primary ingredients—biological: the physical sensation of the sex act and its concomitants; domestic: the social and emotional pleasures of a numerous family; and economic: the productive advantage to a nation and community of maximum population. Franklin's writings on the pleasures of procreation are probably the best known, but he wrote with equal sincerity on its social and economic results.

The concept is epitomized in *Poor Richard* for 1735:

> A Ship under sail and a big-bellied Woman,
> Are the handsomest two things that can be seen common.

In the *Gazette* for the same year (4 March), Franklin printed a semifacetious essay vindicating the marriage state against the attacks of an ill-natured bachelor who had tried to deter his friends from the alleged pitfalls of matrimony. Franklin distrusted and despised the motives of a man who would undertake such an ignoble task. He was "like the wicked Servant," who "wrapt up and hid his Talent in a Napkin, (i.e. his Shirt Tail)." Drawing on conventional fertility symbols, Franklin argued that *"Human Planting* must be more Honourable" than gardening "as the Plants to be raised are more excellent in their Nature, and to bring them to Perfection requires the greater Skill and Wisdom." The opponents of marriage and families, Franklin maintained, were spreading a philosophy of sour grapes. "Like the Fox who could not use his Tail . . . they set up for Advisers . . . and would fain persuade others that the Use of their own tails is more mischievous than beneficial."

Franklin carried on this symbolism in several issues of *Poor Richard,* paraphrasing an epigram he had drawn from an English collection:

[1736:] She that paints her Face, thinks of her Tail.
[1738:] Squirrel-like she covers her back with her Tail.
[1739:] Prythee isn't Miss Cloe's a comical Case?
 She lends out her Tail, and she borrows her Face.

Although Franklin is known to have fathered at least one illegitimate child, he always declared in his writings that marital parenthood is preferable to the indiscriminate kind. Because "dear Papa likes to hear of wedings," his daughter Sally once sent him a list of all his acquaintances who were having them. In *Poor Richard* for 1744 he inserted one of his original sayings:

He that has not got a Wife, is not yet a compleat Man.

He repeated the sentiment on many other occasions. In 1768, congratulating a young man on an early marriage, he wrote: "An odd Volume of a Set of Books is not worth its proportion of the Set, and what think you of the Usefulness of an odd Half of a Pair of Scissors. It cannot well cut any thing. It may possibly serve to scrape a Trencher." Later in France he amplified his metaphor. "Man & Woman have each of them Qualities & Tempers, in which the other is deficient, and which in Union contribute to the common Felicity. Single and separate, they are not the compleat human Being: they are like the odd Halves of Scissors; they cannot answer the End of their Formation." At about the same time he confided to Cabanis in reference to his own marriage that man is a complete being only when he possesses a wife worthy of providing for his happiness.

This is necessary background for the understanding of one of Franklin's notorious writings, his letter, 25 June 1745, on the choice of a mistress in which he defends the paradox that a young man in all his amours "should *prefer old Women to young ones.*" Although this is the part of the letter which has struck the public imagination, it must not be overlooked that in his opening remarks Franklin repeated his usual vigorous praise of marriage. He maintained that marriage is the proper remedy for sexual urges since "it is the most natural State of Man." Joining the scissors simile to his maxim from *Poor Richard*, he argued that it "is the Man and Woman united that make the compleat human Being. Separate, she wants his Force of Body and Strength of Reason; he, her Softness, Sensibility and acute Discernment." Only after this persuasive exhortation to marriage did Franklin proceed to his paradox concerning the superiority of old mistresses. Here are his last four reasons:

5. . . . Covering all above with a Basket, and regarding only what is below the Girdle, it is impossible of two Women to know an old from a young one. And as in the dark all Cats are grey, the Pleasure of corporal Enjoyment with an old Woman is at least equal, and frequently superior, every knack being by Practice capable of Improvement.

6. Because the sin is less. The debauching a Virgin may be her Ruin, and make her for Life unhappy.

7. Because the Compunction is less. The having made a young Girl *miserable* may give you frequent bitter reflections; none of which can attend the making an old Woman *happy.*

8thly and Lastly. They are so *grateful!!*

This witty advice never circulated in Franklin's lifetime and was furtively and surreptitiously passed from hand to hand in the nineteenth century. Only recently has it been rescued from its clandestine existence.

Franklin's next lubricious writing, *The Speech of Polly Baker,* has had a completely opposite history. The most famous literary hoax of the eighteenth century, it was printed and reprinted all over Europe and America and adapted by any number of writers, who took it as a serious sociological document. It is Franklin's most outspoken philoprogenitive piece and, as such, represents an accurate reflection of his opinion, but the narrative by which his ideas are surrounded is pure fiction. Yet the entire world accepted the story as literal truth—and it was even reprinted in one of the most influential books of the century, the Abbé Raynal's *Philosophical History.* Although a fine scholar has published an entire book on the sparse two pages comprising Polly's speech, nobody yet knows when Franklin wrote it. As near as anyone has been able to discover, it appeared for the first time in the London *General Advertiser,* 15 April 1747; yet Franklin himself told Thomas Jefferson that he made it up when he was printer and editor of a newspaper and needed fillers for his columns during the slack season. One would think that he was referring to the *Pennsylvania Gazette,* but Polly Baker is not there.

According to Franklin's fanciful story, Miss Polly Baker had been haled into court "at Connecticut near Boston in New-England," where she was prosecuted for her fifth offense of having a bastard child. Polly had a number of defenses—i.e., she would have preferred wedlock but had been betrayed by her seducer; she had maintained her children by her own industry; and she had neither enticed another woman's husband nor debauched any youth. But her principal plea was that she had actually committed a meritorious deed—useful from the perspective of society; honorable from the perspective of the Christian religion. She begged the civil authority to consider that she had added to "the Number of the King's Subjects, in a new Country that really wants People"; and she reminded the ecclesiastical authority that she had faithfully performed "the Duty of the first and great Command of Nature, and of Nature's God, *Encrease and Multiply*." For this reason, she felt she should have, instead of a whipping, a statue erected to her memory.

Here again Franklin exalts "the Honourable State of Wedlock," but in treating procreation he goes beyond mere approval to the stage of glorification. His intention is partly humorous, but there can be no doubt that he accepted Polly's arguments for maximum procreation on both economic and deistical grounds. Also he was quite probably offering a tardy, discreet and bantering vindication of his own performance of "the first and great Command of Nature" in conceiving his natural child, William.

Franklin used the vocabulary of philoprogenitiveness even in one of his pieces on money-making, *Advice to a young Tradesman,* published in July 1748. After prosaic hints on the value of money and credit, he urged, almost rhapsodically, "Remember that Money is of a prolific generating Nature. Money can beget Money, and its Offspring can beget more, and so on. . . . He that kills a breeding Sow, destroys all her Offspring to the thousandth Generation. He that murders a Crown, destroys all it might have produc'd, even Scores of Pounds." Franklin carried over this imagery even into his autobiography, reporting his discovering "the Truth of the Observation, that after getting the first hundred Pound, it is more easy to get the second: Money itself being of a prolific Nature."

In a later chapter we shall see that Franklin's most important essay on economics concerned the tremendous growth of population in America, a phenomenon which gave him substantial pride and satisfaction.

9. The Electrical Years

A T EXACTLY the same period that external forces were contriving to turn Franklin into a public man, other external forces were operating to turn him into a man of science. In 1743 he saw his first electrical experiment conducted by an obscure and not particularly skilful physician. Ten years later he had become universally recognized as the greatest electrical mind of the age and had been awarded the Copley Medal of the Royal Society. This was a decade of scientific wonders for the entire learned world as well as for Franklin. One of his English friends, Peter Collinson, observed in 1746 that "the Surprising Phenomena of the Polypus" had absorbed the virtuosi of Europe for the past two years and that they had then devoted their attention to electrical experiments, astonishing themselves by investing other human beings with electric fire by the simple process of rubbing a glass tube. In April 1745, the *Gentleman's Magazine* in a glowing "Account of the wonderful discoveries . . . concerning Electricity" rapturously described the same "astonishing discoveries": "The polypus on one hand, as incredible as a prodigy, and the electric fire, on the other, as surprising as a miracle."

Franklin along with the rest of the scientific world marveled at both polyps and electric fire. In *Poor Richard* for 1751 he incorporated a description of the microscopic polyp, explaining its manner of taking nourishment by encompassing other organisms and of procreating by fission. "What is wonderful, and almost beyond Belief is, that it will live and feed after it is turned inside out, and even when cut into a great many Pieces, each several Piece becomes a compleat Polype." Later in the same year Franklin in a work on "The Increase of Mankind" compared the reproductive capacities of a nation to those of a polyp. Perhaps he could have become an eminent protozoologist. But instead of the reproduction of invisible cells, he developed his interest in the production of pyrotechnics.

One would not have expected from the events in Franklin's boyhood that he would develop into the most famous American scientist of his time. In school he had twice failed in arithmetic, although a few years later he took a standard text and mastered it with ease. He also absorbed the modicum of geometry in one or two elementary books of navigation.

He seems to have made his first serious application to practical science in 1725 on his return voyage from London. In addition to playing cards and checkers, he amused himself by taking notes on ocean currents, temperature and meteorological conditions. Four years later he was the first to make what has since become a classic experiment in physics. To prove a definite relation between color and heat absorption, he and a friend placed squares of different-colored cloth on snow and measured the relative depths to which they sank under the rays of the bright sun.

For his *Pennsylvania Gazette,* Franklin wrote detailed accounts of his own observations of several natural phenomena: the effect of earthquakes upon the color of rivers (10 July 1732); the nature of the aurora borealis (29 October 1730); and the behavior of comets (3 March 1742). In October 1743, as a result of waiting to see an eclipse of the moon, he discovered that northeast storms actually moved in the direction from southwest to northeast, that is, opposite to the prevailing wind.

Franklin's first major incursion into practical science was the invention in 1739–1740 of an iron stove which gave off much greater heat than the conventional fireplace and economized greatly on wood. Acting on the principle that "as we enjoy great Advantages from the Inventions of others, we should be glad of an Opportunity to serve others by any Invention of ours," Franklin refused to accept a patent offered by the governor of Pennsylvania. He turned over his plans for manufacture to his friend Robert Grace in gratitude for the loan which Grace had extended him to enable him to open his printing shop. Grace turned out the stoves in quantity, and Franklin to promote their sale advertised them in the *Gazette* and wrote and printed a descriptive brochure, *An Account of the New Invented Pennsylvania Fire Places,* 1744. What is remarkable about this promotional pamphlet is the vigorous literary style—enlivened with a proverb later used in *Poor Richard*—and one or two successful attempts at humor. Iron, we are told, "is always sweet, and every way taken is wholesome and friendly to the human Body—except in Weapons." And with an ironical dig at a notorious English prejudice, which still survives, Franklin remarked, *"That warm Rooms make People tender and apt to catch Cold,* is a Mistake as great as it is (among the English) general."

Although in his pamphlet Franklin professed to be "neither Physician nor Philosopher," he revealed that he had already made a serious and penetrating study of the works of his contemporary Newtonian scientist, J. T. Desaguliers.

In May 1743, Franklin set forth for a visit to Boston and the northern colonies. On the road in Connecticut, he accidentally fell into the company of the most ambitious scientific mind in the colonies, Cadwallader Colden, once a practising physician and author of treatises on botany, mathematics and medicine. Both men were delighted with the encounter. Colden confided to Franklin details of a new printing process which he had invented—a form of stereotyping—and Franklin outlined a scheme for erecting a society at Philadelphia for promoting arts and sciences in the colonies. In the next year he cooperated with other advocates of a learned society to form the group which is considered the nucleus of the present American Philosophical Society.

Colden later wrote to William Strahan, praising Franklin as the most ingenious printer in America, and Strahan replied that his fame had long ago reached England.

After Franklin reached Boston, he attended in May 1743 a demonstration of the new science of electricity by an Edinburgh-trained physician, Dr. Archibald Spencer (wrongly called Adam in most publications). Spencer's course of lectures "surpriz'd and pleas'd" the visiting printer, even though he later came to realize that the experiments had been imperfectly performed. Franklin published an advertisement for Spencer in the *Gazette* when the electrical wizard came to Philadelphia in April of the next year, but he had no inclination to carry on experiments of his own until 1746, when Peter Collinson sent him the account of the electrical wonders from the *Gentleman's Magazine* together with an electrical tube and directions for using it. Early experimenters charged glass tubes by rubbing them with silk.

Collinson, a Quaker merchant and distinguished horticulturist, did more for Franklin's career than any other person. In addition to starting him on his electrical pursuits, he later helped him to attain the office of Deputy Postmaster General of America, the post which in large measure led to Franklin's eventual political eminence. Since Franklin called him his "old friend" at the time of his embarking for England on his second voyage, it is possible that Franklin had met Collinson during his earlier voyage in his teens. It is difficult otherwise to account for Collinson's interest in the American printer.

As Franklin began using Collinson's tube to duplicate the standard European experiments, his house became filled with curious visitors. To diminish the annoyance of these visits, he commissioned local glass blowers to produce other tubes, and soon there were a number of virtuosi performing throughout the city. One of these, an unemployed Baptist minister, Ebenezer Kinnersley, Franklin encouraged to undertake lecture demonstrations for money—even drawing up the lectures and supervising construction of the equipment. Kinnersley's subsequent fame as an electrician in the colonies was exceeded only by that of Franklin himself. In July 1747, the Library Company received from Thomas Penn, proprietor of Pennsylvania, a "compleat Electrical Apparatus," and Franklin immediately took the lead in using it. Finally, Franklin rounded out his personal collection by purchasing all of Spencer's electrical apparatus.

It is still impossible to know with certainty the arrival date of Collinson's present of the electric tube which inspired Franklin's experiments, but it was no earlier than December 1745. In his correspondence with Colden prior to this, Franklin showed an interest in other scientific subjects but did not even mention electricity.

In August 1745, Franklin sent Colden a long critique of an anatomical manuscript of Colden's on the subject of perspiration and the blood stream. To illustrate one of his points, Franklin had set up a rather complicated apparatus consisting of glass tubes and a syphon. He also included a separate enclosure, "A Guess at the Cause of the Heat of the Blood in Health and of the hot and cold Fits of some Fevers." It would seem that if Franklin had already embarked on his electrical experiments, he would not have been able to devote this much attention to anatomical and medical theories. Excusing himself in his letter for presuming to differ from a distinguished physician on medical subjects, Franklin modestly conjectured "that I ought to study the Sciences I dabble in, before I presume to set Pen to Paper."

In November, Franklin wrote again to Colden promising to print at his own expense and risk another of Colden's treatises, an explanation of the causes of gravitation. His policy, he maintained, was to work without gain if he could be the instrument of communicating something valuable to mankind.

In line with his zeal for the promulgation of scientific knowledge, he announced his determination to publish an "American Philosophical Miscellany," but the project never materialized. He was disappointed also with his scientific society: the members were very idle gentlemen who would take no pains. In these projects and in his own experiments, Franklin had been proceeding on the belief that "he who removes a Prejudice or an Error from our Minds, contributes to their Beauty; as he would do to that of our Faces, who should clear them of a Wart or a Wen."

Presumably, soon after writing to Colden, Franklin began duplicating the European electrical experiments and trying some of his own. One of his typical demonstrations was to animate an electrical spider so that he resembled a living one and make him seem to catch at a fly. More spectacularly, he once proposed to entertain a "party of pleasure on the banks of the

Skuylkil" by killing a turkey by electric shock, roasting him on an electric jack, and drinking the healths of the famous electricians of the world from electrified bumpers.

By March 1747 electricity had more completely engrossed Franklin's time and attention than any other study he had ever undertaken. He had little leisure for anything else, he wrote to Collinson, "what with making experiments when I can be alone, and repeating them to my friends and acquaintance, who from the novelty of the thing, come continually in crowds to see them." In the following spring, having reached the age of forty-two, attained financial independence, and fulfilled his civic duties with the successful Association for the defense of Philadelphia, Franklin decided that he was now ready to devote his life primarily to private intellectual and scientific pursuits. He completely gave up his bookseller's trade, put his printing house under the care of his partner, David Hall, and moved to a quieter part of town. As he wrote to Colden, 29 September 1748, he planned "to read, study, make Experiments, and converse at large with such ingenious & worthy Men as are pleas'd to honour me with their Friendship or Acquaintance, on such Points as may produce something for the common Benefit of Mankind, uninterrupted by the little Cares & Fatigues of Business."

Electrical demonstrations, when Franklin first penetrated their mysteries, consisted chiefly in rubbing glass rods in order to produce sparks. At the end of his ten years of experiments, the science had progressed to the understanding of lightning rods and the transmission of electric currents, largely because of two major discoveries made by Franklin himself: the existence of plus and minus charges in electricity, and the identity of electricity and lightning.

Franklin's earliest experiments were made with the Leyden jar—originally a corked bottle partly filled with water, which had been charged through a wire embedded in the cork. Franklin's great discovery was the equilibrium of the plus and minus charges (terms which he himself invented) . As he explained it: "At the same time that the wire and top of the bottle &c. is electrised *positively* or *plus,* the bottom of the bottle is electrised *negatively* or *minus,* in exact proportions: *i.e.* whatever quantity of electrical fire is thrown in at the top, an equal quantity goes out of the bottom." Franklin's language illustrates a close relationship between his scientific theories and his metaphysical ones. In 1725 he had described the equilibrium of pleasure and pain in human experience as a type of balanced plus and minus relationship. "As our *Uneasinesses* are alway's remov'd by some Means or other, it follows that *Pleasure* and *Pain* are in their Nature inseparable: So many Degrees as one Scale of the Ballance descends, so many exactly the other ascends; and one cannot rise or fall without the Fall or Rise of the other." Franklin's mind was geared to systems: he visualized the same regularity in both electrical and psychological phenomena. His electrical theory survived because it could be confirmed experimentally; his psychological theory had to be discarded since it obviously could not be confirmed. Franklin made none of his discoveries by accident: they were all preceded by a carefully wrought theory.

The one great experiment in which Franklin put a hypothesis to the test of observation was his method of proving the identity of electricity and lightning, which Joseph Priestley described as a discovery "the greatest, perhaps, that has been made in the whole compass of philosophy, since the time of Sir Isaac Newton."

Others before Franklin had proposed the hypothesis, but he was the first to suggest a method of proving it. According to his "doctrine of points," lightning or electricity could be attracted from the air during a storm by means of a rod of iron shaped like a needle at the summit of a tall building or by a number of similar points. In his journal, 7 November 1749, he noted, "Let the experiment be made," but he had still not made it when his theories were printed two years later in his monumental London pamphlet, *Experiments and Observations on Electricity.* There was no spire in Philadelphia at that time high enough to attract the electrical charge, and Franklin was presumably waiting for the construction of a steeple on Christ Church. But he got the idea of sending up a kite during a thunderstorm and in June 1752 went out into the country, accompanied only by his son William, in order to avoid the ridicule which he was afraid would have been heaped upon him had he failed. The kite was equipped with a pointed wire to draw the lightning and a metal key at the base of the string. When the kite was aloft in a cloud and the rain had saturated the string, Franklin was able to draw sparks from the key. He had literally brought lightning from the heavens.

In the meantime the eminent French naturalist Buffon had seen Franklin's published *Experiments* and arranged to have them translated. Almost immediately thereafter a French botanist who had recently taken up electricity, Thomas-François Dalibard, performed the experiment, 10 May 1752, from a pointed bar forty feet high in accordance with Franklin's instructions. Although the French experiment preceded Franklin's by a few weeks, he had no knowledge of it and believed that his own kite experiment was the first. Dalibard gave Franklin all of the glory for conceiving the method of bringing electricity from the skies, and Louis XV ordered that the wizard of Philadelphia be sent his compliments and thanks.

The leading French electrician, Jean-Antoine Nollet, however, whose lustre had been dimmed by Franklin's theories, received them with disdain. As Franklin remarked in his autobiography, Nollet "could not at first believe that such a work came from America and said it must have been fabricated by his enemies at Paris to decry his system." Nollet deliberately set about to destroy Franklin's reputation by rigging experiments to make them fail and publishing a series of condescending letters denying the validity of Franklin's theories.

Franklin began an answer but changed his mind, preferring to let his papers "shift for themselves." Shortly after Nollet's letters appeared, he advised a correspondent against expressing resentment against one's adversaries. "In such Cases, the noblest Victory is obtained by Neglect, and by *Shining on.*" With Nollet he easily won the noblest victory. Others took up the defense of his system, and he had the satisfaction of seeing his opponent thoroughly discredited.

On other points besides the nature of lightning, Franklin's electrical studies were inextricably involved with meteorology—

indeed he made little distinction between the two branches of science. He wrote extensively on the causes of earthquakes, on nearly all of the common phenomena of weather, on whether the fresh water in rivers reaches the sea, on whether whirlwinds and water spouts are the same, and on the causes of thunder-gusts. His paper on the last subject was read to the Royal Society in November 1749 and received with serious approval, even though Franklin recorded in his autobiography that it was "laught at by the Connoisseurs." Seven years later another of his papers, *Physical and Meteorological Observations, Conjectures and Suppositions,* was also read to the Royal Society. Here he explained why our breath is visible in cold air, not in warm; why fogs, mists, and clouds remain suspended; why hail is formed in summer; and why snow on the mountaintops in the torrid zone never melts.

Although circumstances forced Franklin to give up his scientific investigations shortly after the publication of his *Experiments,* his scientific curiosity never waned. "This is the age of experiments," he remarked in his autobiography. In 1780 he confided to Priestley that the rapid progress true science was then making sometimes made him regret that he was born so soon. His imagination led him to speculate on the heights which in a thousand years the power of man over matter might be carried. We may, he speculated, "perhaps learn to deprive large Masses of their Gravity, and give them absolute Levity, for the sake of easy Transport. Agriculture may diminish its Labours and double its Produce; all Diseases may by sure means be prevented or cured, not excepting even that of Old Age, and our Lives lengthened at pleasure even beyond the antediluvian Standard." But much as Franklin prized scientific progress, he would certainly have exchanged some advances for certain social reforms. Indeed he once categorically placed political duties above scientific research. "Had Newton been Pilot but of a single common Ship, the finest of his Discoveries would scarce have excus'd, or aton'd for his abandoning the Helm one Hour in Time of Danger; how much less if she had carried the Fate of the Commonwealth." Also Franklin considered the moral world more important than the scientific. To George Whitefield he observed that the discovery of the means of winning the multitudes to virtue would "deserve more, ten thousand times, than the inventor of the longitude."

And what of Franklin's personal reaction to his scientific investigations? Many authors have quoted his words to Collinson: "In going on with these Experiments, how many pretty systems do we build, which we soon find ourselves oblig'd to destroy! If there is no other Use discover'd of Electricity, this, however, is something considerable, that it may *help to make a vain Man humble.*" There is no question that Franklin had his share of vanity—and it was always somewhat of a struggle for him to subdue it. Indeed he had more success in concealing than subduing. When he learned of the compliments of Louis XV, he compared himself to a girl suddenly proud because of the possession of a new pair of garters covered by her petticoats. But after considering his honors, he came to the conclusion that he had "not so much Reason to be proud as the Girl had; for a Feather in the Cap is not so useful a Thing, or so serviceable to the Wearer, as a Pair of good silk Garters."

Franklin was always sensitive about the opinion of others even though he undertook his experiments primarily to satisfy his own curiosity. But he had no feeling of dedication or zeal to advance the future of human knowledge. If his discoveries were accepted by the learned world, he was pleased; and if any of his practical inventions brought to himself and others some degree of ease and convenience, he was pleased also. But he worked primarily for personal satisfaction.

The "first learned Society that took Notice" of Franklin's experiments was not Yale, as Franklin once said, but Harvard College, which granted him the M.A. degree at the instigation of Mather Byles in July 1753. Yale followed suit two months later. The Royal Society awarded him the Copley Medal in November 1753 and elected him to membership in 1756. Some years later, when he had become a member of the council, he had an opportunity to look into the records of his election. His vanity and sense of thrift were pleased together by the discovery that all other members were required to pay initiation and annual fees, but an exception had been made for him—he paid nothing!

For many years, scholars have tried to decide whether Franklin's science was primarily practical or theoretical. For his own opinion, one may point to his question in 1761, "What signifies Philosophy that does not apply to some Use?" One may also suggest that he answered it two decades later in France on the occasion of the first balloon ascent in history. When someone asked what use was the balloon which had just been sent aloft, Franklin replied with typical simplicity: "Of what use is a new-born baby?"

Franklin himself declared that he had "too strong a penchant to the building of hypotheses" since they indulged his "natural indolence." "True philosophy," he insisted, could be founded only on patient and accurate observation, which must always take precedence over conjectures and suppositions. His own efforts he called "philosophical amusements."

Yet his contemporaries compared him to Newton, as I. Bernard Cohen has pointed out, because they realized that he had discovered general laws. He was honored by the Royal Society for his theoretical science—a philosophy of electricity—rather than for his mere physical feat of harnessing lightning. And this is why scientists of our times consider Franklin as one of the most influential exponents of "true philosophy" since Copernicus.

10. School and Society

DURING his electrical period, Franklin's most important public project was that of rallying public support for the Academy. As other citizens responded to his appeals, Franklin realized that the most feasible location for the institution would be the "New Building," erected by the followers of Whitefield. Since the evangelist's visits to the colony were infrequent, and no other preacher could draw such enormous crowds, the "New Building" had become somewhat of a white elephant.

Franklin, as a trustee of both the Building and the Academy, was in an excellent position to negotiate for its conversion. He persuaded the trustees of the preaching house to cede it to the Academy in return for the discharge of its debts and an agreement to maintain a large hall for preaching. As soon as the negotiations were completed in February 1750, Franklin took full charge of renovating the building for its new use. In his memoirs Franklin observed that he cheerfully undertook "the care and trouble of agreeing with the workmen, purchasing materials, and superintending the work," but in the midst of his labors, 13 February 1750, he complained that "In this Affair, as well as in other publick Affairs I have been engag'd in, the Labouring Oar has lain and does lay very much upon me."

One of his most difficult tasks was that of recruiting a headmaster who would combine academic prestige, enthusiasm and administrative skill. Early in July 1750, Franklin and Tench Francis went off to Connecticut to interview such a man, Samuel Johnson, a Yale graduate with an Oxford D.D., who had earned a reputation as philosopher and controversialist as well as teacher. Pleased with Johnson's appearance and scholarly attainments, they offered him the post, 9 August, shortly after their return to Philadelphia. As an inducement, Franklin proposed to print Johnson's philosophical works. Johnson hedged, and Franklin wrote a series of letters, attempting to persuade him to accept. Eventually Johnson declined on the grounds of age and poor health, only to accept the presidency of King's College (Columbia) several months later.

The next serious candidate was William Smith, a Scottish tutor to a wealthy New York family, who had sent Franklin a copy of a utopian tract, *The College of Mirania,* 1753, which he had written to promote higher education in New York. Despite his humble antecedents, Smith had aristocratic inclinations and a great deal of arrogance. Smith needed less persuasion than Johnson, and after returning to England for Anglican ordination he accepted the appointment as rector in the spring of 1754. If there is any man who can be considered the villain in the story of Franklin's life, Smith is that man, as we shall see in subsequent chapters.

Franklin, in his correspondence with Smith and Johnson, freely admitted that he had never been educated himself "(except as a Tradesman) nor ever concern'd in educating others." He never had the least doubts about securing good teachers, assuring Richard Peters that "money would buy learning of all sorts." And he promised Smith that the trustees were "determin'd always to give good Salaries." He viewed the Academy primarily as a salutary cultural influence in the community. "Wise and good men are," he felt, "the *strength* of a state: much more so than riches or arms. . . . And though the culture bestowed on *many* should be successful only with a few, yet the influence of those few and the service in their power, may be very great."

In keeping with his tradesman's background, Franklin believed that education should be offered to others in the community besides future ministers, doctors and lawyers but that the curriculum for these others should be different, particularly in the substitution of English and modern languages for the classical. Later in life he termed Latin and Greek "the quackery of literature." To justify his somewhat novel concept, Franklin published a long essay, *Idea of the English School,* 1751. Designed for boys of from eight to sixteen in age, the curriculum consisted in writing, spelling, reading, public speaking, natural history, composition, ethics and history. As usual, Franklin's most consistently mentioned teaching aid was the *Spectator.*

While placing greatest stress on reading, he gave a much more important place to science (Natural and Mechanic History) than he had in his remarks on the Academy, asserting that "next to the Knowledge of *Duty,* this Kind of Knowledge is certainly the most useful, as well as the most entertaining." And in a letter to Peter Collinson, 4 February 1751, he remarked that he would do his best to have "Natural History establish'd in the Academy" as "a Science of more real Worth and Usefulness, [than] several of the others we propose to teach, put together."

At about this time, Franklin was active also in promoting the Pennsylvania Hospital, printing his *Gazette* essay already alluded to (August 1751) as well as a tract, *Some Account of the Pennsylvania Hospital,* 1754. Franklin did not originate the hospital scheme, however, but was merely one of a group of benevolent citizens engaged. Once again his ingenuity was crucial in raising money. He seems to have invented the fund-matching device popular in our day, persuading the Assembly to grant to the hospital an amount equal to that which it could raise by voluntary contributions. In 1751 Franklin was appointed one of the board of managers of the hospital and first secretary.

In these months Franklin's plans for philosophic retirement underwent a radical change. Immediately after the formation of the Association, he had written to Colden (29 September 1748) that his friends had wanted to elect him to the Assembly but he had dissuaded them, declaring that he "should not serve if chosen." Four years later he took his seat and kept it for thirteen years. Somewhat later, congratulating Colden on his prospects of passing the rest of his days in philosophical retirement (14 September 1752), Franklin could say merely, "I wish for the same, but it seems too distant."

When he vacated his post of clerk, both his son William and Deborah's relative by marriage James Read were candidates to replace him. Franklin must have felt inwardly gratified when his son won out over the persistent Read, whose efforts to secure the post had annoyed Franklin in the past. On 1 October 1751, Franklin was elected alderman of Philadelphia, and one of his first duties was to draft an ordinance regulating town constables and watchmen—the fulfillment of a Junto paper deploring the lack of efficient night-policing of the city. When his mother heard the news of his election, she complimented her son on the respect shown him, but did not know "what the better you will be of it beside the honer of it."

Another of Franklin's schemes came to fruition in March 1752, the founding of a fire insurance company, known as the Hand-in-Hand, of which Franklin was elected president.

We now come to one of the most significant episodes in Franklin's life—his attempt to become Joint Deputy Postmaster General of the American colonies to succeed the incumbent, who was in declining health. William Allen, chief justice of Pennsylvania and married to the daughter of Franklin's friend Andrew Hamilton, used his influence with the postmasters general in London and authorized his agents to advance whatever fees would be necessary to obtain Franklin's appointment. On 21 May 1751, Franklin wrote to Peter Collinson, asking him to use his influence jointly with Allen's. He gave the impression that the annual salary of 150 pounds was to him a secondary consideration—that he coveted the office as a means of increasing his *"Power* of doing Good," particularly in promoting by correspondence his scheme of extending knowledge in the colonies. The salary may very well have been of minor importance, but one cannot help wondering whether Franklin looked upon the position as a means of extending his personal prestige. Almost from the moment of his appointment in 1753, the office brought Franklin opportunities of meeting men "of great place" and advancing his own projects. His letter to Collinson indicates that Franklin did not literally carry out the principle expressed in his autobiography of never asking for, never refusing, or never resigning an office. But he was honest enough in his memoirs, even though repeating his phrase about the "power of doing good," to add that his ambition was flattered by the many offices which came to him at this period, "for considering my low beginning they were great things to me."

As more and more great things came to Franklin, his reputation grew accordingly. Jonathan Todd, a Connecticut minister, spoke of him as one of the chief gentlemen "in the Republick of Letters, whose Parts, Industry and Learning are known in both Englands; and devoted to the Welfare of Mankind." When James Alexander, eminent New York mathematician, sponsored the project of cooperative observation of one of the most significant astronomical events of the century, the transits of Venus across the surface of the sun, he used Franklin as distributing center for his plans because of Franklin's well-known "Love to Literature and the Good of Mankind in General." And the watchful Whitefield, aware that Franklin was growing "more and more famous in the learned world," exhorted him to turn next to the "diligent unprejudiced pursuit and study" of "the mystery of the new-birth."

While going about his projects of local improvement, Franklin also had an eye to the entire American continent and its relationship to the mother country. In common with nearly every English theologian of the century and every economist before Malthus, he firmly believed the verse in Proverbs (14:28), "In the multitude of people is the king's honour," an important aspect of his philoprogenitiveness. In 30 March 1738, he had published an anonymous essay in the *Gazette* equating prosperity with population growth and arguing that the royal interest would best be served by maintaining civil liberties in the colonies. Franklin may have written this important essay himself, and, if he did not, he was indebted to its author for the ideas on population which later gave him world-wide fame as a political philosopher.

According to this essay, Britain sent forth her colonies to extend her trade and sell her goods, which are consumed in proportion to the number of inhabitants. Since "it is an allowed maxim, that wherever Liberty shines, there people will naturally flock to bask themselves in it's Beams," Pennsylvania, known for its liberty, had annually attracted people from Germany and other European nations, and as a result the province had "trebled her inhabitants within these last 20 years." Here much of the colonial increase was attributed to movements of population rather than generation. In *Poor Richard* for 1750, Franklin reported an English computation "that the Colonies on the Continent, taken one with another, double the Number of their Inhabitants every Thirty Years" and asserted that this "quick Increase is owing not so much to natural Generation, as the accession of Strangers." But he added his personal belief that "People increase faster by Generation in these Colonies, where all can have full Employ, and there is Room and Business for Millions yet unborn."

In the next year he formally presented his reasons for the more rapid generation in America than in the old settled countries in a highly influential essay, *Observations concerning the Increase of Mankind, Peopling of Countries, &c.,* which he circulated in manuscript but did not publish until 1755. His argument runs: People increase in proportion to the ease and convenience of supporting a family. This economic facility exists to a high degree in unsettled countries like America. Whatever increases production increases population, and those citizens who aid in the process deserve to be called "Fathers of their Nation." In the American colonies the population doubled in 20 or 25 years, but the process required about 350 years in Europe. In another century, the colonies would outstrip the mother country.

Franklin's essay was reprinted and circulated widely throughout the British Isles, and he became the recognized authority on colonial economics. The impact of his observations of population growth, leading to fears that colonial power would increase with numbers, brought about some of the restrictive measures which England leveled against the colonies and in turn helped to bring on the American Revolution. The peopling theme became almost an obsession with Franklin, and his friend Benjamin Vaughan even considered Franklin's life as portrayed in his memoirs as a symbol of the new world and its "rising people." Because of his essay, Vaughan applied to Franklin a motto from Virgil referring to Jupiter:

Hominum Rerumque Repertor.
"Of men and things the Discoverer."

The concluding remarks of the *Observations,* however, drew the wrath of some of Franklin's critics and even led to his being defeated in an election. In this reprobated passage, Franklin made some unkind comments about Negroes and Germans, objecting on esthetic principles to the black and tawny complexions of African and Asiatic races and preferring "the lovely White and Red" of the Anglo-Saxons. He repudiated the Germans or "Palatine Boors" because they retained their own language and held out against becoming Anglicized. Two years later Franklin amplified his opinions of the Germans and Indians in Pennsylvania in an equally significant letter to Peter Collinson (9 May 1753). He repeated his objections to Germans on grounds of their alien language and reluctance to assimilate and added that their nationalistic exclusiveness made them refuse to participate in defending the colony. Recognizing that the German and English racial stocks were essentially the same, he concluded that the differences between the two nations must "arise from Institution" rather than nature. The Indian distaste for labor and civilized refinements he attributed to the ease by which they could satisfy their needs "by the spontaneous Productions of Nature." For this reason, also, they set little value "on what we prize so highly under the name of Learning."

Labor Franklin considered a fundamental good in society, and the institutions which he recommended were designed to promote or enforce hard work upon the lower orders of society. In regard to industry and frugality, which he regarded as religious duties, he even considered the Germans superior to the English.

In these views, Franklin exposed a conservative tinge to his thought which might even be interpreted as callous. He wondered "whether the Laws peculiar to England which compel the Rich to maintain the Poor" had not encouraged laziness and improvidence. Although acknowledging the Shaftesburian principle that "To relieve the misfortunes of our fellow creatures is concurring with the Deity, 'tis Godlike," he immediately suggested that "the order of God and Nature . . . perhaps has appointed Want and Misery as the proper Punishments for, and

Cautions against, as well as necessary consequences of Idleness and Extravagancy." He approved the institution of workhouses in England so that the poor should no longer be supported in idleness.

In regard to social reform, Franklin took the ultrareactionary view that "whenever we attempt to mend the scheme of Providence and to interfere in the Government of the World, we had need be very circumspect lest we do more harm than good." But in regard to controlling natural phenomena he had no such misgivings. A mere four weeks previously Franklin had ridiculed religious prejudices against lightning rods. "Surely," he had argued, "the Thunder of Heaven is no more supernatural than the Rain, Hail or Sunshine of Heaven, against the Inconveniencies of which we guard by Roofs and Shades without Scruple."

Although Franklin was Philadelphia's outstanding scientist and civic projector, he can hardly be considered an advanced social thinker at this period. His respect for frugality and industry overpowered his benevolence. At the same time we must recognize that Franklin opposed all artificial barriers of rank or social class. When the merchants of Philadelphia organized an assembly for dancing, they attempted to discriminate against the mechanics, whom they considered inferior, by refusing them admission. Franklin ridiculed this snobbish rule so wittily that it was struck out. It would exclude God Almighty, Franklin charged, for "He is notoriously the greatest mechanic in the universe; having, as the Scripture testifies, made all things, and that by weight and measure."

Franklin was able to devote his time to civic betterment because at home everything was just as he liked it, thrifty, tidy and harmonious. His son William, all notions of maritime adventure or military grandeur out of his head, had begun to study law, and Franklin wrote to ask Strahan to enter his name in one of the Inns of Court (6 December 1750). As a dutiful parent, Franklin decided (28 June 1751) to accompany William to London when he should be ready to enter the Middle Temple, where Strahan had enrolled him in February. In the fall of 1751, William made a trip to New England, and Franklin recommended him to the "motherly care and advice" of Jane Mecom. Franklin confided to his sister that William was "indeed a sober and discreet lad of his years, but . . . young and unacquainted with the ways of your place." In Boston, young William made a good impression on Franklin's family and intellectual acquaintances, James Bowdoin in particular, who commended his "good sense, and Gentlemanly Behaviour."

More of a problem to Franklin than his son was his nephew, Benjamin Mecom. Franklin arranged to have him apprenticed to James Parker in 1745 at the age of thirteen. Although a likeable boy, Benjamin immediately showed signs of an instability of character which was eventually to turn into actual insanity. Although Parker treated him well, young Benny delivered himself of more than the usual number of complaints expected from apprentices, frequently stayed out all night, and once tried to enlist with a privateer. Seven years later, Franklin installed him in his Antigua printing office in the spot he had originally designed for David Hall. Benny's querulousness continued, and Franklin regretfully concluded that he had been "too forward in cracking the shell, and producing the chick to the air before its time."

Franklin frequently sent little gifts of money to Jane as well as to his mother. When his mother died in 1752, Franklin thanked his sister and brother-in-law for their "long continued care in her old age and sickness," which distance had kept him from sharing. Revealing his religious optimism or stoicism, he concluded that "She has lived a good life, as well as a long one, and is happy." In the next year, he similarly condoled with his friend Peter Collinson on the latter's loss of his wife. But he did not presume to offer conventional consolations drawn from religion and philosophy. "Natural Affections must have their Course. The best remedy of Grief is Time." Franklin's father had died in January 1745, but we have no record of his feelings when he heard the news. On the stone which he later placed on his parents' grave, he inscribed that his father was "a pious and prudent Man," his mother "a discreet and virtuous Woman."

From now on we shall see a major change in Franklin's mode of living and outlook upon life. Removed from the confining perspective of a small tradesman, he has already become a local politician as well as one of the most important Crown officers in all the colonies, and he has acquired an international reputation as a scientist. He will henceforth travel widely and meet the most substantial citizens of the land, and the area of his thought will become proportionately enlarged.

❖❖*❖*❖*❖*❖*❖*❖*❖*❖*❖*❖*❖*

11. Two Abortive Plans of Union

IN SEPTEMBER 1753, Governor James Hamilton appointed Franklin and two other civic leaders as commissioners to negotiate with the Indians at Carlisle. On arrival they joined the Indians in drinking healths—and then prudently ordered all tavern keepers to sell no more liquor to the Indians until the treaty was concluded. When the business was all over and the ceremonial rum distributed, it took the hundred-odd Indians only a few hours to turn the area into "a Scene the most resembling our Ideas of Hell that could well be imagin'd." The next morning an Indian orator apologized for the carousing with the explanation that the Great Spirit made rum with the express purpose of intoxicating Indians. Franklin agreed that Providence may have appointed rum as the means of extirpating "these Savages in order to make room for Cultivators of the Earth," a view quite in keeping with his kindred one that the poor should be left without relief in order not to interfere with nature.

It has been suggested that this negotiating at Carlisle gave Franklin his start as a diplomat, but the influence of Indian folklore upon Franklin's intellectual development has never been emphasized. He took seriously Indian religious ideas expressed in their treaties, particularly a notion of spirits without bodies rambling under the earth. Also he borrowed the picturesque imagery of an Oneida chief to formulate one of his favorite sayings. The chieftain had exhorted the other Indians to preserve their union and friendship in the words, "Let us keep the Chain from rusting," an Indian cliché. Later Franklin, in describing to Collinson the accord with the Indians, remarked "we brighten'd the Chain with them." His friends in England associated him with the expression, for in 1765 Fothergill gave him a silver cream pot engraved with the motto "Keep bright the chain," which Franklin kept with him throughout his life and bestowed upon a friend in his last will. Finally, Cabanis reported that, in France, Franklin "loved to cite and to practice faithfully the proverb of his friends the American Indians, 'Keep the chain of friendship bright and shining.' "

The frontier Indian treaties represented a very important colonial defense against the menacing activities of the French, who were once more threatening a full-scale war. Franklin was one of the most forceful proponents of the argument that the colonies could not singly combat the enemy but that they must join or die.

The most significant step toward colonial unity before the Revolution was probably the Albany Congress in 1754, a gathering of commissioners from each colony, authorized by the Board of Trade. The commissioners were to devise methods of mutual defense and to confer with the chiefs of the Six Nations. In view of Franklin's previous concern with colonial defense, it was only logical that he should be chosen as a delegate from Pennsylvania. Before leaving Philadelphia, he had formulated an opinion that "Britain and her Colonies should be considered as one whole, and not as different States with separate Interests," a concept more important in his intellectual development than the Albany Congress itself. On the trip to Albany in June, Franklin drew up a plan of union for the colonies, elaborating a matter-of-fact opinion he had expressed three years earlier: "It would be a very strange Thing, if six Nations of ignorant Savages should be capable of framing a Scheme for such an Union, and be able to execute it . . . ; and yet that a like Union should be impracticable for ten or a Dozen English Colonies, to whom it is more necessary."

Although several of the colonies had some scheme to present at Albany, Franklin's plan was the one chosen for approval and recommendation to the various assemblies. The chief point at issue was whether the union should be voluntary or imposed by an Act of Parliament. Franklin had earlier preferred voluntary action but now yielded to the contrary view. He had also been obliged to sacrifice other points, realizing, as he later confided to Colden, that "when one has so many different people with different opinions to deal with in a new affair, one is obliged sometimes to give up some smaller points in order to obtain greater." One can see why Franklin was to emerge as America's greatest diplomat.

Unfortunately all his efforts, as well as those of the entire congress, were in vain. The colonial assemblies were reluctant to relinquish the few powers they held to a uniting body, and not a single assembly approved the plan, not even Pennsylvania. Franklin felt that, had his scheme been adopted, the American Revolution might have been avoided, for the colonies would then have had the strength to defend themselves and there would have been less need for the objectionable taxation subsequently imposed by Parliament. Franklin recognized in his autobiography that pure reason seldom has its way in political decisions. "The best public measures are . . . seldom *adopted from previous wisdom, but forced by the occasion.*" This "wisdom" of Franklin's gives us the key to his career as a public man. In his negotiations, he was always pliable, always ready to take advantage of new occasions as they arose.

That winter, on a trip to Boston on post-office business, he discussed with Governor Shirley the problems arising out of the Albany scheme, the main proposal of which was for a grand council to govern the united colonies. Franklin insisted that the people themselves should have some share in it and that the colonies should not be taxed without their consent. Shirley had an alternate proposal—that the colonies be united to each other by means of delegates to London—a scheme which Franklin welcomed and much later advocated as the only method to keep the colonies within the empire. He and Shirley agreed that the best means of carrying out the proposal would be to allow the colonies direct representation in Parliament. Drawing upon his principle of population growth, the Philadelphia planner visualized the British Empire expanding in strength and wealth through the increase of people in America. Franklin incorporated these theories in three letters to Shirley, which he later published and circulated to promote colonial autonomy. After the Revolution, James Madison affirmed that Franklin had here masterfully brought "within the compass of a nut shell" the reasoning and force of all the succeeding arguments against the claims of the British Parliament.

In Pennsylvania, party lines remained much as they had been in the 1730's when Franklin had begun to use the *Gazette* as a political organ: the proprietary faction still pitted against the Assembly. During the formative years of the colony, feelings had remained under control, since the proprietors had practically no responsibilities, their effective participation in colony affairs being limited largely to reaping their profits. But in time of crisis—when the French and their Indian allies were threatening the western frontiers—the Penns tried to place the entire financial burden upon the residents, insisting that their own properties be exempt from taxation, and at the same time sought to make the Quakers bear the onus for inadequate military preparation. By raising the cry against pacificism, they hoped, according to Franklin, to divert attention from their own avarice and meanness. Franklin, who knew how to deal with the Quakers, was ordinarily able to obtain their financial cooperation, if nothing else. He proposed, therefore, to exclude from the Assembly "Quakerism" or absolute pacificism, but not the Quakers themselves, "who in other Respects make good and useful Members." On this issue Franklin split with his respected friend, William Allen, who cast his weight with the proprietors and indiscriminately condemned the Quakers as responsible for the ills of the colony. Although in a sense Allen later became Franklin's "great enemy," his opposition grew out of public differences rather than personal. The only man who was to carry a vindictive personal grudge against Franklin was "Parson" Smith, who had not yet begun to show his venom.

Wholeheartedly approving neither the governor nor the Assembly, Franklin tried to reconcile their differences. On cordial terms with the new governor, Robert Hunter Morris, whom he had previously known in New Jersey, Franklin worked for governor-Assembly cooperation. Much of his usefulness and popularity stemmed from his ability to moderate between the two forces. Before his election to the Assembly, he had enjoyed a long record of personal acquaintance with the governors, at least two of whom he met on the easy terms of drinking companions. As he wrote to Collinson, 26 June 1755, he stayed in public life only because he was "able now and then to influence a good Measure." Were it not for this, he wrote, "I should be ready to swear never to serve again as an Assembly Man, since both Sides expect more from me than they ought."

Although Franklin retired from his publishing enterprise presumably in order to have time for scientific and literary activities, it turned out that he had even less leisure than before. His appointment as Joint Deputy Postmaster General entailed traveling up and down the coast from Williamsburg to Boston—and he never again passed more than a few consecutive months with Deborah in Philadelphia. In May 1753, he told a friend that he had "never Been more hurried in Business than at present," and in the fall after a ten weeks' journey to the east and two to the west, he complained, "This last summer I have enjoyed very little of the pleasure of reading or writing." In the spring of the next year he visited Maryland on postal business, and in June he attended the political Congress in Albany. After a few weeks at home, he set off in August for a leisurely tour of inspection of the postal service in the north. Franklin's organizing genius—his practical innovations and controls—would eventually coordinate the separate branches in the various colonies and place the entire system for the first time on a paying basis.

While in Boston in December 1754, he appointed his brother John city postmaster and therefore naturally used his home as headquarters. Franklin had no scruples against nepotism: in fact, he strongly advocated preferential treatment in his immediate family, in the Junto, and in the broader circle of the Academy. On his postal trip, moreover, he appointed to the postmastership of Newport, Rhode Island, the son of his brother's friend Vernon, whose money he had "borrowed" in 1724.

Brother John, a year before his appointment, had married a widow, Elizabeth Hubbard, and had gone to live in her homestead, called the Hubbard "mansion." Franklin, when he arrived, was delighted to discover as a fellow guest Catharine Ray, an attractive relative of the Hubbards. At the time, Caty was twenty-three and Franklin forty-eight, a disparity not sufficient to keep Franklin from amorous designs or her from playing up to them. During the day Franklin conducted postal business and discussed the state of the empire with Governor Shirley. At night he flirted and discussed sex with Caty. She seems to have been a tease, who enjoyed exhibiting her virginity. Franklin, who had a sincere respect for premarital chastity, seems to have made a few attempts at authentic love-making and then willingly settled for her games when she resisted the real thing. He established a pattern of daring talk and timid behavior which he was to follow with other women. He found the vicarious pleasure of distantly contemplating the conquest of Caty's virginity more exciting than viewing Deborah's dove-colored silk corsets at close hand.

Caty lived with her aged father and mother on Block Island, a lonely retreat twelve miles off the coast of Rhode Island. On 30 December 1754, Franklin and Caty set off together on a carriage ride from Boston to Newport, Rhode Island, a distance of a good seventy miles. This means that they probably stayed overnight at a tavern, an excellent opportunity for Franklin to have changed the rules of the game if he had wished. But it is certain that he controlled his ardor, because he refers in later letters to liberties she had refused him, and in a particular unequivocal passage he tells her "Your favours come mixed with the snowy fleeces, which are pure as your virgin innocence, white as your lovely bosom, and—as cold." Franklin cherished, nevertheless, a fond memory "of those Hours and Miles that we talk'd away so agreeably, even in a Winter Journey, a wrong Road, and a soaking Shower." Caty, over twenty years later, ascribed a great part of the happiness of her life to the "pleasing lessons" she had received on this sentimental journey.

They seem to have spent a few days at Newport and then continued to the house of Caty's married sister near Westerly, where Franklin was agreeably entertained for several more days. Suddenly Caty was called back to Block Island to tend a sick parent, and Franklin accompanied her to the little skiff which took her out to sea. He stood on the shore, looking regretfully after her until she became indistinguishable even to his telescope.

He now began the final stages of his trip home with great reluctance, indulging himself in short day's journeys and loitering visits on the road. These, he later confided to Caty, "manifested my unwillingness to quit a country, in which I drew my first breath, spent my earliest and most pleasant days, and . . . received so many fresh marks of the people's goodness and benevolence." One of his most agreeable stops was in New Haven where, on 5 February, Ezra Stiles pronounced a Latin oration in his honor in the Hall of Yale College.

When Franklin reached the borders of Connecticut, he began, like Odysseus, to wish for his "good old wife and children."

Caty, back on Block Island, tried to recreate the spirit of their intimacy by sending Franklin a series of indiscreet letters filled with reminiscences of their talks and revelations of her entanglements with other men. Four years before meeting Franklin, she had gone through a similar Platonic experience with a Spaniard, who had exhorted her, after returning to Cadiz, "Preserve a cautious Conduct & put no Confidance in Men. Be prudent, and beg of God to make you a Saint; for which End it is necessary to shun Men, and take care to guard against their Deceits." This is Franklin's translation from her letter, which Caty had kept four years before letting it out of her hands for his perusal. After Franklin's departure she garnered a new crop of lovers and formulated a new set of "prudent Resolutions in the Article of granting Favours." Franklin ironically approved them—but admitted that if he were doing the courting he would have a different opinion. "I should even be malicious enough to say you were too *knowing.*" About himself he reported, "I still relish all the Pleasures of Life that a temperate Man can in reason desire, & thro' Favour I have them all in my Power."

Franklin's answer did not reach Caty promptly, and she tearfully dashed off another letter regretting the thousand things she had said "that nothing Should have tempted me to [have] Said to any body els." She retained enough coquettishness, however, to include some sugar plums, "every one Sweetn'd as you used to like," presumably having been touched by her lips — an eighteenth-century version of *baisers au chocolat*.

Franklin found them so "sweet from the Cause you mention'd" that he could scarcely taste the sugar. He nevertheless felt that he should assume the role of a father and give Caty some sober advice: "Kill no more Pigeons than you can eat." Placing himself squarely out of the competition, he urged her to find a husband. After this, she should spend her time in card-playing, prayers, or learning Franklin's type of philoprogenitive mathematics:

You must practise *Addition* to your Husband's Estate, by Industry & Frugality; *Subtraction* of all unnecessary Expenses; *Multiplication* (I would gladly have taught you that myself, but you thought it was time enough & wouldn't learn) he will soon make you a Mistress of it. As to *Division,* I say with Brother Paul, *Let there be no Divisions among ye.* But as your good Sister Hubbard (my Love to her) is well acquainted with *The Rule of Two,* I hope you will become as expert in the *Rule of Three;* that when I have again the pleasure of seeing you, I may find you like my Grape Vine, surrounded with Clusters, plump, juicy, blushing, pretty little rogues, like their Mama.

With this letter, Franklin enclosed another to his stepniece, Elizabeth Hubbard, interpreting the seal of his letter in an erotic vein. The two hearts of Elizabeth and Caty were to be welded together on an anvil and taken up by a cupid and flown to Franklin. Deborah happened to see this fanciful symbolism while Franklin was still writing and insisted that he add a postscript with her version. "The Cupid represents her Husband, and the Heart in his Hand is hers, which he takes with him where ever he goes, leaving the others for some body else." Although Franklin reported that his wife intervened in a flippant vein, it is not likely that she relished his long-distance flirtation.

Presumably Franklin tired of Caty's epistolary coyness, for in another letter written at about the same time he declined to advise which to choose of two rival suitors. Nor did he reciprocate her effusive compliments but warned that "the most innocent Expressions of warm Friendship, and even those of meer

Civility & Complaisance, between Persons of different Sexes, are liable to be misinterpreted by suspicious Minds." Consequently he ended his letter "coolly in the plain common Form." Although he kept up a sporadic correspondence with Caty until his death, this was the end of the love game.

12. Indian Fighter and Colonial Agent

IN THE spring of 1755, the British Parliament sent from
England a renowned fighter, General Edward Braddock,
with two regiments to rid the western territories of enemy forces
and at the same time to make concerted action by the colonists
unnecessary, thereby frustrating their plans for union. The
Pennsylvania Assembly was not very enthusiastic about the expedition and feared that Braddock, aware of its attitude, would
be prejudiced or resentful. It commissioned Franklin to try to
smooth relations, not in the character of its emissary but as
Joint Deputy Postmaster General and, as such, familiar with
colonial communications. At Frederick, Maryland, Franklin
and his son William, who accompanied him, joined the British
general and almost certainly met for the first time Colonel
George Washington, who was there in the same service. Braddock was impatiently waiting for the delivery of wagons necessary to transport his equipment to the field, and on discovering
that only 25 wagons were available he exploded in exasperation,
declaring that the expedition could not possibly go forward
without at least 150. Franklin thereupon offered to hire this
number in Pennsylvania and set off toward Lancaster and the
western counties, armed with financial powers from Braddock.
In a short time, he had mustered all the wagons and paid out 800
pounds advanced by the general and 200 pounds of his own
funds. The general took the wagons and rolled to a disastrous
defeat, giving the Americans, as Franklin put it, "the first
suspicion that our excellent ideas of the prowess of British
regulars had not been well founded." As soon as the wagon-
owners heard of the defeat, they pressed Franklin for in-
demnification, and he would have been liable to nearly twenty

thousand pounds—enough to ruin him—had the paymaster not honored his commitments. Franklin considered this episode one of the most important in his career, and it was in a sense a heroic venture, entailing the risk of his entire fortune. Certainly he was virtually solely responsible for Braddock being able to go into battle. He formally received the thanks of the Pennsylvania Assembly, and Braddock wrote to the ministry describing Franklin as "almost the only Instance of Ability and Honesty I have known in these Provinces." But because of the unfortunate outcome of the expedition, Franklin never reaped any benefit from these recommendations.

After Braddock's ignominious defeat, it became more and more obvious to the Pennsylvania Assembly that it would have to take measures for its own defense, since the disaster had no more effect upon Governor Morris than "the miracles of Moses had on the heart of Pharaoh." In October 1755 Franklin was commissioned to purchase arms for the frontier settlers, even though he was ill and confined to his room for eight days. In the next month he drew up a Militia Act, providing for an Association similar to that of the preceding war, which was passed by the Assembly in the last week of November. Three weeks later he wrote for the *Gazette* a "Dialogue" to rally support for the proposed militia. With his usual good sense and a somewhat unusual bluntness of speech, he answered the main objection—that Quakers would benefit from the scheme but not contribute. "That is to say, you won't pump ship, because 'twill save the rats, as well as yourself." Franklin's reasoning was forceful and urgent: defend the colony and postpone party contentions. "If good be done, what imports it by whom 'tis done?"

The Indians had burned the Moravian settlement of Gnadenhütten (huts of grace), a mere ninety miles from Philadelphia, and Franklin and two other commissioners were put in charge of a voluntary expedition enlisted under the Militia Act to fortify the frontier. William Franklin went along as aide-de-camp to give the expedition the benefit of his previous military experience. They set out 18 December and arrived about a month later, Franklin passing his fiftieth birthday on the way.

On his first night away from home, Franklin found lodging in an inn. Seeing the landlady about to put very damp sheets on the bed and, as always, worried about cleanliness, he asked her to air them first. Half an hour later she reported the bed ready. Franklin tested it—and jumped out again in just a few seconds. She had aired the sheets on a hedge, and they were "as cold as death, and partly frozen." Since Franklin at this time suffered from the superstition that "mere Moisture, either in Air or in Sheets or Shirts" was pernicious to health, he spent the rest of the night wrapped up in his clothes.

On the way to the frontier outposts, Franklin passed the second week in January 1756 at the principal Moravian settlement of Bethlehem. Taking a keen interest in the matrimonial customs of the sect, he was told that sometimes marriages were arranged by lot but more often the partners were selected by the elders of the community. He appeared satisfied with the answer to his objection to these arranged marriages—that "some of them may chance to be very unhappy." "And so they may," was the answer, "if you let the parties choose for themselves."

While Franklin was away on the frontier, the Associators back in Philadelphia insisted that he be commissioned a colonel, and Governor Morris reluctantly yielded to their demonstrations and signed the papers, 24 February 1756. Although on the field the Moravians called him "General," he then had no official military rank whatsoever, acting under emergency orders from the governor.

On Franklin's birthday, some random Indian scouts harried the expedition, the only time in his life when he was ever under actual fire. At Gnadenhütten, Franklin directed the cutting of timber, the digging of trenches, and the erection of the defenses. Despite heavy rains which prevented work every other day, the fort was brought to "a good defensible condition" in a week. Franklin observed that on working days the men "were good-natured and cheerful, and with the consciousness of having done a good day's work they spent the evenings jollily; but on the idle days they were mutinous and quarrelsome." Noticing also that the men showed little interest in the services held by the Presbyterian chaplain, Franklin suggested that the chaplain take over the functions of steward of the rum and deal it out after prayers. The willing minister carried out the suggestion, "and never were prayers more generally and more punctually attended."

Although the expedition numbered about 130 men, Franklin and his immediate entourage ate delicacies which Deborah regularly sent to the field. In addition to the standard fare of salt pork, they dined on Deborah's roast beef, roast veal, apples and minced pies. At every meal they drank her health, always reminded of her by something at the table. To Deborah, Franklin reported that they slept in warm blankets on deal featherbeds—but in his autobiography he indicated that he slept on hard wooden floors.

The entire operation reveals Franklin's excellent physical condition. It is doubtful that many other public men at fifty, even in Franklin's day, would have been able to lead a military expedition into the rugged wilderness in the dead of winter.

There is no question about the popularity of Franklin with his men. One of his officers wrote, "Mr. Franklin will, at least, deserve a statue for his prudence, justice, humanity, and, above all, for his patience." His men viewed him with admiration, respect and love—which Franklin returned with simple camaraderie. Although by no means exempt from vanity, he did not relish public displays of adulation. On the return from the western expedition, he frustrated the plans of some townspeople to meet him at the city gates, for a sort of triumphal entry, by commanding a quick march which brought them back during the night. When Franklin next reviewed his regiment, the men followed him to his house and insisted on firing some rounds before his door, the force of which broke some of his electrical apparatus. In his memoirs, Franklin remarked that his military title was no less brittle than his glass since all the commissions were soon invalidated by Parliament.

Indeed, the exuberance of his men served to bring him into further disfavor with the proprietor. As he started out on a journey to Virginia in March, the officers of the regiment decided to escort him out of town, and just as he was getting on his horse more than thirty of them, mounted and brightly uniformed, appeared at his door. On the triumphal ride through the city, "they drew their swords and rode with them naked all the way." When Penn in London heard of this, he bristled with jealousy and hurt pride, since no such honor had been paid to him when he visited the province. He immediately complained to the ministry, representing the episode as a proof that Franklin was engineering some kind of a military *coup d'état.*

In commenting to Collinson on this episode, Franklin bared his heart. He had at first wondered whether his dislike of the proprietors may have stemmed from wounded feelings, but now he was fairly certain that he did not "oppose their Views from Pique, Disappointment, or personal Resentment, but . . . from a Regard to the Publick good." Despite the proprietors' charter, laws and wealth, which should have made them adored like demigods, their meanness had brought them to be "Objects of universal Hatred and Contempt." Apologizing for his vanity, Franklin observed that he as a private citizen could "do more Good in their Country than they, because he [sic] has the Affections and Confidence of their People."

Franklin undertook his trip to Virginia to settle post-office business with his colleague, Joint Deputy Postmaster General William Hunter. He was accompanied by his Negro slave, Peter, who fell sick before they reached Newcastle, Delaware. Practically nothing is known about Peter—his age, description, or how Franklin acquired him. But, as might be expected, Franklin was a kind master. He applied the sovereign eighteenth-century remedy of letting blood, placed the ailing slave, wrapped warmly, into a carriage, as he could not bear the motion of a horse, and then put him to bed when they arrived at Frederick, Maryland. By the next morning Peter had almost fully recovered. That same morning Franklin had another opportunity of talking with George Washington, who was returning overland from a visit to New England. Franklin and Peter sailed that same day down the Sassafras River and arrived forty-eight hours later at Hampton, Virginia. On the following day he proceeded to Williamsburg, where he found himself (24

March) in the midst of spring: "Peaches on the Trees as big as Kidney Beans, and Asparagus on the Tables." The spring weather and social life of Williamsburg were such an agreeable tonic that he wrote to Deborah a week later that he was "as gay as a Bird" and not beginning to long for home. He added that he intended to proceed with "Col. Hunter and his Lady" (another Colonel Hunter) to New York in a man-of-war to conduct further post-office business. When Deborah received his letter referring to Hunter "and his Lady," she perhaps felt a pang of uneasiness or jealousy, for she well knew that her husband would never introduce her to society and that nobody would ever have occasion to speak of "Mr. Franklin and his Lady" in any kind of official appearance.

Deborah was used to being left at home and had come to accept the circumstance of her husband's absences outweighing his sojourns in Philadelphia. She was content to look after her modest home and bask in her husband's reflected glory. During his trips, Franklin left Deborah in charge of his accounts—even of the Philadelphia lottery, which entailed her disbursing relatively large amounts. She was familiar moreover with all the routine of the post office and ran it efficiently whenever her husband was absent.

Franklin was accustomed to having Deborah respond instantaneously to his needs, wishes and whims. In November 1756, he wrote to her from Easton, Pennsylvania, where he had attended another Indian Treaty, and expected her to answer by the same messenger. For some reason Deborah failed to reply by return carrier; Franklin wrote back a little peevishly, but covered his pique with the declaration, "I never can be ill natured enough even when there is the most occasion." He had taken the pains to find out from the messenger that the latter had told Deborah at what time he expected to set out and he had lodged next door within easy reach—but she still had not written a letter. Although signing himself "your *loving* husband," Franklin explained in a P.S. that he had *"scratched out the loving words, being writ in haste by mistake, when I forgot I was angry."* Deborah was indeed governed by a firm hand and had reason as she sometimes did to refer to her husband as "my master."

By and large, family affairs were smooth and agreeable. William traveled around with his father on most of his missions. Sally, now thirteen years old, also had begun to show some of her father's commercial sense and had undertaken to sell some London importations in her own right. Franklin took so much pride in her venture that he began negotiations with Strahan to have her appointed American distributor for the *Gentleman's Magazine*.

Even Benny Mecom seemed to be behaving as a Franklin relative should. Having displeased his uncle by suddenly proposing to give up the printing business in Antigua, he redeemed himself in December 1756 by settling his accounts in honorable fashion. With the help of a promissory note which he signed to Franklin, he had acquired title to Franklin's printing press and proposed to take it to Boston, where, Franklin believed, "his Industry & Frugality" would enable him to establish himself anew.

On the political scene, affairs were less placid. Relations between the Assembly and a new governor, William Denny, had been going from bad to worse. When Denny first arrived in August 1756, he seems to have had instructions to offer subtle bribes to get Franklin on the proprietary side. After a ceremonial dinner as part of his reception by the city, he plied Franklin with claret and lavished promises of acknowledgments and recompenses if Franklin would work for political harmony. But Franklin, as usual, insisted that he was at heart friendly to all sides and interested only in the welfare of the whole colony.

When Denny vetoed an appropriation bill in January 1757 because it did not exempt proprietary land from taxation, the Assembly began to talk of Franklin as the most likely man to send to present its grievances in London. On the last day of the month, Franklin informed Collinson that the Assembly had voted unanimously to send him but that he had not yet made up his mind to go. Yet on the same day he wrote to Strahan, implying that he was almost sure to do so: "look out sharp, and if a fat old fellow should come to your printing-house and request a little smouting [job printing], depend upon it, 'tis your affectionate friend and humble servant." Because of his height, Franklin was not really fat but what we would now call strapping.

Shortly afterwards, Franklin ordered sea stores to be put on board a vessel in New York (it was then customary for transatlantic passengers to provide their own food and drink) and was on the point of leaving Philadelphia to embark, when the Earl of Loudoun, commander-in-chief of the British forces in America, turned up in an effort to pressure the Assembly to pass a money bill, including 10,000 pounds to be devoted to his orders. He carried the day, but in the meantime Franklin's packet sailed without him and he lost his provisions. Franklin politely asked when Loudoun would authorize the next ship to sail. The General assured Franklin that the vessel would not be allowed to sail until the next Monday morning. Franklin, not arriving until noon, had some anxiety that the boat might have already sailed, but it was still in harbor. In fact, because of Loudoun's indecision, it was still there seven weeks later.

No two people of characters more opposite than Franklin and Loudoun can be imagined. The methodical, rational and decisive Franklin fumed and fretted in New York, waiting for the procrastinating Loudoun to make up his mind. At the time Franklin "wonder'd how such a Man came to be entrusted with so important a Business as the Conduct of a great Army," but as he saw "more of the great World, and the means of obtaining and Motives for giving Places," his wonder diminished.

While cooling his heels during April and June, Franklin caught up with his correspondence. Soon after arriving, he sent one of his acquaintances, Colonel Henry Bouquet, a letter of introduction to one of his botanical correspondents, Dr. Alexander Garden of South Carolina. Although considering himself an expert punster, Franklin let pass this opportunity without the least effort at joining the two botanical names. Perhaps his spirits were low from waiting around. In his letter to Bouquet, he indulged himself merely with imagining the happiness of "the Folks in Heaven, who tis said, have nothing to do, but to talk with one another, except now and then a little Singing, & Drinking of Aqua Vitae." Then, referring to the refreshing punch made by Garden, "not inferior to the Nectar of the

Gods," Franklin proceeded to "make a Prayer to them, *That whatever I wish for my Friends, shall come to pass.*" Franklin had not forgotten his polytheism, which we shall see he continued to nourish in England.

Having more time on his hands, Franklin sent back to Deborah for some Indian curios he could use as gifts in London, as well as for four different books on chess, including one in French, which he told Debbie to recognize "by the word ECHECS in the Titlepage." Apparently not wanting to have any of his secrets exposed, he particularly ordered her not to "set anybody else to look for them." The ship still not sailing, Franklin crossed to Woodbridge, New Jersey, now the home of James Parker, where Deborah joined him for a few days. Not only Loudoun's procrastination but also rumors of the presence of the French fleet promised further to delay Franklin's sailing. "This tedious State of Uncertainty and long Waiting" almost wore out his patience. He could not remember when he had ever spent time so uselessly.

When the packet finally sailed early in June, it got only as far as Sandy Hook, where it was obliged to wait the sailing of the British fleet. Franklin consumed his sea stores and was obliged to purchase more. These presumbably included alcoholic beverages, for the captain confided to Loudoun before his vessel left the fleet "that Franklin got Drunk one Day and talkt plain language."

Franklin's entourage consisted of his son William, his slave Peter, and William's slave King. The fleet finally set sail in the direction of Louisburg, at the General's orders, and only after five more days was the packet finally allowed to steer for England.

Franklin presumably had in his baggage a copy of *Poor Richard* for every year of publication, since on the voyage he amused himself by detaching most of his proverbs concerning thrift and stringing them together again in a loose narrative to which he gave the title *The Way to Wealth*. He sent it back to Hall, who published it as the introduction to *Poor Richard* for 1758. It has since become the most famous of Franklin's works, being translated into nearly every language and published in hundreds of editions in the English-speaking world. In the narrative, Poor Richard on horseback pauses at a country fair in Pennsylvania to hear the discourse of a new character, Father Abraham, who is haranguing the crowd on taxes and hard times. Just as Whitefield had used the Old Testament Father Abraham to inculcate his doctrine of evangelical Christianity, Franklin used a modern version of the hoary patriarch to disseminate his gospel of thrift and industry. In pithy sentences, for the most part drawn from previous almanacs, the old gentleman exhorts his listeners to abandon the expensive and time-consuming activities of the fair and to dedicate themselves to old-fashioned labor and economy. At the end of his discourse, the people "approved the Doctrine and immediately practised the contrary, just as if it had been a common Sermon." The last sentence should be sufficient indication that Franklin did not intend *The Way to Wealth* as a serious moral work—equivalent to a *way of life*—as it has sometimes been interpreted. Franklin had presented his true convictions a few years earlier in a letter to Strahan, when he exposed the absurdity of "the Pursuit of Wealth to no End." Although Franklin certainly believed in the gospel of thrift and industry and on various occasions seriously recommended that some of his precepts be used as the basis of individual conduct or national policy, *The Way to Wealth* was essentially an intellectual tour de force of the same nature as the magic mathematical squares and circles or the chess problems with which he was also amply supplied on the voyage. Many times in his own career, Franklin showed that he knew the way to wealth but preferred to pursue other values.

13. The First Mission Begins

FRANKLIN arrived in London, 26 July 1757, and as soon as he had found lodging went to interview an eminent Quaker physician, John Fothergill. Having made three visits to America, Fothergill had a great influence among the Friends of both continents and a solid understanding of their political problems. He advised Franklin not to take the grievances of the Assembly immediately to the government but first to try for an amicable accommodation with the proprietors. Franklin then went to visit his old friend, Peter Collinson, and his correspondent of thirteen years, William Strahan, whom he was seeing for the first time.

From Collinson, Franklin learned that Lord Granville, president of the Council, was aware of his mission and wanted to see him as soon as possible. Franklin appeared the next morning and received a lesson in political science: The colonial assemblies had been wrong in considering the King's instructions to his governors as binding upon them but not upon the legislative houses. Drawn up by learned judges and debated in Council, these instructions were the law of the land for the colonies. Franklin replied that it was his understanding that the colonial charters provided that the assemblies should make their own laws and present them to the King. Once the King had assented, he could neither repeal nor alter them, and neither the assemblies nor the King could make laws without the assent of the other. Franklin went back to his lodgings greatly alarmed at the distance separating the two theories. He had previously assumed that the great obstacle to colonial liberty was the self-interest of the proprietors, which he had believed could be overcome by appeal to the King or the Parliament. Now neither the King nor the Parliament seemed sympathetic to the colonists.

He went ahead, nevertheless, with the attempt to persuade

the proprietaries to heed the grievances of the Assembly. Through the agency of Fothergill, he met them at the home of Thomas Penn in an atmosphere of formal politeness which succeeded in changing the attitude of neither side. At the end of the session, the Penns merely asked Franklin to put the Assembly's complaints in writing. When he finally did so after some days, they turned over his document to their solicitor, Ferdinand John Paris, "a proud, angry man," who resented the way Franklin in the Assembly had previously disposed of some of his arguments. Eventually Paris drew up a long message to the Assembly, complaining of Franklin's rudeness (he had omitted the formal titles of the proprietaries in his document) and requesting "some person of candour" to be sent to replace him.

The descendants of William Penn, founder of the colony, had become rather slippery manipulators. For example: they persuaded the Assembly to pay for land they acquired through Indian treaties but refused to pay taxes on any of their holdings. As Franklin put it, the Assembly paid all the cost; the Penns enjoyed all the profit. The family also pretended that the rights which William Penn had accorded to the Assembly to "all the powers and privileges of an assembly according to the rights of free-born subjects of England" were empty promises since the founder of the colony had not been empowered by royal charter to grant them. Franklin, in conversation soon after his arrival with Thomas Penn and his brother, reproached them for this interpretation, arguing that if it were a correct one all the early settlers of the colony had been cheated, deceived and betrayed. He had not forgotten the principle of the *Gazette* essays he had published in 1736, tracing the rights of Pennsylvanians to Penn's charter. Thomas Penn answered merely that it was up to the settlers to have investigated the royal grant for themselves: "if they were deceived, it was their own fault." According to Franklin, Penn made the last remark "with a kind of triumphing, laughing insolence, such as a low jockey might do when a purchaser complained that he had cheated him on a horse." Franklin revealed:

I was astonished to see him thus meanly give up his father's character, and conceived at that moment a more cordial and thorough
contempt for him than I ever felt for any man living, a contempt
that I cannot express in words; but I believe my countenance expressed it strongly, and that his brother, who was looking at me,
must have observed it.

This is one of the few recorded episodes of Franklin's anger
getting the upper hand in disregard of the principles of his
private moral system. From this moment, the struggle against
the proprietors became intensely personal as well as political for
Franklin, and he pursued it with intensity. Before long he
began feeling out Isaac Norris, speaker of the House, to discover
whether sentiment in Pennsylvania would support getting rid of
proprietary government entirely.

One of the proprietary faction from the colony who annoyed
Franklin even more than the supercilious Penns was William
Smith, rector of the Academy. Back in the days when Franklin
was doing his best to hold all elements of the colony together for
the common defense, Smith had distinguished himself by hyster-
ical attacks against the Quakers in order to curry favor with the
proprietors. In the summer of 1756, Franklin wrote cryptically
to Whitefield that education in Pennsylvania would do better in
the colony when Smith should "learn to mind Party-writing and
Party Politicks less, and his proper Business more." A few
months later Franklin was not on speaking terms with Smith
and was charging to his friends that the rector had scribbled
himself into universal dislike by sacrificing the interests of the
Academy to the proprietors. Since his advent the number of
pupils had dwindled to almost one half.

Some time after Franklin arrived in London, the Pennsylvania Assembly charged Smith and a cohort, William Moore,
with libel and clapped them into jail, where they stayed until
the Assembly adjourned. As Anglicans, they had strongly condemned the Quaker pacificism of the Assembly. Smith, on
release, immediately sailed for England to appeal his arrest, to
denounce the Assembly's misuse of powers, and to let loose his
venom against the Quakers and the Assembly's agent, Franklin,

his personal enemy. Franklin called him "Parson" Smith to signify his hypocrisy for trading on his clerical orders to advance his political ambitions.

In April Franklin retaliated upon him with a sly verbal trick. Osborne, a prominent bookseller, asked Franklin confidentially whether Smith's credit was good—since Smith had approached him with a proposal to sell large quantities of books in Philadelphia—which he claimed he could do easily by underselling Franklin's partner, Hall. Franklin told Osborne that his "Townsmen who were Smith's creditors would be glad to see him come back with a Cargo of any kind, as they might have some Chance of being paid out of it." Needless to say, Smith did not get the books, but in the next month the Privy Council upheld his appeal—an indirect blow to Franklin as the Assembly's agent.

In the meantime, Franklin's old friend Ebenezer Kinnersley, who had accepted the position of Professor of English and Oratory at the Academy, wrote to Franklin expressing his dissatisfaction with Smith's philosophy of education. Smith had completely ignored Franklin's ideas about the English school in order to promote classical training, and Kinnersley hoped that Franklin might be able to restore the original intention. Franklin replied bitterly, 28 July 1759, revealing how thoroughly he had been upset by Smith's domination.

Before I left Philadelphia, everything to be done in the Academy was privately preconcerted in a Cabal without my Knowledge or Participation and accordingly carried into Execution. The Schemes of Public Parties made it seem requisite to lessen my Influence wherever it could be lessened. The Trustees had reap'd the full Advantage of my Head, Hands, Heart and Purse, in getting through the first Difficulties of the Design, and when they thought they could do without me, they laid me aside.

Four years later, the trustees themselves recognized that the English school had "dwindled into a School similar to those kept by old Women, who teach Children their Letters." The decline of Franklin's educational enterprise was the first of many disillusionments he was to experience in his long career as a public servant.

Strahan found Franklin and his entourage permanent lodgings, shortly after their arrival in London, in the home of an affable widow of about Franklin's age, Mrs. Margaret Stevenson, on Craven Street. Her only daughter, Mary (commonly called Polly), was then eighteen years old—and had even more of the fresh girlhood charm which had delighted Franklin in Caty Ray. Throughout the next eighteen years, he was to maintain a virtually permanent residence with the Stevensons, and the two households gradually blended into a single *ménage*. Polly played the role of ingenue (combination daughter and flirt), and Mrs. Stevenson played the role of mother and mistress—mothering Franklin as much as her daughter. Franklin called Mrs. Stevenson "my little wife," and if there are no documents proving that she gave him all the privileges of a husband, Strahan was to evince strong suspicions that she did. And with our knowledge of Franklin's early amorous exploits and inclinations, we can hardly come to any other conclusion.

In September, Franklin fell seriously ill with a violent cold and accompanying fever and was confined to his bed for nearly eight weeks. Fothergill was the attending physician and Mrs. Stevenson the nurse. Treatment consisted of being "cupped [bled] . . . on the back of the head" and eating large quantities of medicinal bark—despite which, Franklin's stalwart physique triumphed and he recovered completely.

Among the official dispatches and resolves of the Assembly which Franklin brought to London, he included, as was the custom, a number of private letters. Shortly after his sickness he sought out his old friend James Ralph, "now esteemed one of the best political writers in England" and benefactor of an annual pension of 300 pounds, to deliver the messages of a certain Mrs. Garrigues of Philadelphia, Ralph's daughter by his first wife whom he had deserted when he and Franklin went off to London in 1724. Now remarried, with another child, Ralph was anxious to conceal the first marriage from his present wife.

Franklin willingly cooperated with his old tavern mate and wrote to Deborah to inform Mrs. Garrigues not to attempt to communicate with Ralph again until Franklin should relay a new address, but that Ralph expressed great affection for his American daughter and grandchildren.

As Strahan observed the ease with which Franklin settled into his new quarters in Craven Street, he wondered whether Franklin might follow Ralph's example. Alarmed for Franklin's other family in Philadelphia, Strahan wrote to Deborah, urging her to join her husband in London. "The ladies here," he wrote, "consider him in exactly the same light I do," that is, "perfectly agreeable. . . . Upon my word I think you should come over with all convenient speed, to look after your interest; not but that I think him as faithful to his Joan, as any man breathing; but who knows what repeated and strong temptation may in time, and while he is at so great a distance from you, accomplish?"

Strahan made no attempt to keep his letter a secret from Franklin—and offered to lay a considerable wager that Deborah would come at once. Franklin forthwith reported the conversation to his wife (14 January 1758): "I tell him I will not pick his pocket; for I am sure there is no inducement strong enough to prevail with you to cross the seas." Whether interpreting this as an order or merely remaining subject to a quite natural fear, Deborah gave Strahan a strong negative and in due course received her husband's approbation. "Your Answer to Mr. Strahan was just as it should be. I was much pleas'd with it. He fancy'd his Rhetoric and Art would certainly bring you over." Strahan thereupon observed to David Hall, 10 June 1758, that he was sorry about Deborah's dread of the sea. "There are many Ladies here that would make no objection to sailing twice as far after him."

Even though Franklin preferred his independence in London, he still had tender feelings for Deborah and tried to ease her loneliness. He admitted to her that he found pleasure in the friendship of persons of worth and the conversation of ingenious men but insisted that "at this time of my life, domestic comforts afford the most solid satisfaction, and my uneasiness at being absent from my family, and longing desire to be with them, make me often sigh in the midst of cheerful company." At another time he tried to convey the impression that Mrs. Stevenson represented nothing more to him than a landlady and nurse.

She is indeed very obliging, takes great Care of my Health, and is very diligent when I am any way indispos'd; but yet I have a thousand times wish'd you with me, and my little Sally with her ready Hands and Feet to do, and go, and come, and get what I wanted. There is a great Difference in Sickness between being nurs'd with that tender Attention which proceeds from sincere Love.

As an envoy of the prosperous colony of Pennsylvania, Franklin lived in a rather opulent style; indeed he fared so well that his enemies accused him of extravagance at public expense. Apart from his slave, Peter, transformed into a gentleman's body servant, he kept his own chariot, the hackney coaches at his end of town (near the Strand, but not as fashionable then as now) being "the worst in the whole City, miserable, dirty, broken, shabby Things, unfit to go into when dress'd clean, and such as one would be asham'd to get out of at any Gentleman's Door." He also acquired "a compleat Set of Table China, 2 Cases of silver handled Knives and Forks, and 2 pair Silver Candlesticks," with which he entertained polite company in his lodgings. Some of the meat he served, Deborah sent to him from Pennsylvania. He ate her dried venison for breakfast and rashers of her bacon with green peas for dinner. Mrs. Stevenson felt there was never any so good in England.

The Pennsylvania Assembly had appropriated 1,500 pounds as total expenses for Franklin's mission—presumably to last no longer than six months. At the end of six years, he had still received merely 1,500 pounds. Without the yearly payments he was receiving from David Hall from their printing business, he would not have been able to make ends meet.

During the spring of 1758, Franklin and William spent a week in Cambridge and returned for Commencement at the beginning of July. Franklin's "vanity was not a little gratified by the particular regard shown . . . by the chancellor and vice-chancellor of the University and the heads of colleges." During the second trip he visited the village in Northamptonshire where the Franklins had lived, from time immemorial, and made inquiries about his ancestors. Then he turned toward Birmingham to visit Deborah's relations. Here he enjoyed the company of Mrs. Sarah Salt, "a jolly, lively dame," who resembled Deborah: "her whole face has the same turn, and exactly the same little blue Birmingham eyes." In writing to Deborah about his visit, Franklin asked her to gather her clan together in Philadelphia "and drink the health of your Birmingham friends, for we often drank at Birmingham our friends in Philadelphia."

To Deborah, ever anxious for his prompt return, Franklin gave his health as the pretext for his trips, but he was probably incurably in the grip of wanderlust which he had acquired as a postmaster, traveling up and down the coast of America. Later, at the age of seventy-five, Franklin was still firmly convinced that his health had been in great measure preserved because of the air and exercise which his annual journeys afforded him. He may have been the first man in modern society to recognize the benefit of an annual vacation.

Franklin now began to feel remote from everything in Philadelphia which had once vitally concerned him: civic organization, family and business. In April 1759, he wrote to David Hall that he could not supply him with copy for the next year's *Poor Richard* as he had expected to do. Yet he had begun, in September 1758, a series of letters to London newspapers which he kept up faithfully throughout his sojourn. These took the place of his contributions to the *Pennsylvania Gazette* and exhibit almost as great a variety, even though he had one dominating purpose in mind, to create a climate of opinion favorable to the measures which he was promoting as agent of the Assembly.

Although Franklin ostensibly was sent to represent particular grievances to the Privy Council, his agency before long turned into a propaganda mill—one of the most efficient which had ever operated in London. Franklin acted as a combination publicity office, public relations service and lobbyist. Since the interests of the Pennsylvania Assembly were similar to the interests of all the colonies, most of Franklin's propaganda concerned America at large rather than Pennsylvania alone. As a standard technique, he preached that what was good for the colonies was good for Great Britain. The key note of his writings was "the British interest." Eventually New Jersey, Georgia and Massachusetts also employed him as an agent for routine business—not directly as a propagandist, since this part of his activities he concealed, but as a liaison officer with various governmental bureaus—valuable because of his contacts and growing fame as a statesman.

In the dissemination of propaganda, Franklin's indispensable ally was his fellow printer, William Strahan. A kindred spirit to Franklin, Strahan had also risen by his own labor from humble origins to become a consequential citizen. He accumulated a fortune of 100,000 pounds and served as a Member of Parliament for ten years. Once inviting Franklin to his seat in the House of Commons, Strahan observed that no two journeymen printers had ever met with such success in the world as themselves. Even before their meeting, Franklin and Strahan had playfully concocted in their letters a marriage between Sally Franklin and Strahan's son, William. Strahan was the printer and principal stockholder of the *London Chronicle,* an influential evening newspaper of high literary standards. He gave Franklin nearly carte blanche to use the pages of his newspaper for propaganda items, at least thirty of which originated there. Strahan also printed a number of political pamphlets for Franklin and provided him an entree into the journalistic circle of London.

Franklin had another willing collaborator in a wealthy barrister, Richard Jackson, a gifted writer and political philosopher, whom such observers as Boswell, Johnson and Lamb customarily alluded to as "all-knowing." To Collinson, Franklin owed his introduction to Jackson, a substantial part of his incalculable debt to the philanthropic Quaker, for Jackson was one of the most capable legal minds of his time and a specialist in American affairs. He advised Franklin on the characters and habits of thought of the leading members of the Privy Council and procured for him an invaluable list of acquaintances in and out of Parliament. Eventually Jackson became agent for Connecticut and bought land in that colony with a thought to emigration.

Despite the best efforts of Jackson, Franklin at first had access only to second-string members of the government. Although he made several attempts to see William Pitt, the prime minister, he was always forced to state his business to Pitt's secretaries, who, by their unctuous civilities, drew what information they could about American affairs for their own advantage but gave Franklin himself no satisfaction. Some time during preparations for the campaign against Fort Niagara and Fort Duquesne in 1758, however, Franklin and Jackson prepared for Pitt's consideration a joint set of proposals concerning prime military objectives and methods.

After publishing three preliminary pieces in the *Chronicle*, Franklin prepared for the British lawmakers a monumental volume, *An Historical Review of the Constitution and Government of Pennsylvania*, published in June 1759. The agent and his sturdy collaborators gave their best talents to this ringing defense of the Assembly and people. Franklin supplied the materials, including addresses and petitions he had written for the Assembly; Jackson did the writing; and Strahan took charge of the printing. James Ralph may also have had some hand in the volume, since for many years he was thought to be the author. The Assembly, of course, footed the bill.

The theme of the work is the principle which Franklin had enunciated in his angry interview with the Penns—that the rights of citizens of Pennsylvania cannot be less than the rights of Englishmen. On the title page appeared a notable motto by Franklin drawn from one of the documents he had written for the Assembly: "Those who would give up essential liberty, to purchase a little temporary safety, deserve neither liberty nor safety." According to Jackson, "there is not in any volume, the sacred writings excepted, a passage to be found better worth the veneration of freemen." The book set forth the authors' interpretation of the history of the colony as a continuous effort by the proprietors to diminish the fundamental rights of the people in order to secure their own profit. In a letter to one of Franklin's younger supporters in Pennsylvania, Joseph Galloway, 17 February 1758, he compared his work to an act "in which the Proprietary will be gibbeted up as they deserve, to rot and stink in the Nostrils of Posterity." One unfortunate effect of the book was to eliminate some of Franklin's Quaker supporters because of Jackson's hard treatment of the pacifist wing.

14. Scotland and the Canada Pamphlet

BUT all was not work and struggle for Franklin these days. He enjoyed dinners and drinking sessions with Jackson, played cribbage with Strahan, drank with a society of gentlemen at the George and Vulture tavern, and escorted the Stevensons to the opera. Thomas Penn, somewhat surprised at the moderation with which Franklin conducted his Assembly business, believed that he spent "most of his time in philosophical, and especially electrical matters, having generally company in a morning to see those experiments."

In the summer of 1759, Franklin decided to take William on another excursion out of the capital and to go much farther afield than they had ventured in the previous year. They planned a leisurely journey northward, through Derbyshire, Sheffield and Manchester to Liverpool, and thence into Scotland if time allowed. Franklin would not be slighting his mission, since the government offices had closed, and he could once more plead the advantage to his health of escaping from the London heat. Perhaps there was a little too much heat for William also, in more than a climatic sense. Early in the next year he became the father of an illegitimate son, and it is possible that the expectant mother had become importunate in the days before the projected journey. As great a mystery exists concerning the exact birth date of William's son, named William Temple Franklin, as that of William himself. Temple's tombstone in Père Lachaise Cemetery, Paris, gives it as 1762, but stronger evidence points to 1760, particularly a letter of Franklin's to William, 1 August 1774, asserting that the boy was then "upwards of fourteen."

William, in the summer of 1759, was probably only too pleased to set out with his father, 8 August, in the traveling chaise they had hired.

From Liverpool, Franklin wrote to Deborah on the twenty-ninth of the month that "the Journey agrees extremely well with me," but that they had still not decided whether to continue to Scotland. At Lancaster, their next stop, Franklin received letters which assured him that he could proceed. On 2 September they arrived in Edinburgh, where Franklin's first activity was to look up Strahan, who had been in Scotland for several weeks. Strahan took him to visit a business associate, John Balfour, another printer and bookseller, who did a large mail-order trade. Whether goaded by Balfour's whisky or by the genial conversation, Franklin ordered a large consignment of books for both James Parker and Benny Mecom, presumably without the knowledge of either one. Parker for years afterwards protested that he had not wanted the shipment and could not pay for it. Mecom had no more luck in selling his, and Franklin ended by settling his nephew's account himself.

While in Edinburgh, both Franklin and William were made Guild Brethren and given the Freedom of the City along with four other candidates in a dignified and colorful ceremony. Franklin also visited the university, which he later described as the home of "a set of as truly great men, Professors of the Several Branches of Knowledge, as have ever appeared in any Age or Country."

On 8 September, Franklin and his son went a few miles out into the country at the invitation of Sir Alexander Dick, president of the Edinburgh College of Physicians, to spend the week end at his country estate, Prestonfield.

In the eighteenth century all of Scotland was notorious for its filth, poor accommodations, and indigestible food. The conditions which Franklin had endured on the western frontiers of Pennsylvania may have been more primitive but were certainly cleaner and more salutary. He was delighted, therefore, to exchange the stench, filth and offal of Edinburgh for the munificent hospitality of a country gentleman. It made such an impression upon him that, a few days after leaving Prestonfield, he sent his hosts a short poem of gratitude, recalling in four of its lines:

> Cheerful meals and balmy rest
> Beds that never Bugs mollest
> Neatness and sweetness all around
> Those at Prestonfield we found.

On the fifteenth, Franklin returned to Edinburgh and some time thereafter dined with a literary group at the home of Reverend William Robertson, future principal of the University of Edinburgh and author of a celebrated *History of Scotland*. A fellow guest, the Reverend Alexander Carlyle, noticed that "Franklin's son was open and communicative, and pleased the company better than his father," and "observed indications of that decided difference of opinion between father and son which in the American war, alienated them altogether."

Franklin's alleged taciturnity is one of the paradoxes of his life. Many of the people who knew him remarked on the brevity of his speech—sometimes even absolute silence in the midst of heated discussion. But an almost equal number praised him for his ready wit and flow of agreeable conversation. John Adams charged that he was either vociferous or silent, according to the ends to be gained, probably a very close approximation to the truth. Franklin never could have been the convivial companion and accomplished diplomat that he was without the ability to produce engaging conversation. But he sometimes tired of the game—and preferred to observe others. At the dinner at Robertson's, the conversation had been monopolized by an amateur chemist, who took it into his head to plague the professor of the subject by showing off his own talents. Carlyle described Franklin as "diverted," but he was more probably antagonized. Somewhere—perhaps at this very gathering—Franklin picked up a prejudice against Scottish disputatiousness. In his autobiography he observed that "Persons of good Sense . . . seldom fall into it, except Lawyers, University Men and Men of all Sorts that have been bred at Edinborough."

What is most significant in Carlyle's account is his recollection of the differences in behavior and opinion between Franklin and his son. Other observers had commented on William's pleasing exterior: Strahan, for example, thought him "one of the prettiest young gentlemen" he had ever known. William used his natural endowments to charm both susceptible young ladies and important political personalities. Less bound than his father in loyalty to the Assembly, William from the time of his entering the Inner Temple was consistently seeking preferment, which in England was to be had by acceding to the landed interests—and William was now very much in England as far as his career was concerned.

In the third week of the month, father and son were on their way to Glasgow, where they visited Adam Smith and other notables of that city. They continued northward and then back again to the east and the university town of Saint Andrews. In the preceding February, Saint Andrews had conferred upon Franklin the degree of doctor of laws *in absentia,* and out of gratitude he naturally wished to visit the university which had honored him. This time, on 2 October, he was made a Guild Brother of the town and was possibly received by the faculty of the college.

Franklin paid a visit to one of the students, David Erskine, later Earl of Buchan, who was ill of a fever, and at his bedside advised against his undergoing the common treatment of blistering. More than twenty years later, when Buchan gave Franklin the credit for saving his life on this occasion, Franklin professed to have forgotten it completely.

From Saint Andrews, Franklin returned once more to Edinburgh, where he made the acquaintance of Henry Home, Lord Kames, a distinguished lawyer who in his spare time wrote treaties on esthetics and literary criticism. On the way back to the English border, Franklin stopped by invitation to visit Kames at his country estate in Berwickshire. Here he enjoyed stimulating conversations on philosophical subjects with his host—the kind of talk which "warms the mind, enlivens the imagination, and is continually starting fresh game, that is immediately pursued and taken, and which would never have occurred in the duller intercourse of epistolary correspondence." How different from the forced brilliance of the intellectual showoffs he had encountered with Alexander Carlyle!

After leaving Kames, the Franklins crossed the English border and spent some days touring the weaving establishments of Yorkshire. They returned to Craven Street—William perhaps to his paramour, Franklin to Mrs. Stevenson—on 2 November 1759, a bleak and foggy day, bringing to a conclusion, Franklin later told Kames, "six weeks of the densest happiness I have met with in any part of my life."

While Franklin had been in Scotland, Wolfe's momentous victory for the British forces in America had occurred at Quebec. The capitulation of that fortress meant virtually the end of French power on the continent. The British colonists rejoiced because they would have no more exposed frontiers to worry about and no more Indians stirred up by an alien nation. Franklin rejoiced both as a Briton and as a colonist. Swayed by his theories of population, he believed that "the foundations of the future grandeur and stability of the British empire lie in America." From the St. Lawrence to the Mississippi, America, he predicted, would be peopled by British subjects within a century. Britain itself would grow in population through the resulting increase in commerce, and the Atlantic would be covered by British shipping. But these happy results would come, he warned, only if Britain retained Canada at the Peace Treaty. If the British negotiators let it slip through their fingers in return for other concessions, the American colonies would continue to be harassed by the Indians and the dream of empire would never become a reality.

A strong party in England argued for the giving up of Canada, however, for reasons which Franklin combatted "every day and every where." These strategists asserted that Canada was too large to settle, not worth the having, and that British possession would incite other nations into an envious coalition.

In his earlier contributions to the *London Chronicle*, Franklin had argued against softening the war effort and warned against the dangers of a premature peace. In April 1760, with some help from Jackson, he published his most famous political pamphlet, *The Interest of Great Britain Considered with Regard to Her Colonies,* a work worthy of comparison to the *Historical Review.* Just as he had written his first economic pamphlet in 1729 from the perspective of the "true Interest" of Pennsylvania, he now looked at the true interest of the empire. The Caribbean sugar island of Guadeloupe, as well as Canada, had fallen to the British, and the politicians were discussing which of the two England should choose to keep at the peace treaty. Franklin argued forcefully against the opinions that the products of Guadeloupe would be more valuable to the British economy than the land of Canada, and that guaranteeing the colonies safety from the Indians would make them so strong that they would eventually demand political and economic independence. As early as 1758, the British attorney general, Charles Pratt, had expressed this fear to Franklin. In his pamphlet, Franklin's main point was that the security of the entire empire—England as well as America—required that the French be entirely evacuated from the continent. The objection concerning eventual American independence he answered satirically: a much better way of checking American population (the rise of which he had dramatically demonstrated in many publications) would be to enjoin the colonial midwives "to stifle in the birth every third or fourth child." Seriously he pointed out that it was a great error to think that the colonies could not be filled without draining England of its people or its wealth. As the empire prospered, he argued, so would the motherland.

Remembering the ill-fated Albany Plan, he pointed out in addition that there was slight chance that the colonies could ever unite for any cause short of the most grievous tyranny and oppression. With a mild and just government, the colonists would always remain dutiful and obedient. To round off this promise, Franklin added one of his typical axioms, made to seem proverbial: "The waves do not rise but when the winds blow." He later used this "proverb," which he had adopted from Waller's line, "The seas are quiet, when the winds give o'er," to symbolize the American grievances which led up to the Revolution.

Strahan printed a thousand copies of Franklin's pamphlet,

which the author paid for. The work sold well, and Franklin confided to David Hall that he had "gain'd some Reputation by it," but he had "more Pleasure in the Hopes of it's doing some Service to the Colonies." As we know, Franklin's opinion prevailed at the peace negotiations—even though his pamphlet had little influence on the outcome.

That summer Franklin tasted other fruits of success in his immediate objective of taxing the proprietors' lands. He had hoped to take another vacation in Scotland and even venture into Ireland, but his litigation confined him in London until the middle of September. Governor Denny in Pennsylvania had finally signed an appropriations bill including levies on the Penn estates. Enraged at what they considered a betrayal of their interests, the Penns fought before the Privy Council to block royal confirmation. During their fulminations, Franklin remarked to William Pitt:

Between you and I, it is said, that we may look upon them all [the proprietors] to be a Pack of d----d R[asca]ls; and that unless we bribe them all higher than our Adversaries can do, & condescend to do every Piece of dirty Work they require, we shall never be able to attain common Justice at their Hands.

After days of pleading on both sides, Lord Mansfield took Franklin aside and asked for his personal assurance that the act would do no injury to the proprietary estate. After Franklin put this guarantee in writing, the proprietors agreed to the act and it received royal sanction. The Assembly had reason to be pleased with its special agent.

Deborah, however, had other feelings. She had heard in the beginning of the year disquieting rumors of her husband's private life—probably details of his intimacy with Mrs. Stevenson. Franklin wrote, 27 June 1760, of his concern that she should be afflicted by these "idle Reports." "Be satisfied," he assured her, "that while I have my Senses, and God vouchsafes me his Protection, I shall do nothing unworthy the Character of an honest Man, and one that loves his Family." This pledge, one may notice, did nothing to deny the rumors and gave Franklin plenty of room for future indulgence.

In his letter to Deborah, Franklin reported that he had been elected member and chairman for that year of a philanthropic society, particularly devoted to Negroes, called the Associates of Dr. Bray. At the meeting which he attended, 1 May, only seven others were present, including the famous lexicographer, Dr. Samuel Johnson. The two doctors probably conversed formally but mutually backed away from any kind of intimacy. It would be hard to imagine two less similar personalities than the urbane Franklin and the pompous Johnson.

Franklin was probably the only member of the Associates owning his own slave. The best Franklin could say about Peter at that time was that he behaved as well as could be expected in a country where servants were often spoiled. "He has as few Faults as most of them," Franklin remarked, "and I see with only one Eye, and hear only with one Ear."

Franklin's relations with Strahan had been so amicable that the latter had proposed a business partnership as well as a marriage between Sally and his son—both arrangements which Franklin recognized as exceedingly advantageous. Franklin declined the proposals, however, giving as reasons his affection to Pennsylvania because of long-established friendships and Deborah's "invincible Aversion to crossing the Seas." Leaving it to Deborah's discretion whether to communicate the marriage offer to Sally, he solemnly promised her that he would not even consider settling in England and leaving his family in America. But, although he had no way of knowing, this is virtually what he was going to do for the next fifteen years. From the time of his first arrival in London, he never stopped talking of his longing for the domestic comforts of his Philadelphia household, but except for an interlude of two years he never returned to them until just before the Revolution.

In England he had almost as many relatives as in the colonies. In the preceding year, one of the English branch of the Franklins had died, and the small estate had been divided into seven equal shares among the survivors, including Franklin. He immediately turned his part over to two cousins, "they being ancient Women & poor." He wrote to his sister Jane, 9 January 1760, on the remarkable ravages which death had been making in their family. Of his parents' thirteen children who had grown to adulthood, only three were now living. "As our number diminishes," he urged, "let our Affection to each other rather increase: for besides its being our Duty, tis our Interest; since the more affectionate Relations are to one another, the more they are respected by the rest of the World."

During this year, Polly Stevenson asked Franklin to become her tutor, and he was happy to oblige—not only to be able to try out his theories of education but to increase their intellectual intimacy. Much of the teaching had to be done by correspondence, since Polly lived as a companion with her aunt in Wanstead about ten miles out of London. Franklin frequently drove Mrs. Stevenson in his carriage to visit her daughter—enjoying their rural tête-à-têtes at the same time.

Polly also made herself useful to her mentor as a copyist. She it was who transcribed some letters on electricity which Franklin sent to a French physician, Dr. Jacques Barbeu Dubourg, for publication in his *Gazette d'Épidaure,* a twice-weekly medical journal.

One subject on which Polly needed no instruction was composition. She wrote a polished, correct and vibrant style unblemished by the juvenile phrasing and erratic spelling which Franklin had been accustomed to in his correspondence with Caty Ray. In Polly's letters, Franklin was always delighted by "the Ease, the Smoothness, the Purity of Diction, and Delicacy of Sentiment." The subject matter also was radically different. With Caty, Franklin had been forced to confine himself to her immature confidences and the trivia of domestic affairs. With Polly, Franklin discussed such subjects as the functioning of barometers, the usefulness of insects, and the operation of tides in rivers. Polly understood Franklin's explanations and answered with admirable theories of her own. But Franklin cautioned her against being carried away by her scientific prowess, repeating the conviction he had already expressed to his electrical collaborators that moral duties are more important than science. "The Knowledge of Nature may be ornamental, and it may be useful," he admonished, but "there is no Rank in Natural Knowledge of equal Dignity and Importance with that

of being a good Parent, a good Child, a good Husband or Wife."
Characteristically Franklin chided Polly for her resolution to
remain single. If they should broach moral philosophy as well as
natural, he suggested, he would lecture her a little on that score,
that is, his favorite theme of philoprogenitiveness. Franklin
could not resist an equivocal proposal even if in jest. In an
apparently harmless letter of the next month on insects, Franklin slipped in the risqué sentence, "The usefulness of the
cantharides or Spanish flies, in medicine, is known to all, and
thousands owe their lives to that knowledge."

On another occasion when they had been disappointed of a
projected evening at the theatre to see *School for Lovers,*
Franklin regretted that when Polly was "so desirous of studying
in that School it should not be open." He almost ventured, he
confided, reading to her "a few Lectures on the Subject myself."
Even in his most intimate personal letters in all stages of his life,
Franklin combined the anomalous ingredients of blatant moralizing and sly ribaldry.

15. Holland and Home Again

IN THE second week of August 1761, Franklin and William, accompanied by Richard Jackson, set out for a vacation in Holland, their first visit to the continent. After a smooth voyage, they visited all the principal towns of Holland and Belgium. At Brussels, in the private laboratory of Prince Charles of Lorraine, "full of Art & Nature," they saw an apparatus for trying Franklin's electrical experiments. William was dazzled by the "Magnificence & Riches of the Roman Catholic Churches" but disdainful of the convents for English ladies of quality. The nuns at one of them did not "look very inviting & on the contrary appeared like Cross Old Maids who had forsaken the World because the World had first forsaken them."

At the Hague they were invited to dine with the English ambassador, Sir Joseph Yorke, in the company of most of the foreign ministers. And on another evening they dined at the home of Count Bentinck, "the Head of the Nobility in Holland." In Amsterdam they visited the endowed homes for old people, still an important tourist attraction. Franklin approved the institution of the Dutch homes, unlike schemes of government aid since the inmates had purchased with their own funds the right to end their days in them.

For William, the most disagreeable circumstance in Holland was the continual smoking of the natives. "I dont Recolect," he wrote, "that I saw more than one Dutch Man without a Pipe in his Mouth, & that was a fellow who had hung in Chains so long that his head had drop'd off. There Very Children are taught Smoakin from the Moment they leave Sucking."

The return passage, on which the Franklins embarked during the third week of September, was stormy and disagreeable. Upwards of fifty passengers of different nations crowded below decks on account of the strong winds. Referring to the labeling of baggage, William followed the punning example of his father in humorous remarks about his seasickness.

> I can assure you that . . . there was no such thing as *Inside Contents unknown* for my part what ever I might have been formerly I think I must now be one of the best natur'd Men living, as Old Neptune & Colus took that opportunity of depriveing me of Every bit of Gaul I had in my Body.

Perhaps the ship was filled to capacity to accommodate returning Englishmen and foreign visitors en route to the coronation of His Majesty George III, which was to take place on 22 September. Before leaving London, Franklin, who had great faith in the wisdom and virtue of the young monarch, had providently secured two places for viewing the procession, and father and son arrived two or three days before the great day. William did not use the place provided by his father, however, since someone gave him a ticket enabling him "to see the whole Ceremony in the Hall, & to walk in the Procession quite into the Abbey." We do not know whether Franklin also had a privileged position. Perhaps the situation was symbolic of the days to come when the son would be within the precincts of the throne and the father on the outside.

In the last week of April 1762, Franklin visited Oxford University by invitation and received the honorary doctorate of laws, and William, who accompanied him, received the master of arts. While at Oxford, he saw more evidence of Parson Smith's chicanery, a malicious letter about Franklin to the president of St. John's College designed to keep Franklin from his doctor's degree. Later, at Strahan's house, Franklin faced the rancorous educator and forced him to disavow his charges. But Smith kept up his virulent campaign, dispersing throughout London the story most likely to upset Franklin, that many of his friends in Philadelphia had turned against him. Franklin later theorized to Polly Stevenson that he had himself made Smith his foe by the most honest method of acquiring enemies—"doing him too much kindness." But he was willing to keep Smith as an enemy—since, as he added, it is convenient to have at least one, who by his readiness to revile on all occasions, makes one always careful of one's conduct. Franklin firmly decided, however, not to allow anyone to persuade him to another meeting with Smith. He expressed his scorn by inscribing some verses on the title page of a collection of pious pieces published by Smith in London. The verses by Paul Whitehead began with the couplet

> Full many a *peevish, envious, slanderous* elf
> Is in his works, Benevolence itself.

Franklin had announced to Deborah in March his imminent departure from England, and he gradually spread the news among his acquaintances. One of these, David Hume, praised him (10 May) as "the first philosopher, and indeed the first great man of letters" for whom Britain was indebted to America. Many others attempted to dissuade him from leaving, including his dear friend Strahan.

Anticipating the pleasure of being reunited with Deborah, Sally, and his other connections in Philadelphia, Franklin confided to Polly Stevenson that he felt "a little like dying Saints, who, in parting with those they love in this World, are only comforted with the Hope of more perfect Happiness in the next." He used the same metaphor in a letter to Kames but kept it less personal by omitting any reference to Deborah. "I am going from the old world to the new; and I fancy I feel like those, who are leaving this world for the next: grief at the parting; fear of the passage; hope of the future."

In his last letter to Polly, Franklin revealed the hopes he had once entertained that she might have married William and "become his own, in the tender Relation of a Child." But William had preferred to seek easy conquests for routine amusement and a lady of wealth and position for marriage. And Polly perhaps had been too dazzled by the father to settle for the son. William was not sailing with his father but was remaining in England to cement his own political and matrimonial interests.

The closer Franklin came to sailing, the more acute became his pain at leaving England. Reason called him to America, he wrote to Strahan, but inclination had carried the day for England. He now had decided to make this "one vibration" and return to England to settle forever. "Nothing will prevent it, if I can, as I hope I can, prevail with Mrs. F. to accompany me." His former talk about Deborah's fear of the ocean was in part a pretext to justify leaving her at home. She would have crossed the sea any time her master so desired.

Embarking at Portsmouth, Franklin sailed by way of Madeira, where he observed the agricultural conditions and stocked up with vintage grapes for the rest of the journey. On the next leg of the voyage, Franklin observed his cabin lamp—a glass tumbler, the bottom third filled with water, the middle third with oil, and the top third empty. His perception of the tranquility of the oil over the tumultuousness of the water gave him the hint for a later experiment of stilling a large body of water by spreading oil over it.

Arriving in Philadelphia on 1 November, Franklin had the pleasure of finding his family well and receiving a cordial welcome from his friends "as hearty and more numerous than ever." Smith's malicious reports had been entirely false. In the previous month Franklin had been re-elected to his seat in the Assembly, which had adjourned without appointing a new agent in order to await his advice. Although Franklin was naturally pleased with the succession of personal friends coming to congratulate him, he was also aware that Smith represented a strong faction and had based his disparagement of Franklin's mission on somewhat more than personal animosity. The governor at that time, James Hamilton, son of Franklin's old friend, Andrew Hamilton, had never been on anything but good terms with the returning agent. Yet he caustically summarized the anti-Franklin view in an amusing letter to a mutual friend, Jared Ingersoll of Connecticut.

I cannot find that his five years' negotiation, at a vast expense to the Province, hath answered any other purpose with respect to the public, than to get every point that was in controversy determined against them. Yet what is this to Mr. Franklin? Hath it not afforded him a life of pleasure, and an opportunity of displaying his talents among the virtuosi of various kingdoms and nations? And lastly, hath it not procured for himself the Degree of Doctor of Laws, and for the modest and beautiful youth his son, that of Master of Arts?

Franklin's prestige was undoubtedly not helped very much when the news trickled over—probably on the same convoy which brought Franklin—that William had been constituted royal governor of New Jersey on 22 August 1762. Nepotism in itself would have caused few eyebrows to be lifted in the colonies—but it was somewhat odd that the son of the man sent by the Assembly of one colony to remonstrate against the behavior of its governor should be himself appointed as governor of a neighboring colony.

Despite the known political adroitness of the "modest and beautiful youth," he would probably never have advanced so far without his father's prestige. It has even been suggested that the Penns had a hand in the appointment, thinking that it would serve to soften Franklin's opposition to the ruling powers of Pennsylvania. But John Penn, nephew of the proprietor, Thomas, exploded indignantly in a letter to William Alexander, a Crown officer in the colonies, 3 September 1762:

The whole of this business has been transacted in so private a manner, that not a tittle of it escaped until it was seen in the public papers. . . . I make no doubt but the people of New Jersey will make some remonstrance upon this indignity put upon them. . . . If any *gentleman* had been appointed it would have been a different case.

Franklin in later life affirmed that he had not been at all pleased by his son's efforts to obtain the post and had remonstrated against his growing aristocratic tendencies. In the midst of William's solicitations at the court, Franklin told him the parable of his childhood purchase of a whistle and of his searing chagrin at discovering its minimal value. "Think of what the whistle may one day cost you," Franklin enjoined his son. "Why not become a joiner or a wheel-wright, if the estate I leave you is not enough? The man who lives by his labor is at least free." But William had been too much infatuated by the title of excellency to heed his father's plebeian advice.

On his return to Philadelphia, Franklin found that the city had greatly increased in its buildings—and he was told that there had been a proportionate increase in population, but, to him, the streets seemed "thinner of People," owing perhaps to his "being so long accustomed to the bustling crowded Streets of London."

After months in his spacious Craven Street lodgings and visits to some of the great mansions of Britain, he decided that it was time for him to enjoy more comfort at home, and he began letting contracts for the construction of a new house which he envisaged as a model home for the nation. He wrote that because of its "Convenience, Security against Fire and cheapness, . . . it may be considered a kind of Pattern House by future Builders, within the Power of Tradesmen and people of moderate Circumstances to imitate and follow." On the surface it looked as though Franklin was really home to stay. His son wrote to Strahan, 25 April 1763, "My mother is so entirely averse to going to sea, that I believe my father will never be induc'd to see England again."

Early in 1763, Franklin submitted his accounts to the Assembly. During his six years in England, 15,000 pounds had passed through his hands, two-thirds of which concerned matters not connected with his mission. He was able to account for slightly over 200 pounds which had been spent in printing costs for propaganda pieces, but he had kept no record of his entertaining lawyers and other political acquaintances at tavern dinners—nor had he yet received a penny in the way of salary. The Assembly promptly reimbursed him for all his expenditures and allowed him due compensation for his time and pains, an action which confounded his enemies, who had been circulating lurid reports of his extravagance.

During his absence, Franklin's coquettish friend Caty Ray had finally settled on a suitor, William Greene, whom she had married and already given two children. Franklin revived his old philoprogenitive joke but this time ascribed it to Deborah, who, he alleged, supposed that Caty "learnt *Addition,* in which you most often have Occasion to say, *One that I* CARRY, *and two, makes Three.*"

William, soon after his appointment as governor of New Jersey, had married in London Elizabeth Downes, a polished and aristocratic beauty worthy of William's good looks. Franklin, on hearing the news, expressed to Caleb Whitefoord, a neighboring resident of Craven Street, his hopes that William would make a good governor and a good husband, "for I know he has good Principles and good Disposition." Almost immediately after the marriage, William and his bride sailed for their new post, landing in Philadelphia, where they were welcomed by Franklin and other civic dignitaries. In February 1763, Franklin accompanied the new governor and the new bride to New Jersey.

Despite his long absence, Franklin had not given up his postmastership, and in April he set off on a journey of inspection to Virginia. Then in June he continued in the opposite direction throughout New England in order to regulate and improve the service, this time taking his daughter for company. Sally, now almost twenty years old, had become "quite a woman with many amicable accomplishments," and Franklin delighted in showing her off. But Franklin, unlike some of his biographers, never made any claims for Sally's beauty. Indeed, as Deborah's daughter, she was probably always homely, the adjective which one outspoken observer applied to her when she had reached her forties.

In company, father and daughter gave informal concerts, Sally singing and playing the harpsichord and Franklin playing the glass harmonica, an instrument which he had invented some time before. By friction on a row of crystal glasses the instrument gave off resonant, bell-like tones. Franklin's favorite compositions were the simple melodies of Scottish songs, which he preferred to the ornate elaborations of Italian arias.

Franklin made the trip from Philadelphia to New York by road and sent for Sally to join him by ship. In his absence Deborah had been opening his mail from England (perhaps with the suspicions of a jealous wife), but Franklin did not rebuke her. Instead he gave his approval, 16 June, on the grounds that it must give her pleasure "to see that People who knew me there so long and so intimately, retain so sincere a Regard for me." To judge whether this was ironic or sincere, one would need to know whether Franklin was expecting any letters from the Stevensons. All we know is that, not long after this, Franklin urged Mrs. Stevenson to join him in Philadelphia—but that she did not accept the invitation.

Franklin and Sally left New York late in June, traveling by light carriage and saddle horse, which they took turns riding. They were accompanied by John Foxcroft, newly appointed Joint Deputy Postmaster General. Somewhere on the road, Franklin fell from his horse and severely injured his shoulder, his years of riding in coaches in London apparently having diminished his equestrian skill. They reached Warwick, Rhode Island, early in July, and Franklin had the pleasure of seeing Caty Greene, surrounded by her children, "the happy situation" he had formerly wished for her. One of Franklin's older brothers, Peter, now postmaster at Newport, had also come to Warwick for the reunion. Since Franklin and Sally spent the whole month of August in Boston, he had the opportunity of renewing his ties with his sister Jane.

He had originally planned to keep "bachelor's hall" in Boston, in a house which he had inherited from another sister, Elizabeth, in settlement of money he had long ago advanced. Jane, however, insisted that he stay with her in a boardinghouse she kept a few doors away from their childhood home. Franklin accepted for himself but proposed that Sally stay with Jonathan Williams, a prosperous merchant, his and Jane's nephew by marriage, "as there is a harpsichord, and I would not have her lose her practice." Acquainted with the bleak and sordid atmosphere of Jane's boardinghouse, Franklin probably invented the harpsichord as an excuse to arrange more suitable surroundings for his impressionable young daughter and at the same time to spare Jane's sensitive feelings.

A few days after arrival in Boston, Franklin and Foxcroft proceeded to Portsmouth, New Hampshire, on their postal tour, while Sally remained to practise her music. On this trip, Franklin had another fall from horseback which dislocated his shoulder, an accident which he was almost ashamed to admit. Ruefully he told Caty Greene, 5 September, "I am not yet able to travel rough Roads, and must lie by a While, as I can neither hold Reins nor Whip with my right hand till it grows stronger." Jane nursed him with such tenderness and solicitude that he later teasingly accused her of tyranny. Thanking her for her care, he playfully pretended to feel emancipated in his new surroundings, "where I am allow'd to know when I have eat enough & drank enough, am warm enough, and sit in a Place that I like, &c. and no body pretends to know what I feel better than I do my self."

On 13 October, Franklin and Sally began their return journey, stopping once more at the Greenes' in Warwick and with other friends at Newport, Westerly, New London and New Haven. After only one day in New York, they spent the next day at Woodbridge, New Jersey, with James Parker and another day at Burlington with William, who met them twenty miles on the road. They arrived in Philadelphia on 5 November, Franklin having covered almost two thousand miles in seven months, nearly all of it by horse and carriage over rough roads. His fatigue, however, had not by any means disposed him against travel, for in December he was still favorably inclined to accept Strahan's offers and return to England.

One of the considerations which had served to keep him in the colonies—one stronger than friends and family ties—was a project of developing a "Slice of Territory" to be settled between Pennsylvania and the Mississippi. Even before his mission to England, Franklin had dreamed of leading a colony to the Ohio, and during his English residence he had been involved in an abortive application for a grant of land. Now he asked Jackson whether there were any prospects of securing a crown grant. Franklin, confident of his ability to engage a number of settlers in the colonies, believed that they should strike while the iron was hot. He had already discussed projects of settlement with various promoters and had asked Hall to publicize them in the *Gazette*. His accident may have led him to feel, however, that he was not in good shape for frontier pioneering, for in December 1763 he announced a change of heart: "I could have been of Use in procuring Settlers;—but begin to think myself too old to engage in new Projects that require Time to become advantageous."

He was not encouraged even by a reported cessation of Indian hostilities on the frontier, believing that peace should not have been concluded before "those Villains" had been made "to smart sufficiently for their perfidious Breach" of the last one. Pennsylvania had been the first colony to fulfill its requisition of a thousand men to fight the Indians under a British command, and Franklin urged Jackson (24 December 1763) to mention the circumstance wherever it might serve to help the colony: "let us be prais'd a little by way of Encouragement to be good Boys for the future."

When Franklin had first returned from England, he believed that the colony had too much money in circulation, leading, he thought, to idleness and extravagance. By the end of the year, however, he had changed his mind, and he delivered in the Assembly a long speech in favor of a money bill, presumably the longest speech in his career. The Penns also supported the paper currency but wanted it to be legal tender to everyone but themselves. This, Franklin felt, was manifestly unfair—and he publicly expressed his contempt for the Penns in no uncertain terms: "whatever our Distresses are, the Proprietor has no Bowels; he never relents." Franklin proposed, therefore, to issue an interest-bearing currency which would be legal tender in all cases except perpetual contracts—a device which would put the proprietors on the same footing with the rest of the colony but still not force them to accept the paper money. Despite Franklin's oratory, the Assembly voted for the proprietors' plan rather than Franklin's. Franklin considered himself "but a very indifferent Speaker," and tradition verifies that he was never very persuasive before a large audience.

16. A Bitter Election

MORE urgent matters than a money bill were to face Franklin and the Assembly during the next year, 1764, the most turbulent and probably the most disappointing of Franklin's career. Constantly occupied with public care and turmoil, Franklin accomplished nothing of any importance in science and neither added to his circle of close friends nor enriched the friendships and family ties he already possessed. Although his political leadership was invaluable to the community, it was involved with acrimonious disputes and trivial issues which produced no glorious episodes or solid achievements. Not only did Franklin receive no additional honors or marks of esteem but, for the first time in his life, he felt the impact of mass hostility and realized that respectable people—not only isolated grudge-bearers such as William Smith—could regard him with animosity.

Franklin was caught in two simultaneous political struggles: one, open and violent; the other only latent, but far more significant in its ultimate effects. The first was between the advocates of the existing proprietary government and those who wanted to be governed directly by the Crown. The second conflict was between local economic interest and Parliament. At this time, Franklin assumed that the interests of royal government and the people of the colony were identical; he was soon to discover that they were opposed.

Late in December 1763, the city had been shocked by alarming news of horrible rioting on the frontiers, this time caused not by the Indians but by lawless whites. Frenzied bands in Lancaster County had murdered twenty innocent Indians, living peacefully under government protection. Instantaneously "the Spirit of killing all Indians, Friends & Foes, spread amazingly thro' the whole Country," the populace in general approving the massacre. When Franklin learned that the rioters planned to organize a mob of 1,000 men and descend into Philadelphia to wipe out 140 converted Quaker and Moravian Indians living there, he wrote a pamphlet to check the murderous spirit and strengthen the hand of the government. His moving *Narrative of the Late Massacres in Lancaster County* exposed the inhumane details of the murders and appealed to the white population to discriminate between enemy Indians and those who had been living peaceably in their midst. With extensive quotations from Pope's *Odyssey,* Franklin called on his fellow citizens to observe the sacred rites of hospitality. He warned the perpetrators of the wicked slaughter that "the dying Shrieks and Groans of the Murdered, will often sound in your Ears: Their Spectres will sometimes attend you, and affright even your innocent Children!"

Franklin's powerful appeal brought about a sudden and remarkable change in public opinion. He forthwith formed another defense Association to support the governing authority, signed its roster himself, and procured the signatures of hundreds of others. The governor at this time, John Penn, nephew of the proprietor, was newly arrived from England. From their first meeting, Franklin treated him with the utmost respect as the organ of government and promoted in the Assembly "a ready compliance with every thing he proposed or recommended." During the Indian crisis, the governor turned to Franklin as the most stable force in the community, using Franklin's house as headquarters and staying up with him during two consecutive nights. Penn unhesitantly offered Franklin command of the militia, but Franklin preferred to carry a musket as a symbol of obedience to strengthen the governor's authority. Yet when the determined militia faced the rioters, Franklin acted as spokesman. At the confrontation, the power of authority dominated and the insurgents quietly dispersed with their guns and tomahawks. Within the space of twenty-four hours Franklin had been, in his own words, "a common soldier, a counsellor, a kind of dictator, an ambassador to the country mob, and on his returning home, nobody again."

The harmony between the governor and his people was not

to last. As Penn continued to insist on preferential treatment of family lands in all tax measures, the Assembly lost patience and directed Franklin to draft a "Petition of the Freeholders and Inhabitants," asking the royal government to take over the province from the proprietors. Late in May, the Assembly chose Franklin as its speaker, and a number of the members proposed sending him back to England with the petition, feeling that he might be a better person to present it than Jackson, who had been appointed Franklin's successor as agent. Franklin assured them that Jackson would be as tender and careful of their interests as he himself, but at the same time he asked Jackson, 1 June, whether in his opinion it would be in any way useful or necessary for him to go over. Franklin acted the part of a sincere and conscientious man. Even though his desire to see his English friends made him desirous of the trip, he was "very unwilling the Publick should by that means be put to any unnecessary expense."

To support the petition and get the maximum number of signatures, Franklin wrote a tract, *Cool Thoughts on the Present Situation*. In accordance with his title, he avoided all aspersions or personalities, arguing merely that the ills of Pennsylvania were inherent in the system of proprietary government itself—the Penns being no better or worse as men than other rulers. So anxious was he to be rid of the proprietary system that he discounted the disadvantages which might be expected from Crown rule, some of which he had first suggested in his letters to Governor Shirley back in 1754. In private letters to Jackson, moreover, he had recognized the conflict of interests between Parliament and colony which were already coming into the open. Parliament had decided to maintain a permanent garrison to keep the Indians under control—and these troops had to be paid for. Franklin admitted that some form of taxation was necessary and advocated that the duties be placed on luxuries and on items which would not destroy trade with other colonies. He sanguinely hoped that Parliament would realize that what was bad for Pennsylvania would be bad for England as well. As he put it to Collinson, 30 April, "What you get from us in Taxes you must lose in Trade. The Cat can yield but her skin. And as you must have the whole Hide, if you first cut Thongs out of it, 'tis at your own Expense."

The proprietary party argued that the proposed change in government would not only entail the sacrifice of liberties and privileges but would also saddle the colony with the expense of buying out the entire holdings of the Penns. The proprietary faction worked also on religious prejudices, stirring up the fears of Quakers and Presbyterians over the possible introduction of Anglican bishops. Also, they courted the western Presbyterians, those who had engaged in the Indian riots, by reminding them of the way they had been condemned by the Quakers.

Franklin's buoyant belief that a Crown government would set everything to rights was not shared in England by Jackson. Soberly he reminded his friend (11 August) that although the present king was "a Prince of the most boundless Grace," he would not live forever, and power might come into the hands of profligate ministers who would exploit and tyrannize the province. Jackson was not opposed to the petition, but he saw a little more clearly than Franklin that its success might not greatly ease the lot of the colony.

Jackson expressed these same opinions in conversation with one of the staunchest supports of the proprietors, William Allen, who was then in England. Hoping to keep a burgeoning rift between Franklin and Allen from becoming irreparable, Jackson gave the latter as he was about to embark for America a letter for Franklin as well as oral messages. Soon after Allen's arrival in Philadelphia, Franklin called on him with a cordial greeting of welcome, but as soon as he was ushered into a large company of fellow greeters, Allen launched into a political discourse, holding up as bugbears the obstacles attendant upon Crown government, particularly the prospect of paying 100,000 pounds for the Penn lands, a figure which he asserted Jackson had requested him to communicate. (This Jackson later denied.) In Quaker circles, also, Allen began abusing Franklin by unfairly representing a private conversation that had passed between them many years before—presumably charging Franklin with having sought to stifle the Quakers in the days when he was writing *Plain Truth*. Franklin thereupon refused to have anything more to do with his former patron, declaring to Jackson, 1 September, "With me . . . a second Confidence is impossible where the first has been betrayed." In a later cutting description, Franklin suggested that Allen had nothing to warrant his high judicial reputation but his appearance. "He has the wisest look of any Man I know—and if he would only nod and wink, and could but hold his Tongue he might deceive an Angel."

As time grew close to the Assembly elections on the first of October, the parties readied themselves for a hard-hitting and foul campaign. In these days no one came near Franklin but his own followers. He wrote to Strahan that the proprietary faction would "ere long either demolish me or I them. If the former happens, as possibly it may, Behold me a Londoner for the rest of my Days." His chief supporter and party whip in the Assembly was Joseph Galloway, a young lawyer who had represented Franklin's views while Franklin was in England. When another lawyer, John Dickinson, published a proproprietary speech with a preface by Franklin's inveterate enemy, William Smith, Galloway rejoined by publishing an antiproprietary speech with a caustic preface by Franklin. Here Franklin's language was so savage that he even apologized to Jackson for it. His most infuriating passage was a mock epitaph to the proprietors composed of phrases drawn from the Assembly's resolves and messages. Charging that the proprietors "suffer'd their Colony to welter in its Blood" rather than abate their dishonest pretensions, Franklin excoriated them as a reprehensible instance of "human Depravity and Ingratitude."

Franklin's ingenuity worked against him, however, for his opponents retaliated by pillorying him in a mock epitaph of their own, published as a pamphlet, *What Is Sauce for a Goose Is Also Sauce for a Gander*. Here appeared the brutal charges that William's mother had been an abandoned street woman and that Franklin had once proposed a scheme "to demolish the Quakers entirely." The crucial tactic of the Allen faction, however, was to reprint the part of Franklin's *Observations concerning the Increase of Mankind* in which he had asked: "why should the Palatine Boors be suffered to swarm into our

Settlements and, by herding together, establish their Language and Manners, to the Exclusion of ours?" The German voters were told that Franklin had called them "a *Herd of Hogs.*"

The election was the most bitterly fought in the history of the province. The polls opened at nine in the morning and could not be closed until six the next day. Both sides had spies watching—and at three in the morning the race was so close that both groups sent out to bring in the lame and aged in litters and chairs. Franklin and Galloway lost the election by 26 votes out of nearly 4,000 cast—one thousand Germans, influenced by the "Palatine Boor" passage, according to Franklin, voting against them who would otherwise have been their supporters. But Franklin's friend Collinson believed that he had been defeated by the frontier Presbyterians—the Indian killers. According to one observer, "Mr. Franklin died like a philosopher. But Mr. Galloway agonized in death, like a mortal deist, who has no hopes of a future existence."

Yet even though Franklin was defeated personally, his party won and at the first sitting of the Assembly he was appointed agent to assist Jackson in presenting its petition to the Council. John Dickinson, in opposing the nomination, described Franklin as the man in the whole world "most obnoxious to his country" and argued that a true patriot, when any doubt existed about his popularity or effective usefulness, would voluntarily retire from public life. Then when the minority group for which Dickinson spoke published a formal protest, Franklin retaliated with his last fling against his opponents, *Remarks on a Late Protest against the Appointment of Mr. Franklin as an Agent for this Province.* In his earlier writings he had confined his wrath to the proprietors and governors, but now he ruthlessly exposed the villainy of their local instruments such as Allen and Smith, particularly their efforts to maim or murder the reputations of all who stood in their way.

The work did not appear until he was already at sea, leaving him with the final word: "I wish every Kind of Prosperity to my Friends; and I forgive my Enemies."

According to an eyewitness, "a very great Number of the reputable Inhabitants of this City and County" saw Franklin off on 7 November 1764. On his embarking, he was saluted by "a Number of Cannon, and the Huzza's of the People; and an Anthem was sung" to the tune of *God Save the King*.

> O LORD our GOD arise,
> Scatter our Enemies,
>   And make them fall.
> Confound their Politicks,
> Frustrate such Hypocrites,
> *Franklin,* on Thee we fix,
>   GOD Save us all.

He was rowed on board the Ship *King of Prussia* . . . by Ten Freeholders of the White-Oak Company, in their Barge, they attending on Purpose; in short, the Respect that was paid to this great and truly deserving Patriot, can hardly be set forth, nor the Joys shewn on the Occasion, be express'd.

Franklin's enemies kept up their vilification after his departure, however, in more pamphlets and in "saying and doing Things to destroy his Character that would make even Devils blush." Eventually one of Franklin's friends, John Hughes, put a stop to their open calumny by undertaking to pay to the hospital ten pounds for every charge against Franklin they could maintain if they would pay fifteen pounds for every falsehood he could prove against them. Presumably Hughes was never called upon to pay a penny.

All this wrangling and contention depressed even such a hearty and optimistic soul as Franklin. At various trying periods when his disgust at the opposition tactics would reach a peak, he had considered moving to some other colony or returning to live in England for the rest of his life. During his most gloomy moments, he even questioned the integrity of human nature, at one time (14 March 1764) advising his physician friend, Fothergill, to give up his healing trade.

To be hurried about perpetually from one sick chamber to another [he wrote] is not living. Do you please yourself with the fancy that you are doing good? You are mistaken. Half the lives you save are not worth saving, as being useless, and almost all the other half ought not to be saved, as being mischievous. Does your conscience never hint to you the impiety of being in constant warfare against the plans of Providence? Disease was intended as the punishment of intemperance, sloth, and other vices, and the example of that punishment was intended to promote and strengthen the opposite virtues. But here you step in officiously with your Art, disappoint those wise intentions of nature, and make men safe in their excesses.

Some readers have interpreted this gloomy language as ironical in order to reconcile it with Franklin's more frequent optimism. Unquestionably this somber emphasis was only temporary, but it shows, nevertheless, the rigorous side of Franklin's character: a conviction of moral rottenness, reminiscent of Calvin, and a fatalistic acquiescence in human suffering, precursive of Malthus. We shall see later that, during the Revolutionary War, Franklin actually opposed a medical service for the army. His bitter mood reappeared in the summer of 1764, for in condoling with his sister Jane on the death of her married daughter he could find nothing more comforting to say than merely, "She is doubtless happy—which none of us are while in this Life."

17. Performance in Parliament

O N THE thirty days' voyage to England—a remarkably fast crossing for those days—Franklin had respite from political harassment and opportunity to draw conclusions from his experiences of the past year. Up to that time he had enjoyed universal popularity, thanks to his good humor, easygoing disposition, ready wit and propensity to laughter. The disagreeable bouts with William Smith and the proprietors had been interludes which he had been able to brush off as inconsequential. Now he realized that he could not count on any man's good will. Interest or party could set even his friends against him.

His last act before the vessel put out to sea had been to write Sally in this vein, reminding her that he had many enemies—all on the public account, but enemies, nevertheless, and very bitter ones.

You must expect their enmity will extend in some degree to you, so that your slightest indiscretions will be magnified into crimes, in order the more sensibly to wound and afflict me. It is therefore the more necessary for you to be extremely circumspect in all your behavior, that no advantage may be given to their malevolence.

One act of prudence he particularly recommended was going constantly to church—no matter who the preacher was.

The notion had once occurred to Franklin to take Sally on this trip with him, but he had thought better of it—probably more because she might have been in the way of his gallant attentions to the Stevensons than because of any opposition of Deborah's.

From Portsmouth, where he landed, Franklin went directly to Mrs. Stevenson's in Craven Street, traveling the seventy-two miles in a single short winter day. He may have taken his speedy journey as a good augury for the coming months. Since his

English "wife" was not at home, Franklin sat comfortably in the parlor to wait. But he had forgotten the caprices of the English climate. Despite Mrs. Stevenson's customary attention and a woolen dressing gown which Franklin had borrowed for his voyage, he caught a most violent cold which plagued him for almost two weeks. This gave him more time to contemplate the political situation of America and his role in it.

Although Franklin's principal business was to present his petition, he was nevertheless cognizant of the serious threat to the colonial economy inherent in Parliamentary plans to tax the colonies for the financing of new defense measures. As an alternative to the Stamp Act then under consideration, Franklin proposed to the ministry, some time before March 1765, a variant of the currency scheme he had published almost twenty-five years previously in his *General Magazine.* Currency would be emitted on real estate, as in the earlier plan, but all the profits would be returned to England instead of being retained by the colonies. This scheme would both keep currency circulating in the colonies—always a thorny problem—and provide a revenue tax which the colonists would not find displeasing. Since the proposal follows closely Franklin's magazine article, it is reasonable to believe that he conceived the plan of revamping it before leaving Philadelphia and that he framed it to fit the new situation on his ocean voyage. Within three months of his arrival in London, he wrote to John Ross, lawyer and member of Franklin's Pennsylvania regiment, that he had "been of late so much engaged in our general American affairs that it was necessary to let what particularly related to our Province to sleep awhile for the present." On the same day, 14 February, he told David Hall, "The Stamp Act, notwithstanding all the Opposition that could be given it by the American Interest, will pass." Pass it did—and Franklin continued for a short time his efforts to have his currency scheme accepted as a substitute.

Franklin's experience with ministers, men of letters, and the British population in general had revealed that they suffered as much from ignorance as misunderstanding of America. He realized that he could hardly expect British public opinion to take a realistic view of American problems without having a realistic knowledge of America itself. So many absurd news items about the new world had appeared in the press that he decided to retaliate by his favorite method of education by hoax. In the *Public Advertiser,* 22 May 1765, he ironically defended some of the most ridiculous items and added some of his own. He confirmed, for example, reports of the establishment of a cod and whale fishery on the Great Lakes.

Cod, like other Fish, when attacked by their Enemies, fly into any Water where they think they can be safest; . . . Whales, when they have a Mind to eat Cod, pursue them wherever they fly; and . . . the grand Leap of the Whale in that Chace up the Fall of Niagara is esteemed by all who have seen it, as one of the finest Spectacles in Nature.

He gave a similarly facetious reply to the exponents of the old notion of biological degeneration, who seriously objected that the American "Sheep have but little Wool, not in the whole sufficient for a Pair of Stockings a Year to each Inhabitant." Franklin insisted in a joke borrowed from Herodotus that "the very Tails of the American Sheep are so laden with Wool, that each has a Car or Waggon on four little Wheels to support and keep it from trailing on the Ground." Actually Franklin may have used the method of ridicule in this instance because serious economic argument or statistics would have failed. Three years later his son reported statistics from New Jersey to confirm

the Opinion which some entertain of the Colonies not having Wool enough to make every Person in them a Pair of Stockings. There has at this Session been laid before the Assembly an exact Return of all the Slaves, Cattle, Sheep, &c. in the Province, whereby it appears evidently upon Computation that even in the Counties where there are the most Sheep, there are not Three Pounds of Wool for every Householder. So that if we consider the Number of Women, Children, & Servants, &c. we shall find that there is not enough to make each of them a Pair of Garters.

Franklin found pleasure in his tall tales, and he enjoyed recounting them to gullible Europeans. Several times the eminent French physician Cabanis heard Franklin tell that he had observed in the forests of North America a sort of bird which, like the horned screamer or the horned lapwing, carried two horned tubercles at the joints of the wings. These two tubercles at the death of the bird become the sprouts of two vegetable stalks which grow at first in sucking the juice from its cadavre and which subsequently attach themselves to the earth in order to live in the manner of plants and trees.

Franklin's health remained good, although in the spring of 1765 he suffered an attack of gout which kept him at home for two weeks. The experience gave him some misgivings about the common notion that gout was not really a malady but a benefit, saving the victim from worse afflictions which might be fatal. As his gout later became chronic, he became more ready to adopt the theory that it was a salutary condition.

In July he returned a favor to his childhood friend, Mather Byles, who had promoted Franklin's academic degree at Harvard, by successfully supporting Byles for a degree in divinity at Aberdeen, describing his old friend as "a Gentleman of Superior Parts & Learning, an Eloquent Preacher, and on many accounts an Honour to his Country." At another Scottish university, Edinburgh, Franklin had intervened so often in behalf of similar honors for American clergymen that he began "to feel a little unwilling to apply again immediately to the same University in favour of another, lest they should think me troublesome." He decided in 1767 to apply to Glasgow for his next candidate. Toward William Smith, however, he kept his animosity as vigorous as his benevolent sentiments toward other clergy, particularly preventing some dissenters from donating to Smith's academy by charging that it was not truly interdenominational.

At first Franklin wrote frequently to Deborah about various family concerns, perhaps because he found it slow work to get back into London society—and the peaceful domestic life he had just left looked good. He bought Debbie china and curtains and worried about the painting of his new house. Deborah, for her part, resigned herself to being as happy as possible by staying at home while her husband was "not here to make me quite so." She continued to treasure Franklin's less and less frequent letters, labeling one of them "a *husband Love letter*" and reading it over and over. By the middle of 1765, when Debbie had moved into her new house, Franklin had readjusted to the tempo of London life and breathed a new spirit of urbanity. Now he had pious words about "continuing to do Good to our Fellow Creatures, without Regarding the Returns they make us, whether Good or Bad. For they are all his Children, tho' they may sometimes be our Enemies." Writing to his old Junto friend, Hugh Roberts, he shrugged off "the Bird-and-Beast People"—his enemies—and all their pecking, snarling and barking. And to another old acquaintance he gave an even more cavalier opinion of the malice of his adversaries: "all their Arrows shot against us, have been like those that Rabelais speaks of which were headed with Butter harden'd in the Sun."

These same adversaries had occasion for a new volley of arrows when the much-dreaded Stamp Act became law. Franklin reported to Charles Thomson, a political associate in Philadelphia, 11 July, that he had taken every step in his power to prevent it—that nobody had greater interest than he to oppose it (the act worked harder on printers than anyone else). "But the Tide was too strong against us. The nation was provoked by American Claims of Independence, and all Parties joined in resolving by this act to settle the point." Franklin had his letter printed in the *London Chronicle* to justify himself at home, but his enemies charged that it indicated nothing but his acceptance of a *fait accompli*. His cause was not helped, moreover, when it was known that he had nominated his loyal defender, John Hughes, to be stamp collector in Philadelphia. Even Jane Mecom felt a great shock at the appointment.

Jane was having great difficulty these days in adapting the doctrine of Alexander Pope, "Whatever is, is right," to her own hard life. In fifteen months she had been bereaved of four near and dear relations. "Nothing but trouble can you hear from me," she lamented. Franklin's comforting letter in reply gave her renewed feelings of gratitude and admiration. Despite his high position and the constant labors required of him, he had been not only "the best of Brothers but . . . a Tender Father to me & mine." Since Jane was now saddled with a half-dozen needy relations who could contribute little or nothing to their keep, she asked Franklin for advice on how to make ends meet. Could he suggest any business she might undertake or, if she was too old herself, which might be suitable for her two daughters? Franklin responded generously to this and every other appeal from his younger sister, motivated not only by the family tie and his inherent generosity but also by the thought that he also had been born into her drab kind of world and had it not been for the circumstances which raised him to his high social station he would be there still.

The longer Franklin stayed away from Philadelphia, the more unpopular he became at home—now not only with the disgruntled "Bird-and-Beast People" but also with the ordinary citizens and tradesmen, who were beginning to feel the pinch of the Stamp Act. His enemies charged that he had proposed the act himself and that he stood to gain from every stamp sold—and his silence seemed to verify the charges.

Indeed, Franklin was not unwilling to reap personal advantage from his inside knowledge of Parliamentary activities. He sent his partner, David Hall, a large quantity of printing sheets which could be stamped at a cheaper rate than that of his competitors, but his thrifty calculations were foiled when an order went out that paper could not be stamped in America and the lot had to be returned to England.

Hearing that William Allen had publicly accused him of opposing repeal of the Stamp Act, Franklin answered that he might as well have been accused of planning "Adam's fall and the Damnation of Mankind." He took all this adverse criticism philosophically, however, reflecting that if he were now being undeservedly condemned there were other times when he had been praised beyond his merits. "These are the Operations of Nature," he told his sister Jane (1 March 1766). "Take one thing with another, and the World is a pretty good sort of a World." Falling back on his old doctrine, he consoled himself that true happiness is internal, depending "more upon one's own Judgment of one's self, on a Consciousness of Rectitude in

Action and Intention and in the Approbation of those few who judge impartially than upon the Applause of the unthinking undiscerning Multitude, who are apt to cry Hosanna today, and tomorrow, Crucify him."

His enemies, he wrote to Galloway (8 November), were merely making themselves ridiculous by the absurdity of their charges. "Dunces often write Satyrs on themselves, when they think all the while that they are mocking their Neighbours. . . . Dirt thrown on a Mud-Wall may stick & incorporate; but it will not long adhere to polish'd Marble."

Franklin not only lost face but also the good will of his townsmen, most of them now convinced that he had turned against them. Reports even reached William Franklin that mobs were intent upon burning Franklin's new house, and he urged Deborah and Sally to take shelter in Burlington. But Deborah stood her ground against the threatened danger and with the aid of her relatives turned her house into a virtual arsenal. She was willing to fight physically for her husband's honor, as she loyally reported after the confusion had died down: "I said, when I was advised to remove, that I was very sure you had done nothing to hurt anybody, nor had I given any offense to any person at all, . . . but if any one came to disturb me I would show a proper resentment."

Aware as we now are of Franklin's incessant lobbying against the Stamp Act and his many letters to the press, we may well ask the question: why did he not publicly own his writings against the Stamp Act so that his townspeople would know the struggle he was making in their behalf? First of all, his writings would have lost much of their effect had they not been anonymous. Furthermore, as an employee of both the Assembly (agent) and the Crown (deputy postmaster), Franklin had a split loyalty. When it later became necessary to make a choice, he never hesitated to throw in his lot with the people of America, but at this time he saw no reason for sacrificing his personal interests. He still had hopes, moreover, of participating in the development of western lands—as an investor, if not as a settler.

Not able for these reasons to expose his publishing ventures,

Franklin engineered instead a spectacular demonstration of his loyalty to both Crown and Assembly. This time he was not a mute in the play but the star actor.

The colonists had reacted to the Stamp Act, as Franklin predicted they would, by refusing British goods and services, and as a consequence British producers, traders and shippers began to suffer and then to feel common cause with the Americans. They combined forces and persuaded Parliament to open hearings on the commercial havoc created by the act. When the hearings began in January 1766, Franklin was everywhere, "attending Members of both Houses, informing, explaining, consulting, disputing, in a continual hurry from morning to night." As Pitt began his speech on the question, neither Franklin nor anyone else knew which side he would support, but after he used the term "unhappy act," Franklin rejoiced.

The stage was now set for his own appearance as an expert witness on America before the House of Commons on 13 February. Franklin, bringing realistic knowledge of a world which existed only in imagination for most of his audience, swayed the Parliament of this ancient kingdom by his simple logic and self-confident demeanor. In replying to his questioners, Franklin's reasoning was so clear and his knowledge so inclusive, as one Englishman put it, that he seemed to be a "Master examined before a parcel of school-boys." He appeared to such great advantage because, as he later admitted, the performance was rigged from start to finish.

Friendly members were primed to ask questions designed to elicit the responses which Franklin wished to have broadcast. Adversaries naturally had the same right to submit their queries, but Franklin could anticipate their line of reasoning. By means of his carefully planted questions, Franklin was able to tell the House that unless the act were repealed there would follow "a total loss of the respect and affection the people of America bear to this country, and of all the commerce that depends on that respect and affection." In answer to one questioner he affirmed that the Americans would never pay the stamp duty except by force of arms, and to another he asserted that no military force could compel the people to buy the stamps. When asked what substitute he would propose when the Crown needed money, he fell back on the old system of each colony granting the necessary aid—and he assured his audience that it would never be refused.

As supplementary information, Franklin repeated his statistics of American population doubling at a tremendous rate. Finally, by means of a dialogue on economic self-sufficiency, he brought the proceedings to a close with the epigrammatic sharpness of the epilogue of a play.

Q. What used to be the pride of the Americans?
A. To indulge in the fashions and manufactures of Great Britain.
Q. What is now their pride?
A. To wear their old cloaths over again, till they can make new ones.

Franklin's performance was a mad success. The Marquis of Rockingham told a friend of Strahan's "That he never knew Truth make so great a Progress in so very short a Time. From that very day, the *Repeal* was generally and absolutely determined." Franklin saw to it that the proceedings were fully transcribed and printed under the title, *The Examination of Doctor Benjamin Franklin*. Edition followed edition, both in England and the colonies. Extracts were published in the *London Chronicle* and the *Gentleman's Magazine;* and the work was even reprinted by the French physiocrats as proof of the validity of their theories, particularly that taxes on commerce are nearly always passed on to the consumer. Not only was Franklin's damaged reputation thoroughly rehabilitated in Pennsylvania—he became a European celebrity as an economic theorist.

The Stamp Act was indeed repealed in less than a month, but the repeal brought in its wake sinister repercussions, particularly an affirmation that Parliament had the right to legislate for the colonies "in all cases whatsoever"—a declaration which momentarily passed unnoticed but which eventually led to revolution itself. Another difficulty, somewhat minor—there was talk of requiring that every document drawn up during the period when the act was in force must have a stamp in order to defray expenses. Franklin thereupon argued in a *Chronicle* squib that this proposal would be as difficult to enforce as the original act and engender as much hard feeling. It reminded him of the story of a Frenchman brandishing a red-hot iron, who used to accost strangers on a bridge across the River Seine with many compliments. "Pray Monsieur Anglois, says he, Do me the Favour to let me have the Honour of thrusting this hot Iron into your backside?" The Englishman naturally retorts with an angry negative, to which the polite Frenchman replies, "If you do not chuse it, I do not insist upon it. But at least, you will in Justice have the Goodness to pay me something for the heating of my Iron." Franklin told the story in conversation as well, and it became his best-known anecdote, circulating in England and France. Eventually an expanded version appeared in the *Massachusetts Centinel,* 1 November 1788, as a tribute to Franklin but expanded with a number of "Damn your souls" in the dialogue. The embellishment reminded Franklin of hearing the story of a dispute between Queen Anne and the Archbishop of Canterbury, in which each disputant swore three or four thumping oaths in every sentence. When one of the hearers expressed surprise at their language, the storyteller interjected, "O no, *no,* . . . that is only my way of telling the story."

Scholars have raised the question whether Franklin at this time held a consistent political theory on which to base his appeal for American rights. Did he ground American rights on the original charters (as he had in the *Gazette* in the 1730's); did he maintain (as he had in his letters to Governor Shirley) that Americans, like other Englishmen, could not be taxed without representation; had he conceived the radical theory of natural rights; or did he conceive of the colonies as semi-independent organisms in a federal empire, owing allegiance to the Crown but not to Parliament? In everything else but politics Franklin had a prior theoretical basis for his conduct. In politics, he planned his strategy as he went along, always with an eye to that which was workable and acceptable rather than to the ideal. Probably at this time, therefore, Franklin still had not arrived at a consistent theory of American rights. This is not to say that Franklin never cherished principles, goals or ideals—merely that in his political career he had no theoretical plans for securing his aims. As he said in his autobiography, "The best public measures are . . . seldom *adopted from previous wisdom, but forced by the occasion.*"

Just a few months after the repeal of the Stamp Act, he declared to Lord Kames that the concept of British sovereignty over the colonies was ambiguous and that no clear idea of the foundation on which it existed had been established. Whether or not Franklin had clearly thought through the theory of American claims, he asserted in May 1766 that the best practical method of resolving American discontent would be to provide the colonies representation in Parliament. Realistically, he admitted that the Parliament was not disposed to grant this status at present, but he predicted that when America had become strong enough to convince Parliament to grant it, America would refuse.

Franklin continued to speculate on economic questions not directly related to the welfare of the colonies, publishing in the *Chronicle* (November 1766) an essay of primarily English application, *On the Price of Corn, and the Management of the Poor.* Pretending to be an English farmer, he declaimed against laws designed to keep food cheap and encourage manufactures by forbidding the export of agricultural products. To the argument that this operates for the welfare of the poor, Franklin replied that "the best way of doing good to the poor, is, not making them easy *in* poverty, but leading or driving them *out* of it." Like a modern crusader against the principle of social security, he recorded his observation "that the more public provisions were made for the poor, the less they provided for themselves, and of course became poorer. And, on the contrary, the less was done for them, the more they did for themselves, and became richer." In reference to charity hospitals, almshouses for the aged, and a tax on the estates of the rich to support the poor, Franklin solemnly declared:

The day you passed that act, you took away from before their eyes the greatest of all inducements to industry, frugality, and sobriety by giving them a dependence on somewhat else than a careful accumulation during youth and health, for support in age or sickness.

(Presumably his cherished Philadelphia hospital was not for the poor!)

How are we to explain this attitude in a spirit demonstrably benevolent and progressive in other directions? One might argue, perhaps, that he was merely reflecting one of the traditional dogmas of mercantilism—the theory of the utility of poverty. On the contrary side, a case might be made that Franklin was really on the side of social progress by viewing his arguments as a defense of the new economics of laissez-faire and free trade against the stultifying effects of the outmoded mercantilist theory.

Without question this is a partial explanation, since Franklin later regarded with approval many of the doctrines of the French physiocrats. But this still does not account for his opposition to social aid for the sick and aged. This opposition or prejudice probably stemmed from his early environment, which placed such a premium on individual labor and enterprise that he was blinded to the need for helping those whose natural endowments were inadequate. Almost monthly he was receiving accounts of distress from his own sister—at her wit's end to support her immediate family and various hangers-on. Since no outside help was available to Jane, Franklin probably saw no reason why it should be extended to strangers. His own economic rise had been hard but steady, and he attributed it mainly to his principles of thrift and industry, making no allowances for his intellectual genius and physical stamina. He assumed that the rest of mankind was cast in the same superior mold as he himself.

Franklin gratified his benevolent impulses through individual acts of charity rather than through social humanitarianism. This, of course, makes them none the less benevolent. A good example was his kind attention in transatlantic voyages to steerage passengers. Franklin distributed small quantities of tea, chocolate, fruit and other delicacies to relieve their dejection, restore health, save life, and make the miserable happy.

At the beginning of this year (1766), Franklin passed his sixtieth birthday, entering, as he put it to Deborah, in his fourth score of years, and he congratulated himself and her on "the great Share of Health" they both enjoyed. Immediately after the repeal of the Stamp Act, when it was no longer necessary for the colonies to boycott British goods, he sent her a new gown. Informing her of his declaration to Parliament that the Americans could make clothes of their own before their old ones were worn out, he was reminded that the last time he was home he owned at least twenty pairs of breeches.

In the middle of June, Franklin set out with a physician friend, Sir John Pringle, on a journey to Pyrmont, a mineral spa in Germany. To Deborah, he gave his by now habitual excuse of needing the air and exercise for his health, attributing a newly discovered feebleness and ailing periods during the winter and spring to the lack of a journey in the previous year.

High point of the tour was a visit to the university town of Göttingen, where both Pringle and Franklin were elected to the Royal Society of Sciences. Here at dinner with Johann David Michaelis, then a student in his twenties, Franklin shone forth on his favorite theme of population growth in America. When Michaelis predicted that the colonies would inevitably seek independence from England, Franklin denied it with such fervor that Michaelis was indelibly struck by Franklin's earnest, intelligent and highly expressive face. Lessing came to Göttingen that same summer, but Michaelis preferred the two Englishmen—and Franklin more than Pringle—perhaps, he later theorized, because he considered Pringle a mere physician but Franklin a practical philosopher and great scientist. More probably he succumbed, without realizing it, to the charm of Franklin's personality.

On his return from the continent, Franklin found a letter awaiting him from a certain Sarah Broughton in Philadelphia, complaining about a debt of over thirty pounds which Deborah had owed for seven years. To make matters worse, Deborah had replied to this lady's remonstrances "that she did not know me, and that I might write to you she was a hegehog, [a shrew]. Now sir I don't think her a hegehog," Sarah continued, "but in reality she has shot a great many Quills at me." We do not know what Franklin did or thought about Sarah Broughton's protest. He probably recognized that old age had not made Deborah any less cantankerous and then shrugged it off.

More disturbing news concerned the defection of his partner Hall into the camp of Allen, Smith and the proprietors. William Franklin was quite satisfied, 13 November 1766, "that he has no Friendship for you, & is as great an Enemy to your side of the Question as ever Smith was. All the Difference is that Smith is so openly, & the other covertly—a meer Snake in the Grass." Franklin's friends Joseph Galloway and Samuel Wharton had entered into a partnership with another printer, Goddard, to publish a newspaper, the *Pennsylvania Chronicle,* to sponsor the Franklin policies in opposition to the *Gazette,* and were keeping an editorial position open for Franklin if he should care to join the enterprise on his return to Philadelphia.

Franklin was also grieved to hear news of the death of his brother Peter in July, news which he had been expecting to hear ever since the spring. He wrote immediately to the widow, turning over to her one of his houses and making arrangements for her support. As he was soon to be reminded by Jane, he and his sister were now the last two left of the thirteen brothers and sisters who had once sat around the family table in Boston. But in England Franklin's domestic circle had grown—thanks to his irresistible love for children. In the spring of the year, his uncle's grandson Thomas, a dyer in Leicestershire, brought his only daughter, Sally, then about thirteen years old, to see Franklin in London. Both Franklin and Mrs. Stevenson were captivated by her "sweet, obliging Temper," and Franklin gladly acquiesced in Mrs. Stevenson's suggestion that she remain at Craven Street "for a little Schooling and Improvement." Franklin received ample compensation for his care. Sally was nimble-footed and willing to run errands and wait on him, so that for some years he was able to do without a manservant. Sally remained with her "cousin" Benjamin until her marriage, developing into a fine girl worthy of her distinguished kinsman.

At some time during these same months, Franklin learned of the existence of William's illegitimate son, who had been placed in the charge of Strahan just before William returned to America to take over the governorship of New Jersey. Franklin's paternal affections were too strong to permit the child to live among strangers, and soon William Temple also joined the Craven Street household, Franklin prudently allowing William to pay for his maintenance and education. Polly and Mrs. Stevenson, recognizing the strong physical resemblance between the child and his grandfather, immediately penetrated the secret but pretended to be ignorant until Franklin voluntarily admitted the relationship somewhat later.

18. Reduced Revenues

AFTER repeal of the Stamp Act, the Pennsylvania Assembly ordered Franklin to transfer his attentions to another objectionable trade restriction, the Currency Act of 1764, which perpetuated the traditional colonial handicap of an insufficient legal tender. Franklin drew up a skilful rebuttal of all the arguments against colonial paper money and drafted a substitute bill to be presented in Parliament, but he warned his constituents that, because of the ill-humor against America, there was little chance of its being enacted. Franklin's writings had been so well circulated in America, however, that public opinion once more began to rally around him—one enthusiastic admirer, Samuel Smith, even declaring that "all the provinces in North America ought to make it worth your while to reside in England as long as you live."

In the same month as his examination before Parliament, Franklin presented to Grenville his revamped currency scheme and then, subsequently deciding that it would not be much more welcome to the colonies than was the Stamp Act, talked it down to the ministry. To his great surprise, over a year later, when Townshend, Chancellor of the Exchequer, proposed various duties for American revenue, Grenville scorned them as piddling measures compared to a design he would submit: "make paper money for the colonies, issue it upon loan there, take the interest, and apply it as you think proper." Townshend, taken aback, muttered that he was just about to present something very similar himself. Franklin and the startled merchants who had combined with him to defeat the Stamp Act held back their currency petition, therefore, lest it be attached to this kind of a revenue scheme. Fortunately for Franklin, the proposal was allowed to stay buried. Had it been resurrected and ascribed to

Franklin, it would undoubtedly have exposed him to another round of abuse and opprobrium in America.

In order to abate some of the animosity already stirred up against the Americans by reports of organized opposition to the Stamp Act and of the refusal of New York to quarter troops, Franklin tried in various *Chronicle* pieces to convince public opinion that the Americans had contributed substantially to the prosperity of the empire and that their grievances were real and legitimate. But he had no exalted view of the literary merits of these communications. Comparing them to the past parings of his nails, he considered them ephemeral things, "written occasionally for transient Purposes, and having done their Business, they die and are forgotten." The attitude of Parliament, of the ordinary newspaper, and of the coffeehouse politician had begun to make Franklin feel like a second-class citizen. Every Englishman, considering himself a King of America, seemed to be concerned with the discipline, punishment and rebuke of Americans. The standing maxim of the English seemed to be: "you exist only for our sakes." Americans had fought in the war, for example, but were not to conceive themselves equally entitled with other British subjects to such fruits of victory as fisheries. One reason for the appeal of the theory which Franklin later developed that America owed allegiance to the King, not Parliament, may be that it restored colonial self-esteem by putting the American on a level with his English brother.

In April 1767, Franklin received an almost incoherent letter from Deborah, filled with concern over Sally. Apparently Franklin had advised Sally to make friends, and, taking him at his word, she had acquired 'a boy friend. Deborah was distrustful—used the word "hate" about the young man—and reproachfully declared, "I am obliged to be father and mother." In the next month, Deborah informed her husband that a certain Mr. Bache had begun to express an interest in Sally. Franklin had written so seldom to Deborah that she felt abandoned, complaining that she even had to learn of Franklin's plans from her neighbors. In July she wrote that some "say you will come home this somer; others say not. I cante say any thing as I am in the darke and my life of old age is one Continewed state of suspens."

From William, Franklin learned more specific details about Sally's suitor, Richard Bache, an extremely small-scale merchant, originally from Preston, Lancashire. William thought his prospects were not good, and he unequivocally opposed the match. Indeed, he told Franklin that he had heard that Bache was "a mere Fortune Hunter, who wants to better his Circumstances by marrying into a Family that will support him." Actually Bache had originally been engaged to another girl, Margaret Ross, who died in August 1766 and had asked him on her deathbed to marry her intimate friend, Sally Franklin.

All Franklin could do was to leave the affair to Deborah's judgment and advise her that, if she decided the marriage was suitable, to carry it through as soon as possible—but with frugality and economy. His eighteen-year partnership with Hall had just expired, and he was afraid that he might even lose the post office, which would cut down their income to their rents and interest. This would mean the end of Deborah's comfortable housekeeping and their lavish entertaining. This was no time, Franklin wrote (22 June), to consider "an expensive feasting Wedding." Deborah should be guided by his own scale of living: as frugal as possible, "not to be destitute of the Comforts of Life, making no Dinners for anybody, and contenting myself with a single Dish when I dine at home."

This bleak description—product of a thrifty mood and William's dire hint of a fortune hunter—had no more real relationship to Franklin's actual life than had the parsimonious proverbs of Poor Richard. Between March and July of this year, Franklin ordered from one supplier alone, two barrels of best beer and eight and one-half of table beer. Best beer cost thirty shillings the barrel; table beer ten—relatively every bit as expensive as it is now. We cannot know how much of this enormous quantity Franklin drank himself, but he was assuredly not depriving himself. All his pretensions to the contrary, Franklin was an experienced toper. One night, for example, when Lord Clare invited him to dinner, they each drank a bottle and a half of claret.

Franklin made no greater effort to abstain from erotic pleasures. When the young Philadelphia artist Charles Willson Peale was studying painting in London in 1767, he took advantage of his father's previous acquaintance with Franklin to call upon the doctor without an introduction. Finding out where Franklin lodged, he went to the Stevensons' house alone and was shown into a room where Franklin "was sitting with a young Lady on his knee." We have no way of determining whether this young lady was Polly or a lady of the town. All we know is that a pencil sketch of Peale's, presumed to be the one which he made to record his impression of this visit, depicts a robust gentleman seated in a compromising posture, his right hand at the lady's neckline and her left hand resting on the gentleman's breeches.

When writing to Deborah about the proposed marriage of his daughter, however, Franklin was feeling his age and worried about his security when he should be even older. "If we were young enough to begin Business again, it might be another Matter;—but I doubt we are past it." In this mood, Franklin thought only of the frugality and care required to live on their investment earnings so that they could leave the entire principal to their children. He hoped Bache would not expect much of a dowry before their death. "I can only say, that if he proves a good Husband to her, and a good Son to me, he shall find me as good a Father as I can be." He could manage 500 pounds for Sally's clothes and furniture, but for the rest the couple must depend on their own industry and care.

Two months later, Franklin's spirit of economy had extended to his English family. Thomas Franklin had proposed that Franklin take English Sally back to America with him, but Franklin felt disinclined "as the Care of educating other People's Children is a Trust too weighty for us as we grow old." He had heard nothing more about his daughter's engagement— only that Bache had suffered a financial loss—and suggested that she be sent to London, probably thinking that this would give her the opportunity to forget her suitor.

But even these family worries could not upset the optimism which Franklin had acquired in England, nor could a new letter from his sister, questioning his estimate of the goodness of the world. Jane had used as an argument against his cheerful philosophy the unjustified abuses he had received from his countrymen, but Franklin counted them instead among his honors. "One cannot behave so as to obtain the Esteem of the Wise and Good, without drawing on one's self at the same time the Envy and Malice of the Foolish and Wicked, and the latter is a Testimony of the Former." Franklin refused to condemn the world "in the Lump because some bad People live in it." His hapless sister soon had more reason to bemoan the sufferings of this life, for in September her youngest daughter, Mary, died at the age of nineteen. Franklin, in condoling with her, sympathized understandingly with her particular grief in a sorrow which millions before and after have been called upon to bear. "Natural Affections will have their Course," he observed, "and Time proves our best Comforter."

Shortly after this, Franklin invented a new phonetic alphabet and reformed system of spelling, which may very well have come into his mind while he was struggling through the crude phonetic spelling of his wife and sister. In a sense, his innovation was an example of his love for persons of ordinary capacities, to facilitate written expression for them and spare them embarrassment. Also it represented his linguistic conviction that conventional spelling is irrational. "Polly knows," he once told Mrs. Stevenson, "I think the worst spelling the best." And he confided to Polly, with whom he corresponded in the new script, that it was intended primarily for those "who do not spell well." Franklin took his reformed alphabet seriously—and did not, as previous writers have alleged, drop it almost immediately as a capricious fad. He had type made up for printing it, which shortly before his death he turned over to Noah Webster, hoping that the younger man would pursue the reform.

At about this time, the Grand Duke Leopold of Florence commissioned one of his countrymen, Philip Mazzei, to obtain two Franklin stoves. Mazzei went directly to their inventor, who was kind enough to help in the quest but warned that it would be difficult to find the stoves, since most artisans, "not wishing to be mere copyists, were given to introducing changes." After visiting many stores with no success, they came by accident upon a small shop with a stove almost like Franklin's. Franklin persuaded the shopkeeper to come to his lodgings to make a model of the authentic Franklin stove, and the artisan soon became rich selling them. Mazzei was amazed by Franklin's taking time out from his political affairs to design stoves. The House of Commons even consulted Franklin as a technical heating expert, and he designed "some Pipes &c to keep a proper Degree of warmth allways in the House in Winter." He also supervised the installing of lightning rods on St. Paul's and the Royal Exchange.

When the Abbé Morellet later visited Franklin's lodgings in London, he also was impressed by Franklin's stove and by the successful manner in which Franklin mingled scientific research with his broad political views. Much later in France, Morellet, Turgot and Franklin frequently discussed the theory of stoves, and Morellet made successful experiments of his own.

On 28 August, Franklin with his friend Pringle set off for a six weeks' visit to Paris—to transact "a little private commission," to see some more of the continent, and to enjoy an annual change in scene for his health's sake. In the days immediately prior to his departure, Franklin had seen a good deal of the French minister plenipotentiary, Durand, who invited him to dinner, visited him in return, and treated him with great civility. But Franklin was a long way from becoming a Francophile. Still, judging France by his experiences on the Pennsylvania frontier, he fancied "that intriguing nation would like very well to meddle on occasion, and blow up the coals between Britain and her colonies."

Almost all we know about Franklin's journey comes from a sprightly letter to Polly Stevenson (14 September), so long that it cost Polly a shilling to receive it (postage then being paid by the addressee, not the sender). At Dover, a number of passengers who had never before been on the water partook of a hearty breakfast. "But they had scarce been out half an Hour, before the Sea laid Claim to it, and they were oblig'd to deliver it up. So it seems there are Uncertainties, even beyond those between the Cup and the Lip." Franklin embraced the theory—contrary to that generally held today—that seasickness is less likely on an empty stomach.

On both sides of the channel the travelers suffered so many impositions from boatmen and porters that Franklin could not decide which were more rapacious, the English or the French, although the latter had, "with their Knavery, the most Politeness." Throughout the rest of his tour, Franklin was agreeably impressed by the French politeness, so universally praised in the eighteenth century, at least. As a stranger, he had as much deference shown him as would have been accorded to a lady in England. "Why don't we practise this Urbanity to Frenchmen?" he demanded. "Why should they be allowed to outdo us in anything?"

Both Franklin and Pringle had the honor of being presented at court to Louis XV, Franklin as an eminent scientist and Pringle as physician to the English Queen. At the palace of Versailles, they attended the *Grand Couvert,* a supper which the King and Queen ate in public. Ushered through the crowd of spectators, the two Englishmen were allowed to stand directly behind the King and Queen—the King talking a good deal to Pringle and merely taking some notice of Franklin (perhaps because only Pringle spoke fluent French). Although flattered by the royal courtesies, Franklin affirmed that "no Frenchman shall go beyond me in thinking my own King and Queen the very best in the World, and the most amiable." Franklin also attended the Parisian art galleries but did not presume to comment on the paintings, since he did not profess to be a connoisseur. Art and dancing are about the only subjects of any kind in which Franklin had no talent (although he sometimes made some rough sketches of his own).

Nor was Franklin much interested in "old buildings and monuments." He once confessed that if he could find "in any Italian travels a receipt for making Parmesan cheese, it would give me more satisfaction than a transcript of any inscription from any old stone whatever." In Paris, Franklin paid close attention to the construction of ordinary dwelling houses, chiefly of stone with slate or tile roofs—details which interested him from the perspective of fire prevention. He also observed to the printer Baskerville that the French had been so reduced by war that "so far from being able to pursue schemes of taste, . . . they were unable to repair their public buildings, and suffered the scaffolding to rot before them."

Not in the least a gourmet, Franklin remained indifferent to French or any other cuisine, but he picked up an invaluable general rule, still serviceable, which he passed on to a friend a few years later:

in travelling foreign Countries . . . avoid as much as possible all Disputes, & . . . be contented with such Provisions and Cookery, as you meet with in the Inns, so you will have the best the Country affords in the Season, which you cannot know so as to direct, and if you attempt to direct the Cookery they will not understand or be able to follow your Orders, & whatever Difficulties you put them to they will be sure to charge you extravagantly for.

As a result of the Parisian atmosphere, Franklin underwent a transformation in personal appearance—being changed into a real Frenchman by his tailor and wigmaker. "Only think," he wrote to Polly, "what a Figure I make in a little Bag-Wig and naked Ears! They told me I was become 20 Years younger, and look'd very galante." Facetiously he added that since, in Paris, the mode was to be sacredly followed, "I was once very near making Love to my Friend's Wife." And from what we know of Franklin we may conclude that there may have been as much truth as jest in the observation.

Apart from his occupation with gallantry, Franklin also had many serious conversations with scientists and economists. He was entertained by Berthier, a physicist who later said that he had been a "Frankliniste" without knowing it, as well as by Dalibard, whom Franklin generously complimented by describing as "the first of Mankind, that had the Courage to attempt drawing Lightning from the Clouds." Franklin also established personal contact with Dubourg, who had already printed some of his scientific letters and was to become the first editor of his works.

Just a few months prior to his visit, Franklin's letter *On the*

Price of Corn had appeared in *Ephémérides du citoyen* in a translation communicated by a certain "Abbé M.," probably Abbé Morellet, soon to become one of Franklin's most intimate friends. The *Ephémérides* was the semiofficial organ of the physiocrats, a group of benevolent economists who believed that agriculture was the basis of prosperity and that taxes should be kept low to encourage it. Benevolent as they were, they shared Franklin's opposition to public welfare projects, and they later reprinted a number of Franklin pieces against social security. Nearly every writer on Franklin's economic theories has repeated the words of du Pont de Nemours in the *Ephémérides:* "Who does not know that the English have today their Benjamin Franklin, who has adopted the principles and the doctrine of our French economists?" But no one quotes Turgot's rebuke of du Pont in which he asserted that there was no foundation for this claim and that, particularly on the question of colonies, Franklin's opinions were "not at all in harmony with the true principles." Although Franklin did not meet du Pont de Nemours during his first visit to Paris, he spent some time with the arch-priest of the physiocrats, François Quesnay (with whom he found communication difficult) , and with the elder Mirabeau. On returning to England he published a number of pieces advancing physiocratic notions, particularly *Positions to be Examined, concerning National Wealth.* Here his most important statement concerned the three ways by which a nation could acquire wealth: war, which is robbery; commerce, which is cheating; and, agriculture, "the only *honest* way, wherein man receives a real increase of the seed thrown into the ground, in a kind of continual miracle, wrought by the hand of God in his favour, as a reward for his innocent life and his virtuous industry."

While in Paris, Franklin received a note from Caleb Whitefoord, his neighbor on Craven Street, who had been commissioned by Mrs. Stevenson to ask Franklin if he would mind hiding away in his bagwig a few yards of French lace and thread for "Clandestine Importation." We must assume that Franklin found this violation of His Majesty's Customs against his principles but that Mrs. Stevenson nevertheless got her lace, for shortly after Franklin returned to London he published in the *Chronicle* (24 November) a tirade against "SMUGGLING, and its various Species." His ostensible purpose was to help put money into the British treasury and thus reduce the amount required in taxes from America. He castigated those people who consider themselves *"honest Men"* but who are nevertheless willing to defraud the government of its revenues by smuggling or by purchasing smuggled goods from others. With direct reference to Mrs. Stevenson, Franklin asked:

Is any Lady asham'd to request of a Gentleman of her Acquaintance, that when he returns from abroad, he would Smuggle her home a piece of Silk, or Lace, from France or Flanders? Is any Gentleman asham'd to undertake and execute the commission? No. Not in the least.

Franklin's moralizing converted Polly, who wrote from the seaside that his arguments had caused her to turn "a deaf ear to all the invitations to smuggling," but Mrs. Stevenson defended her own occasional lawbreaking as motivated not by mere selfishness or avarice but rather in honest resentment at bureaucratic waste. Franklin's main target, however, was the average Englishman, who thought nothing of breaking the laws his own Parliament had made yet condemned the Americans as rebels and traitors for every minor infraction of laws which they had no hand in making. Franklin was still smarting over the injustice of indiscriminate charges leveled against his countrymen.

19. Stern Economist

IN THE beginning of 1768, a fundamental change took place
in the British overseas administration—the creation of a
distinct department for American affairs, headed by a secretary,
Lord Hillsborough, a minister who had hitherto taken a rather
neutral position concerning the policies Franklin had been
promoting. Franklin had heard rumors that he was himself
being considered for the post of undersecretary but discounted
them.

On 17 February Franklin had an interview with Hillsborough on the currency question and found the new minister on
his guard. Hillsborough was one of the tribe of men who, trying
to please everyone, abound in smooth answers and assurances of
good will. With Franklin he persisted in his neutralism, carefully avoiding either negatives or affirmatives. At a later interview Hillsborough let Franklin know that he suspected him of
being the author of the American "Farmer's" *Letters* (John
Dickinson's legalistic argument against Parliamentary right to
tax the colonies), which Hillsborough considered "extremely
wild." Franklin was not flattered. He felt that nobody had
settled the relationship between Britain and the colonies, neither the Pennsylvania "Farmer" nor the Boston writers. At that
time he was inclined to believe that the best case would be an
extreme one: either Parliament could make all laws for the
colonies or it could make none, and he preferred the latter view.
As he wrote to William (13 March 1768), this position could be
defended by considering the colonies as "so many separate
states, only subject to the same king, as England and Scotland
were." In his private speculation over the past two years, Franklin had been developing this theory of the King as the sole
unifying authority between colonies and mother country—and
he was soon to use it publicly. Despite his earlier political

opposition to Dickinson, Franklin arranged an English edition
of the *Letters,* adding a somewhat timorous preface of his own,
probably a device to obtain an open-minded reading by opponents of the American cause.

By July Franklin had learned not only that he would not be
elevated to be undersecretary but that he was in real danger of
losing his postmastership—not because of his continued residence in England but because of his political activity: his being
"too much of an American." When Franklin's friends in high
places discovered that his tenure was insecure, they sounded him
out on his feelings about accepting some even higher post in
England. This indulged Franklin's vanity, and, since he thoroughly enjoyed the comforts and sophisticated society of London, he would certainly have jumped at the chance to stay there
as a government official. He even played the game of courtier or
place seeker. He told one of his friends, an emissary of the Duke
of Grafton, "that having lived long in England, and contracted a
friendship and affection for many persons here, it could not but
be agreeable to me to remain among them some time longer, if
not for the rest of my life." There was no nobleman, he added in
due form, to whom he could, "from sincere respect for his great
abilities and amiable qualities," so cordially attach himself, or
to whom he should so willingly be obliged, as to the Duke of
Grafton. Yet Franklin was too much of a political realist to place
much reliance on even the best-intended assurances of patronage, and he privately resigned himself to returning to Philadelphia. He assured William (2 July 1768) that "so great is my
inclination to be at home, and at rest, that I shall not be sorry if
this business falls through, and I am suffered to retire with my
old post."

In August Franklin had an interview with Hillsborough on
the petition for changing Pennsylvania to a royal government,
and once more they "parted without agreeing on any thing."
But Hillsborough's "partiality for Mr. Penn" now seemed so
strong that Franklin decided to press the matter no further
during his administration. Also he carried on a personal campaign against Hillsborough in the press, which had little effect
because of the triviality of the issues. In other more important

pieces, Franklin continued his efforts to show the unreason-
ableness of oppressive and restrictive duties in America and to
expose the British attitude toward America as that accorded to a
subject people. With an impressive array of new statistics, he
demonstrated the financial value of trade with the American
colonies in order to stress the absurdity of blindly insisting on
"an impractical right of taxing them" when long experience had
shown that they gave voluntarily upon requisition from the
throne. In his most effective piece, *Causes of the American
Discontents before 1768,* introduced by his motto "The Waves
never rise but when the Winds blow," he described himself as
"an impartial historian of American facts and opinions"—the
view which he generally held of his propaganda. He still felt that
he was writing in the interests of the entire empire rather than
America alone. It was his English countrymen who were at
fault: "so far from conceiving that what is best for mankind . . . may be best for" America, they were studying to
establish their separate advantage over the colonies. Franklin
had talked and written "so much and so long on the subject"
with so few results that he became momentarily discouraged—
"weary of talking and writing." His impartiality had done nothing but make himself suspect: "in England, of being too much
an American, and in America, of being too much an Englishman."

Although Franklin was not often seen at the English court,
he was gratified in October 1768 to be invited to dine with the
monarch of another nation, Christian VII of Denmark, then
visiting England and traveling under the assumed name of
Prince of Travendahl. Franklin was impressed by "his great
Affability & Condescension, and the Pleasure he appears to take
in every thing he sees"—a characteristic naturally appealing to
Franklin, who had it himself. At table Franklin was placed near
the King, only Lord Moreton, president of the Royal Society,
intervening. Moreton kindly acted as interpreter since Franklin
at that time still had no fluency in the language of diplomats,
French. The questions which the King asked "were such as
shew'd an inquisitive mind and a good Understanding." During
the second course, large groups of people were allowed to pass

through the room, as the custom was, to see the King at dinner, and Franklin shared the public gaze. He wrote of this reception to his son—who would readily sympathize with a little vanity over association with the great—but cautioned William not to allow his letter to circulate outside the family, "for it will not be decent in us to talk of these kind of Things."

There is a tradition that during this same year Franklin visited the scene of his earlier labors, Watts's Printing House in Lincoln's Inn Fields, where he consorted with the workers. "Come my friends," he allegedly declared, "we will drink together: It is now forty years since I worked like you at this press, as a journeyman printer." He then presumably sent for a gallon of porter and drank with the men, "Success to Printing." Source of the legend is a plaque on Franklin's press itself, now in the Smithsonian Institution. This apocryphal tale lacks the ring of truth not only because of the date (why would Franklin have delayed his visit to Watts's establishment many years after returning to London?) but because in this year Franklin was much more inclined to hobnobbing with royalty than with the proletariat.

This was the period of popular demonstrations in favor of John Wilkes, who had been denied his seat in the House of Commons because of a libel against the government. Whether or not Wilkes was a demagogue, as his enemies charged, there is no question that the common people followed him almost to the point of worship. But for Franklin at this time, the common man was a menace to order and the Wilkes demonstrations were lawless riot and confusion. All Franklin could see was:

Mobs patrolling the streets at noonday, some knocking all down that will not roar for Wilkes and liberty; courts of justice afraid to give judgment against him; coal-heavers and porters pulling down the houses of coal merchants, that refuse to give them more wages; sawyers destroying saw-mills; sailors unrigging all the outward bound ships, and suffering none to sail till merchants agree to raise their pay.

Franklin looked out the window and saw "a great mob of coal porters, . . . carrying a wretch of their business upon poles to

be ducked, and otherwise punished at their pleasure for working at the old wages." This was symbolic to Franklin that the
common people had lost "all respect to law and government . . . and every thing that used to keep them in order."
Not only did Franklin now feel no solidarity with the working
class, he felt strong opposition. His own antecedents were nothing to the purpose. Probably in America in Franklin's day no
proletarian class as such existed. We remember that no social
distinctions had intervened between Franklin as a journeyman
printer and Governor Keith or subsequent governors. When
Franklin returned to England, he identified with the gentry
rather than the workers.

There is no question that Franklin never liked Wilkes, and
in this antiproletarian mood he published in the *Gentleman's
Magazine* (April, 1768) another of his reactionary economic
essays, *On the Labouring Poor*. Once again launching out
against laws for the relief of the unfortunate, he charged that
they improperly invest the poor "with an inheritance, as it were,
in all the estates of the rich." In the vein of Mandeville,
Franklin echoed the stock arguments used innumerable times
before and since, that relieving the poor encourages laziness and
that raising wages fosters drunkenness.

Giving mankind a dependance on anything for support, in age or
sickness, besides industry and frugality during youth and health,
tends to flatter our natural indolence, to encourage idleness and
prodigality, and thereby to promote and increase poverty. . . .
[The working class] consider every encrease of wages, only as
something that enables them to drink more and work less; so that
their distress in sickness, age, or times of scarcity, continues to be the
same as if such laws had never been made in their favor.

All this does not mean, of course, that Franklin lacked
compassion for the poor or suffering humanity. But he consistently held out against indulging any kind of economic dependence. In his autobiography he relates that one morning he
found in front of his door on Craven Street, a poor woman "very
pale and feeble as just come out of a Fit of Sickness," who was
sweeping his pavement with a birch broom. When he asked by

whom she had been engaged, she replied, "Nobody; but I am very poor and in Distress, and I sweeps before Gentlefolkses Doors and hopes they will give me something." Franklin promised to give her a shilling if she would sweep the whole street—and in three hours she returned to collect her wages. Franklin was willing to relieve this poor woman because she conformed to his notions of initiative and industry. Another person more tenderhearted might have given her the shilling without requiring the work. Franklin not only let her sweep the entire street but sent his servant out to see whether she had done it properly. Typical of Franklin is his reason for telling the story of the street cleaner: not to encourage acts of individual charity or illustrate the need for social benevolence but to trace the origin of one of his civic projects—that of keeping the streets of London and Westminster clean.

On another occasion the rector of St. Martin's Parish, Dr. Saunders, went from house to house during a severe winter soliciting contributions to buy coal for poor families. Franklin admitted that he gave "but little, very little" even though considerably more than his wealthy proprietary, Thomas Penn. Franklin originated many works of public and private charity when his sensibilities were touched, but he still tended to hold every individual responsible for his own economic condition.

Franklin gave a slightly more mellow cast to his economic theories, however, in a subsequent *Chronicle* piece (June 1768), a highly fanciful hoax combining satire, economic theory, religious speculation and Indian anthropology. This imaginative creation is unique not only in Franklin's career but in all literary history. Franklin labeled his work, *Extract from an Account of the Captivity of William Henry in 1755, and of his Residence among the Senneka Indians six Years and seven Months till he made his Escape from them,* passing it off as a summary of a Boston publication. That is why previous biographers have failed to identify it as Franklin's. The idea came to him from an essay in Bradford's *American Magazine* thirty years before, and he embellished it with his experiences at the Indian Treaty in Carlisle. In the narrative, the pretended William Henry engages in lengthy philosophical and moral conversations with Old Canusatego, the counselor and chief of the

village—a character drawn from the real chieftain whom Franklin had known on the Pennsylvania frontier. One day William
Henry listens to a young warrior's discourse on creation. Nine
Oneida warriors see a "beautiful young Woman descend naked
from the clouds." Recognizing her as "the great Manitta's
Daughter," they give her broiled venison to eat—and she reas-
cends into the clouds, first telling them to return to the same
place in twelve moons. They do so and find growing "where
she had pressed the ground with her right hand, corn; where
with her left hand, beans; and where her back parts had pressed
it, there grew tobacco." This recital is greeted by laughter from
the warriors, and Old Canusatego calls it a foolish Oneida tale.
To correct this faulty cosmogony, the grave chief with an air of
dignity and authority gives the true account of the beginnings
of his country. There is not a single "great good Manitta," he
affirms, but several. "If there were but one, how unhappy must
he be without friends, without companions, and without that
equality in conversation, by which pleasure is mutually given
and received." These gods live in the sun and moon, love each
other as brothers, and visit and converse with each other. Each
god or "good Manitta" is devoted to his own land and takes care
of peopling it. (All this is strongly reminiscent of Franklin's
youthful articles of belief and shows that he had not given up his
polytheistic notions.) The five Indian nations sprang from the
fertile fields of Onondaga, which the good Manitta had sown
with five handfuls of red seeds, like the eggs of flies. From these
seeds came forth little worms which penetrated the earth and
were united with spirits which had never seen the light.

Manitta watered the earth with his rain, the sun warmed it, the
worms with the spirits in them grew, putting forth little arms and
legs, and moved the light earth that covered them. After nine moons
they came forth perfect boys and girls. Manitta covered them with
his mantle of warm purple cloud and nourished them with milk
from his finger ends. Nine summers did he nurse, and nine summers
more did he instruct them how to live. [Even Franklin's anthropo-
logical fantasy was colored by his philoprogenitiveness.]

In the economic section of his allegory, where Franklin
exalts free trade, he seems to show more concern for human
values than in his sterner economic writings. The five Indian

nations lived happily as long as they communicated "freely to each other as their wants required, all the good things that had been given them." But the great evil Manitta caused each nation to hold back the product which it had in more abundance than the others and to demand greater quantities of the other nation's product in return. At this selfish behavior, the father in the sun hurled denunciation in thunder.

Wretches, said he, did I not freely give to each of you different kinds of good things, and those in plenty, that each might have something in his power to contribute to his brother's happiness, and so increase the happiness and strengthen the union of the whole; and do you now abuse those gifts to oppress each other; and would one brother, to make himself *in imagination* more happy, make four brethren *in reality* more miserable.

This rebuke accompanied with drastic punishment made the Indians reform their evil ways, and "from that time down to the present day, it has been an inviolable rule and custom among the nations, that *every Brother is welcome to what a Brother can spare of the good things which the great Spirit has caused to spring for him out of the earth.*" This seems to be a statement of social responsibility for economic distress within the community, but we must be careful to read it in context. It is an allegory concerning nations, not individuals within the same nation, and even then its force is enervated by the qualifying phrase, "what a Brother can spare."

While Franklin was elaborating his Indian cosmogony and reflecting on his polytheistic theology, he worried very little about his family in Philadelphia. In January 1768, Deborah received the first letter from her husband in almost five months. She answered on the next day, addressing him as "My Dearest Dear Child." She had previously sent him quantities of Indian and buckwheat meal, apples, cranberries and nuts, perhaps in response to his letter urging household economy. Sally had gone ahead with her marriage to Richard Bache in the preceding October. In February 1768, Franklin wrote to Jane that he would have wished better prospects for Sally, and in August he wrote sternly to Richard Bache, explaining that he had previously answered none of the young man's letters because he had looked upon him "as an instrument of bringing future unhappiness on my child by involving her in the difficulty and distress that seemed connected with your circumstances, you having not merely nothing beforehand, but being besides greatly in debt." Only the passage of time had made him relent sufficiently to write these sober words and to express the hope that his son-in-law might retrieve his losses by "industrious Application to business." In the spring of the next year, however, Franklin became reassured. He had received a visit from one of Bache's sisters, a comely young lady, and now he was satisfied that Sally had made a good connection. No better way of winning over Franklin at any age than sending a handsome young girl.

Benjamin Mecom, after unsuccessful runs with his printing press in Boston, New York and New Haven—with varying degrees of help from his uncle—had just installed himself at Philadelphia (in 1768). None of his family realized that his erratic behavior stemmed from a mental disorder which would eventually end tragically. So Franklin could not understand "how so very sluggish a creature" could maintain a family in Philadelphia.

And William, who was producing no legitimate issue, began to develop tender feelings for William Temple and wrote to ask Franklin's sentiments about bringing the child back to America when he should return, proposing to pass off Temple as the son of a poor relation whom he had adopted as his own. Franklin had no objection as long as William continued to pay for his son's upkeep. Later he reminded William that he owed a considerable sum for the "Maintenance & Education of Temple; but that his Friends will not grudge when they see him."

During this year (1768) Franklin's health was remarkably good, even though he did not make his customary long summer journey. As he entered the winter season, he remarked that it was his fourth one free of gout. At the age of sixty-three, he felt that his constitution was actually on the mend. Walking tired him less than formerly, and he felt stronger and more active. Yet he was under no illusion that he would grow young again, and he realized that every additional day of life was uncertain. "I know that men of my Bulk often fail suddenly."

One day in reading the newspapers, Franklin came upon the surprising report that he had been appointed as agent for Georgia, a colony which he had never visited and where he had few contacts. Late in June 1768 he received official notice from Governor Wright of Georgia, who at the same time informed Hillsborough that Franklin had been chosen as a compromise candidate to put an end to a dispute between the two houses of the Georgia legislature. Within six months of Franklin's appointment, the "agent for Georgia" presented to the London Board of Trade a "Memorial in Relation to the Silk Culture in Georgia," advocating the paying of bounties and seeking expert technological guidance. One cannot be sure whether this agent was the one appointed by the province, Franklin, or the Crown agent, Dr. John Campbell, but it is more likely to have been Franklin since at the same time he was very much concerned with promoting silk culture in Pennsylvania. Georgia had the same interests as Pennsylvania in seeing the repeal of the obnoxious revenue acts, and Franklin wrote to Noble Wymberley Jones, Speaker of the Georgia Commons, 7 June 1769, that some hope existed for such an outcome and "that gradually every Obstruction to that Cordial Amity, so necessary for the Welfare of the whole Empire will be removed." The great obstacle he saw was the prestige of Parliament—reflecting "the Pride Natural to a great Nation, the Prejudices that have so universally prevailed here with Regard to the Point of Right, and the Resentment at our disputing it."

The Americans had been so successful in their boycott of British goods that Franklin began to think that they would derive more benefit from continuing to rely on their industry and frugality than from resuming extensive trade with England. If the colonies became economically independent, he wrote to an ardent defender of colonial rights, Dr. Samuel Cooper of Boston (27, April 1769), "this handicraft, shop-keeping State, will, for its own sake, learn to behave more civilly to its Customers."

To inform English public opinion, Franklin kept up in the

newspapers his defense of the character and attainments of Americans. Still he had nothing but good to say of the body of the English people: "of a noble and generous Nature, loving and honouring the Spirit of Liberty, and hating arbitrary Power of all sorts." And he could scarcely conceive of a king of better disposition than George III, "of more exemplary Virtues, or more truly desirous of promoting the Welfare of all his Subjects." On the King's official birthday, Franklin and Samuel Wharton "went to Court Together, dressed in rich Silks &c. and made a very genteel Appearance." One of Franklin's Philadelphia acquaintances observed that he looked "heartier than ever I knew him in America and has a most surprising influence, and is as much talked of as in America." For Franklin, Parliament was the great villain—made up, as he had written to Kames on New Year's Day (1769), of selfish men supposedly doing good but actually serving their private interests.

Franklin was also called upon to vindicate his own integrity as an agent against published charges that a Crown-appointed postmaster whose son was a royal governor must obviously be a tool of the ministry. Ridiculous as such an accusation must have seemed to anyone in the government, Franklin was obliged to write an anonymous letter to the London *Gazetteer* (17 January 1769), defending himself and some of his countrymen against the alleged inconsistency of agitating against Parliamentary duties while at the same time seeking places and pensions. In exasperation he affirmed that Americans had not been taught "that the interests of their King and his subjects are so contrary and incompatible, that an honest man cannot serve the one without betraying the other."

On the same day the *Public Advertiser* published a bitter assault by Franklin directed against those in England who had proposed to use military force in order to collect revenue in the colonies. By means of a table of the costs of subduing the colonies, he demonstrated that such an attempt would be far too expensive, even if successful.

Toward the end of the year (1769), shortly before the reconvening of Parliament, Franklin with the aid of Strahan made a vigorous effort to achieve total repeal of the objectionable duties. Strahan prepared seven questions concerning what measures would need to be taken to restore harmony in American relations, and Franklin wrote out a detailed reply. The great problem was to repeal the taxes while still preserving the dignity of Parliament. He assured Strahan that the two aims were not mutually exclusive. If Parliament had made an error it should correct it. "The Honour and Dignity of the British Legislature will not be hurt by such an Act of Justice and Wisdom." To Franklin, the wisdom and conduct of a legislature should be the same as that of an individual and measured accordingly. "It is the Persisting in an Error, not the Correcting it, that lessens the Honor of any Man or Body of Men."

In his other answers, Franklin sketched the theory of the sovereignty of the King, not Parliament, and affirmed that the only way of composing the differences with the colonies would be to restore the situation which existed before the Stamp Act. More concerned with practical adjustments than metaphysical prerogatives, Franklin granted the people of Britain the right to intervene in the financial affairs of America so long as they never exercised it. (In an earlier letter to Galloway, he had compared this right to "the Claim of the Spanish Monarch to the Title of King of Jerusalem.") Finally, Franklin warned that ministerial rigidity would lead to mutual provocations and eventual separation, prophesying almost step by step the events which actually brought on the Revolution. The circulation of this colloquy in Massachusetts was decisive in Franklin's being chosen in the next year agent for that colony.

At home, the new topic of conversation was a baby, Benjamin Franklin Bache, born to Sally, 12 August 1769. On the last day of the month he was baptized at Christ Church in Philadelphia, William and his wife standing for him, a Mr. Boynton serving as proxy for Franklin, and Deborah in good enough health to attend for herself. According to William, "he is not so fat & lusty as some Children at his Time are, but he is altogether a pretty little fellow, & improves in his Looks every Day." To Deborah, this meant that he resembled his grandfather, and she hastened to convey these tidings to Franklin, knowing they would bring him pleasure.

From Boston, Jane as usual had no happy intelligence—but she still wrote without complaining. If her brother had been born under a lucky star, hers was certainly ill-intentioned. Just before the Stamp Act, she and her daughter had begun to manufacture artificial flowers for "Ladyes Heads & Boosomes," in order to supplement their boardinghouse income. She asked Franklin whether Mrs. Stevenson would be willing to send her some worn cloth lining or old handkerchiefs dyed in bright colors which could be used in the process. Franklin's wardrobe, she was afraid, would not be shabby enough for this lowly purpose. Mrs. Stevenson and Polly accordingly saved their old materials and sent them to Jane, probably out of regard to Franklin. But just as the little business seemed to promise some success, the Americans began their antibuying campaign, practising Franklin's favorite virtues of industry and frugality on a massive scale and wiping out Jane's potential market. Mrs. Stevenson was dilatory in correspondence, and Franklin apologized, explaining that she "scarce ever can prevail on herself to write a Letter to anyone" (29 September 1769). Jane had written that "all the Assistance of Reason and Religion" had scarcely been sufficient to keep up her spirits. Franklin replied that it was well she had such aids, but reason would be of more use if it "could enable us to *prevent* the Evils it can hardly enable us to *bear*." In an unusual mood for one of the most committed rationalists of the whole Enlightenment, he admitted that he had "sometimes been almost tempted to wish we had been furnished with a good sensible Instinct instead." Perhaps he was discouraged by the failure of his logic to convert the ministry. In the same vein he wrote to Polly Stevenson (2 September) that "there are certain Circumstances in Life, sometimes, wherein 'tis perhaps best not to hearken to Reason."

※◇※◇※◇※◇※◇※◇※◇※◇※◇※◇※◇※

20. Dr. Doubleface

SOME Englishmen believed that the Americans were inconsistent in constantly clamoring for the rights of Englishmen
for themselves while at the same time denying practically all
rights to their Negro slaves. To defend his countrymen, Franklin published in the *Public Advertiser* (30 January 1770) a
dialogue between an American and two hostile Britons. Admitting the evils of slavery, Franklin argued that it had been
brought to America by the English and even at that moment
Parliament refused to sanction laws in the colonies to discourage
the slave trade. These are strong arguments, but Franklin
devoted more space to the specious one that servitude in Britain
was worse than in the colonies. Pointing to the English miners
who "dig Coal . . . in those dark Caverns under Ground,
unblessed by Sunshine," he accused the English of making
miners virtual slaves "and their Children after them." He was
certainly no advocate of slavery, but, as we well know, arguments like his were later widely used in its defense. In debates in
other areas he would never have agreed that two wrongs make a
right. This is one of the least admirable of Franklin's propaganda pieces.

He did much better two years later, publishing in the
Chronicle, 20 June 1772, a denunciation of the hypocrisy of
Britons who took pride in their virtue and liberty for setting
free a single Negro in their courts while by their laws promoting
the Guinea slave trade, "this pestilential detestable traffic in the
bodies and souls of men."

Only gradually did Franklin revise his conception of
Negroes as an inferior race, which he had expressed in his essay
on the increase of mankind. In December 1763, as a result of
visiting a Negro school, he had acquired "a higher Opinion of
the natural Capacities of the Black Race" than he had ever

before entertained. "Their Apprehension," he then observed, "seems as quick, their Memory as strong, and their Docility in every Respect equal to that of white Children."

Franklin made his most positive and decisive call for colonial action in 1770 in a private letter (18 March) to Charles Thomson, a leader of the Philadelphia merchants, who was appealing to popular sentiment and enrolling the lower ranks of tradesmen and mechanics to enforce the nonimportation agreements. Thomson saw to it that Franklin's letter was printed and widely circulated in Philadelphia and Boston and read aloud in public meetings. Here Franklin openly repudiated "the idle notion of the dignity and sovereignty of Parliament" and charged that the Bedford party wished for a pretense to order a massacre in the colonies. He pointed out that if the colonists now let down their nonimportation agreements, they could never hope to use such a device in the future—whereas if they kept it up they would never again need to use it. His urgent appeal was persist! persist! persist!

The irate ministry, considering Franklin's position irreconcilable with his loyalty as a Crown officer, execrated him as "Dr. Doubleface" and "the Judas of Craven Street." According to the ministry, Franklin was a shrewd temporizer, constantly on the fence, dedicated neither to the Crown nor to the colonies. And it is true that, until almost the last minute before the outbreak of the Revolution, Franklin played the role of a moderate. Despite his republican pronouncements during the Revolution, he had never been on the radical side while in England.

Although the ministry considered him a disloyal and ungrateful public servant, Franklin steadfastly refused to resign his postmastership, facetiously observing to Jane Mecom (30 December 1770) that he was "deficient in that Christian virtue of resignation." In justifying his tenacity, he pointed out that the office before his tenure had been so badly managed that it never even produced the salary it was supposed to pay. He had worked hard to put it on its feet, and he felt he deserved to be continued in office. But whether the ministry dismissed or retained him, he would adhere firmly to his rule "never to turn aside in public affairs through views of private interest; but to go straight forward in doing what appears to me right at the time."

The issue was simple as Franklin put it in his most concise exposition in the *London Chronicle* (8 November 1770) : the Americans were not disloyal and they had always been willing to give aid to the Crown according to their ability; but always they had thought "that they themselves have alone the right of granting their own money, by their own Representatives in Assembly met, and that the Parliament of Britain hath no right to raise a revenue from them without their consent."

During this year Deborah was particularly dispirited, despairing now of ever seeing her husband again. Her only consolation lay in little Benny Bache, whom she lovingly called "King Bird." Franklin, perhaps realizing her low spirits, asked a number of acquaintances from London going to Philadelphia to call upon her. These included a milliner and mantua maker; a portrait painter, Henry Benbridge; and a future bishop, William White.

Richard Bache had gone to Jamaica to investigate the possibilities of settling himself in business there—a prospect which did not please Franklin, who lost no time in expressing his opposition. Sally immediately complied with his wishes that she remain in Philadelphia, and she persuaded her husband to return. "Your last letter has determined me," she wrote to her father (May 1770). "No Sir; your Child will not give you pain; she will stay and prove to you through life what she really is—Your Dutiful and Affectionate Daughter." Some people would say that Franklin was somewhat unreasonable in asking this sacrifice, particularly when he had been living in another country for many years. But Franklin with his patriarchal notions took Sally's acquiescence as a matter of course. His chief family worry seemed to be that Deborah would humor her grandson too much and possibly spoil him.

Jane Mecom had visited Philadelphia soon after Benny's birth, scrutinizing him closely for resemblances to his grandfather, but could find none except good nature and a sweet smile. This was the first meeting of Jane and Deborah, and it must have made Jane realize even more than before how unlucky she had been in her own life. Here was Deborah, a woman of her own social station and much less intelligent, living in conditions of comfort and security which she had never dreamed of for herself. As she wrote to Franklin, "I am convinced Poverty is Intailed on my Famely Prehaps for wise Ends & I Indvour to be content."

Jane's letters may have been poorly spelled; Deborah's were often incoherent. Franklin in his correspondence with his sister discussed political principles and issues; and they both mentioned books they had been reading. Franklin affirmed that she wrote better than most American women. But the Franklin-Deborah correspondence has absolutely nothing intellectual to illuminate it. Essentially the same is true of the letters between Franklin and Sally, who resembled her mother more than her father. When Franklin had an intelligent girl such as Polly Stevenson under his tutelage, he pushed her to achievement. But in writing to Sally and Caty Ray Greene, he made no such demands. Although Jane had not had the opportunity to develop her intellectual capacities, she was in comparison with Deborah a female savant, and both she and Franklin fully realized it.

During the year 1770, Franklin had a good deal of trouble with his health. Throughout the first quarter he suffered from a disagreeable giddiness, which was replaced by an attack of gout. Then in the fall his arm began to pain him again. But approaching his sixty-fifth year, he took comfort "that nothing can pain me long."

Polly Stevenson had become a June bride, marrying a young physician, William Hewson, with Franklin's approval and blessing. The marriage unfortunately brought on a rift in the relations between Polly and one of her closest friends, Dorothy Blount, who fancied a grievous neglect and complained to Franklin. He tried to heal the breach by teasing Polly about their increased intimacy. "Your old Dolly and I," he quipped, "have agreed to love each other better than ever we did, to make up as much as we can our suppos'd loss of you."

Polly with her husband soon returned to Craven Street,

taking over management of the house when her mother went away for a short visit in September. During Mrs. Stevenson's absence Franklin wrote his famous *Craven Street Gazette,* a newspaper in miniature devoted exclusively to their household, which Franklin wrote daily for four days as a parody of the ordinary periodicals to which he had been submitting his political articles. Typical is the following item for Sunday, 23 September:

Dr. Fatsides [Franklin] made four hundred and sixty-nine turns in his dining-room, as the exact distance of a visit to the lovely Lady Barwell [one of Polly's young friends], whom he did not find at home; so there was no struggle for and against a kiss, and he sat down to dream in the easy-chair, that he had it without any trouble.

On Tuesday the *Gazette* featured the piece of important intelligence "that the amiable and delectable Companion, Miss D[orothea] B[lount], had made a Vow to marry absolutely him of the two [Franklin or a friend, John Hawkesworth] whose Wife should first depart this Life." Consequently each of the gentlemen "sincerely wished Health & long Life to the other's Wife." Later, in France, after Deborah had been dead for several years, Franklin revamped this theme of changing wives in a bagatelle addressed to Mme. Helvétius. Since Deborah was still living while Franklin was writing on Craven Street, he was demonstrating rather openly that his connubial attachment was not very strong. The *Gazette* is nevertheless a gay and charming *jeu d'esprit,* as much a satire of Franklin himself as of the London press. Not only did he have a superb sense of humor but also the capacity to treat himself lightly, one of his most endearing qualities.

❖❖*❖*❖*❖*❖*❖*❖*❖*❖*❖*❖*

21. Temporary Tranquility

THE year 1771 is the only one of Franklin's agency in England during which he published no propaganda pieces in the British press. He deliberately refrained, thinking that the battle had been won. "Just at this Juncture," he wrote to Samuel Cooper (30 December 1770), "perhaps 'tis more prudent to be quiet, to stir no new questions, to let heats abate; and when men are cooler, Reason may be better heard." He had in his hands, however, a piece to prove "that every lady of Genoa is not a Queen of Corsica," in other words, that every citizen of England was not King of America, but he presumably passed his article around among his friends for advice and then never published it. At least no printed work of this nature has yet been identified.

Franklin thanked Cooper, one of the most ardent defenders of colonial rights in Massachusetts, for his unexpected appointment as agent of that colony, describing it as one of the greatest honors accorded to him. The appointment had been as much of a surprise, and somewhat of a setback, to a young Virginian then in England, Arthur Lee, who had expected the agency for himself. But since Franklin believed that he might leave England any day, Lee was given a reversionary appointment, providing that he should take up all responsibilities at Franklin's leaving. Lee became more and more resentful of Franklin as events forced the agent to keep postponing his departure. But at the time of the appointment, Lee admitted that Franklin's "abilities are so extraordinary that I do not wonder he meets with so much estimation." Eight years later Lee's pride and ambitions were again to come into contact with Franklin and lead to his vociferously questioning the older man's abilities.

Franklin's optimism led him to report to Thomas Cushing, speaker of the Massachusetts Assembly (5 February 1771), that the doctrine of the right of Parliament to tax America had practically been given up, although no formal renunciation of the claim to do so could be expected. Franklin's rosy outlook seemed to have pervaded his attitude toward life in general. At least his belief in providence, from which he had never been shaken, supported his faith in human nature.

Upon the whole [he wrote to his sister (17 July)], I am much disposed to like the World as I find it. I see so much Wisdom in what I understand of its Creation and Government, that I suspect equal Wisdom may be in what I do not understand: And thence have perhaps as much Trust in God as the most pious Christian.

Yet, with Lord Hillsborough, Franklin seemed to be making no progress, having come to the conclusion that "the Colonies could expect neither Favours nor Justice during his Administration," his character being "Conceit, Wrongheadedness, Obstinacy, and Passion." To relieve his annoyance after a particularly disagreeable interview with the secretary, Franklin wrote out the minutes of their conference in dialogue form. Hillsborough, because of his doctrine that an agent could be appointed only by the General Court with the assent of the governor, had refused to accept Franklin's credentials. After some minor fencing, Franklin affirmed that he saw no reason why the governor's consent should be necessary.

L.[ord] H.[illsborough] (*With a mixed look of anger and contempt.*) I shall not enter into a dispute with YOU, Sir, upon the Subject.

B.F. I beg your Lordship's pardon; I do not presume to dispute with your Lordship; I would only say, that . . . the concurrence of the governor does not seem to me necessary. It is the business of the people, that is to be done; he is not one of them; he is himself an agent.

L.H. (*Hastily.*) Whose agent is he?

B.F. The King's, my Lord.

Despite considerably more skirmishing, Hillsborough persisted in refusing to accept the agent's credentials, and Franklin departed, observing that whether his appointment were acknowledged or not he could be of little use while Hillsborough's intransigent attitude existed. If his dramatized account is accurate, it well corroborates Franklin's analysis of his own character: "costs me nothing to be civil to Inferiors, a good deal to be submissive to Superiors."

Although Franklin was by and large optimistic about the likelihood of Parliament's eventually taking a reasonable attitude toward the colonies, he presented a dismal outlook to the Massachusetts Committee of Correspondence, 15 May 1771, seeing in the system of customs to be erected in America, "the seeds sown of a total disunion of the two countries." With his practical view of human character, he predicted that the separation would come about through the rapaciousness of petty customs officials. Only needy men would leave England to become customs officers; they would mask their greed with insolence, stir up hatred, take out their resentment maliciously, and incite reprisals, which would in turn draw more severity and acts of oppression from England. With this lugubrious picture in view, Franklin advised Thomas Cushing, a member of the committee (18 June 1771), that the colonies should immediately decide upon measures of resistance to Parliament —the only question was whether these measures should be abrupt or gradual.

At home, Deborah was recovering from a complete loss of memory, which she had suffered for several days in the previous year, a relapse which she attributed to her loneliness. William had written to his father that "her memory has failed her much and she becomes every day more and more unfit to be left alone."

Perhaps in reaction to her temporary loss of faculties, she began trying during her convalescence to impress her husband with her business acumen, particularly by buying a bill of exchange for thirty pounds at an advantageous discount, which she sent to Franklin for collection. Instead of showing pleasure, he replied with a firm letter acquainting her that he had given strict orders to Hall and his other friends not to advance her more than thirty pounds a month for household expenses, which he felt would be ample for her needs since she regularly received in addition the rent from seven or eight houses which he owned. Franklin's colleague in the post office, Foxcroft, had consequently refused to advance her the money to buy the bill, and she had then appealed—successfully—to Hall.

Deborah's mental lapses may be offered in excuse for Franklin's limiting her funds, but he reprimanded her also, as he said, "because you never have sent me any Account of your expences, and think yourself ill-used if I desire it; and because I know you were not very attentive to Money-matters in your best Days." With unnecessary asperity, Franklin added, "I do not like your going about among my Friends to borrow Money." Lonely Deborah, pining away for her "dear Child," was not likely to have had her low spirits much improved by this letter.

As a result of Franklin's rebuke, Deborah began sending him receipts for all the money she disbursed, but as Franklin began to receive them he professed to be satisfied with her accounts, probably realizing that he had already been harsh enough.

During the previous year, Franklin's grandnephews, Josiah Williams and Jonathan Williams, Jr., had come to live in London under Franklin's care, the first to study music, the second to learn the ways of the business world. Happy with their company, Franklin "never saw two young men from America more prudent and frugal" than they. Jonathan, in particular, pleased Franklin with his excellent turn for business and accounts, which he had applied to put all of Franklin's records in order.

Franklin also extended moral support and encouragement to another young American, the artist Charles Willson Peale, who several years previously had sketched Franklin with a young girl on his lap after surprising him in that compromising position. Now Franklin advised him how to succeed in his profession. Apart from urging Peale to acquire "great Industry and Frugality," applicable to all of Franklin's protégés, he gave other counsel particularly appropriate to artists and, one might add, to prostitutes: work hard and charge high prices while still young and still enjoying peak physical powers. "The Arts have always travelled Westward," Franklin concluded, "and there is no doubt of their flourishing hereafter on our side the Atlantic."

On 18 May, Franklin and Jonathan Williams, Jr., set out on a journey to Manchester, Sheffield and Birmingham, in the company of a Dutch scientist, Jan Ingenhousz, and an English electrical experimenter, John Canton. They returned in time to be in court on the King's birthday, 4 June. Franklin reported to Deborah that the journey, as usual, had been of great value to his health, the air and exercise having given him fresh spirits. His visit to the clothing manufacturers in Yorkshire had convinced him of the natural impossibility, considering the growth of American population, that England could continue much longer as outfitters for America.

One of the most plausible of the Franklin anecdotes has him visiting the clothing factories of Norwich, where one of the manufacturers, proudly displaying his wares, comments, "Here is cloth for Italy; this is for Germany, this for the West Indies, and this for the American continent." Franklin, noticing that the weavers were half-naked or wearing patched and tattered clothing, turned to the proud owner and asked, "And don't you make anything for Norwich?"

Almost immediately after returning to London, Franklin left the city again to spend a week in the middle of June at the country residence of Jonathan Shipley, bishop of St. Asaph. Like many prelates in the eighteenth century, Shipley seldom visited his charge but preferred to establish a permanent abode elsewhere. His was a country residence at Twyford, in southern England, a good distance from St. Asaph in Wales. When Franklin first met Shipley is not known, but he became an intimate friend after this first visit, attracted most probably by the bishop's five daughters, ranging in age from eleven to twenty-three. His favorites were Catherine, eleven, and Georgiana, fifteen. The latter was gifted with some of the intellectual precocity which Franklin had admired in Polly Stevenson, and he later sent her one of his books as a mark of his "Regard for her philosophic Genius."

Probably Franklin was thinking of the Shipley girls a few months later when he recalled the advice of a wise old man "to chuse Wives out of a Bunch; for where there were many

Daughters, . . . they improv'd each other, and from Emulation acquir'd more Accomplishments, knew more, could do more, & were not spoil'd by parental Fondness like single Children."

Franklin gave Georgiana a live squirrel called Mungo, which Deborah had sent from America, but it eventually escaped from captivity and was killed by a dog. Franklin then sent Georgiana an epitaph in the vein of Thomas Gray's ode "On the Death of a Favourite Cat." Franklin's parody in "the monumental style and measure, which, being neither prose nor verse, is perhaps the properest for grief" revived the literary form which he had used with disastrous results in the election of 1764. It begins with the conventional "Alas! poor MUNGO" and concludes with a Gray-like moral:

> Learn hence,
> Ye who blindly seek more liberty,
> Whether subjects, sons, squirrels or daughters,
> That apparent restraint may be real protection;
> Yielding peace and plenty
> With security.

Such an epitaph, Franklin concluded, would be far more decent and proper than a poetic elegy, such as:

> Here SKUGG [a common 18th century
> Lies snug,   name for all squirrels]
> As a bug
> In a rug.

This famous phrase seems to be another of Franklin's original creations.

Franklin returned to Twyford for another visit late in July and stayed throughout the first two weeks of August. This turned into one of the most significant periods in Franklin's life, for in this quiet country atmosphere he began writing his memoirs and completed the first and most important part. Nobody knows why he began his autobiography at this time—or even why he undertook it at all. In addressing it to his son, he explained that he had always had pleasure in obtaining little anecdotes of his ancestors and he assumed that William would find equal pleasure in learning the circumstances of his father's life. Also Franklin thought that his posterity might profit from understanding the means by which he had elevated himself from poverty and obscurity to relative affluence and celebrity.

Since William was already acquainted with many of the details of his father's early life, Franklin probably had his grandson William Temple Franklin even more in mind, for Temple, then eleven years old, lived at Craven Street during school vacations and took up much of Franklin's thought and attention. Franklin, moreover, may have been inspired to write his memoirs by the chance purchase two or three weeks before of a collection of books and pamphlets formerly owned by his uncle Benjamin, these mementos and thoughts of his own ancestors leading him to set down his life for his posterity.

It is doubtful that Franklin at this time had any thought of publishing his work. Indeed, a strong indication that he was not reminiscing for the public appears in a passage drawing attention to his digressiveness: "I used to write more methodically. But one does not dress for private company as for a public ball." If there is anything at all about Franklin's style which calls for apology, it is only this lack of order. Otherwise it has the same qualities of smoothness, clarity and brevity which he had demanded in his youthful journalistic days. With no models to follow, Franklin unfolded a fascinating narrative garnished with proverbial wisdom and incisive comments on universal human characteristics. One might even say that Franklin established the genre of modern autobiography.

His achievement is all the more remarkable when we consider the short length of time in which the first part was written—two weeks or less. He wrote as the thoughts came, clear and vivid, and with practically no revision. In the midst of a lively family circle like the Shipleys, Franklin could not devote all his time to writing in seclusion, nor would he have wished to.

On the day when he was preparing to return to London, Mrs. Shipley insisted that he remain another day to celebrate the birthday of Benjamin Bache. At dinner, attended by all five daughters and a clergyman's widow over one hundred years old, the chief toast of the day was Master Benjamin Bache, which the venerable old lady began in a bumper of dessert punch. Mrs. Shipley proposed "that he may be as good a Man as his Grandfather," Franklin protested he hoped Benny would be much better, and the bishop finished with "We will compound the Matter, and be contented if he should not prove *quite so good*."

Early the next day Franklin set out for London by coach, taking with him the eleven-year-old Catherine, who was going back to school. They passed a lively day together, arriving in London at six in the evening. Acquainting Mrs. Shipley of their safe arrival, Franklin summarized the progress of their friendship. "The first stage we were rather passive. I tried several topics of conversation, but none of them would hold. But after breakfast we began to recover spirits and had a good deal of chat." Most of it concerned the husbands Catherine wished for her sisters: a country gentleman for Georgiana, a rich city merchant for Betsy, an Earl for Emily, another nobleman for Anna Marie, and for Catherine herself "an old man of 70 or 80," who would take her when she was about thirty and leave her a rich widow. Franklin could easily have projected himself into the role.

Ten years later Franklin still remembered his "little Fellow-Traveller, the sprightly Kitty, with whose sensible Prattle" he had been charmed and entertained.

In many ways the ride with Kitty was a duplication of an earlier one with Caty Ray—merely a greater spread of ages. One cannot help thinking also of a famous literary journey throughout the United States in which a middle-aged man and a nymphet patronize motels and jukeboxes. Yet there is no reason to assume any of the perversion of Humbert Humbert in the paternal philosopher of Philadelphia. During his entire maturity, Franklin loved to have children of all ages and both sexes around him. Loving the role of *pater familias,* he was not overly concerned with the constituency of the family.

A few days after depositing Catherine in London, Franklin set out on another vacation trip, this time to Ireland and Scotland, accompanied by his old friend Jackson. On 5 Sep-

tember they disembarked on the Irish coast, proceeding immediately to Dublin. After a "plentiful dinner of fish," Franklin
was seized with violent vomiting and a looseness which continued as long as he stayed in the country.

Most of the Irish who entertained him belonged to the
faction known as "Patriots," advocates of an independent parliament, who, recognizing their parallel circumstances with America, were eager to show friendship to its distinguished representative. Franklin naturally tried to strengthen their friendly
feelings toward America and suggested that by combining their
interests they might both obtain more equitable treatment
from England. On 10 October, Franklin and Jackson visited the
Irish Parliament, two days after the opening ceremony. Jackson
was immediately admitted to the floor because of a rule extending this courtesy to members of the English Parliament. Franklin was about to proceed to the visitors' gallery when the speaker
informed the house of his presence, describing him as an
American gentleman of "distinguish'd Character and Merit, a
Member or Delegate of some of the Parliaments of that
Country," and asked whether for the purpose of seating they
should regard the American Assemblies as equivalent to English
Parliaments. The whole house responded with an enthusiastic
affirmative, and Franklin was led to the floor. As this was the
highest mark of public esteem so far shown to Franklin, his
vanity must have been measurably gratified, even though he
later represented the honor as a mark of respect to his country,
not to him as an individual.

A few days later the travelers were invited to dine with the
Lord Lieutenant of Ireland and discovered Lord Hillsborough
as a fellow guest. Hillsborough greeted Franklin with extreme
cordiality, as though trying to overcome the reserve which had
previously existed between them. Then he invited both Franklin and Jackson to stay at his estate if they should travel
northward, urging the invitation so politely that they were
forced to accept. Franklin later said he had no intention of going
near the village of Hillsborough, but when he and Jackson were
about to part company—Jackson to go to Hillsborough and he
to visit a friend in another village—no post chaise could be

found for Franklin, and he was obliged to proceed with Jackson. Hillsborough entertained them at his house with a thousand civilities for five days.

In his conversations, the secretary tried to appear more of an Irishman than an Englishman, agreeing with Franklin that it was wrong to restrain American manufactures. He claimed the bounty on silk, an inducement to encourage its production, as his brain child and consulted Franklin about granting another on wine. His attentions to his guest extended as far as putting his own cloak around Franklin's shoulders so that he might not catch cold and instructing his son to take him for a forty-mile sight-seeing tour. Franklin could not understand the reasons for all this cordiality, since Hillsborough apparently did not try to sway him to reduce his efforts in behalf of American rights. If Arthur Lee, the reversionary agent from Massachusetts, had heard of Franklin's sojourn at Hillsborough, he would have felt vindicated in the charge he had made in June that Franklin was not only temporizing but that he was actually a tool of Lord Hillsborough.

When Franklin looked back upon his Irish experiences, his strongest impressions seem to have been "of the poverty and beggary of the poor inhabitants on that side of the water." He noticed that a small part of the nation were "extremely opulent, living in the highest Affluence and Magnificence: The Bulk of the People Tenants, extreamly poor, living in the most sordid Wretchedness, in dirty Hovels of Mud and Straw, and cloathed only in Rags." Comparing this condition with the even distribution of wealth in New England, "where every Man is a Freeholder," Franklin concluded that the benefits of trade were not sufficient to compensate for its evils. If a civil society were to be judged by Ireland and the weaving districts of England, he would never advise a nation of savages to accept civilization.

In the Possession & Enjoyment of the various Comforts of Life, compar'd to these People, every Indian is a Gentleman: And the Effect of this kind of Civil Society seems only to be, the depressing Multitudes below the Savage State that a few may be rais'd above it.

This depressing spectacle of Irish poverty, however, did nothing to change Franklin's opinion that the state should not administer social welfare. He believed in economic legislation for the benefit of the colonies but not for the relief of social misery.

Franklin parted company with Jackson in Ireland and proceeded alone to Edinburgh, where he arrived on 26 October. For the first night he was "lodg'd miserably at an Inn" but was afterwards rescued by "that excellent Christian David Hume," who, "agreeable to the Precepts of the Gospel," received Franklin in his newly finished house. During the next four weeks in Scotland, Franklin spent most of his time with a young Rhode Island lawyer and future delegate to the Continental Congress, Henry Marchant. His chief activities were dining around, shoping and talking. Some time after the middle of November, he received a letter from his son-in-law Richard Bache, who was now visiting his mother in Preston, Lancashire. This decided Franklin to cut short his Scottish visit and return to London by way of Preston in order to meet Sally's husband for the first time. He arrived on 24 November and was agreeably received by Mrs. Bache, "a most stately well looking serious Lady," sixty-eight years of age. She must have met with Franklin's approval in at least one regard, for she had borne twenty children by her husband, whom she had buried twenty-five years previously.

Richard, whom Franklin found to his liking, had hoped that Franklin could help him obtain some government office in America, but Franklin spoke against it, preferring that all his relatives appear "in an independent situation, supported by their own industry." (He had changed his mind completely about the appropriateness of nepotism, which he had practised on a wide scale before coming to England.) Richard had brought 1,000 pounds sterling with him, and Franklin advised him to invest it in goods to be sold in Philadelphia, and as an earnest of his confidence and good will he gave his son-in-law an additional 200 pounds to invest. To Sally, he explained that her husband, as a businessman rather than a place holder, would be "more independent, more a Freeman, and less subject to the Caprices of Superiors." He hoped that Sally would not be too proud to be serviceable to her husband as Deborah had been to him.

Late in November, Franklin returned to Craven Street, with Richard as his traveling companion. Just before setting out he wrote in a very cheerful strain to Polly Stevenson Hewson, from whom he had received a detailed description of her first child, Franklin's godson, who was just cutting his first teeth. Franklin was prodigiously pleased to hear that the child resembled him in many particulars. Polly had written:

He is generally serious, no great Talker, but sometimes laughs very hearty; he is fond of being in his *Birthday Suit,* and has not the least apprehension of *catching cold* in it; he is never troubled with the *Airophobia,* but always seems delighted with fresh Air.

This is a reference to Franklin's nude air baths, which he kept up through his old age, and which he had apparently practised more than once in Polly's view. Amused by the resemblances which Polly had noticed, Franklin remarked, "I am persuaded there is another, which you have omitted, tho' it must have occur'd to you while you were putting them down"—an anatomical allusion neither esoteric nor very delicate.

In prescribing a regime for rearing his godson, Franklin indulgently advocated that the child be given everything he liked:

I think it of great Consequence while the Features of the Countenance are forming; it gives them a pleasant Air, and, that being once become natural and fix'd by Habit, the Face is ever after the handsomer for it, and on that much of a Person's good Fortune and Success in Life may depend. Had I been cross'd as much in my Infant Likings and Inclinations as you know I have been of late Years, I should have been, I was going to say, not near so handsome; but as the Vanity of that Expression would offend other Folk's Vanity, I change it, out of regard to them, and say a great deal more homely.

The likings and inclinations in which he had recently been crossed were probably for kisses desired of Polly and her girl friends. He was certainly not referring to Mrs. Stevenson, who never denied him anything. Elsewhere in his letter, Franklin alluded humorously to Mrs. Stevenson in reference to Polly's revelation of "a certain Lady's having entertain'd a new Gallant, in my Absence." Not in the least surprised or jealous, Franklin remarked blithely—and probably with much truth—"I have been us'd to Rivals, and scarce ever had a Friend or a Mistress in my whole Life, that other People did not like as well as my-self."

Franklin was in excellent spirits, his traveling having had the therapeutic effect he expected. Even though he wrote to Sir Alexander Dick "that I grow too old for Rambling, and that 'twas probable I should never make such another Journey," he described his trip to his sister in a quite contrary vein as "an agreeable tour with a pleasant companion," which despite six weeks of visceral looseness had contributed materially to the establishment of his health.

When Franklin returned to London, he made several cour-tesy calls upon Hillsborough to thank him for his summer hospitality, but Hillsborough would not even receive him. Franklin then stopped trying, after he was haughtily turned away by the porter on one of the secretary's levee days, even though a number of coaches stood outside the door. As Franklin put it, Hillsborough "threw me away as an orange that would yield no more juice and therefore not worth more squeezing." This ingenious metaphor was not original with Franklin. Twenty years earlier Frederick the Great had said of Voltaire, "I shall have need of him for another year at the most; one squeezes an orange and throws away the skin."

Throughout the next year Franklin worked on two fronts to bring about Hillsborough's downfall. He prepared for the press a thorough analysis of the secretary's administration of Ameri-can affairs, charging that at all stages he had sought bad ends by improper methods. His Lordship's greatest mistake, Franklin affirmed, was refusing to receive petitions expressing the colo-nies' grievances—and his opposition had led directly to the nonimportation agreements and other protest measures. Frank-lin never published this piece because Hillsborough resigned as the result of a crushing blow to his prestige which Franklin administered in another area—that involving western settle-ments in America.

Since 1763, when he and Jackson had tried to get a Crown grant of western lands, Franklin had maintained his interest in the western territories. He had subsequently joined in a gigantic scheme, embracing a score of the most influential speculators

and administrators of England and the colonies. Under the
titular leadership of Thomas Walpole, a London banker and
nephew of the former prime minister, they formed the Grand
Ohio Company and in 1772 petitioned the Board of Trade for a
grant of twenty million acres of land. Franklin had to keep
behind the scenes, since some of his letters to America which
had been made public had made him "a little obnoxious to the
ministry," but his advice was asked at every step. Strahan
thought that Franklin's lukewarm temper stemmed from a
growing reserve joined with a "natural Inactivity." He once
heard Franklin in his own house "propose to Mr. Wharton to
strike his Name out of the List, as it might be of prejudice to the
undertaking." Hillsborough, president of the Board of Trade,
had at first been thought favorable to the project, but when the
petition (signed by Walpole, Franklin, John Sargent and
Samuel Wharton) was presented, the board handed down a
detailed unfavorable report. Franklin thereupon drew up an
answer, which was presented to the Privy Council. Against
Hillsborough's two principal objections, he urged that the
project involved no conflict with Indian claims and that the area
could be settled so as to maintain trade intercourse advantageous to England. Swayed by Franklin's argument (1 July
1772), the Privy Council granted the petition, a tremendous loss
of face for Hillsborough, although he may have been overrid-
den not so much because of Franklin's persuasiveness as because
of the presence in the scheme of powerful and influential
Englishmen. Franklin himself refused to take any credit but
pointed out to William that "Hillsborough's brother ministers
disliked him extremely, and wished for a fair occasion of tripping up his heels." Hillsborough, mortified by the council's
decision, resigned as American secretary and was replaced by
Lord Dartmouth.

For Franklin then, nothing could have made his situation
more agreeable. As he wrote to William, 19 August, he had

a general respect paid me by the learned, a number of friends and
acquaintances among them, with whom I have a pleasing intercourse; a character of so much weight, that it has protected me
when some in power would have done me injury, and continued

me in an office they would have deprived me of; my company so much desired, that I seldom dine at home in winter, and could spend the whole summer in the country-houses of inviting friends, if I chose it.

Some time earlier he had written to Samuel Cooper in a similar strain: "I have, thanks to God, a Competency, for the little Time I may expect to live, and am grown too old for Ambition of every other kind but that of leaving a good Name behind me."

Although, during 1772, Franklin did not make any single long journey, he visited a number of his friends in their country seats. During April he was guest of a liberal intellectual Whig, the Earl of Shelburne, at Wycombe, where he met for the first time the Abbé Morellet, a deistical French clergyman fast earning an international reputation as an economist. With Morellet, Franklin discussed economic theory, science, ethics and music, but in few words and at rather lengthy intervals. Few men better than Franklin, Morellet later reported, exemplified the maxim that a wise man never wastes either his time or his words. At Wycombe, Franklin applied the knowledge he had acquired about oil and water on his return voyage to America in 1762. Pretending to calm the turbulent waters of a wind-swept stream by a flourish of a bamboo cane, he actually dropped some oil from a hollow in its base, which produced the apparent miracle. A superstitious farmer, thinking he had seen a divine sign, asked Franklin what he should believe. The amused conjuror answered, "Nothing except what you see."

Another of the Shelburne circle with whom Franklin developed cordial relations was the dissenting minister, educator and scientist, Joseph Priestley, whom he had previously visited at Leeds in the spring of 1769. In September 1772, Priestley was trying to decide whether to accept a post as Shelburne's librarian, and Franklin explained how he could come to a decision through a system of "prudential algebra," listing reasons for and against in parallel columns to determine which side was of greater weight. This device, which Franklin himself once used to decide whether to stay in England or return to America, provides still a further example of his methodical mind.

In June and July 1772, Franklin took his usual summer vacation, visiting Cumberland, Westmoreland, Yorkshire and the coal mines at Whitehaven. His observation of the vegetation-covered rock in these mines led him to form a theory of the formation of the earth, which he later discussed with the Abbé Soulavie in France and presented formally in a paper read at his own American Philosophical Society.

22. *Postmaster No More*

IN HIS activities as a colonial agent, Franklin had almost imperceptibly allowed the defense of Massachusetts to take precedence over his Pennsylvania concerns. Indeed, after he resumed writing letters to the press in 1772, most of them were concerned with New England, an almost inevitable consequence of the more vociferous resistance to Parliamentary restrictions in Boston than in Philadelphia. Having accepted the Massachusetts agency, Franklin was willy-nilly placed in the forefront of the American radical movement. Also, because of Massachusetts he became the scapegoat in the most sensational political scandal involving America before the Revolution.

Early in 1773, Franklin supervised the publication of an English edition of *The Votes and Proceedings* of the Boston town meetings, which affirmed certain inviolable rights of the colonists and protested against their being infringed. He added a preface asserting that the English people had a right to know what the ministry had tried to conceal from them—that the people in America were united in discontent over their maltreatment by Parliament. As he reviewed the situation, the repeal of the Stamp Act had restored harmony temporarily, only to have the flame of hostility rekindled by the short-lived Townshend duties and the tax on tea, which was retained. The obnoxious customs regulations to enforce the latter caused the Americans to patronize smugglers from other nations and to abstain rigidly from all English imports. The net result for England was a costly customs system, producing virtually no revenue, and the hastening of a decline in the East India Company almost to the point of ruin.

Further to arouse the English nation, Franklin turned once more to satire. In September 1773, he published ironical *Rules by Which a Great Empire May Be Reduced to a Small One*, a

summary of the most grievous policies of the colonial administration presented as maxims in the most blunt, colloquial
language. For example, the empire reducer should always suspect the provinces of treason and rebellion and, by quartering
insolent troops, provoke the rising of mobs. "By this means," he
advised, "like the husband who uses his wife ill *from suspicion,*
you may in time convert your *suspicions* into *realities."*

A few days later, with the connivance of the publisher of the
Public Advertiser, Franklin perpetrated in the news columns a
hoax similar to the forgoing satire. As an item of "Foreign
Intelligence," Franklin presented *An Edict by the King of
Prussia* in which that monarch claimed the island of Britain by
virtue of its having originally been colonized by Germans. The
King ordered the British henceforth to pay a duty of four and a
half per cent on all goods imported and exported, to abandon
completely iron manufacture, wool production and hatmaking,
and to receive into their midst all criminals which Prussia
wished to transport. These regulations, the monarch assumed,
should be considered "just and reasonable" since each was
copied from British statutes for the government of Ireland and
America.

For his summer vacation in 1773, Franklin visited Sir
Francis Dashwood, Baron Le Despencer, at his country estate at
West Wycombe. Dashwood was Joint Postmaster General of
England and had been introduced to Franklin in 1769 by
Governor Denny. Franklin delighted in his luxurious surround-
ings, finding the gardens a real paradise, but most of all he
appreciated "the facetious and very intelligent Conversation" of
his host.

On the day the newspaper with his satire arrived, the poet
Paul Whitehead, who was also in the company, came running
into the breakfast parlor with the paper in his hand. "Here!"
says he, "here's news for ye! *Here's the King of Prussia, claiming a right to this kingdom!*" Everybody was amazed as Whitehead proceeded to read aloud. But after getting through a few
paragraphs, the shrewd poet turned to Franklin and said, *"I'll
be hanged if this is not some of your American Jokes upon us."*

Both pieces met enthusiastic response from both the Ameri-

can and British public, the *Rules* attaining even more popularity than the *Edict*. In sending them to his sister, Franklin
explained that, growing tired of meekness and smooth words, he
had saucily held up a looking glass so that some ministers could
"see their ugly Faces, & the Nation its Injustice."

Franklin was acutely concerned about his own financial
affairs, since his salary from Pennsylvania, on which he chiefly
depended, had not been reaching him regularly. On paper he
received 1,200 pounds a year from the four colonies he represented, but Georgia paid him only 100 pounds the first year and
nothing thereafter. From Massachusetts he had never received a
farthing, because the governor had control over the agent's
salary and would not sanction payment. Franklin wrote to
Galloway, therefore (6 January 1773), that he would be grateful
for any amount the House could send and that he would
continue to serve the colony as long as he could afford to
continue in London.

When Franklin passed his sixty-seventh birthday, he
confided to Deborah that it seemed "but t' other Day since you
and I were rank'd among the Boys & Girls, so swiftly does Time
fly!" Even at this advanced age he said he regularly swam in the
river every evening during the summer months for two or three
hours.

Deborah continued to cater to her husband, sending him so
many apples that he at one time had six barrels on hand. In
many ways, however, he seemed thoughtless in return. A French
edition of his works having appeared during the year, Franklin
mentioned it to Debbie with a description of the frontispiece, a
print with "so French a Countenance that you would take me
for one of that lively Nation." Then he added bluntly, "I think
you do not mind such things or I would send you one." Even
Debbie might be hurt by such a reference to her intellectual
limitations.

At that moment her mental and physical condition had
declined so badly that Sally had taken over running the household. Franklin exhorted his daughter to keep exact accounts,
and in order to encourage habitual economy he reminded her
that whatever a child saves of its parents' money would be its

own some day. "Study Poor Richard a little," he advised, "and you may find some Benefit from his Instructions."

Clearly, therefore, the gospel of thrift was not a product merely of Franklin's years as a tradesman but a lifetime conviction. During the American Revolution, he even seriously advocated that English copper coins be replaced by new ones bearing Poor Richard's proverbs.

The French edition of Franklin's works had been prepared by Dr. Jacques Barbeu Dubourg, a Paris physician and one of Franklin's most sincere adulators. In addition to all of Franklin's electrical pieces, it contained several political and philosophical works printed for the first time in a collected edition and some pieces printed for the first time anywhere. Among the medical subjects which Franklin discussed in this edition was the hygienic value of his air baths and a related theory that "the causes of colds are totally independent of wet and even of cold."

Franklin's summer host, Le Despencer, a notorious rake and debauchee but an excellent postmaster, found his chief amusement these days in presiding over the blasphemous rites of his Hell Fire Club and reconstructing an ancient church in West Wycombe. Like Franklin, he was fascinated by Christian rituals which he could not accept intellectually. During their conversations, he persuaded Franklin to collaborate with him in about as unlikely a project for the two deists as could be imagined, editing and publishing a revised edition of the Episcopalian Book of Common Prayer. Although, like many other deists in Anglican circles, Franklin did not literally accept the Thirtynine Articles, he certainly believed in prayer for himself as well as for others. He viewed the project, therefore, as a labor of utilitarian reform and probably also derived from it something of the satisfaction he encountered from his literary hoaxes.

The book was printed in the same year as its conception, 1773, under the title *Abridgement of the Book of Common Prayer*. Franklin wrote the preface, explaining that the editors were attempting to promote worship, not to impede it, and that they wished to curtail only the length of the service, not the practice of religion. The actual revision consisted of nothing but abbreviation, not a single word of the original text being changed. But the stripping was done along deistical lines, eliminating mystical doctrines and metaphysical subtleties. Apart from the pleasure which the editors found in their work, the experiment was a failure. Some copies were given away, practically none were sold, and the rest became waste paper.

Franklin had always assumed that all the measures enacted by Parliament to the detriment of the colonies had been proposed by the ministry, but one day toward the end of 1772 one of his English friends assured him that the restrictions he most complained of had been projected, proposed, solicited and obtained by "some of the most respectable among the Americans themselves." As proof, Franklin's friend turned over to him a collection of anticolonial letters written by the American-born governor of Massachusetts, Thomas Hutchinson, and the lieutenant governor, Andrew Oliver. Franklin immediately transmitted these letters to the Massachusetts Committee of Correspondence, and from this moment he took a much firmer stand in his negotiations and letters to the press. He began talking of the growing strength of America in wealth and numbers, warning his Boston friends of the need to preserve military discipline and quoting the Italian proverb, "Make yourselves Sheep, and the Wolves will eat you." Also he began to perceive for the first time that George III himself favored the harsh policy toward the colonies.

Franklin's new firmness further widened the divergence between his political attitude and his son's; William did not share his opinion of the heinousness of the Hutchinson letters. Franklin accepted the fact that his son was "a thorough government man" and did not try to change his views. He only wished him "to act uprightly and steadily, avoiding that duplicity, which in Hutchinson, adds contempt to indignation." Since Franklin realized so clearly the extent of his son's involvement with the administration, it is hard to account for the extreme bitterness he felt later on when William remained loyal to his principles and interest at the outbreak of the Revolution. Father and son had long since chosen separate camps.

Franklin's summer at West Wycombe was probably the last period of relaxed tranquility which he enjoyed in England. During the spring, the Hutchinson letters which Franklin had sent to Massachusetts had, contrary to his express instructions and stipulations, been published and had stirred up violent feelings both in America and England. The Massachusetts House of Representatives immediately passed resolutions asking for the removal of Hutchinson and Oliver, sending to Franklin a petition to that effect to be transmitted to the King.

In the meantime William Whately, brother of the man to whom the letters were supposed to have been written, and John Temple, a customs official, carried on a debate in the newspapers over who had transmitted the letters to America. Denial of complicity by both men led to their fighting a duel, in which Whately was slightly injured. When Franklin heard that the duel would be resumed as soon as Whately should recover, he decided that it was his responsibility to prevent it, and accordingly he revealed in a letter printed in the *London Chronicle*, on Christmas Day 1773, that he alone was the person who had obtained the letters and transmitted them to Boston. Immediately the wrath and resentment of the ministry descended upon Franklin.

At a meeting of the Committee for Plantation Affairs on 11 January 1774, Franklin was ordered to submit copies of the Hutchinson letters and required to prove that they were authentic. A further hearing was scheduled for the twenty-ninth of the month. The newspapers began carrying attacks and invectives against Franklin, rumors circulated that he would be seized and sent to prison, and his friends hinted that the scheduled hearing had as its purpose to blacken his name so that he could be stripped of his post-office place without giving the appearance of injustice. He was also told that the petition was to be rejected with epithets, the Assembly censured, and the governor honored.

Everything took place just as predicted.

The Privy Council met at Whitehall in a narrow room, known as the Cockpit, hardly larger than a private living room and furnished with a long table at which sat the councilors—a record number of thirty-six present at this occasion—purposely invited as though as to a bullbaiting. Everyone else stood, including Franklin and the solicitor general Wedderburn, who defended the Massachusetts governors. The president of the council sat at the head of the table with his back toward a fireplace which jutted out to form a small recess on each side. Franklin stood in the recess at the left of the president, and Wedderburn stood somewhere on the opposing side of the table. The only member of the council openly friendly to Franklin was Lord Le Despencer, but some of Franklin's friends, including Priestley and Shelburne, had crowded into the room as onlookers.

Without doubt the ministry had decided in advance that Franklin wielded too much power in the colonies and that he had been involved with too many disaffected petitions. To them, his sending the Hutchinson letters back to Massachusetts was the act of an irresponsible troublemaker. Also his ceaseless trumpeting the growing strength of America had aroused fears of American independence. Since American population increase could lead to independence and Franklin never stopped talking about this increase, he became inevitably associated with that unpleasant concept. The ministry judged, therefore, that the time had come to cut him down.

The proceedings began quietly enough with a reading of the petition for the removal of Hutchinson, the supporting resolves, and the governor's letters. Next, the counsel whom Franklin had engaged spoke on the general discontent of the people of Massachusetts and argued that for efficient administration as well as the peace of the province it was necessary to have Hutchinson and his lieutenant removed.

Then Wedderburn, renowned for his sharp tongue and ruthless will, launched into a survey of the last ten years of the history of Massachusetts in a tirade larded with "invective ribaldry," which he heaped upon Franklin for nearly an hour. Although the ostensible purpose of the hearing was the petition for the removal of Hutchinson, Wedderburn passed over everything except Franklin's alleged provocative policies and the manner in which he had gained possession of the letters. Franklin, he charged, was solely responsible for all the ill will between the Assembly and the governors, and in acquiring the letters he had stooped to the level of a common thief. Franklin's "deliberate malevolence," Wedderburn thundered, could be matched only by a character in Young's tragedy *Revenge,* who gloated:

> I forged the letters; I disposed the picture;
> I hated, I despised, and I destroy.

Yet Franklin's malevolence was not without plan: he was "so possessed with the idea of a Great American Republic" that he fancied himself as an ambassador rather than agent and used the "language of the minister of a foreign independent state." Wedderburn's delivery was as offensive as his words. He shouted and raged with such intensity that "the ear was stunned at every blow." The audience "seemed to enjoy highly the entertainment and frequently burst out in loud applause."

During the whole time, Franklin stood "like a rock in the same posture, his head resting on his left hand," and abided "the pelting of the pitiless storm." He said not a word. Although the rules forebade him to interrupt, he could have made a formal reply, but he declined. He also refused to be examined. The pendulum had swung completely from the triumph of his friendly examination over the Stamp Act.

Franklin had a number of reasons for keeping silent. He fully realized that he was before a hostile body, which had prejudged him. Nothing he could say would change its opinions. Also, he was not a good speaker, and even for propaganda purposes a reply would serve no useful purpose. He might have argued that the hearing concerned only the petition and that the question of his possession of the letters was irrelevant—but Wedderburn had successfully tied the two together. His only defense against the charge of theft was that it was common practice to intercept letters of political importance, and that some of his own letters had also been apprehended and made public. Yet this could not change the fact that he was guilty of possessing private letters not addressed to him—and there was no way of warding off the abuse.

Nobody likes to be called names in public, and Franklin's silence was an extraordinary feat of endurance. No doubt he mentally repeated from his scheme of moral perfection his precepts for moderation ("Forbear resenting injuries as much as you think they deserve") and humility ("Imitate Jesus and Socrates"). An ordinary human being would have exploded with rage. Yet as Franklin left the room, he whispered in Wedderburn's ear, "I will make your master a LITTLE KING for this." To one of his friends, he remarked, "That was a handsome discourse which the buyer has not finished paying for. It can turn out to be more expensive than he thinks."

That night when Franklin took off his suit of figured Manchester velvet, he probably already viewed it as a symbol of the ordeal he had been through. He was later to wear the suit as a token of his vindication.

The next day, as Franklin expected, he received a letter informing him that he had been dismissed from his office of deputy postmaster general.

Franklin's immediate reaction, naturally enough, was extreme resentment, and he thought of evening the score. Three days later, informing William of his dismissal, he clearly revealed that he hoped that his son would resign as governor of New Jersey in protest. Although not expressing his wish directly, Franklin pointed out that since William's salary had never defrayed expenses he would be better off settled on his farm, a more honest and honorable employment because more independent. "You will hear from others the Treatment I have receiv'd," he wrote. "I leave you to your own Reflections and Determinations upon it."

But as Franklin's many friends came to Craven Street purposely to express their regard for him and their repugnance to the council, he gradually accepted the situation with his usual equanimity. Pleased to discover that his good reputation had carried the day over Wedderburn's scurrility, he revealed that he "felt the Advantage of a good Conscience, which wonderfully supports a Man on such Occasions."

In a little more than two weeks, therefore, he wrote again to

William, now directly advising him not to resign. "Let them take your place if they want it. . . . One may make something of an Injury, nothing of a Resignation."

Whatever his father's wishes, it is doubtful that William could have been induced to resign his governorship. He had already had sharp differences with his father over British policy, and Wedderburn's abuse had not changed the issues. Later in the year, when they disagreed over the justice of later American remonstrances and British retaliation, Franklin exposed his opinion of his son's misplaced loyalty (7 September 1774) in language even more tart than before: "you, who are a thorough Courtier, see every thing with Government Eyes."

Before writing to Thomas Cushing about the grueling day at the Cockpit, Franklin waited over two weeks—undoubtedly to let his emotions cool and to keep from revealing the extent of his bitterness. "What I feel on my own account," he finally wrote, "is half lost in what I feel for the public." If the government had reached the point that petitions and complaints of grievances had become so obnoxious that it struck down the mere pipe which conveyed them, Franklin despaired that peace and union could be maintained throughout the empire.

In writing to his sister just two days later (17 February 1774), Franklin struck a more personal note. "Intending to disgrace me, they have rather done me Honour." His only fault, he said, had been too great attachment to the interests of America, and his dismissal was merely a testimony to his incorruptibility.

In his most urbane commentary, a letter to his scientific friend, Jan Ingenhousz (18 March), Franklin treated the affair as a commonplace political show. The populace "love to have a good character cut up now and then for their entertainment." It was merely Franklin's turn to be abused by the ministry, but he had lost thereby no honor, respect or affection. This was probably the version which Franklin hoped that Ingenhousz would circulate among his scientific acquaintances on the continent.

To Cushing, Franklin wrote in a far more worried strain the next month (16 April). Still relatively unconcerned over his own treatment, he reported that the "Torrent is still violent against America." He had heard that copies of some of his previous letters had been declared treasonable, an absurd accusation, but in view of the past he would not wonder "if less than a small lump in my Forehead is voted a Horn." In the press he had actually been called "OLD TRAITOR FRANKLIN" and described in terms originally applied to Falstaff as "this living emblem of Iniquity in Grey Hairs."

Although Franklin himself kept a "cool, sullen silence" about Wedderburn's abuse, he was delighted to read in the *Public Advertiser,* 16 February 1774, a brilliant retort to Wedderburn's cleverest stroke, where he had called Franklin in Latin, instead of a man of letters, a man of "three letters," *homo trium literarum,* referring to the three-letter word for "thief," *fur.* Franklin's defender in the *Advertiser* (who may have been Franklin himself) published the epigraph from Dubourg's edition of Franklin's works, *Il a ravi le feu des Cieux* (he stole fire from the skies), and granted that in this sense Franklin was indeed a thief "much more impudent and audacious" than Wedderburn had insinuated.

In the long run, Wedderburn's abuse turned out to be the best thing that ever happened for Franklin's reputation in America. The sympathy aroused by his appearance as a political martyr magically restored Franklin's early prestige, which had been sadly tarnished by the Stamp Act and by suspicions that he had done very little to prevent its passage. Now at home he was once more a hero.

23. Friction Increases

AFTER the Cockpit ordeal, Franklin in letters and reports began to change his tone, giving up talk of persuasion, compromise and petition. His emphasis was now all on economic necessity. England needed America more than America needed England, a conclusion which he felt had been amply demonstrated by the success of the nonimportation agreements. Franklin's stiffening attitude came not only from personal disillusionment with the ministry but also—and perhaps primarily—from political developments in America. The Boston Committee of Correspondence organized in 1772 had spread in the next year to the other colonies. In December 1773 the citizens of Massachusetts organized their notorious tea-dumping in Boston Harbor; and in May 1774 Virginia called for a congress of all the colonies, which led to the first Continental Congress, convening at Philadelphia in September. Some Englishmen even thought that the increased resistance of the colonies was a consequence of the scurrilous treatment given to Franklin.

Franklin held to his belief that the empire was greater than England, but the ministry persisted in exalting England over the empire. Even worse, the ministry portrayed the American struggle for rights as rebellion and the people as rebels. Resentful of the rage of the ministerial writers, Franklin prepared an exposé of their efforts to persuade the public "that this War with the Colonies (for a War it will be) is a National Cause, when in fact it is merely a ministerial one." From these words, it is not clear whether Franklin was himself threatening war or merely predicting that ministerial policies would bring on a conflict. Probably he intended it both ways. Later in the same essay he charged that the gross calumniators of the Americans wanted the English "to imbrue our Hands in Brothers' Blood."

A foolish general had boasted in Franklin's hearing that with a thousand British grenadiers he could "go from one end of America to the other, and geld all the Males, partly by force and partly by a little Coaxing." Franklin bristled at this arrogant militarist, who took the Americans "for a species of Animals very little superior to Brutes," another variant of the foolish doctrine of biological degeneration. Even his friend Strahan, fatuous and gullible in patriotic matters, seriously reported to Franklin that he had heard news "of a Scotch Sergeant's having alone met a party of 40 American Soldiers, disarm'd them, and brought them Prisoners into Boston."

In retaliation, Franklin wrote two satires for the *Public Advertiser,* recently identified by Verner W. Crane. One of these (15 April 1774) ironically characterized the colonists as "a dastardly Set of Poltroons," who although descended from British ancestors were "degenerated to such a degree that one born in Britain is equal to twenty Americans." The companion piece (21 May) proposed that General Gage at the head of five battalions of "intrepid Sons of Britain" and a company of sow-gelders proceed through all of the towns of America, castrating all the male inhabitants. Indignantly Franklin charged that such a campaign would conform "to the modern Maxim . . . that it is better that ten innocent Persons should suffer than that one guilty should escape."

In August 1774, Franklin visited William Pitt, Earl of Chatham, at his country estate in Kent. The great statesman, then in the Opposition, expressed esteem for the American people and wished with Franklin that a "good Understanding among the different Parts of the Opposition" might lead to a restoration of harmony with the colonies—but admitted that he had little hope for such a political coalition. Franklin spun out his favorite theme of the never-ending expansion of the colonies, affirming that except for the warped policies of the ministry they "might have gone on extending our Western Empire, adding Province to Province, as far as the South Sea." Repeating from his satirical *Rules by Which a Great Empire May Be Reduced to a Small One* his principle that empires begin to crumble at their extreme outposts, Franklin argued that the British system had been so far preserved only because the provinces had been in great measure allowed their own government. There was, Franklin assured Pitt, as yet no sentiment whatsoever in America for becoming an independent state.

But in talking with fellow Americans, Franklin showed his toughening attitude. Josiah Quincy Jr., who had been sent over from Boston to check on Franklin as well as on the political situation in general, wrote back reassuringly in November 1774:

Dr. Franklin is an American in heart and soul. You may trust him; —his ideas are not contracted within the narrow limits of exemption from taxes, but are extended upon the broad scale of total emancipation. He is explicit and bold upon the subject, and his hopes are as sanguine as my own, of the triumph of liberty in America.

This is the earliest known indication of Franklin's expressing a sentiment for independence, although he may have intended merely "dominion" status. A few weeks earlier Franklin had expressed to Jonathan Williams his pleasure in the zeal with which the other colonies had supported New England. Even though they might desert her and all Europe were to join Britain in attempting to enslave her, he was confident that "she would finally succeed."

Early in December 1774, Hillsborough raged in the House of Lords that "there were then *men* walking in the streets of London, who ought to be in Newgate, or at Tyburn." Although mentioning no names, he made it clear that he meant Franklin and Quincy.

Immediately after his drubbing at the Cockpit, Franklin felt that he should resign his various agencies but soon changed his mind—realizing that the colonies still needed his services. He actually had ceded his Massachusetts agency to Arthur Lee, but the latter was not so desirous of the job as he formerly had been, for he immediately went off on a year's tour of France and Italy, and Franklin felt obliged once more to resume care of Massachusetts affairs. Even though in the fall of the year he felt some apprehension that he might be put into prison, Franklin decided that he should await the results of the Continental Congress before leaving England.

Many of the candidates for election to Parliament had subscribed to a pledge to repeal the coercive acts against America, but Franklin had little faith that the temper of the government would change. Cynically he observed to Cushing, 10 October, that, since most of the members bribed or bought their way in, they would be obliged to sell their votes to the ministry to reimburse themselves. Franklin argued that America could easily buy "the whole Parliament, Minister and all"— a theme which he later delighted to repeat during the Revolution. He even suggested ironically that Parliament be done away with entirely since it was nothing but a tool of the ministry.

Although Franklin had no way of knowing it at the time, perhaps the greatest service he performed for his native country in this year was to encourage the emigration to Pennsylvania of a former customs inspector, who was thirty-seven years old and had failed in every career he had so far tried. His name was Thomas Paine, and he had been introduced to Franklin by a member of the Excise Board. Franklin gave Paine a letter to Richard Bache, asking his son-in-law to give Paine his utmost assistance in finding employment as a clerk, schoolmaster or surveyor. Paine was to become one of Franklin's most loyal admirers and perhaps his closest rival in praising the glories of nature in America and the excellence of American government.

Another young man whom Franklin liked, Polly's husband, Dr. William Hewson, died in May as a result of cutting himself while making a dissection. He left a wife and two children with a third on the way. Polly's only consolation was that at about the same time she became rich by the death of the aunt to whom she had been companion for many years.

In July Franklin wrote to acquaint Debbie with these details, and in September he wrote again to administer a mild rebuke for her failing to write to him during the last nine months. Although admitting that she may have been subject to some indisposition or may have been expecting him to arrive home any day, he peevishly added that many other old friends had dropped him a line on the chance of reaching him and asked, "Why might I not have expected the same Comfort from you, who used to be so diligent and faithful a Correspondent, as to omit scarce any Opportunity."

Debbie probably never read this complaint, for she died on 19 December as the delayed reaction to a paralytic stroke she had suffered four years earlier. In the autumn she had told William that she did not expect to live another summer and would not see her husband again unless he returned that winter. William believed that "her disappointment in that respect preyed a good deal on her spirits." He told his father that because of severe snowstorms he had arrived for her funeral only a half hour before the corpse was taken to the cemetery. William and Bache were the chief mourners, and Hugh Roberts and other old friends were "carriers." Although Franklin may have been upset by this news, it is possible that he accepted it calmly, for he had been writing philosophically about the imminence of his own death for at least five years.

On his sixty-ninth birthday, 17 January 1775, Mrs. Stevenson gave Franklin a festive dinner, attended by a number of ladies and gentlemen. Then in the next month came the sad tidings of Deborah's death which, rather than any political developments, finally determined Franklin to return to America. At this time he had no notion of an absolute break with England, for he told Dr. Richard Price, a dissenting clergyman sympathetic to the colonies, that he might return the following winter.

The British government now began to realize the importance of Franklin's personality as a political force far transcending the relatively minor official post which he held. Secretary Dartmouth, therefore, arranged for two separate social groups to attempt to enroll him as a peacemaker. Early in November, Franklin's old Quaker friend Fothergill, now Lord Dartmouth's physician, sent another long-standing Quaker friend, David

Barclay, a rich merchant, to sound out Franklin on the means to pursue in order to restore harmony. A few days later Fothergill asked Franklin whether he would draw up a written plan, and he accordingly produced a brief statement of terms which might bring about a durable union. Fothergill and Barclay then went over it with him, giving their opinion as to how much would be acceptable to Parliament, and then promised to submit a revised version to Dartmouth.

In the meantime, personalities closer to the government instituted parallel negotiations in an even more devious manner. At a meeting of the Royal Society in November 1774, one of its members approached Franklin with a challenge to a chess game from a lady who had heard of his prowess in the game and wished to meet him. Two or three weeks later, Franklin went to the house of this lady, the sister of Richard Lord Howe, prominent rear admiral and M.P. Franklin enjoyed a pleasant evening and accepted an invitation for another day, thinking that nothing but his conversation and chess skill were involved. At the second meeting, during the course of a chat over a mathematical problem and the New Parliament, which had just convened, the lady asked him what was to be done about the dispute with the colonies. "They should kiss and be Friends," was Franklin's typical reply; "what can they do better?" On Christmas Eve, when Franklin was paying a courtesy call, Mrs. Howe (she had married a Howe) introduced him to her brother, who immediately began to compliment Franklin, affirming that no man was better equipped than he to reconcile the differences with America. Professing to be merely an independent member of Parliament, Howe began to pump Franklin about the means of restoring harmony. Franklin answered that he also had a sincere desire to heal the breach and that he would not allow his personal injuries to interfere—his fixed policy, as he had said on other occasions, was never to mix private feelings with public affairs. In response to Howe's request, he then agreed to draw up more terms or propositions for discussion.

Two days after Christmas, Howe revealed that he had seen Franklin's plan prepared for Barclay and had found it too favorable to the colonies. Assuring Franklin that no one suspected him of being led by a selfish motive, Howe indicated that Franklin might "with reason expect any Reward in the Power of Government to bestow" if he would submit a more acceptable paper. This, according to Franklin, is what the French call "Spitting in the Soup" (i.e., looking after one's own interest). Franklin did as asked. Then, early in January 1775, Fothergill and Howe independently told him that the Ministry considered the plan each had in hand to be inadmissible.

Later in the month Pitt escorted Franklin into the House of Lords to hear him speak in favor of removing troops from Boston, a proposal which was defeated. On 29 January, exactly one year from the day when Franklin had been publicly traduced in the Cockpit, Pitt called upon him at Craven Street to discuss a plan for reconciliation, which Pitt had drawn up. The great statesman stayed nearly two hours, leaving his coach plainly visible to people coming home from church, and Franklin admitted that the visit flattered his vanity "not a little."

Two days later Franklin returned Pitt's visit with remarks on the plan. Although he stayed four hours, he succeeded in changing only one word in the written proposals, Pitt doing practically all of the talking. Later, Franklin cited Pitt's behavior at this interview to prove that those who shine most brilliantly in public eloquence exhibit gross ineptitude in the discussion of details and handling of great affairs. Franklin, of course, represented the converse.

On the following day (1 February), Pitt in an excellent speech presented his plan in the House of Lords, once more introducing Franklin as an auditor. Lord Sandwich, a longstanding opponent of Franklin and the colonies, immediately urged that the plan be contemptuously rejected on the ground that it was obviously not the work of a British peer but of an American. Staring Franklin in the face, he said that "he fancied he had in his Eye the Person who drew it up, one of the bitterest and most mischievous Enemies" his country had ever known. Franklin, with his long practice in controlling and disguising his feelings, kept his countenance as immovable as if his features "had been made of Wood." Pitt very generously came to Franklin's defense, resenting the injurious reflections on a gentleman "whom all Europe held in high Estimation for his Knowledge and Wisdom, and rank'd with our Boyles and Newtons; who was an Honour, not to the English Nation only, but to Human Nature." As he listened to these words, Franklin experienced even more difficulty in keeping "an unconcern'd Countenance." But despite Pitt's eloquence and weighty character, the Lords refused even to consider his proposal.

The whole performance gave Franklin an "exceeding mean Opinion" of hereditary legislators. They appeared to him "to have scarce Discretion enough to govern a Herd of Swine." There would be more propriety, he felt, "in having (as in some University of Germany) *Hereditary Professors of Mathematicks.*" This analogy Franklin used frequently in later propaganda, and it provided Thomas Paine the hint for a similar comparison in *The Rights of Man*. In 1775 Franklin had no better opinion of the elected House of Commons, the members buying votes for election and then accepting bribes from the ministry.

A day or two later at Fothergill's, Barclay summarized for Franklin some of the observations which the ministry had made upon his various points, but in doing so he rubbed Franklin the wrong way, by dropping hints about possible rewards and honors. When he suggested that America urgently needed to come to terms because of the ease with which Britain could burn its coastal towns, Franklin almost lost his temper. Revealing that most of his own property consisted of houses in these towns, he heatedly dared the government to make bonfires of them any time—he would never alter his resolution to defend the rights of his country. The pressure of these negotiations— anger and anxiety—began to disturb his rest, however, and he confided to one of his friends that "whatever robs an old Man of his Sleep, soon demolishes him."

On 20 February, Lord Howe told Franklin that the ministry was thinking of sending Howe himself as a commissioner for settling the differences in America, and he proposed taking Franklin with him as an adviser. At this or some other meeting when Howe led Franklin to believe that a reconciliation might soon take place, Franklin literally shed tears of joy. But his ardor cooled when Howe once more dangled offers of various rewards, including payment of all his back salary as agent for Massachusetts. Franklin replied that any such arrangement would automatically cancel his usefulness by making him appear to be under the influence of a bribe.

Some time in the next few days came the news of Deborah's death, and Franklin made his decision to return to Philadelphia to look after his private affairs. He told Howe, therefore, that if Howe were not going to America as a commissioner, he would be forced to leave by himself on the first available ship. On 7 March, Howe replied that there would be no commission for the time being but that he hoped that he could count on Franklin's cooperation if he were sent later.

At about this period Franklin attended another debate in the House of Lords, where he heard with disgust another tirade on biological degeneration, "many base Reflections on American Courage, Religion, Understanding, &c. in which we were treated with the utmost Contempt, as the lowest of Mankind, and almost of a different Species from the English of Britain."

Franklin was utterly tired of this kind of talk. He had already written in the *Public Advertiser,* 7 February 1775, a reply to a similar speech in the House of Commons in which a "certain North British Colonel" had affirmed that Americans were inferior "in Devotion to Women, and in Courage." Franklin answered with his favorite theme, "the rapid Increase and Population of America"; this circumstance contrasted with the decrease in England and Scotland would certainly show, he argued, which of the two peoples was "most effectually devoted to the Fair Sex." With characteristic irony, Franklin added an observation which reveals that he had heard many conversations on seduction: "that upon this Subject to talk much, and to do little, are inseparable." As for courage, the military history of America had shown that the British regulars, "vain boasters," had in nearly every engagement been totally routed by their enemies until rescued by the American provincials.

In another session of the Lords, Franklin listened with disgust as Lord Sandwich commended Dr. Johnson's *Taxation*

No Tyranny in which the Court pensioner had recommended that Indians be hired to assassinate American farmers and that Negro slaves be urged to cut their masters' throats.

The irresponsible speeches in the House of Lords aroused Franklin to the point of going back to his lodgings and drawing up an intransigent personal protest against closing the port of Boston. Fortunately, before sending it to Dartmouth, he showed it to Thomas Walpole, who looked at him as if he thought Franklin had gone out of his senses. Walpole cautioned him that the protest might be interpreted as "a National Affront" and lead to dangerous consequences to Franklin's person. Not eager to exasperate the ministry any further, therefore, Franklin kept his protest to himself.

This acute sensitivity to criticisms of America was a new development in Franklin's personality. He had always loved his country; now he became a superpatriot. With obvious pride he reported to Charles Thomson (5 February 1775) the plaudits accorded the American Congress by some members of the House of Lords, particularly Pitt's designation of it as "the most honourable Assembly of men, that had ever been known." He told James Bowdoin, 25 February, that the eyes of all Christendom were upon America and that the issue of the contest would be of the utmost significance to all mankind. And on the same day in a letter to Galloway, he contrasted the extreme corruption of the old rotten state of England with "the glorious publick Virtue so predominant in our rising Country." Henceforth, until his death, the virtue and glory of America was to become for Franklin a parallel theme to its rising population.

By this time Franklin had certainly begun to think in terms of America cutting herself loose from England and of appealing for foreign aid in doing so. Before returning to America he wrote a *Dialogue between Britain, France, Spain, Holland, Saxony and America,* summarizing the issues between Britain and the colonies and predicting that the other countries would furnish military aid to America. At the end of the dialogue the European nations in a chorus accuse Britain of base and unjust treatment of her own mother (Saxony) and children (the colonies) . This was certainly more than a whisper of independence even though Franklin still hoped that the separation could be averted.

Franklin dined with Josiah Quincy, Jr., on 3 March, the eve of the latter's return to America, and privately discussed political developments for three hours. Very significantly, Franklin spoke out against leaning on France or Spain for aid. Arthur Lee had already made contact with Beaumarchais and was trying to arrange French participation in an actual American separatist movement. But Franklin, who claimed intimacy with the Spanish and French ambassadors, characterizing the latter as "a shrewd, great man," opposed taking "any step of great consequence, unless on a sudden emergency, without advice of the continental congress." Presumably he believed that, if necessary, the colonies could go it by themselves, for he argued that New England alone could hold out for ages against England. But Franklin was for moderation and compromise, as he had been all along.

Two days before sailing, Franklin instructed Mrs. Stevenson to turn over all his Massachusetts papers to Arthur Lee and wrote to his successor that, although he might possibly return to England in the autumn, he would never again accept the agency.

According to Mason Weems, who met Franklin shortly after this time, Strahan tried to keep Franklin from returning to America, arguing that it would soon be filled with tumult and bloodshed. Franklin replied with the since-famous phrase, "No, sir, where liberty is, there is my country." These words came to be associated with Franklin throughout the rest of the Revolution; so there is no doubt that he used them at one time or another, but we have no authority to support Weems that he spoke them to Strahan at this particular moment. The closest parallel in his published works is a comment on the European libertarian movement in 1789 in a letter to Samuel Moore, Secretary of the London Society for promoting Arts, Manufactures, and Commerce (5 November). Here Franklin expressed the hope "that a lover of liberty may find *a country* in any part of Christendom."

Franklin spent his last day in England with Priestley, looking over a number of American newspapers and directing his friend which articles to extract for the British press. "In reading them, he was frequently not able to proceed for the tears literally running down his cheeks." He had just received a note from Fothergill admitting that the ministry was hardened against America and considered it in no other light than "a larger Field on which to fatten a Herd of worthless Parasites."

Franklin sailed with his grandson Temple on 21 March, arriving in Philadelphia 5 May, after a voyage so calm that a London river boat could have accompanied them for the whole distance.

24. Preparations for War

O N THE morning after Franklin's arrival in Philadelphia, he was appointed by the Pennsylvania Assembly a delegate to the Continental Congress. Almost the first thing he then did was to write a cold note to his son, expressing his disappointment that William had not resigned his post as governor of New Jersey. "While you are in it I know you will execute it with fidelity to your master," he wrote, "but I think independence more honourable than any service." Franklin probably had a premonition that when America separated from Britain he would at the same time be separating from his son.

Still, the rupture did not take place immediately. Franklin sent Temple off to live with his father in New Jersey, where he was received and acknowledged as son and heir. But Franklin never relinquished the hold he had attained on his grandson's affections. He made arrangements for Temple to enter the Philadelphia Academy in the fall and furnished a room for him in his own house.

Franklin later spent a night drinking with his son and one of his son's best friends, Joseph Galloway, Franklin's former supporter in the Assembly but now becoming as firmly welded to the Tory position as William himself. According to Galloway's later recollection, the "glass having gone about freely, the Doctor at a late hour, opened himself, and declared in favour of measures for attaining to Independence." He did his best to persuade the younger men to follow his lead but had absolutely no success.

From the moment of his arrival, Franklin found nearly all of America a virtual armed camp. In Philadelphia the tradesmen drilled in the fields at five in the morning and at six in the evening, before and after their regular work. There were three volunteer battalions, an artillery company, and a troop of light horse. To Franklin, the unanimity of spirit was amazing. Every morning from six to nine, he met with a Committee of Safety, appointed by the Assembly, then immediately proceeded to the Continental Congress, which kept him busy until four. Its members, Franklin proudly wrote to Bishop Shipley, "attend closely without being bribed to it, by either salary, place, or pension, or the hopes of any." Giving way to his new-found super patriotism, Franklin asked the bishop to reflect "on the difference between a new, virtuous people, who have public spirit, and an old corrupt one, who have not so much as an idea that such a thing exists in nature."

To his English friends, Franklin wrote about the British defeat at Lexington and Concord, gleefully describing it as a retreat of twenty miles in six hours. The retaliatory burning of Charlestown, Massachusetts, he considered a brutal, infamous act, worse than any ever committed by the Indian savages. Although admitting to Shipley that he was ashamed to contemplate revenge, he could not disguise his determination that his people should exact full reparation for every evil done to them. "You see I am warm," he wrote; "and if a temper naturally cool and phlegmatic can, in old age, which often cools the warmest, be thus heated, you will judge by that of the general temper here, which is now little short of madness."

On 3 June, Franklin was appointed to a Congressional committee of five members, including John Jay, to draw up a petition to the King of England, justifying the reasonableness of the American cause. So far as we know, this is the first meeting of Franklin with Jay, a New York lawyer almost forty years Franklin's junior. They were later to become close friends as diplomats and peace negotiators in Europe.

On 25 June, Franklin drew up a bill in the Continental Congress, never enacted or inscribed, replying to English charges that the Americans were guilty of ingratitude. Two days later he wrote to an English business acquaintance that America would give the English "one Opportunity more of recovering our Affection and retaining the Connection"—a sincere petition of Congress—but he feared that it would be the last. The British had already begun the house-burning which he had predicted in his talks with Barclay, and Franklin now angrily assumed that the ministry was wicked enough to burn every house in America.

In a similar vein of restrained rage, he wrote to Strahan, accusing him and the British people of fratricide.

You are a Member of Parliament, and one of that Majority which has doomed my Country to Destruction.—You have begun to burn our Towns, and murder our People.—Look upon your Hands! They are stained with the Blood of your Relations!—You and I were long Friends:—You are now my Enemy,—and I am—Yours,—B. Franklin.

Franklin's editors have indicated that this letter was never sent. Indeed it is probable that Franklin never intended that it should reach his friend and that he wrote it entirely as a propaganda piece without any reference to his real feelings toward Strahan. He saw to it that it was published in France and America, and it became one of his most famous letters. But Strahan never let it interfere with their friendship.

In July 1775, Franklin voted against a proposal in the Continental Congress to "provide a Medical Chest for the army," perhaps still motivated by his general opposition to all forms of governmental aid to individuals. To the surprised delegates, however, he merely related in his defense an anecdote of Dr. Fothergill, "who being desired by a philosophical friend to say candidly whether he thought Physicians of real service to mankind, replied by observing that he must first know whether his friend included old women among Physicians; If he did he thought they were of great service."

Franklin's sister Jane had fled from Boston during the occupation by General Gage, going first to Providence and then to Warwick at the invitation of Caty Ray Greene and her husband. Franklin, filled with solicitude, immediately wrote to assure her of his readiness to look after her needs, and William offered a refuge in Amboy. Franklin, although strongly wishing the pleasure of her company, was not sure how long Philadelphia would be safe from invasion or how long his public duties would allow him to remain at home. He reported that Sally's second son, William, now two years old, was "an Infant Hercules." And probably giving Jane as great a shock as she had received from the invading British, he casually remarked, "I have brought over a Grandson with me, a fine Lad of about 15"—probably Jane's first news that William Temple even existed.

On 2 August, the Congress adjourned for a month, leaving Franklin with the responsibility of setting up a new general post office and attending an Indian Treaty on the Ohio before the new session. On 30 September he was appointed member of a committee to confer with Washington on the provisioning and regulating of the continental army. They proceeded directly to headquarters in Cambridge, Massachusetts, arriving at night on 15 October. General Nathanael Greene, who met him on the following day, regarded him all evening with silent admiration, reporting to a friend that "Attention watched his Lips and Conviction closed his Periods," probably another way of saying that Franklin was taciturn, the reputation which he henceforth almost universally acquired in his diplomatic negotiations.

On the way back from Cambridge, Franklin stopped at Warwick to visit the Greenes. While in the neighborhood he spent some time at the home of Catharine's uncle, Judge Philip Greene, and attempted to play the same games with Betty, the thirty-three-year-old spinster daughter of the house, as he had long ago enjoyed with her cousin Caty. But now both Franklin and his intended playmate were too old for avuncular sex. Betty refused to go horseback riding with Franklin and made her distaste so obvious that her father called her rude and ordered her to accept the next invitation. They had their ride and Franklin made an unsuccessful pass, for on their return "Betty informed her honored father of the result of the day's outing in these words: 'Don't you ever ask me to ride with that old fool again.' "

Franklin continued on his way to Philadelphia, taking his sister with him as well as Caty's son Ray, then ten, who was to enter the Philadelphia Academy. For Jane, the journey with her distinguished brother was one of the highlights of her life. His conversation was to her "more than an Equivelent to all the fine wether Emaginable."

At Providence someone asked Franklin whether the Congress was negotiating with a supposed French commissioner in Philadelphia. Although conversations were then going on with Franklin's knowledge, he adopted a pose of diplomatic innocence (an attitude which became invaluable to him later in France) and answered, "How could such a Thing be before Independency was declared?"

On the last leg of the journey, Franklin, Jane and little Ray stopped at Governor Franklin's "magnificent" house in Perth Amboy, the last known meeting between father and son until after the war.

In November 1775, the Congress appointed Franklin to a Committee of Secret Correspondence, organized to explore the possibilities of foreign aid. Franklin was a logical choice because of his great reputation among the scientific societies of Europe. As Philip Mazzei put it, he was in a position "to obtain greater consideration than all Congress put together—the latter body, at that time, being known only by name."

As we have seen, Franklin in England did not agree with the radical wing which hoped to get support from European courts in the struggle against Parliament, but when he was won over to this tactic—probably by the outbreak of hostilities—he put all his abilities and influence into the effort. In December, he wrote to two of his continental contacts, sounding out their reaction to the notion of supporting the colonists. First of these was a Swiss writer, Charles W. F. Dumas, then residing in Holland, who hearkened to Franklin's appeal and served the Congress with a small remuneration until the end of the war. The second correspondent was Prince Don Gabriel of Spain, who had sent Franklin a gift edition of his translation of Sallust. In his letter to the Bourbon prince, Franklin very cleverly suggested that the "first Efforts of a rising State" might "furnish materials for a future Salust."

Some time during November 1775 a stranger appeared in

Philadelphia, seeking to impart confidential information. Congress appointed Franklin, Jay and Jefferson to meet with him in Carpenters' Hall, where they learned that his name was Achard de Bonvouloir and that he had come from the King of France to offer unofficial support in the struggle against England. This support must remain absolutely secret, but it would be tangible, consisting of arms, ammunition and money. By meeting with this French agent, Franklin entered into a new career, which he would not leave before becoming the greatest American diplomat of the Revolution and America's most famous citizen abroad.

Franklin's most brilliant literary contribution of the year was another hoax, but this time his purpose was serious and patriotic. Published in the *Pennsylvania Evening Post*, 14 December 1775, his hoax consisted of the presumed epitaph of John Bradshaw, a strong-minded British defender of liberty. Bradshaw had presided at the trial ordering the execution of Charles I, and his ashes had allegedly been buried on a high hill in Jamaica to preserve them from "the rage against the Regicides exhibited at the Restoration." In the last line of his epitaph, Franklin created another of his axiomatic marvels: "REBELLION TO TYRANTS IS OBEDIENCE TO GOD." According to John Adams, Franklin later proposed it for the Great Seal of the United States. The ingeniousness of the hoax is that, in addition to vindicating the rebellion of the colonists against George III, it enabled Franklin to get back at the ministerial writers for having coupled Whiggism and Presbyterianism in their abuse of the Americans. In his English letters to the press, Franklin had already reminded his readers that Presbyterians had saved their country "from the Tyranny of the Stuarts." Now he suggested that they were still capable of resisting oppression. Only in this political sense did Franklin ever have anything good to say about the Presbyterians.

Despite these varied activities, Franklin took a less active part in political affairs, while Congress remained undecided on a foreign policy, than he had played previously either in Pennsylvania or England. Now he was primarily a witness of events rather than an initiator or participant. Although he willingly served wherever his countrymen asked his aid, his great talents at first were dissipated or wasted. At best, he was a counselor—in the framing of the Declaration of Independence; at worst, he was a mere local official—in the Pennsylvania Committee of Safety.

In this committee he was called upon to design a pike for infantrymen to be used against British bayonets, to decide upon means of obstructing the river approaches to Philadelphia against enemy vessels, to supervise distribution of captured enemy lead, and to perform routine administrative chores. Even in Congress he served on merely functional committees to inquire into lead production and salt making. Franklin himself considered his design for the river obstructions, "or *chevaux de frise,* to be of great importance," and he later proudly reported that they had held up the English advance for seven weeks.

In February 1776, Franklin resigned from his Pennsylvania offices in order to devote all of his time to Congress, having been appointed a commissioner to Canada in an effort to convince the northern provinces to join the struggle against British tyranny. Of all the British territory on the American continent, Canada was the only place where Franklin had no connections and where his great name gave him no extraordinary measure of prestige. To send a man of Franklin's years and ability on such an exhausting expedition—up the Hudson in a heavy snowstorm and across the half-frozen Lake Champlain—was one of the most reckless examples of human waste in the Revolution, particularly since even at the outset the mission never offered any great prospect of success. Franklin and his two fellow commissioners arrived in Montreal late in April, where they were coolly received, the Canadians being dubious about the success of the continental army and inclined to believe that their Catholic religion would be better respected by the British than by the puritanical Americans. Franklin, soon realizing the hopelessness of the situation, started back to Philadelphia alone but was overtaken on the way by John Carroll, a Catholic priest who had accompanied the commission as an aide and as living proof to his Canadian coreligionists that Congress respected their faith.

Franklin daily grew more feeble and without Carroll's "friendly assistance and tender care" would have been unable to manage on the road. About the only valid accomplishment of the journey was the cementing of the friendship between the aged deist and the young priest, which later had something to do with Carroll's being appointed the first Roman Catholic bishop of the United States.

When Franklin returned to Philadelphia early in June, in debilitated condition with a disagreeable breaking out on his skin, he made an oral report to Congress that no help could be expected from Canada. But this made no difference to the belligerent mood and intransigent thinking of the members.

On 7 June, Richard Henry Lee submitted a resolution affirming that the United Colonies were independent and absolved of all political connection with the British Crown. Four days later, a committee consisting of Franklin, Jefferson, John Adams, Roger Sherman and Robert R. Livingston was appointed to frame a declaration to the effect of Lee's resolution. The committee could hardly have been more oddly assorted, chosen, it would seem, primarily for geographical reasons; but it turned out to be suited for the task in hand.

Even though Franklin and Adams came from similar backgrounds, they never understood each other. And even though they were later forced to cooperate on a diplomatic mission to France, they were about as personally incompatible as any two statesmen could be. Adams was twenty-nine years younger than Franklin, but in all their relations Adams behaved with the soberness and sometimes crotchety irritability of an old man and Franklin with the openness and accommodating ease of a young one. As far back as 1756, shortly after Adams had graduated from Harvard, he admired Franklin as a "prodigious Genius cultivated with prodigious Industry." Four years later he praised Franklin's "amazing Capacity for Business, His Memory and Resolution, Amidst so much Business as Counsellor, Post Master, Printer, so many private studies, and so many Publick avocations." Despite this foundation for a harmonious relationship of merited respect on one side, cordial cooperation on the other, Adams could not overlook Franklin's human frailties when he came to know the older man better—and once having sat in judgment upon Franklin, he decided that Franklin was not his superior and began to resent every circumstance which placed Franklin above him in the eyes of the world.

Between Jefferson and Franklin, however, despite an even greater difference in age, there was never the slightest friction at any time. They responded warmly to each other at first meeting, and Jefferson became in a sense Franklin's disciple as well as his loyal friend, regarding him as "the ornament of human nature." When Jefferson went to Paris in 1784, he remarked that he could only succeed Franklin at the French court, not replace him.

Since Jefferson's previous writings had been recognized for their "peculiar felicity of expression," the committee asked him to draw up the preliminary draft of the declaration of independence. Perhaps the labor of composition would have been delegated to Franklin had he not been recovering from his arduous Canadian journey. As it was, he wrote to George Washington on 21 June, that he knew little about what was going on in the Congress except that a declaration was being prepared. Jefferson proceeded entirely on his own, showing his text separately to Franklin and Adams before reporting to the full committee. Neither made any sweeping alterations. Franklin's major change was in the phrase "we hold these truths to be sacred and undeniable," which he shortened to the more forceful "we hold these truths to be self-evident." He similarly changed "arbitrary power" to "absolute Despotism" and "deluge us in blood" to "destroy us."

After the committee reported to the Congress on 28 June, that body made a number of drastic revisions before the final text was adopted on 4 July. Jefferson was extremely sensitive to these "depredations," as he called them, and confided his chagrin to Franklin. The older man comforted his colleague by telling him that he had himself been so much afflicted by having his own writings mauled that he had adopted as a rule, whenever in his power, "to avoid becoming the draughtsman of papers to be reviewed by a public body." He once knew an apprentice hatter, about to go into business for himself, who planned a handsome signboard with the inscription "John Thompson, Hatter, makes and sells hats for ready money." Before ordering the sign, he showed his proposed inscription to a number of friends, who word by word whittled away his text until nothing was left but " 'John Thompson' with the figure of a hat sub-joined."

Franklin might also have reported an experience of his own which he remembered from his tenure in the Pennsylvania Assembly. On one occasion he had drawn up and read at a public meeting a proposal for some kind of action. A carpenter, who was present, "took it into his hands, & dividing the sheet into two, said of one leaf, *This I think is enough, & will answer.*"

In the popular mind, Franklin's role in the adoption of the Declaration of Independence is associated with a purely apocryphal legend. According to Jared Sparks and earlier biographers, John Hancock is supposed to have urged unanimity by affirming, "There must be no pulling different ways; we must all hang together." Franklin replied, "We must, indeed, all hang together, or most assuredly we shall all hang separately."

Four days after the adoption of the Declaration, Philadelphia elected Franklin as a delegate to a convention to frame a constitution for Pennsylvania, and he was shortly after elected as its president. Although modern writers have minimized Franklin's personal participation in the Pennsylvania convention (and he was certainly absent much of the time because of his national duties), many of his contemporaries considered him to be the guiding philosophical light of the resulting constitution, particularly the provisions for a plural executive council and a unicameral legislature. According to Thomas Paine, Franklin told the convention that a system of two houses is "like putting one horse before a cart and the other behind it, and whipping them both. If the horses are of equal strength, the wheels of the cart, like the wheels of government, will stand still; and if the horses are strong enough, the cart will be torn to pieces." Whether or not the convention in adopting unicameralism acted out of deference to Franklin, there is no question that he opposed a system of two houses.

The debates over the Pennsylvania government extended themselves over many weeks without agreement, during which time life in the community proceeded smoothly and evenly. Eventually, according to the Abbé Morellet, Franklin warned his fellow legislators "that in the midst of our present anarchy life goes on just as before. If our disputes continue, take care lest the people realize that they can easily dispense with our services."

During the sessions of the convention, the leading Anglicans of the community invited Franklin to a meeting at the home of his old enemy, William Smith, to discuss the future of the College of Philadelphia. Since the Declaration of Independence had cut all political ties of the Anglican church with England, the Anglican trustees were afraid that popular sentiment might demand that the college be administered henceforth by the state or by some other religious denomination. Franklin had already resumed superficially polite relations with Smith—as a consequence of the latter's election to an office in the American Philosophical Society—and he not only attended the meeting but "cheerfully promised" to propose to the convention "an article drawn up by Dr. Smith, securing all chartered rights" to the incumbent trustees. The maneuver failed, however, to retain Smith in office. Dismissed in favor of a Presbyterian provost, he almost immediately announced loyalty to the Crown and sat out the war as a despondent Tory, brooding over his ancient animosities.

In the meantime, Franklin's old acquaintance Lord Howe had been placed in command of the British fleet in America and was sent to join his brother, General William Howe, to carry out negotiations for a peaceful settlement prior to initiating large-scale warfare. On 12 July, Howe sent Franklin an official statement of his mission along with a personal letter in which he indiscreetly revealed that the primary interest of the British in retaining America was to prevent its trade "from passing into foreign Channels."

Franklin took full advantage of this slip in his reply and in subsequent propaganda. Franklin, of course, did not need Howe to tell him that commercial relations with America were all-important to England, and this was the inducement he was later to use in seeking an alliance with France. Since Howe's authority did not go beyond "Offers of Pardon upon Submission," Franklin declared that all negotiation would be pointless. Also he observed, in accordance with his realistic view of human nature, that the British had injured the Americans too atrociously to be able to "pardon" them. The guilt of the British would impel them to break the spirit of those they had persecuted. Regretfully, Franklin formally abandoned the endeavor he had long been exerting, "with unfeigned and unwearied Zeal, to preserve from breaking that fine and noble China Vase, the British Empire;" for he "knew, that, being once broken, the separate Parts could not retain even their Shares of the Strength and Value that existed in the Whole, and that a perfect Reunion of those Parts could scarce ever be hoped for."

Some days later, an American general, Sullivan, taken prisoner on Long Island, carried a message to Congress that Lord Howe, although not empowered to deal with Congress directly, wished to have a private conference with some of its members. The Congress appointed Franklin, Adams and Edward Rutledge for the purpose, and they proceeded to the rendezvous in New York scheduled for 11 September. They found the roads congested with soldiers going to join Washington, and the inn at New Brunswick where they stopped for the night was so crowded that Adams and Franklin were obliged to share a tiny room with an equally tiny window. Adams, like most of his contemporaries, had a fear of the night air and closed the window tight. But Franklin protested that they would be suffocated with it shut—that the air indoors was worse than that outside. Persuading Adams to open the window and come to bed, Franklin talked them both to sleep expounding his theories of air baths and of colds.

At the conference itself Howe had actually no authority to offer anything more than he had previously proposed in his letter to Franklin, and the committee was no more inclined than Franklin to find the conditions of return to Crown rule acceptable. Both Franklin and Adams shone as wits. When Howe remarked that if America should fall he should feel and lament it "like the Loss of a brother," Franklin bowed and replied, "My Lord, We will do our Utmost Endeavours to save your Lordship that mortification." At Howe's admission that he had no power to receive the three Americans except as private individuals, Adams rejoined, "Your lordship may consider me, in what light you please; and indeed I should be willing to consider myself, for a few moments, in any Character which would be agreeable to your Lordship *except that of a British subject.*" Somewhere along the way Howe referred to the advantages which Britain hoped from America, "her commerce, her strength, her men," giving Franklin the opportunity to introduce his favorite theory of peopling: "Aye, my lord, we have a pretty considerable manufactory of men." As it eventually became clear that Howe could offer nothing until the colonies returned to their former allegiance, the Americans flatly stated that they were now independent states and could be treated with on no other terms.

That put an end to all negotiations; Lord Howe's brother became a soldier once more; and the war broke out in earnest. The English captured New York City and Long Island; and all over the country incidents erupted between patriots and Tories. Among the latter, Franklin's son had been put under guard at his farm in Burlington and later sent to Litchfield, Connecticut, for greater security. Despite this change in his son's fortunes, Franklin did not disown him or otherwise reveal his chagrin. Perhaps he grudgingly respected William for proving that he could remain a good government man in foul weather as well as fine. In his will Franklin had left William all his books and papers. Far from changing this bequest, he left the trunk containing them, including the manuscript of his autobiography, in the custody of William's friend Galloway, who had moved into the country, a place less likely to be molested by British troops than Franklin's own home.

Notwithstanding his paternal forbearance, Franklin still wanted to keep at a minimum his son's influence over the young and impressionable William Temple Franklin, who was living with his stepmother at Perth Amboy and had asked Franklin's permission to join his father. After some consideration, Franklin decided (19 September) that he could not approve such a journey—giving no reasons except the need for Temple to continue with his studies at this crucial age when he was to lay the foundations of his future. "If this Season is neglected, it will be like cutting off the Spring from the Year."

Temple, therefore, assumed that Franklin had suspicions that he might carry "dangerous Intelligence" to his father, an assumption which hurt Franklin a little. "You could have suspected me," he wrote three days later, "of a little tender Concern for your Welfare." The pretext Temple had offered for the journey was that of taking a letter to the governor from his wife. But the wise Franklin thought that the project arose from the boy's wanderlust, disinclination for schoolwork, and a sincere desire, which Franklin by no means blamed, "of seeing a Father you have so much Reason to Love."

25. Secret Diplomat

AFTER his appointment to the Committee of Secret Correspondence, Franklin's most important work consisted in preparing the preliminary stages of negotiation with France, even though he had opposed calling on foreign governments before the Declaration of Independence. Working through his old philosophical friend Dubourg, undeniably one of the first French supporters of the American Revolution and one of the most zealous, Franklin supervised the official contact with Vergennes, French secretary of foreign affairs, and laid the ground for all subsequent French aid extended to America.

Nobody in the Congress wanted a political alliance with France, Franklin perhaps least of all. What was desired and vitally needed was military and economic aid of all kinds. The French on their side had realized for many years the potentialities of an independent America for weakening their traditional British enemy and had sent their secret agent, Bonvouloir, to Philadelphia early in 1775.

Before leaving on his fruitless expedition to Canada, Franklin had been in touch with two other French agents, Penet and Pliarne, who had offered to exchange military supplies for tobacco and other products. Franklin told Penet to carry out the French side of the negotiations in collaboration with Dubourg and to trust nobody else. In June 1776, Dubourg arranged for Penet and Pliarne to handle a shipment of arms from the royal arsenal. Vergennes knew of all these activities, and supported them, but had to keep governmental concurrence secret. He particularly cautioned Dubourg to be circumspect in all dealings: "One can dissimulate certain things which one cannot authorise." Despite his precaution, Dubourg's American sympathies came to the attention of Lord Stormont, the English ambassador in Paris. Writing to his superior, Lord Weymouth, in London (24 July 1776), he complained of Dubourg's "regular Correspondence with Doctor Franklin," and his circulating "all those Reports to our Disadvantage."

In March 1776, the Committee of Secret Correspondence appointed Silas Deane as an agent to France, and Franklin wrote his instructions. He was to go directly to Dubourg, "a man prudent, faithful, secret, intelligent in affairs," who would introduce him to Vergennes and to other American sympathizers. In his negotiations he should stress the advantages to France of American trade which "was rapidly increasing with our increase of people" and find out whether France would be willing "to enter into any treaty or alliance with them, for commerce or defense, or both."

Shortly after the Declaration of Independence, Franklin was appointed to a committee to draw up a treaty to be proposed to France. Other members were Dickinson, John Adams, Benjamin Harrison and Robert Morris. In their discussions, Adams contended forcefully against "an alliance which might embarrass us in after times, and involve us in future European wars." According to Adams, *"Franklin, although he was commonly as silent on committees as in Congress, . . . ventured so far as to intimate* his concurrence with me in *these sentiments."*

After the terms of a treaty had been agreed upon, the next step was to present it to France. On 26 September, Congress in secret session appointed Franklin and Jefferson to join Silas Deane, already in France, as commissioners. When Benjamin Rush, who sat next to him, congratulated him on the appointment, Franklin compared himself to the remnant of a piece of cloth of which the shopkeepers would say, "You may have it for what you please." "Just so," Franklin remarked, "my country may command my Services in any way they choose."

Now all the more anxious to keep Temple away from his father, Franklin wrote two days later asking him to return to Philadelphia immediately, "something offering here that will be much to your Advantage if you are not out of the Way." He had in mind taking Temple to France but for security reasons could not be more specific.

One can imagine the dismayed reaction of Franklin's family

and friends when they learned of his new mission. A year before, when Jane heard that Franklin might return for further negotiations in England, she had remonstrated, almost in panic, "You Positively must not go, you have served the Publick in the way beyond what any other man can Boast till you are now come to a good old Age & some younger man must now take that Painfull service upon them [sic]. Dont go, pray Dont go." Now he was a year older, and about to embark on a voyage in which he ran a solid risk of being hanged for treason if apprehended by an enemy ship. But he was more concerned about his country than his own fate. On the day of his embarkation (25 October 1776), he wrote, "I hope our people will keep up their courage. I have no doubt of their finally succeeding by the blessing of God, nor have I any doubt that so good a cause will fail of that blessing."

Franklin decided to take the six-year-old Benjamin Franklin Bache with him as well as the sixteen-year-old Temple. They crossed in cold weather in the *Reprisal,* a vessel so frail that it was lost on its return voyage. Accommodations were so "miserable" that Franklin was almost "demolished." En route they were pursued by British men-of-war, and they themselves captured two small British prizes. Later Franklin described the *Reprisal* as "a miserable vessel, improper for those northern seas," and charged that he was so badly fed that "on his arrival he had scarce strength to stand."

When they entered Quiberon Bay on 29 November, adverse winds kept the vessel from proceeding up the Loire to the port of Nantes. Franklin landed 3 December by means of a fishing boat at the coastal village of Auray, which appeared to him "a wretched place." He wrote immediately to Deane, acquainting him of the new commission and also informing him that Arthur Lee had been named as a replacement for Jefferson, who could not leave Virginia.

On the two-day trip by carriage to Nantes, Franklin was struck by the appearance of some peasant women he encountered on the way. "They were all of fair white and red complexions," he noted, "but one among them was the fairest woman I ever beheld." The voyage had fatigued and weakened him, but

he recovered strength fast after landing. At Nantes he received
the first taste of the nationwide adulation which was to charac-
terize his sojourn in France.

As soon as Franklin reached Paris, 21 December, Dubourg
sent cards to his acquaintances all over the city, heralding the
arrival of his distinguished friend. Two days later, Franklin and
his fellow commissioners Deane and Lee sent a formal note to
Vergennes, announcing their presence and asking for an opportunity of presenting their credentials. On Christmas Day, Stormont reported sourly to his chief, "I have already observed to
your Lordship that Numbers of People resort to him [Franklin],
but there are very few Persons of Condition among them."

Franklin was under orders to obtain recognition of American independence, a treaty of commerce, military assistance,
and, if possible, French entry into the war as an ally. Most
important was the military alliance; least important, the commercial treaty. To be sure, the latter was all that America had to
offer on her side, and Franklin in his first interview with
Vergennes pretended that this was all he was interested in
discussing. Vergennes was not deceived, although a little surprised. "I don't know whether Mr. Franklin told me everything," Vergennes wrote to the French minister in Spain, "but
what he did say is not very interesting in regard to the circumstances of his country." The petition for a commercial treaty was
so "modest" that it did not really cover anything which the
Americans "did not already enjoy." Vergennes found this modesty praiseworthy, if predicated merely on the dislike of being
burdensome to a power whose aid they hoped to obtain, but he
wondered whether it was not really based on "political
considerations"—as it actually was.

Realizing that England could not afford to allow France and
Spain to take over American commerce, the Americans assumed
that this circumstance alone would bring about a breach between England and the other two powers. This rupture, Vergennes foresaw, "by changing the theme of the war, would
naturally lead the English to recognize the independence that
they now dispute with the colonies without burdening them
with an eventual defensive alliance such as a new nation has to

avoid because it can form itself and prosper only in a long era of peace." This in a nutshell was Franklin's diplomatic strategy, and Vergennes grasped it immediately. Since his own policy of revitalizing French prestige rested upon reducing British commercial power, Vergennes was willing to support the American struggle for independence. For some time, however, French aid had to remain secret. The "cry of the nation" was for the *Insurgens,* as the Americans were called in France, but the court was reluctant to risk a war with Britain. For this reason, Franklin had not been invited to Versailles, the French fearing to upset the British ambassador, Stormont, who was making vigorous protests against Franklin's even being allowed in Paris.

Other channels, however, were available. Over a year previously, Arthur Lee in London had met the French dramatist and man of pleasure, Caron de Beaumarchais, and convinced him of the ultimate victory of the colonists. In September 1775, Beaumarchais had composed a memoir to Louis XVI, predicting a successful revolution in America, and at the same time had laid plans for an investment company to aid the colonies and earn a profit for himself. Before Franklin's arrival, Dubourg and Beaumarchais were vying with each other to win the favor of Deane and Vergennes. By the time Franklin arrived on the scene, Beaumarchais had already set up a dummy trading concern, Roderigue Hortalez & Company, which was to be the instrument of shipping supplies to the colonies. Franklin had many conferences with Beaumarchais and with another more solid and prominent investment broker, Donatien Leray de Chaumont. But when he saw the French ministers, he did so at night in the greatest secrecy. Franklin found no difficulty in deferring to their wishes for discretion. As he remarked to Arthur Lee, "It is necessary to gratify the desires, and in some Sort comply with the Humours, of those we apply to."

Chaumont offered to Franklin as a residence and office a wing of his mansion, l'Hôtel Valentinois, "a fine airy House upon a Hill," situated at Passy, then "a neat Village on a high Ground, half a Mile from Paris," but in our day the most elegant section of the city. Franklin enjoyed "a large Garden to walk in" only a few steps from the Seine, where he swam almost daily in good weather. His appetite was good and he slept soundly, thanks to the "French Cookery," which agreed with him better than the English. He supposed that this was because the French used "little or no Butter in their Sauces," an indication that he had not become a connoisseur in matters of cuisine. Franklin soon became accepted as a member of the Chaumont family and playfully began calling the daughter of the house his wife.

Soon after taking up residence, Franklin was visited by one of his neighbors, a fellow scientist and political philosopher, Jean Sylvain Bailly, who had taken him for a model and hoped to become a kind of French Franklin. After entering the salon, Bailly lapsed into silence, respectfully waiting for his host to begin the conversation. Eventually he offered Franklin a pinch of tobacco, which was refused. After two hours of silence, Bailly got up to leave—and Franklin's only words as he showed out his visitor were "fort bien." Bailly loved to tell this story and, confirming the legend of Franklin's taciturnity, frequently said that "fort bien" were the only words that he had ever heard from Franklin when no other company was present.

During his first months in Passy, Franklin spent most of his evenings at home, amusing himself by playing chess with a priest employed as a tutor in the Chaumont family. According to the grandson of Franklin's landlord, they once played all through the night until they had exhausted their supply of candles.

We are indebted to another clergyman, the Abbé Flamarens, for the most famous description of Franklin in France, which appeared twice in contemporary periodicals and circulated widely:

He has a handsome physiognomy, glasses always on his eyes, very little hair, a fur cap, which he always wears on his head, no powder, but a neat appearance. Extremely white linen and a brown habit are his sole ornaments.

We note particularly Franklin's fastidiousness, a trait from his youth—and the absence of powder, a very new development. Since nearly everyone else wore a powdered wig, Franklin emphasized his natural locks in a self-description, which he sent to a friend of Mrs. Stevenson, a certain Mrs. Emma Thompson then living at Lille (8 February 1777):

Figure me in your mind as jolly as formerly, and as strong and hearty, only a few years older; very plainly dress'd, wearing my thin gray strait hair, that peeps out under my only *Coiffure,* a fine Fur Cap, which comes down my Forehead almost to my Spectacles. Think how this must appear among the Powder'd Heads of Paris!

The French placed great importance on Franklin's laying aside "the wig which formerly in England hid the nudity of his forehead and the useless adornment which would have left him at the level of the other English." To them, his bare head represented "the simplicity and the innocence of primitive morals." A much better explanation is that Franklin was suffering from a scurvy of the head which he had originally acquired in Ireland and which spread or contracted according to the quantity of salted meats and cheese in his diet. Living chiefly on salt beef during the passage to France, Franklin found that the scurvy had spread over most of his body. He probably left off wearing his powdered wig as a form of treatment. On one occasion, he used even this trivial circumstance to advantage. At a Parisian salon when he bared his head and displayed his long hair, his hostess remarked, "You must be deprived of wigs in Philadelphia." Franklin then replied, "We have a greater need of men than of wigs." Certainly he had no scruples against either the foppishness or the expense of artificial hair, for there still exists a stiff bill rendered to him in 1772 covering the manufacture and care of his wigs.

Franklin humorously confided to Mrs. Thompson that he wished every French lady and gentleman would follow his example of combing his own hair and pay him half the money saved by dismissing the hairdressers. He could then enlist these *friseurs* and with the money saved take them to England to dress the heads of the ministers and privy councilors, who were a little deranged. This was one of Franklin's favorite jokes, which he repeated to Turgot in a slightly different form. If everyone in the French nation would agree not to have his hair curled and not to use powder for the duration of the war, he proposed, "your wig-makers will form an army, and you can maintain them with the fees you will save, and the grain which would otherwise go to make powder will serve to nourish them."

Franklin also showed Mrs. Thompson that his gallantry was still very active. To her queries about Brussels and Lille as prospective dwelling places, he replied that a single woman such as Mrs. Thompson could maintain herself comfortably anywhere—and himself in the bargain—but he conjured her not to invite him in earnest to come to live with her, for being on official business he ought not to comply, but he was not sure that he would be able to refuse.

Another of his feminine acquaintances resident in France, Mrs. Juliana Ritchie, warned him that he was continually surrounded by spies. Admitting the probability of the report, he shrugged it off by citing a rule which he felt would prevent any inconvenience from the circumstance: "to be concern'd in no Affairs that I should blush to have made publick." If he were sure that his valet were a spy—as he probably was—Franklin would not dismiss him for his espionage if he liked him otherwise.

A much greater hindrance to Franklin than British spies was the horde of French and other adventurers who wanted to make a career out of fighting in the American army. So many aspiring officers, each a veritable Caesar, besieged and badgered Franklin and the other American commissioners that their time was "cut to pieces by personal Applications, besides those contained in dozens of Letters, by every Post." As a result "scarce one in a hundred" of the applicants received as much as "a simple Recommendation to Civilities." Franklin wrote to a friend that he was terrified by the noise of every coach entering his court. "I am afraid to accept an Invitation to dine abroad, being almost sure of meeting with some Officer or Officer's Friend, who, as soon as I am put in good Humour by a Glass or two of Champaign, begins his Attack upon me."

Even though the aspiring officer might be a gallant and able soldier, Franklin explained, to refuse his request would be much kinder than to give any kind of recommendation. But to satisfy those applicants who insisted on some kind of document, Franklin prepared a model letter declaring he knew nothing of the bearer, not even his name. Explaining that it was not uncommon in France for one unknown person to bring "another equally unknown, to recommend him; and sometimes they recommend one another"—Franklin referred the recipient to the bearer himself "for his Character and Merits, with which he is certainly better acquainted than I can possibly be." Franklin's model letter was a mixture of pleasantry and efficiency, like much else in his personality. As a young man traveling in America, he had similarly devised a set speech which he uttered as soon as he entered a strange inn or tavern: "My name is Benjamin Franklin, I was born at Boston, am a printer by profession, shall return at such a time, and have no news—Now what can you give me for dinner?"

In France Franklin refused to answer many of the letters of solicitation, and when he did answer, he sometimes forgot himself to the point of insult. But he had the prophetic insight to recommend, sight unseen, the nineteen-year-old Marquis de Lafayette to Washington's special care. Lafayette's family, apprehensive that the young man's benevolent instincts might lead him to bestow his money on unworthy recipients, hoped that some "discreet friend" could be persuaded to take charge of his funds, and Franklin asked Washington to become the friendly banker. Washington's warm response, as everyone knows, was salutary for both Lafayette and the American cause.

Another pressure upon Franklin, almost as insistent as the military, was the literary. Scores of aspiring French writers sent Franklin manuscripts for approval or dedicated their works to him with the hope of receiving favorable public attention. Sometimes Franklin acknowledged these dedications, particularly if written by acquaintances or eminent literary men; most frequently he ignored them. Since these adulatory inscriptions came entirely unsolicited amid the press of necessary business, one can excuse Franklin for neglecting most of them. He seems to have been heartless, however, in his treatment of the Chevalier de Berny, a retired army captain of Strasbourg, who sent Franklin an entire book, carefully inscribed by hand and carrying a highly complimentary dedication to Franklin and a page of poetry honoring him for being chosen to represent the thirteen states in Europe. Franklin accepted the book, filed it with his correspondence, but made no acknowledgment whatsoever to de Berny. The disappointed author sent a series of pathetic letters—eight during nine months—expressing his chagrin in being denied both an acknowledgment of his gift and any answer to his letters. Franklin may have felt that de Berny belonged to the class of well-meaning Europeans who "make shoes for feet they have never measured," but he seems to have been unusually callous in not at least acknowledging the old man's tribute.

Franklin had one of his own letters similarly disregarded when he sent Stormont an incensed protest over the British treatment of American prisoners, who were forced to serve on British naval vessels or transported to remote points in Africa and Asia. Stormont, pretending not to have opened the letter, sent it back with the insulting note, "The King's Ambassador receives no Letters from Rebels but when they come to implore His Majesty's Mercy."

Franklin got his revenge by inspiring a propaganda story, which made the rounds of the *beau monde,* reached Vergennes himself, and quickly became crystallized in a newspaper anecdote. Once Stormont

told a French nobleman, that six battalions in Washington's army had laid down their arms. The nobleman applied to Doctor Franklin, to know whether the story was a truth (*une vérité*), to which the Doctor answered, *"Non, Monsieur, ce n'est pas vérité, c'est seulement un Stormont."*

This answer gained such circulation among the wits of Paris that the word *stormont* became the court phrase for a lie.

When Franklin learned of the rout suffered by the Hessian troops at Trenton in the wake of Washington's victory on Christmas Day 1776, he similarly exposed the viciousness of the mercenary system by means of a bitter hoax, *The Sale of the*

Hessians, printed in the French press. In a fictitious letter, the Count de Schaumbergh writes to his representative in America, expressing delirious joy that three-fourths of his men had been killed and must be paid for by the English and their ranks filled with new recruits.

Since some commentators throughout Europe had been maintaining the British-inspired fiction that Franklin was in large share personally responsible for the war, Franklin assured his Dutch friend Jan Ingenhousz that he had "long laboured in England, with great zeal and sincerity, to prevent the breach that has happened." But at present he was not come to France to seek peace—only assistance in the struggle against British injustice and tyranny. Old as he was, he flattered himself that he would live to see his country "settled in Peace and Prosperity, when Britain shall make no more a formidable Figure among the Powers of Europe."

Even before Franklin's arrival in France, Turgot, eminent economist and retired finance minister, had sent to du Pont de Nemours (5 June 1776) the Latin epigram which became the most famous line ever written about Franklin, *Eripuit cælo fulmen, sceptrumque tyrannis.* (He snatched the lightning from heaven and the sceptre from tyrants.) Turgot later came to visit Franklin, escorted by the Duc de La Rochefoucauld, who had met Franklin many years previously in London. During the course of the year, they had serious discussions over economic policy. The eminent financier tried to convince Franklin of the advantages of direct taxes over indirect so that America would not follow the example of England and base its economy on indirect taxation, but Franklin believed that in economics at least the British system was preferable.

In the last few months before leaving England, Franklin had met the secretary of the Earl of Shelburne, Benjamin Vaughan, who became one of Franklin's warmest admirers. A liberal Whig, he also became one of the most ardent supporters of the American cause. Late in December 1776, Vaughan sent to Franklin in Paris some newspapers as evidence of his interest in America. These probably contained defamatory articles, since

Vaughan affirmed, like Ingenhousz, that his great affection made him sensible to all insults cast upon Franklin. Within the next two weeks, Franklin wrote to Polly Hewson, "I have just seen in the Papers 7 Paragraphs about me, of which 6 were Lies."

In September 1777, Vaughan came to Paris, hoping to re-establish contact with Franklin. He had in addition certain commercial interests to promote, and he may well have been commissioned by the pro-American forces in Parliament as an unofficial liaison agent to explore the possibilities of resuming peace negotiations. For this reason, Franklin could not let the French authorities—or the vigilant internal spy system—see him on too friendly terms with a British emissary. The only place he could think of "where a Meeting with me would not occasion Speculation" was the swimming pool which he regularly attended. Then, as in our day, Parisians bathed in "a large white wooden Building upon a Boat in the River opposite to the Tuilleries." The attendants knew Franklin by sight but did not realize that he was the eminent philosopher or Bonhomme Richard, as he was more familiarly called. Vaughan was to inquire merely "for an old Englishman with grey Hair."

Another Englishman friendly to the Americans was David Hartley, son of the famous philosopher and a member of Parliament since 1774. After Franklin's arrival in France, Hartley continued their friendly correspondence "with sentiments of good will to both countries," but Franklin assured him (14 October 1777) that sentiment in America now regarded the entire British nation, not merely the ministry, as responsible for the barbarities of the war. "You are no longer the magnanimous and enlightened nation, we once esteemed you, and . . . you are unfit and unworthy to govern us, as not being able to govern your own passions." The best means of changing American opinion and preparing the way for an eventual peace, Franklin advised, would be to adopt humane methods of treating American prisoners—allowing the Congress "to send or employ a commissary to take some care of those unfortunate people."

During all this time, the French government was a pleased witness of the difficulties which the British were having with their former colonies—but was not sure enough of an American triumph to consider entering into the treaty which Franklin was empowered to offer. Indeed, since Vergennes could not openly even acknowledge Franklin's presence in Paris, Franklin had been officially instructed not to show himself at public gatherings. Official timidity manifested itself in other ways. A bookseller, Ruault, had dedicated to Franklin in 1777 *The Works of Bernard Palissy* (a French scientist of the Renaissance) , describing Franklin as a philosopher who had penetrated into the secrets of politics as well as nature. But royal permission and approbation of this dedication were abruptly revoked.

On one public occasion Franklin despaired so much of receiving adequate or timely enough aid from the French that he threatened a French nobleman with the consequences of letting America go it alone. After a dinner in September 1777 at which wine had overcome Franklin's customary patience and taciturnity, he rebuked the Comte de Lauraguais: "There is nothing better to do here than to drink; how can we flatter ourselves . . . that a monarchy will help republicans revolted against their monarch?" This was indeed a pertinent question, frequently raised at the time. Bluntly Franklin said that he was sorry that the French tried to have it both ways—to exhaust England and keep a new empire from rising.

In order to be more surely, more promptly independent, to guarantee ourselves from the horrors of war, and from the future dangers of obtaining liberty by our own strength [Franklin declared], I should have liked that the strength of France had prevented us from knowing the whole extent of ours: I should have liked, for the good of the two hemispheres, that we had been connected, from the first, in general commerce, through the interest of France.

Despite the forced seclusion in which Franklin lived, he was much sought after and entertained. At first he was extremely circumspect concerning military news from America. A wit at a dinner party, hoping to draw him out, remarked, "One must admit, monsieur, that it is a great and superb spectacle which America offers us today." "Yes," replied Franklin modestly, "but the spectators do not pay." Although Franklin's command of French was not extensive, he enjoyed the theatre. One day in

July when he expressed the desire to see Molière's *Amphitryon* and *Pourceaugnac,* two plays not often presented that season, the players announced a kind of command performance for Franklin—and succeeded in filling the entire hall by four in the afternoon.

By the end of the year, the news of Burgoyne's surrender at Saratoga had given the American cause a new prestige, and Franklin appeared more and more in public. He received the homage of the grave and serious at a public meeting of the Academy of Sciences (12 November) and the acclaim of the gallant and frivolous at the opera. At the same time Franklin cast off the reserve which had previously hedged in his conversation about the war. He openly criticized as a blunder Howe's tactics in focusing on the Congress and cleverly remarked "that it was not he who had taken Philadelphia, but Philadelphia who had taken him."

The final triumphant outcome of Franklin's deft handling of the French diplomats and of news from the battlefields was the signing of the treaty of friendship and commerce—which Congress had sought since September 1776. On 8 December 1777, Conrad Alexandre Gérard of the Ministry of Foreign Affairs admitted to the three commissioners, Franklin, Deane and Lee, that the King's council was now ready to negotiate a commercial agreement and an alliance, and both sides began to consider terms. Franklin had more trouble in pleasing Arthur Lee, however, than satisfying Gérard. The scrupulous Virginian accused Franklin of being dilatory in preparing the documents because he dined out every night. On 18 January, Gérard presented the treaties as acceptable to the French. Lee, as usual, found a detail to offend his scruples, but Franklin finally convinced him that the treaties were honorable. One can understand Lee's suspicions of Franklin and Deane, which eventually erupted into open animosity. When both Franklin and Lee had been in England, it was Lee who had urged seeking French aid, Franklin who had opposed it. After Franklin returned to America in 1775, Lee remained in London working for American interests—even after the Declaration of Independence—to the detriment of his financial affairs and at a great risk to his life. Yet in all relations with French society, diplomatic and intellectual, Franklin was universally acclaimed and Lee virtually ignored.

When the documents were ready for signing, 5 February, Franklin prepared for the ceremony by donning the coat which he had worn on the day Wedderburn abused him at Whitehall—now faded and somewhat tighter. Gérard at the last minute asked that the ceremony be deferred until the next day, and Franklin's entourage wondered whether he would again wear the symbolic coat. Although he had been heard to say "that he was not insensible to injuries, but that he never put himself to any trouble or inconvenience to retaliate," he admitted to Deane the next day—while wearing the coat—that he was indeed giving it "a little revenge."

On 20 March, Louis XVI symbolically announced the treaty to the world by receiving the commissioners at court. This time Franklin wore a new suit—impeccably clean as always—and plain as had become his custom in France. Still without ornamentation (wig or ceremonial sword), he was mistaken for a Quaker. On this as on almost every public appearance, the French public assumed that he represented the moral simplicity of a primitive society. Vergennes and the court diplomats knew that this simplicity was deceptive, this innocence an illusion, but they were delighted nevertheless to witness Franklin's personal triumph at the moment when the United States of America was being recognized for the first time before the world as an independent nation.

26. *Les Françaises*

ALTHOUGH there is no doubt that Franklin enjoyed his
political triumphs—receptions at court; dinners offered
by ministers, diplomats and fellow scientists—these gala affairs
did not take place every night. Franklin's greatest social pleasures came, as usual, from his feminine companions, the earliest
of whom were Mlles. Biheron and Basseport, to whom he had
been introduced by Dubourg. Mlle. Biheron, distinguished as
the first woman to make a career by modeling human bodies in
wax, was a precursor of the famous Mme. Tussaud. An intelligent woman, dedicated to science, she earned the patronage of
several doctors but lacked the feminine attributes to captivate
Franklin. She belonged to a category of useful Frenchwomen of
a certain age, who, in his own words, were "so ready to do you
service, and from their knowledge of the world know so well
how to serve you wisely." Franklin valued these women, he said,
because they had no designs upon his person, but he had his
own clearly defined designs upon certain other Frenchwomen.

After Franklin had been living in Passy for about a year, he
developed intimate friendships with two accomplished ladies
living close to him, one noted for her charm and beauty, the
other for her wit and wide acquaintance in the literary world.
The charmer was Mme. d'Hardancourt Brillon, a matron in her
middle thirties, "one of the handsomest women in France,"
according to Mrs. John Adams, and married to a somewhat
indifferent husband twenty-four years her senior, who was occupied with his own love affairs. The lady of the salon was Mme.
Catherine Helvétius, widow of the materialist philosopher, then
in her late fifties. Franklin, in his seventies, seriously courted
both ladies. As a general rule, he dined at least once a week with
Mme. Helvétius and visited Mme. Brillon every Wednesday and
Saturday. By and large, Mme. Brillon supplied the place for-

merly occupied by Caty Ray and Polly Stevenson, while Mme. Helvétius—closer to Franklin's age and more appropriate for actual lovemaking—replaced Mrs. Stevenson. Turgot was Franklin's rival for the hand of Mme. Helvétius, and on one occasion all three went through great emotional turmoil when Franklin pressed her to marry him. With Mme. Brillon marriage was out of the question, but Franklin constantly urged her to grant him more favors than her intellect alone could provide. Whether he succeeded in his aim we shall never know, but if, as some critics assert, their relations were "almost certainly platonic," it was only because the lady wanted to keep them that way. The evidence of Franklin's past life and his ardent pursuit of Mme. Helvétius indicates that he would have enjoyed physical contact with Mme. Brillon as well. If Franklin was constitutionally able, he meant business when he made advances to Mme. Brillon, and the evidence indicates that he was in excellent shape for a man of his age—witness, for example, his swimming in the Seine with his grandson.

"All his proportions proclaim the vigor of Hercules," wrote du Pont de Nemours somewhat later, "and at the age of 75 years he still has the suppleness and nimbleness of his character." John Adams remarked that at the age of seventy-odd Franklin "had neither lost his Love of Beauty nor his Taste for it." He even cited Franklin's sexual proclivities as rendering him unfit for his diplomatic post. "You may depend upon this," he wrote to one of his supporters in the Continental Congress, Elbridge Gerry (3 September 1783) , "the moment an American minister gives a loose to his passion for women, that moment he is undone; he is instantly at the mercy of the spies of the court, and the tool of the most profligate of the human race." The French conceived of Franklin as a patriarch, but he did not always behave like one.

Franklin's relations with Mme. Brillon were curiously two-fold, one side paternal, the other frankly erotic. In one role he gave her advice on her family affairs and delivered moralistic sermons. In the other he behaved as an ardent suitor. One cannot say which of these was dominant. But even when Franklin approached Mme. Brillon as her "good Papa," he blended an incredible combination of Don Juanism and moralizing—probably because he enjoyed both strains and both came naturally.

In one of his earliest epistles to Mme. Brillon, 10 March 1778, Franklin revived his playful philoprogenitiveness, although he no longer saw himself as the great procreating force. "People commonly speak of *Ten* Commandments," he wrote. "I have been taught that there are *twelve*. The first was, *Increase* and *multiply* and replenish the Earth. The *twelfth* is, A new Commandment I give unto you, *that ye love one another.*" He hoped that his "keeping religiously these two Commandments, tho' not in the Decalogue," would compensate his so often breaking the one forbidding coveting one's neighbor's wife which, he confessed, he broke as often as he saw or thought of his lovely spiritual guide, Mme. Brillon. To bolster his suit, he cited the opinion of "a certain Father of the Church," another of his mythical authorities, "that the most effectual Way to get rid of a certain Temptation, is, as often as it returns, to comply with and satisfy it." Almost a century later Oscar Wilde made a similar remark: "The only way to get rid of a temptation is to yield to it."

In most of their dialogues, Franklin talked roguishly about his physical needs and Mme. Brillon—definitely a tease—talked self-righteously about her virtue. She may in actuality have been as virtuous as her pose, but John Adams, who was shocked by meeting the mistress of M. Brillon at the family table, believed also that "Madame Brillon consoled herself by the Amitie of Mr. Le Vaillant" [probably Franklin's close friend Le Veillard].

Once Franklin recounted the story of a beggar asking a rich bishop for alms. The bishop refused even the most trifling coin but offered instead his benediction. This the beggar spurned, arguing that if it had been worth anything the bishop would not have parted with it. According to Franklin, Mme. Brillon was trying to put him off with the same kind of niggardly Christian charity. "Rich like an archbishop in all the Christian virtues and morals," she could have sacrificed to him "a small part of one of them without the loss being visible." Mme. Brillon replied that Franklin was a sophist and his argument founded on a false principle. The kind of charity he had asked of her could be found anywhere, she maintained, and he would not suffer by her refusals. She had given him her friendship—and had loved him as a daughter should love her father. The other treasure which had been entrusted to her— her virtue—she was obliged to guard for ever and could not relinquish even to him.

This way of arguing, Franklin refuted in turn by an allegorical tale. If one begged the loan of horses from a friend, who replied that he would like very much to oblige but was afraid that the journey would damage his horses, would not one be justified in assuming that he prized his horses more than his friendship? But if one were to lend one's horses willingly, it would be logical to assume that the lender loved his friend more than his horses. And Franklin was ready for the sacrifice of his own "large and handsome" steeds.

On another occasion Franklin remarked that if he were the angel Gabriel he would like to carry Mme. Brillon on his wings. His friend replied that even then she would not travel with him although "no longer very young nor a virgin." She was "afraid of miracles happening, and miracles between women and angels might not always bring a redeemer."

Franklin lived on the best of terms with M. Brillon, a plump tall man who admired him both as a distinguished philosopher-diplomat and, as he once said, a connoisseur of feminine flesh. Like Franklin, M. Brillon suffered from the gout. Toward the close of 1780, when Franklin was immobilized by a severe attack lasting eight weeks, Mme. Brillon dedicated to him a verse fable entitled "The Sage and the Gout," suggesting that the enjoying of too many mistresses had something to do with the malady. Franklin characteristically replied that the reverse was true: when he was young and enjoyed the favors of the sex more than at that moment, he had no gout; therefore if the ladies of Passy would show "more of that species of Christian charity" which he had often recommended in vain, he might rid himself of the ailment. Mme. Brillon affected to criticize his logic. One could say with equal reason, she affirmed: "when I threw myself out of the window, I did not break my leg." Her only consolation for gout and other pains was patience. "We are in the midst of frosts, and must wait patiently for the bright sun, and while waiting, amuse ourselves in the moments when weakness and pain leave us some rest." She offered to make Franklin's waiting as easy as possible and in a very tantalizing and equivocal phrase suggested that she would even go as far as his kind of Christian charity. Only Mme. Brillon's original French conveys the piquancy of her wordplay, which undoubtedly delighted its recipient "vous ne douttés surement pas que je ne m'en acquitte de mon mieux pour vous, jusqu'à la charité chrétienne, c'est à dire votre charité chrétienne *exclusivement.*"

As an exercise in patience, Franklin wrote a dialogue of his own, *Between the Gout and Mr. Franklin,* now interesting chiefly because of its depiction of the manner in which Franklin passed his time at Passy. In the morning, instead of working up an appetite for dinner by salutary exercise, he read books, brochures or gazettes, for the most part not worth the pains. Then he dined grandly: "four cups of tea and cream with one or two slices of bread and butter and the butter covered with slices of smoked beef." After dinner he sat at his desk, writing or talking to people on business, and finally playing chess for two or three hours. Even when visiting Mme. Brillon, he failed to take advantage of the hundred steps in her garden leading from the terrace to the lower plain. Installing himself on the terrace at six o'clock, he praised the beautiful view, called for tea and the chessboard, and remained glued to his seat until nine o'clock.

Franklin wrote his dialogue in French, one of a series of exercises in which he engaged in order to master the language. When Mme. Brillon complimented his style—more successful, she felt, than the cold purity of grammarians—Franklin was encouraged to send her other efforts in the language. He humorously referred to his difficulties with genders.

Masculine and feminine things (apart from moods and tenses) have been giving me trouble for 60 years. I once hoped that at 80, I could be delivered, but here I am at 4 times 19 [1782], which is very close; nevertheless these French "feminines" still disturb me. This should make me happy to go to paradise, where they say these distinctions are abolished.

With Mme. Brillon, Franklin enjoyed all the fresh pleasure of a young lover—and went on living from day to day as though he would live forever. The great pains that he took to learn French can be explained only by his youthful disposition. He refused to be satisfied with conversational French, which would have sufficed for his business relations, but wrote out endless exercises, translations and original pieces to master grammar and idiom.

When Franklin visited the house of Mme. Brillon, she and her friends and daughters sometimes entertained him with instrumental and vocal concerts, which he called his "Opera." After one of these sessions in August 1778, during which they had discussed the controversy then raging between the rival music schools of Gluck and Piccini, Franklin exposed the triviality of the controversy by means of a meditation on "The Ephemera" as emblems of human life. One of these little flies, while priding himself on his personal longevity—the great age of seven hours—lamented nevertheless the brevity of existence and, by showing the limited effect of his political struggles and philosophical studies, illustrated the negligible importance of all human concerns. Franklin based his moral reflections on an essay he had taken from a British periodical, *The Freethinker,* and published in the *Pennsylvania Gazette* in 1735, a remarkable illustration of his power of memory. For him, life was a continuous whole. In his old age he remembered and understood the problems of youth as well as many of his own early exploits.

His famous story of the whistle grew out of a tender letter which Mme. Brillon wrote to him in the autumn of 1779, when she was away from Passy and felt nostalgia for their Wednesday and Saturday nights—the teas, chess, music and kisses. Only the conviction of happiness in another life, she reflected, can help us bear the ills of this one. But in the meantime, she reasoned, "let us get all the good we can out of this poor world of ours."

Perhaps since his friend was out of reach, Franklin answered

in a highly serious tone instead of repeating his ordinary ama-
tory symbols. We might, he suggested, draw more good from
this world than we do, and avoid the greater part of our miseries,
if we could keep from false estimates of the value of things. To
illustrate his point, he told the now-familiar story of his childhood purchase of a whistle and stressed the universal folly of
paying too much for one's trinkets.

One of the pleasant pastimes which Franklin shared with
Mme. Brillon was his favorite game of chess. On one Saturday
night when Mme. Brillon was taking her bath, he and Le
Veillard began playing while she was in her covered tub, and
Franklin was so carried away with the competition that he kept
her in that uncomfortable position for hours. He prided himself
on his good play and his exemplary conduct during the game,
going so far as to print a set of rules, *The Morals of Chess,* the
earliest of a number of little pieces which he called bagatelles
and printed on a private press which he had set up in his
headquarters at Passy. Franklin seemed in practice, however, to
have been a bad loser and a rude opponent. Apparently he
made no attempt to conceal his impatience when his adversaries
took a long time in moving, drumming on the table with his
fingers as though playing the piano. This habit was so disagreeable that his host Chaumont once tactfully observed that Franklin had forgotten to condemn one bad practice in his *Morals of
Chess.* When Franklin asked what it was, Chaumont explained
by making the gesture. Franklin replied, "Nonsense, it is a
bagatelle, not worth speaking about." His rationalism apparently did not extend to his own foibles.

Franklin, who always regarded himself as possessing an
optimistic attitude toward life, wrote for Mme. Brillon a commentary on the "two Sorts of People in the World, who with
equal Degrees of Health & Wealth and the other Comforts of
Life, become, the one happy, the other unhappy." Here he
expanded observations he had made back in his early days in
Pennsylvania concerning two of his friends named Potts and
Parsons. The economically privileged Parsons "always had the
means of happiness, without ever enjoying the *thing;* the other
had always the *thing,* without ever possessing the *means.* Par-

sons, even in his prosperity, always fretting; Potts, in the midst of his poverty, ever laughing." Franklin concluded, therefore, "that happiness in this life rather depends on internals than externals; and that, besides the natural effects of wisdom and virtue, vice and folly, there is such a thing as a happy or an unhappy constitution."

Most of Franklin's bagatelles written for Mme. Brillon represented an attempt to amuse through useful truth or, as Georgiana Shipley put it, by means of "conversation badinante et réfléchie." The one which enjoyed greatest vogue in France was a brief parable entitled simply *Conte,* a tale advocating religious toleration which Franklin adapted from a sermon he had heard Whitefield deliver in Pennsylvania many years before. A man of good will, but no religion, dreams of entering heaven. St. Peter orders the applicants of each sect to join their coreligionists, but Montrésor has none. "Enter any way," says the saint; "and find a place where you can." Mme. Brillon had her own version.

When I go to paradise, if St. Peter asks me of what religion I am, I will reply—of that in which one believes the Eternal Being perfectly good and indulgent—of that in which one loves those who resemble the Eternal Being. And I loved with idolatry Dr. Franklin. St. Peter will say: I am sure. Enter and take a place near Mr. Franklin. You will find him seated near the eternal.

One Wednesday during a week when Franklin had been working until four every morning, he visited Mme. Brillon after a heavy meal and stayed on the terrace, half dozing, half talking with another of her neighbors, while she descended to the garden below. Realizing that he was almost exhausted with fatigue, Franklin went home before eight o'clock and before Mme. Brillon returned to the terrace. When she discovered that her favorite guest had skipped away, she blamed her neighbor and protested to Franklin the next day. She repeated these jealous scenes so frequently that Franklin drew up a playful treaty of peace for her consideration. As a preamble, he pointed out that she was being unreasonable in refusing him everything physical in their love (except a few polite kisses) and at the same time begrudging him other feminine companions. His admiration, esteem, respect and even affection could be shared with other ladies, he said, without in any sense diminishing the amount he felt for her—just as the sweet sounds she produced on the piano could be heard by twenty people, and each would receive equal pleasure. Eventually Mme. Brillon saw his point and was able to admit that "all women love you, because you love them all."

Regardless of the extent to which Franklin succeeded in persuading Mme. Brillon to grant the intimacies he was constantly pursuing, he met a firm rebuff in an almost equally persistent attempt to arrange a marriage between William Temple Franklin and Mme. Brillon's daughter Cunégonde. Having spoken privately to M. Brillon without success, Franklin then wrote a persuasive letter to Madame, urging the match.

His personal motive, he said, was the strong attachment he felt for the entire Brillon family, and he wished to conserve by the marriage the tender ties of their friendship. So great was his desire for the union that he was willing to abandon his own daughter and remain for the rest of his life in France—further evidence that he had never had great affection for Sally. "Having almost lost my daughter by the vast distance between us," he wrote, "I hope to find one in you and another in your daughter to care for my old age if I remained in France and to close my eyelids after my death."

Brillon père in an initial interview with Franklin made two objections to his proposal: the possibility that Billy might take Cunégonde back to the United States, and the difference in religion. Franklin disposed of the first objection by affirming his own intention to remain in France for the rest of his life. He shrugged off the second with the typically deistical maxim that all religions are the same—it is only the trappings which are different. A stick of sugar candy could be wrapped in blue, green or yellow paper, but it is only the sugar itself which counts.

One might think that the Brillons would have considered it a great honor to ally themselves by marriage with Franklin, but even with his concessions they politely rejected the match. They gave as reasons that Billy would find it impossible to give up his national connections and remain in France; that M. Brillon needed a son-in-law who would carry on his business; and that the difference in religion still mattered. Even though they agreed philosophically with Franklin, they were obliged to follow the customs of their own country. It may be that the Brillons had more important reasons which they left unexpressed. Perhaps they recognized an element of instability in Billy's character. He had become known in Paris for cultivating the airs of a dandy, and public opinion was sometimes shocked by the discrepancies between Franklin's sage and patriarchal bearing and his grandson's open hedonism. Perhaps also they were deterred by Billy's illegitimacy, a circumstance which Franklin could hardly have kept secret. If the Brillons shared the common European obsession with family background, their attitude may have had something to do with Franklin's later writings against hereditary aristocracy.

Franklin left less of a record of his relations with Mme. Helvétius than with Mme. Brillon—perhaps because they were more serious and more compromising. But we learn many details of the liaison from several French men of letters who were friends of both parties. These include Turgot, Cabanis, and the Abbés Morellet and de La Roche.

Turgot, the tough economist who had written the famous Latin epigram about Franklin, had been in love with Mme. Helvétius even before her marriage—and after she became a widow he revived his suit with as much ardor as before. Cabanis and the two abbés resided with Mme. Helvétius on her estate at Auteuil, furnishing a permanent core for her salon, which was called The Academy in honor of the more than thirty members of the French Academy who attended regularly. The Abbé de La Roche was a former Benedictine whom Helvétius had converted to a secular way of life and who remained attached to Mme. Helvétius through gratitude. Cabanis, a protégé of Turgot, had come to Paris to study medicine. In January 1777, when Franklin passed his seventy-first birthday, Cabanis was twenty, the Abbé de La Roche was thirty-seven, and Morellet was fifty, a significant ladder of years if the rumors about Mme. Helvétius had any foundation. John Adams, in viewing the lady's "handsome" masculine entourage, caustically remarked, "The Ecclesiasticks . . . I suppose have as much power to Pardon a Sin as they have to commit one, or to assist in committing one. Oh Mores! said I to myself."

Mme. Helvétius never showed any outward preference to any one of her retinue, and all joined Franklin in paying homage to her as Notre Dame d'Auteuil. All three looked up to Franklin and wrote valuable recollections after his death. During the agreeable luncheons when Franklin came to visit, they discoursed on topics befitting their intellectual attainments —morality, politics and philosophy. Franklin used his charm and coquetry on Mme. Helvétius; the Abbé Morellet, regaling himself with rich cream, used his formal logic to prove propositions which nobody believed. All were so happy, according to the Abbé de La Roche, that they would have renounced future paradise in order to keep on living this way for eternity. Indeed, Franklin once sent Mme. Helvétius a note indicating that if he were called to paradise that morning he would ask permission to wait until after one o'clock to receive a kiss which she had promised earlier at Turgot's house.

Franklin also tried his hand at some of the unconventional logic in which Morellet excelled. "In sharing other things," he remarked to his hostess, "each one of us has only one part; but in sharing pleasures with you, my portion is doubled. The Part is greater than the whole." He once spoke of their being "4 Mesdames Helvétius" and proposed to keep one of her selves "at his house for life," allowing the other three to remain at Auteuil for Cabanis and the two abbés.

Speaking for men of learning of all sorts, Franklin told Mme. Helvétius that they found "in your sweet society that charming benevolence, that amiable attention to oblige, that disposition to please and be pleased, which we do not always find in the society of one another. It springs from you; it has influence on us all, and in your company we are not only pleased with you, but better pleased with one another and with ourselves."

At times Franklin would offend the good lady—or she would

pretend to be offended. "Sitting in state on her sofa," she would extend "graciously her long, handsome arm" and say " 'la; baisez ma main: je vous pardonne,' with all the dignity of a sultaness." Franklin once remarked that he and the deceased husband of Mme. Helvétius had loved the same studies, "the same friends, *and the same wife.*"

The degree of intimacy which Mme. Helvétius openly revealed in her relations with Franklin may be judged from the shocked narrative of Abigail Adams (Mrs. John Adams) in 1784.

. . . She ran forward to him, caught him by the hand: "Hélas! Franklin"; then gave him a double kiss one upon each cheek, and another upon his forehead. When we went into the room to dine, she was placed between the Doctor and Mr. Adams. She carried on the chief of the conversation at dinner, frequently locking her hand into the Doctor's, and sometimes spreading her arm upon the backs of both the gentlemen's chairs, then throwing her arm carelessly upon the Doctor's neck.

I should have been greatly astonished at this conduct, if the good Doctor had not told me that in this lady I should see a genuine Frenchwoman, wholly free from affectation of stiffness of behavior, and one of the best women in the world. For this I must take the Doctor's word; but I should have set her down for a very bad one, although sixty years of age, and a widow. I own I was highly disgusted, and never wish for an acquaintance with ladies of this cast. After dinner she threw herself on a settee, where she showed more than her feet. She had a little lap-dog, who was, next to the Doctor, her favorite. This she kissed, and when he wet the floor she wiped it up with her chemise. This is one of the Doctor's most intimate friends, with whom he dines once every week, and she with him.

Franklin seems to have pushed his romantic proposals with greatest ardor during the last months of 1779. One evening in September of that year, he was responsible for disarranging the "beautiful hair" of Mme. Helvétius, which was always a source of pleasure and admiration to him. The next morning he sent a note, half apologetic, half audacious.

. . . If that Lady loves to spend her days with him, he would love as much to spend his nights with her; and as he has already given her many of his days, although he has so few of the remainder of his to give, she would seem ungrateful never to have given him a single one of her nights, which pass continually as pure loss, without giving happiness to anyone, except Poupon [a cat or lapdog].

Early in the next year Franklin made it clear that he wanted marriage, and he pressed her so far one evening that she declared her determination to remain single for the rest of her life. This "barbarous resolution" disturbed Franklin so much that he dreamed—or said he dreamed—that he had died and been transported to the Elysian Fields. Here he talked to Helvétius and was surprised to learn that the philosopher was completely uninterested in news of his widow. He had taken a new partner, who turned out to be Franklin's former wife, Deborah, whom Franklin described as less beautiful than Mme. Helvétius but with as much wit and good sense. When Franklin attempted to claim her, she spurned him with the callous remark that nearly half a century with him had been enough—now she had a new connection for eternity. Franklin applied his dream to his pursuit of Mme. Helvétius by appealing, "Let us avenge ourselves."

Franklin reworked this story from his *Craven Street Gazette*, as a means of recovering from the blow of the refusal of Mme. Helvétius, and allowed copies to circulate which he had printed on his private press in order to create the impression that he had been only partly serious in his courtship—that he was governed by gallantry rather than passion. For this reason, his letter found its way into the *Correspondance littéraire* of Grimm and his collaborators, where it was published in April 1780.

But Franklin's courtship was no joke either to him or to Mme. Helvétius. In the wake of Franklin's continued declarations of love, her tranquility was so upset that she decided to leave Paris and spend the summer at Tours. Turgot, who reported her "rather bad condition" to du Pont de Nemours, found this decision highly reasonable, "not only for her own tranquility" but also to re-establish calm in Franklin's head, which was "agitated so improperly."

Franklin himself had written more than twenty years previously, "Old Age . . . is subject to Love and Follies as well as Youth." The "Amours of Age," he had observed, may seem ludicrous to others, but to the old they are highly serious. This was the last emotional turbulence of his life. When Mme. Helvétius returned to Auteuil, Franklin had resumed his philosophical detachment, and the luncheons continued with undisturbed harmony.

From the moment of Franklin's arrival in Paris, his fame continued to grow, particularly among the common people, thanks in great measure to two separate translations of *The Way to Wealth* (one by Barbeu Dubourg) which enjoyed a tremendous vogue, the people associating Poor Richard with his creator. Clay medallions of various sizes bearing Franklin's portrait were sold in incredible numbers, "some to be set in the lids of snuffboxes, and some so small as to be worn in rings." As he wrote to his daughter (3 June 1779), "these, with the pictures, busts, and prints, (of which copies upon copies are spread everywhere,) have made your father's face as well known as that of the moon." Even Louis XVI succumbed to the mode to the extent of presenting one of the court ladies a handsome chamber pot with Franklin's physiognomy on the inner base. Giving in to his penchant for punning, Franklin deduced from the number of dolls made in his image that he was truly *"i-doll-ized* in this country."

In return, Franklin was pleased with the French character, particularly the politeness and civility he encountered on every hand. He found the French "a most amiable Nation to live with," a people free from a national vice such as English pride or Scotch insolence. As he wrote to Josiah Quincy (22 April 1779):

They have some Frivolities, but they are harmless. To dress their Heads so that a Hat cannot be put on them, and then wear their Hats under their Arms, and to fill their Noses with Tobacco, may be called Follies, perhaps, but they are not Vices. . . . In short, there is nothing wanting in the Character of a Frenchman, that belongs to that of an agreeable and worthy Man.

The ladies, conforming to the tradition of politeness, he explained to his niece (11 October 1779), were particularly attentive.

Somebody, it seems, gave it out that I lov'd Ladies; and then every-body presented me their Ladies (or the Ladies presented themselves) to be *embrac'd*, that is to have their Necks kiss'd. For as to kissing of Lips or Cheeks it is not the Mode here, the first, is reckon'd rude, & the other may rub off the Paint. The French Ladies have however 1000 other ways of rendering themselves agreeable.

One of them, Mlle. Le Veillard, the young daughter of the superintendent of the Passy water system, urged him to be bolder in his approaches to French girls. They were, she affirmed, more interested in kissing him than he assumed. In future, she advised, he should take it as a good sign when a French girl made no resistance and should immediately become more enterprising.

John Adams for all his stern morality was jealous of Franklin's success with the French ladies. He complained to Mercy Warren, poetess and historian, that Frenchwomen "have an unaccountable passion for old age, whereas our countrymen, as you know madam, have rather a complaisance for youth, if I remember right." It had not occurred to him that perhaps men and women in France would prefer sexual partners with the maturity which experience brings.

Despite the admiring ladies and friendly priests with whom Franklin was surrounded, he still was not sufficiently enamored of his French surroundings to wish the Gallic way of life to be impressed upon his younger grandson, Benjamin Franklin Bache. In the spring of 1779, Franklin sent him to Geneva so that, as he explained to several friends, his grandson could be educated as a "Presbyterian as well as a republican" and thus be fitted for his future life in America. Almost ten years old, Benny had learned Latin, writing, arithmetic and dancing and spoke French better than English. He traveled to Geneva in the company of a kindly Swiss gentleman, Cramer, who later treated him as one of his own family. Quite significant is the fact that Franklin sent his grandson out of France, a country he knew well, to Switzerland, a country he had never visited, entirely because of his belief that in Geneva "the proper Principles" prevailed.

⟡⟡*⟡*⟡*⟡*⟡*⟡*⟡*⟡*⟡*⟡*⟡*

27. *Private and Official Diplomacy*

IN FEBRUARY 1778 Franklin took his grandson to visit Voltaire, who had just returned to Paris, after a long exile, to receive the homage of the literary world. At the bedside of the great *philosophe,* Franklin asked him to bestow his blessing on the wide-eyed boy, a symbolic benediction of the new world by the old which instantly became the talk of all Europe. Virtually every writer who has portrayed the scene has indicated that William Temple Franklin, then approaching his eighteenth year, was the grandson for whom Franklin asked Voltaire's blessing. Yet all evidence indicates that it was the eight-year-old Benjamin Franklin Bache, a much more suitable recipient. Franklin in his writings does not refer to the incident, but Voltaire discusses it in two letters. Although the patriarch was very ill, twenty visitors besides the Franklins were at his bedside when Franklin made his request. According to Voltaire, he said merely "God and Liberty," and the witnesses shed tears of sensibility. In the eyes of a contemporary journalist, however, both philosophers had contrived a cynical and irreligious show, and Franklin's request was "indecent, puerile, low and . . . of a derisive impiety."

Two months later, the two sages performed again at a public meeting of the Academy of Sciences. Franklin, as usual, was clad in the utmost simplicity: a plain suit of dull yellow cloth, a white hat, blending with his grey hair. His corpulent body appeared enormous in contrast to Voltaire's emaciated skin and meager bones. The audience, delighted at seeing the two patriarchs side by side, screamed for some formal recognition of the historic significance of the encounter. John Adams, one of the spectators, wrote that neither of our philosophers seemed to divine what was wished or expected; they however took each other by the hand. But this was not enough. The clamour continued until the explanation came out: *Il faut s'embrasser à la française*. The two aged actors upon this great theatre of philosophy and frivolity then embraced each other by hugging one another in their arms and kissing each other's cheeks, and then the tumult subsided.

All Europe thereafter, said Adams, spoke of the sublime spectacle of Solon embracing Sophocles.

Another sharp-tongued observer, Mme. d'Épinay, reported that "as soon as Franklin and Voltaire appeared at the theatre, in the parks, or at the academies, the shouting, the clapping of hands, never finished. When princes appeared—no commotion. But Voltaire sneezes, Franklin says 'God bless you,' and the din begins all over again."

But on 30 May, Voltaire died. He and Franklin had been members of the same Masonic lodge at Passy, the Nine Sisters (the Muses), and after Voltaire's passing the membership considered Franklin as filling the void in their group. In a printed testimonial, the officers announced their pleasure in welcoming Franklin, the friend of the great man who had passed on. To them, Franklin was "a *philosophe* for whom the old world had long envied the new, who knew how to conquer the terrifying mysteries of both Nature and politics: a man useful to the entire universe by his labors, protector and lawmaker of his country by his courage and enlightenment." Later in the year, when the Nine Sisters held a commemorative ceremony for Voltaire, Franklin and the authors of a eulogy and a tableau were crowned with laurel wreaths, after which all three went to place their wreaths at the foot of Voltaire's bust.

In his official life, Franklin's greatest burdens were two of his American associates, particularly his fellow commissioners Arthur Lee and Ralph Izard. The latter, a native of South Carolina, had been appointed commissioner to Tuscany but had to wait in Paris for that court to recognize American independence. Both Lee—with some reason—and Izard—with absolutely none at all—nurtured ill feelings against Franklin, on the grounds that he held too much power in his hands and that he carried out negotiations with the French court without consulting them sufficiently.

In January 1778, in consequence of overlooking Izard's advice on some minor aspect of the treaty, Franklin received a querulous letter complaining of his lack of politeness and sincerity. Franklin tried—but not very hard—to smooth his colleague's ruffled feelings by a mitigating letter offering the maxim that one should "always . . . suppose one's Friends *may be right* till one *finds* them wrong." Two months later, Franklin was still attempting to make up for the supposed slight. According to Jefferson, "Izard hated Franklin with unparalleled bitterness," and Franklin had a hard time coping with his sullenness. Since it was Franklin's policy not to return anger for anger or not to exhibit his feelings if anger should arise despite his care against it, he disposed of his scorn for Izard by drawing up another literary hoax, a *Petition of the Letter Z,* presumably "From 'The Tatler,' No. 1778." Actually it is an imitation of the remonstrance of the family of the "ixes" in Steele's *Tatler* 35, a further example of Franklin's extraordinary memory. In Franklin's satirical *jeu d'esprit,* "the letter Z, commonly called *Ezzard, Zed,* or *Izard,*" argues that since he is as eminent as any other letter, there is no reason "why he should be treated as he is, with disrespect and indignity." Z petitions, therefore, that he be placed at the head instead of the tail of the alphabet and that he be substituted for S in the word *wise.* The Tatler decides, however, "That Z be admonished to be content with his station, forebear reflections upon his brother letters, and remember his own small usefulness, and the little occasion there is for him in the Republic of Letters."

In his marginal notes, Franklin explained that Izard, jealous of Lee's being appointed commissioner for France, showed himself as "little, hissing, crooked, serpentine, venemous" and then accused Lee of having the same characteristics. Since Izard never saw this squib, it had no effect upon his ill-feeling. Franklin later admitted that he could have avoided Izard's enmity "by paying him a compliment," but he never bothered to do so.

Lee, equally resentful of Franklin's popularity with the

French court, proved much more troublesome to Franklin, since he was vested with more authority than Izard—on paper as much as Franklin himself. When Lee early in 1778 suggested that Jonathan Williams, Jr., be appointed a commercial agent at Nantes to replace the deceased incumbent, Thomas Morris, Franklin received the suggestion coldly and advised his grand-nephew not to accept the post—he did not "wish to be much oblig'd to" Lee "and less to be a little oblig'd." Later events showed the wisdom of Franklin's attitude.

The Thomas Morris at Nantes was a brother of Robert Morris, the Philadelphia financier. The restless Lee soon discovered that Silas Deane, the original commissioner, had been carrying on private commercial transactions for Robert Morris in addition to negotiating for the Congress. He grew suspicious that Morris and Beaumarchais were involved in a swindle and communicated his suspicions to Congress. Franklin at first took Deane's side. When Congress recalled Deane for an inquiry into his affairs, Franklin wrote to Henry Laurens, president of the Congress (31 March 1778), "I have no doubt, that he will be able clearly to justify himself. . . . I esteem him a faithful, active, and able Minister." The next day Franklin wrote to Lee protesting against his insinuations that both Franklin and Deane were guilty "of Negligence or Unfaithfulness." Lee then learned that Gérard, recently appointed minister to the Congress, was to accompany Deane to America, and was outraged that he had not been consulted. Informing Franklin that he considered the arrangement a personal affront (2 April), he asked sarcastically whether this was the example which Franklin in his "superior wisdom" thought proper to set "of order, decorum, confidence, and justice." When Franklin received this letter, implying that its author was "the only careful, honest Man" of the three commissioners, he was unable to contain himself. "I do not like to answer angry Letters," he wrote (3 April). But he felt called upon to warn Lee that his "Sick Mind, . . . forever tormenting itself, with its Jealousies, Suspicions & Fancies" would drive him to real insanity unless he could control it. By putting these sentiments on paper Franklin relieved his own feelings and therefore did not send the letter.

The next day, when he had calmed down even more, he answered Lee's objections point by point with great moderation.

Lee could be obnoxious to Franklin not only because of his suspicions and accusations but because of his powers as joint commissioner. He even proposed that Franklin accept joint auditing of expense accounts and that he examine Deane's private mail, proposals which Franklin indignantly rejected.

In July 1778, Franklin wrote to James Lovell of the Committee for Foreign Affairs protesting against the folly of maintaining three commissioners at the French court (four, if the interfering Izard were to be counted). Although three may have been needed for the treaty, Franklin argued, the subsequent business did not justify the expense of three separate accounts. Humorously Franklin suggested that each spent nearly as much as Lord Stormont, notorious in Paris for his stinginess. When the British ambassador was recalled consequent to the Franco-American treaty, he placed an advertisement in the newspapers offering for sale a large quantity of unused table linen. The Paris wags found this quite credible, for Stormont was never known to have entertained. John Adams, arriving as Deane's replacement, 9 April 1778, turned out to be even more economical than Stormont, and Franklin had to persuade him that the cost of clothes should be "reckoned among expenses for the public." In the article of frugality, Poor Richard had to take second place to Lee and Adams.

Franklin received Adams with great cordiality, which was only natural since, as Adams remarked in his diary, until then they had "always agreed in their Opinions and Sentiments of public affairs." Franklin took Adams with him wherever he was invited—to dinner with Turgot on the evening of his arrival, to meet Mme. Brillon on the next evening, and to a similar social gathering virtually every day. In less than two weeks, Adams's New England conscience began to bother him, and he wrote in his diary, "These incessant Dinners and dissipations were not the Objects of my Mission to France."

Adams soon learned about the feud between Franklin and Lee, which he characterized as disagreeable and pernicious in its effects both at home and abroad. When Izard tried to turn

Adams against Franklin by denouncing him as a "man of no Veracity, no honor, no Integrity," Adams at first adopted a neutral position. He acknowledged that there had been disputes in Pennsylvania and England concerning Franklin's "moral and political character" even though "he had generally maintained an honorable character in the world." Before long, however, Adams leaned more and more to the Lee-Izard side.

Late in May, Adams complained in his diary that the

Life of Dr. Franklin was a Scene of continual discipation. . . . It was late when he breakfasted, and as soon as Breakfast was over a crowd of Carriages came to his Levee . . . with all Sorts of People. . . . These Visitors occupied all the time, commonly, till it was time to dress to go to Dinner. He was invited to dine abroad every day and never declined unless when We had invited Company to dine with Us.

Adams always went with Franklin until he began refusing invitations so that he could find time to study French "and do the Business of the mission." Obviously he considered Franklin's dinner engagements one form of dissipation, not realizing that Franklin was conforming to diplomatic custom. He was an expert at conducting high finance and high politics with glass in hand.

After the signing of the treaty, the chief function of the commissioners was to keep pressing for more and more French money and aid to be channeled to America. Franklin turned over the account keeping to Adams but took sole charge of another vital function, which he was forced to keep secret—even from his fellow commissioners. This was the negotiation with Great Britain for an eventual peace. Almost from the moment of the French treaty, Franklin stayed in contact with a stream of private and official peace emissaries from England. Before the end of 1778, he had, according to rumor, received twenty of these "ambassadors." One of them was James Hutton, a leader in the Moravian church, highly esteemed by George III, who had been with Franklin on his military expedition in 1755–1756. Franklin had absolutely no proposal to offer. All he would say was that peace could be obtained if Britain would drop all pretensions to sovereignty, but it would not be a lasting one unless Britain also tried to regain the respect and affection which America formerly felt. Later he told Hutton, as he was to impress upon all the other British emissaries, that if England failed to make peace with America before going to war with France, America would remain faithful to its ally and refuse a separate peace.

Shortly afterwards, David Hartley, a Member of Parliament who had been trying to secure humane treatment of American war prisoners, wrote to Franklin, urging him not to allow American gratitude toward France to lead his nation into a permanent pro-French attitude. Franklin replied with a famous allegory:

America has been *forc'd* and *driven* into the Arms of France. She was a dutiful and virtuous Daughter. A cruel Mother-in-Law turn'd her out of Doors, defam'd her, and sought her Life. All the World knows her Innocence, and takes her part; and her Friends hope soon to see her honourably married.

Frequently Franklin regarded his country metaphorically. Later that year he spoke against moves to seek alliances and aid from other European courts on the grounds "that a young State like a young Virgin, should modestly stay at home, & wait the Application of Suitors for an Alliance with her. . . . Our Virgin," he continued, "is a jolly one; and tho at present not very rich, will in time be a great Fortune." England he called a bull, which needed to be kept quiet and orderly. Franklin's political metaphors were more than mere figures of speech. He actually believed that political relationships were essentially of the same nature as personal relationships, and a large measure of his success as a diplomat came from his profound human understanding. Throughout his negotiations he constantly stressed the parallel between the personal and the political.

Franklin distinguished Hartley and his other friends from the war party in England, but he exhorted Hartley, as spokesman for the Whigs, not to "join with the Tories in supporting and continuing this wicked War against the Whigs of America." When Adams got wind of the correspondence with Hartley, he remonstrated with Franklin against carrying on political discussions. Franklin tactfully explained that he could do nothing to prevent Hartley from coming to Paris but offered to decline engaging in private conversations.

In the midst of the communications from his personal friends, Franklin received a mysterious packet labeled "Secret and Confidential—Read this in private." It turned out to be an appeal for Franklin to support a plan of reconciliation in return for which the British court would grant him and his confidants places, pensions and peerages. Although the missive was signed "Charles de Weissenstein," Franklin believed that it originated with George III himself. He was instructed to reply by dropping a letter at a prearranged time in the church of Notre Dame for a stranger who would be known by a rose in his hat. Franklin indignantly repudiated these furtive dealings coupled with dishonorable rewards—doubly reprehensible since they were proffered at the very moment the British court was sending commissioners to treat openly with the Congress.

This court had seemed to be willing to try violence to dispose of Franklin if bribery did not work. Hartley warned him in the spring to be on his guard, but Franklin answered that "having nearly finished a long life" he set "but little value on what remains of it. . . . Perhaps the best use such an old fellow can be put to, is to make a martyr of him." He was careful enough, however, not to respond to an anonymous note in May, asking him to meet the writer in the Jardins des Eaux at Passy, realizing that "some bad purpose" was intended. Reports of his assassination had been anonymously circulated in London, indicating that his fears and suspicions had a solid basis. But Franklin was more disturbed by the gadflies Izard and Lee than by British threats.

In the meantime, Deane, back in Philadelphia, had published "An Address to the People of America," 5 December 1778, exposing the factionalism which had torn apart the American government and charging that Congress had refused to listen to his defense. When Adams heard about it in February, he told Franklin to his face, knowing full well that Franklin had taken Deane's side over Lee, that "it was one of the most wicked and abominable Productions that ever sprung from an human heart."

Early in 1779, Franklin received the welcome news that Congress had accepted his recommendation of limiting the commissioners to one and that he had accordingly been appointed sole plenipotentiary. Acquainting his grandnephew Jonathan Williams, Jr., with the development, 13 February, Franklin expressed his pleasure that the appointment "was not obtained by any Solicitation or Intrigue on my Part" and affirmed that he had not written a syllable to any person in or out of Congress "magnifying my own Services or diminishing those of others"—an honest claim which Lee, certainly, would never have been able to match.

The latter, unable to accept the older man's appointment with good grace, expressed his pique by refusing to give up a number of official papers which he had at various times taken from Franklin's house. In going through the accounts, Franklin had come across a note in Lee's handwriting on the back of one of Jonathan Williams's statements, affirming his conviction that Williams had in his hands over one hundred thousand livres of public funds—in more direct language, that Franklin's relative was an embezzler. Franklin's misgivings about Lee's being involved in the appointment of Williams were now amply justified. But he realized that Lee's accusation was a touchy subject, transcending wounded sensibilities and petty reprisals. When huge amounts of public funds were in question—received and dispersed for the most part in great secrecy—it was necessary to subject the honesty of any individual under suspicion to a rigid scrutiny, completely without regard to rank or connections.

Franklin immediately wrote to Lee (13 March 1779), asking his reasons for believing that Williams had public funds in his possession, so that justice could be done and the money recovered. Two weeks later, after Lee had refused to comply with this request, Franklin drew up another letter, challenging Lee to produce or retract. Repudiating all suggestions of favoritism toward his nephew, he affirmed "that a Rogue living in a Family is a greater Disgrace to it than one *hang'd out* of it." But, on the other hand, if Williams were innocent, justice demanded that his name be cleared immediately. At the last minute, Franklin did not send Lee the letter, "merely to avoid a continu'd Altercation, for which I had neither Time nor Inclination, and he abundance of both."

Actually Franklin had no doubts whatsoever about his nephew's integrity, and he ordered an immediate inquiry to settle the matter. He believed that he could have avoided a good deal of Lee's ill will if he had not shown his own good will toward Deane. Lee's nasty insinuations were subsequently investigated by a group of impartial merchants at Nantes, who exonerated Williams completely.

Franklin had no real uneasiness about the concomitant efforts of Lee and Izard to injure him in Congress, trusting in his good name, the affection of the people, and the justice of Congress. He was surprised to learn, however, that his two enemies had attacked him for using his grandson, William Temple Franklin, as his secretary. Their objections were based not on nepotism but on the theory that Temple could not be trusted because of the Tory principles of his father. Later Franklin discovered that his friend Daniel Roberdeau had used this argument in the Pennsylvania delegation against the appointment of Franklin as plenipotentiary and carried it so forcefully that Pennsylvania was the only state to vote against him. The apparent repudiation by his own state—a situation which Franklin could not understand at his distance from Congress—was not really a lack of confidence but a reflection of the havoc the Deane imbroglio had created in local politics. As a result of the investigation into Deane's affairs, Pennsylvania dramatically split into two factions—the wealthy merchants such as Robert Morris, who supported Deane, and the citizens' groups, led by Paine and Roberdeau. Although Paine never criticized Franklin, his former patron, Lee's innuendos of connivance between Deane and Franklin temporarily turned popular opinion away from Franklin.

Yet Franklin resolutely refused to take sides in the altercation in which Lee accused Deane of peculation and Deane resolutely denied the charges. He wrote to James Lovell (17

October 1779) that if Deane had embezzled or used public money for his own interests "I give him up." But "as yet, I think him innocent."

As late as 30 March 1782, after Deane had published in England a series of letters hostile to Congress, Franklin still voiced no suspicions of his financial integrity. As Deane continued to sit "croaking at Ghent, chagrined, discontented, and dispirited," Franklin condemned him only for turning against his friends and losing faith in their principles. But he coldly reminded him that his own countrymen now considered him as having abandoned the cause of his own country "and as having with Arnold espoused that of its enemies." In Franklin's opinion, Deane had blighted his life by allowing his resentments and passions to overcome his reason and judgment. Yet in writing to Robert Morris, 14 December 1782, Franklin still believed that "poor unhappy Deane" had been hardly dealt with over his accounts.

Franklin's enemies touched a vulnerable spot when they attacked him through his grandson. Franklin exposed the effects of their "malignant natures" in a rare display of feeling in a letter to his son-in-law Richard Bache, 2 June 1779.

It is enough that I have lost my *son;* would they add my *grandson?* An old man of seventy, I undertook a winter voyage at the command of the Congress, and for the public service, with no other attendant to take care of me. I am continued here in a foreign country, where, if I am sick, his filial attention comforts me, and, if I die, I have a child to close my eyes and take care of my remains.

Having voluntarily sent his younger grandson to Geneva, Franklin was all the more dependent upon William Temple.

Because of his gout, Franklin was unable to go through the ceremony of presenting his credentials as sole plenipotentiary to Louis XVI until 23 March 1779. After his audience, he went the rounds visiting the royal family with the other ministers and was on his feet so much that he was disabled for almost another week. Ruefully he remarked to one of his friends, "There seems . . . some Incongruity in a *Plenipotentiary* who can neither stand nor go." But he consoled himself with the reflection that physicians had not made up their minds whether gout "is a Disease or a Remedy."

Franklin's commission had been brought to him by Lafayette, who returned to his native land covered with glory. This was probably Franklin's first meeting with the young nobleman who had bled for America and left it with universal applause. In the ensuing months, as Franklin planned a land-sea operation to be conducted jointly by Lafayette and John Paul Jones, he spent many happy hours with the French military leader.

During August, Lafayette took charge of preparations in Le Havre for an actual attack upon English soil, and William Temple Franklin, who was also in Le Havre, became so excited over the campaign plans that he asked Lafayette whether he could participate in the action. Lafayette then suggested to Franklin that the young man be made his aide-de-camp, a proposal which Franklin passed along to Vergennes, at the same time expressing his own willingness that his grandson "should embrace this Opportunity of improving himself, in seeing the excellent Discipline of the Armies of France, hoping he will thereby be render'd more capable of serving his Country & our Common Cause." Louis XVI immediately granted Temple the uniform of an aide-de-camp, but since the operation was never carried out he presumably never wore it.

When Adams learned that Franklin had been appointed sole plenipotentiary, he saw himself stranded in Europe with no job and no duties. Franklin advised him to wait for Congress to appoint him to some new post and to send him a new commission, but Adams with typical suspicion and lack of charity thought that Franklin was trying to detain him in Europe to prevent him from revealing to Congress his poor opinion of Franklin's handling of the Paris mission. He returned to America, therefore, sailing in June 1779 with the new French plenipotentiary to America, the Chevalier de La Luzerne, and his secretary Barbé-Marbois. In lengthy conversations on the long voyage, Adams tried to poison the latter's mind against Franklin. "As a Legislator of America," Adams said, "he has done very little. It is universally believed in France, England, and all Europe, that his Electric Wand has accomplished all this Revolution but nothing is more groundless." Soon after arriving in America, Adams repeated his grievances to Thomas McKean, a Pennsylvania congressman, revealing his own jealousy and envy. Franklin, he charged, "knows too little of American affairs, of the politics of Europe, and takes too little pains to inform himself of either to be sufficient for all these things—to be ambassador, secretary, admiral, consular agent. . . . He is too old, too infirm, too indolent and dissipated to be sufficient for the discharge of all of the important duties." Franklin would have been the first to agree that he had too many functions to perform, but the dissipation existed only in Adams's provincial interpretation of Franklin's social life.

As the months passed, Franklin became more and more optimistic over the outcome of the war—and many times predicted a mass emigration from Europe after victory. As he wrote to Samuel Cooper, 22 April 1779, "We have only to persevere to be great and happy." His only general criticism of his country was directed against its "extravagant Luxury." When orders from America for large quantities of tea and "Gegaws and Superfluities" passed his desk, he felt shock and disappointment. This he made clear in letters to political leaders—and made his sentiments even more emphatic to his family. "The Folly of our People, and the Avidity of our Merchants," he told Josiah Quincy (22 April 1779), "concur to weaken and impoverish our Country."

When his daughter asked him to send her some black pins and feathers from France, he refused to cater to her extravagance. "If you wear your cambric ruffles as I do, and take care not to mend the holes," he suggested, "they will come in time to be lace; and feathers, my dear girl, may be had in America from every cock's tail." Here Franklin was attempting to impose the same double standard on his daughter which he had formerly applied to Deborah. If Franklin's own court clothes were simple, he was motivated by preference, not thrift. For once Sally did not take her father's rebuke in silence but justified her desire for "a little finery." She had been invited to the French

ambassador's balls as well as to a day's festivities with General
and Mrs. Washington, and she spiritedly replied to her father,
"You would have been the last person, I am sure, to have wished
to see me dressed with singularity."

The standard of living which Franklin enjoyed at Passy,
although not grandiose, was certainly ample and eminently
comfortable. Receipted bills and contracts with his kitchen staff
provide vivid testimony. His *maître d'hôtel* agreed to furnish
for each of his dinners:

a joint of beef, veal or mutton; fowl or game; two kinds of relish,
two kinds of vegetables, and a platter of pastry, with hors d'oeuvres
of butter, pickles, radishes etc.; for dessert two kinds of fruit in
winter and four in summer; two fruit preserves; one platter of
cheese, one of biscuits, and one of bonbons; ice cream twice a week
in summer and once in winter.

In February 1778, Franklin had more than a thousand
bottles in his wine cellar of the following varieties: red Bordeaux wine 85 bottles; sherry 148; white Bordeaux 34; red
Bordeaux 1761 vintage 15; red Bordeaux bottled at Passy 159;
champagne 21; sparkling wine 326; red Burgundy 113; ordinary
red wine 209; ordinary white wine 10; half bottles of unknown
vintage 12; rum 48. In September of 1782, his inventory showed
1,203 bottles. When we contrast these inventories with those of
his barrels of beer in London, we come to the unmistakable
conclusion that both Franklin's taste and his standard of living
had risen greatly in the intervening years.

In Passy Franklin wrote new drinking songs, sending copies
to both the Abbé de La Roche and the Abbé Morellet, and he
dedicated to the latter a humorous dissertation in French expounding the merits of wine-drinking over water-drinking and
appealing to his friend never to embarrass him by offering to
mix water with his wine.

One of Franklin's dinner guests on 1 March 1779, the Duc de
Croÿ, reported an excellent cuisine amid surroundings which
reflected simplicity and economy. Among other dishes, there
were two kinds of hot fish, an excellent pudding, and pastry for
dessert. Franklin, who at the time was recovering from an attack

of gout, consequently ate only a single daily meal but a copious one. He consumed large slices of cold meat and drank two or three bumpers of good wine. Franklin had enormous sums of money under his personal control, and he believed that a minister of a sovereign state should make a good appearance in the world.

In addition to supervising all the commercial transactions between Paris and Philadelphia for continuing the war effort, Franklin was responsible for the financial disposition of all American vessels and privateers which touched at French ports, a staggering burden even with the aid of his grandson. When John Adams returned to America, Franklin urged him to press upon Congress the need of appointing consuls to assume all mercantile business. Even the main business of the mission—supplying the revolutionary armies on a credit furnished by the French court—proceeded largely on trust. Franklin placed orders, hoping that the funds would be available to pay them, and paid bills, assuming that the merchants had delivered the goods.

One can understand why a man like Deane could be accused of peculating enormous sums of money and nobody be able to prove or disprove the allegations. Franklin wrote to John Jay in October that he had not been able to obtain a sight of Beaumarchais's accounts, and even if he had them in his possession he would not have been competent to interpret them.

In addition to struggling to keep funds available to pay bills pouring in upon him from all parts of Europe, Franklin was caught up in bitter dissension between John Paul Jones and Pierre Landais, a French captain enlisted in the American navy. Jones and some of Landais's men accused Landais of firing into his own flagship during an engagement, and both sides appealed to Franklin for adjudication. Franklin, recognizing that a clash of personalities was involved, referred the matter to Congress for decision, while trying to maintain both captains in active service. He wrote to Sartine, French minister of marine (20 March 1780), virtually exonerating Landais; yet in addressing Landais himself (12 March), Franklin termed him so litigious and quarrelsome that peace and order could not prevail under his command. In the contrary emphases of these letters Franklin revealed both his generosity and honesty.

Franklin removed Landais from command of his ship, the *Alliance,* and replaced him by Jones. But instead of sailing for America as ordered, Jones returned to Paris, and during his absence Arthur Lee persuaded Landais to seize command again and sail to America with Lee as a passenger. Lee presumably wanted to reach Congress to place charges against Franklin before any of Franklin's explanatory documents could arrive. In America, there was even talk that he had bribed the crew of the vessel. At this time, Franklin believed that Lee was "the most malicious enemy I ever had," perhaps not realizing that Parson William Smith was a deadlier one. Smith was motivated by intense hatred and envy; Lee merely by a quarrelsome nature and an overblown sense of self-importance. Smith cared nothing about distorting truth if he could score against his enemy. Lee, despite all his faults, was as honest as John Adams. Even Franklin admitted that Lee's "charges are so frivolous, so ill-founded, and amount to so little, I esteem them rather as panegyrics upon me."

As soon as Lee and Landais arrived in America, Lee circulated the report that the captain was insane. Franklin agreed that the accusation was well founded—as would have been equally the same accusation brought by Landais against Lee. "For tho' neither of them are permanently mad, they are both so at times."

Franklin was thoroughly disgusted with the temperamental exhibitions and personal ambitions of his ship captains, writing to his grandnephew (27 June 1780), "I will have absolutely nothing to do with any Squadron Project. I have been too long in hot Water, plagu'd almost to Death with the Passions, Vagaries, and ill Humours and Madnesses of other People." Even the intrepid John Paul Jones fell under his displeasure and was given essentially the same advice which Franklin had previously offered to Izard. "If you should observe on occasion to give your Officers and Friends a little more Praise than is their Due, and confess more Fault than you can justly be charged with, you will only become the sooner for it, a Great Captain."

John Adams came back to Paris in February 1780 with a new appointment as commissioner to take charge of eventual peace negotiations. The frigate he sailed on also carried a gift box for Franklin of two dozen bars of handmade crown soap from Jane Mecom. Adams and Franklin lived on polite terms in Paris, even though neither Adams nor the Congress at first informed the older man of the nature of the younger man's mission. Unfortunately, Adams, who was temperamentally unable to sit idly by waiting for the end of the war, tried to push himself forward as an adviser to Vergennes without Franklin's knowledge. In so doing, he ran afoul of Vergennes and virtually destroyed his usefulness at the French court. Since nobody at this time was in a position to talk peace, Adams began writing unsolicited letters to Vergennes about military and diplomatic affairs completely out of his province, affirming in essence that France should not expect gratitude from the United States since French aid to the American cause produced equal benefit to France. To make matters worse, he proposed to continue offering his advice and sentiments directly "in person or by letter to your excellency, without the intervention of any third person." Vergennes, instead of welcoming Adams's opinions, found his correspondence unauthorized and impertinent and turned it over to Franklin with the request that he report it to Congress for censure.

Franklin thereupon assured Vergennes that Adams's behavior and opinions represented his personal indiscretion and not instructions from Congress and that Congress would moreover deplore them. To Congress, Franklin duly reported that Adams had offended the French court and added that his interference represented one of the inconveniences of having more than one minister at the same court: "the Impressions made by one, and intended for the Service of his Constituents may be effaced by the Discourse of the other." Franklin had followed—and affirmed that he would continue to follow—a policy of expressing unfailing gratitude toward the French court; whereas Adams advocated "a little apparent Stoutness, and greater air of Independence and Boldness in our Demands."

Franklin then informed Adams of Vergennes's request to have the distasteful correspondence brought before Congress and at the same time gave Adams the opportunity "to write something for effacing the Impressions" his opinions had made, but Adams preferred to let them speak for themselves. He, nevertheless, felt injured, aggrieved and resentful.

Vergennes, in the meanwhile, prevailed upon Congress to instruct Adams to clear everything with the French ministers. His instructions actually called upon him "to make the most candid and confidential communications upon all subjects to the ministers of our generous ally, the King of France; to undertake nothing in the negotiations for peace or truce without their knowledge and concurrence; and ultimately to govern yourselves by their advice and opinion." Vergennes also pulled strings in Philadelphia to have Franklin appointed as a joint peace commissioner, so that eventually the negotiations would be conducted by Adams, Jay and Franklin.

Franklin's continued loyalty to the French court decided his opinion on the most knotty political question confronting the American nation in 1780—whether America would continue the war for the sake of her allies beyond the point where a peace would be advantageous for her alone. Thomas Paine in his *Common Sense* had set forth the doctrine that American interest would be best served by disentanglement from European political affairs—a doctrine which John Adams accepted and carried even further. David Hartley, in the midst of the war, astutely realized that the disentanglement doctrine would support his arguments for an early peace and separation of America from France. On 29 June 1779, he sought to convince Franklin that "there is no common sense" in the Americans "entangling themselves in all the Gothic crusading follies of European nations, amongst whom the only definition of man seems to be a fighting animal, or the gladiator of God's creation to mangle and destroy his works." Franklin in reply (2 February 1780) admitted to holding "a very singular Opinion, . . . that there hardly ever existed such a thing as a bad Peace, or, a good War," but declared that this opinion would not dispose him to make any improper concessions. Unequivocally he declared that "the Destruction of our whole Country, and the Extirpation of our whole People" would be "preferable to the Infamy of abandoning our Allies."

28. *Abuse and Vindication*

THE winter which began in December 1780 ushered in the
most difficult year of Franklin's life, during which several
times he lost his genial good humor and bitterly resented the
apparent ingratitude of his countrymen. During the two previous months he had been incapacitated by the torment of the
gout, and, even after the attacks had subsided, his tender feet
and feeble knees made going up and down stairs exceedingly
difficult and inconvenient. On one occasion he was even forced
to decline a dinner engagement with Vergennes because of the
strict diet he had been forced to adopt. While recovering the use
of his limbs, he received the disheartening news from America
(10 January 1781) that his enemies had been plotting to move
in Congress for his recall. In England, the report was even
circulating that Franklin had resolved to return to America to
confront and refute his envious and malignant accusers. The
dismal tidings from home combined with the effects of his long
illness made Franklin feel his age, and he even predicted to
Vergennes that he would not long have any concern in worldly
affairs.

Yet during the same period, when the weary diplomat
detected a melancholy tone in the correspondence of Charles
Dumas, acting as the American agent in Holland, Franklin
exhorted him to be of good courage and recommended walking
as "an excellent thing for those whose employment is chiefly
sedentary."

The rumbles in Congress had of course been initiated by
Lee and Izard, who had started a campaign against Franklin as
soon as they landed in America. Since their complaints were
based on nothing more substantial than misunderstandings and
personal jealousy, they were of necessity vague and general.
Izard, however, insinuated that Franklin had engineered

"something criminal in money matters" respecting the crew of the *Alliance,* and when pressed to account for Franklin's motive had feebly answered that he had wanted to assist his grand-nephew, Jonathan Williams, Jr., in making a fortune.

Although few besides Lee would have joined Izard in affirming that "the political salvation of America depends upon the recalling of Dr. Franklin," other Americans wondered whether perhaps there were some substantial reasons for replacing him, for instance, his advanced age. More important was his entanglement in the controversy between Deane and Lee, which Thomas Paine, as a critic of Deane, had kept on the front page of American newspapers throughout 1779. Paine even engaged in an altercation with Sally Franklin Bache over Deane, and feeling ran so high that he would no longer thereafter remove his hat to her. Although Paine kept his former patron's name out of his attacks on Deane, Lee himself saw to it that Franklin's friendship and tacit support of the luckless diplomat came to the full attention of Congress. Franklin for once had misjudged the tide of affairs, having unequivocally declared that there was nothing against Deane except "Prejudices that Time will cause to vanish by showing they were groundless." Paine and Lee thundered so furiously against Deane that they drowned out his weak defense before Congress.

Unfortunately Franklin was somewhat like Deane in having no one to look out for his interests in Congress. Harassed by his mercantile and consular duties, lacking a secretarial staff, alternately tormented by the gout and titillated by the dinners and receptions of his feminine friends and diplomatic associates, he kept his reports to Congress at a minimum. When Gérard had been French minister in Philadelphia, he had noticed that Franklin "never writes," and Vergennes soberly conceded that Franklin's "age and his love for tranquillity give him an apathy incompatible with the business with which he is charged, which is all the more painful to me as there are important matters about which this minister keeps silent, while the good of the cause would require that he transmit his opinion to the Congress." The members of Congress, losing contact with their representative in the nation's most crucial diplomatic service, naturally developed doubts of his efficiency. Franklin enjoyed his role as a diplomat but constantly complained about the need of performing consular duties as well. In mercantile matters, he admitted, he was like a man walking in the dark.

Although only Massachusetts and South Carolina approved the motion to recall Franklin, Congress showed its lack of confidence by voting to send an envoy extraordinary to Paris to support Franklin's appeal for French aid. Chosen for reasons of psychological propaganda, the new envoy, Colonel John Laurens, was an experienced military man and son of a former president of Congress, Henry Laurens, who had been taken prisoner by the English and was at that moment suffering in the Tower of London. Since Colonel Laurens had personal knowledge of the needs of the army, it was thought that his representations would carry authority and persuasiveness. Unfortunately he was only twenty-six years old and not skilled in either diplomacy or human relations. Informing Thomas Paine that he lacked sufficient acquaintance with political affairs and the resources of the country to undertake the mission, he asked Paine to accompany him as his secretary, but John Witherspoon and some other congressmen, nettled by Paine's difficult personality, opposed the request and another South Carolinian, Major William Jackson, was chosen instead. Paine obligingly went along anyway, paying his own expenses.

Although Franklin reacted with normal resentment to the humiliating news of Laurens's appointment (13 February), he sat down to address another appeal to Vergennes, one of the most astute letters in the diplomatic history of the Revolution. By his adept portrayal of the distress in America, coupled with renewed warning of the dangers of British victory, Franklin made it seem impossible for France to do anything else but increase its material assistance. Forcefully he introduced Washington's appraisal of the situation: one of two things was essential, either America must sue for peace or receive "the most vigorous Aid of our Allies, particularly in the Article of *Money*." Should this aid not be given in time, Franklin solemnly warned, the English would recover the American conti-

nent and become "the *Terror of Europe*." This was virtually
the only time in the easygoing diplomat's negotiation with the
French court that he deviated from his steadfast policy of
showing constant gratitude in order to apply the pressure of life-
or-death urgency and exposure to a common threat, the rarity of
the appeal undoubtedly counting as an important element in its
effectiveness.

In addition to the pressure from Congress for reports and
increased funds, which weighed heavily on Franklin's spirits, he
was also beset by local creditors and agents, who daily presented
notes and invoices for payment and kept him in a flurry of worry
and irritation. While waiting for a reply from Vergennes, he
wrote, 22 February 1781, with grim humor to Adams, who was
attempting to negotiate a treaty in Holland, that if his endeavors
should fail and his notes not be backed up, he would be "ready
to break, run away, or go to prison with you, as it shall please
God."

His patience running short, Franklin wrote again to Vergennes, asking in a businesslike manner exactly what he should
report to Congress might be expected in French aid. This time
Vergennes immediately granted an audience. He explained that
the King and his advisers strongly opposed any American attempt to borrow money anywhere in Europe, since the effort in
other countries would depreciate American credit and compete
with the court's own financing, but that the King would contribute as an outright gift the amount of six million livres.
Franklin's diplomacy had once more triumphed. He had obtained as a gift that which Laurens would have been glad to
receive as a loan—and he had made his coup before Laurens
landed on French soil. But as Franklin reported his success to
Samuel Huntington, president of Congress, he concealed any
note of self-satisfaction. He devoted half of his letter to a
personal concern, however, a request that Congress would both
replace him and provide some permanent employment as a
diplomat for William Temple Franklin. As reasons for wishing
to be relieved of his duties, he gave his age, his poor health, and
his service of fifty years in public affairs. He also proposed to

submit his accounts for examination as well as Deane's—even
though he may have been hard put to produce Deane's if he had
ever been called upon to do so.

It is more than likely that the shrewd ambassador submitted
his resignation to force Congress to make a definite choice
between him and his enemies. Congress would either have to
accept his resignation or repudiate and silence the Lee-Izard
faction. Without any doubt Franklin hoped that Congress
would take the latter course, but he was psychologically
prepared to be replaced, admitting to John Adams "that another may easily be found" who could better execute his duties.
He kept an eye open for suitable candidates, once writing to
John Jay that he hoped Jay would be his successor and at
another time asking Lafayette to advise Congress on the subject
when the time came to appoint "a fitter Man." As soon as Jay
learned of Franklin's resignation, he wrote to the president of
Congress, urging that it not be accepted; he soberly testified
that the great man's letters bore no mark of age and that his
reputation and respectability were everywhere acknowledged in
Europe. Franklin certainly had no desire to return to America
immediately, for he had requested permission to remain in Paris
as a private citizen at least as long as the war should last. He was
not afraid of being caught up in the American turmoil but felt
that Europe was a better milieu for spending "the Evening of
Life more agreeably in philosophic Leisure." He had even
tentatively considered a tour of Italy and Germany with his
grandsons.

Laurens, Paine and Major Jackson landed at L'Orient on 9
March and were met by Jonathan Williams, Jr., who rode with
Paine as far as Nantes. Paine spoke freely as usual about his
personal likes and dislikes, admitting that he stood on the side of
Lee and regretted Franklin's support of Deane. Williams found
Paine to be a "pleasant as well as a sensible man" despite his
adherence to the wrong party. When the group arrived in Paris,
Franklin did all in his power to make Laurens at home and
assure the success of the mission. The young envoy was indefatigable and "took true Pains," but "he *brusqu'd* the Ministers

too much." On one occasion he grossly violated protocol by addressing Louis XVI at a court function. All that Laurens succeeded in obtaining by himself was permission to float a loan of ten million livres in Holland on the credit of the French court. When Laurens and Paine embarked for America on 1 June, taking with them two and a half millions in silver, however, both attributed the gift to the efforts of Laurens alone.

Franklin generously reported to Congress, 14 May 1781, that Laurens's "indefatigable Endeavours . . . brought the good Dispositions of the Court to a more speedy Determination of making an addition than could well have been expected so soon after the former Grant." But he explained more bluntly to William Carmichael, 24 August, that since the promised Dutch loan had not been negotiated, Laurens "in fact obtained nothing." Franklin's less tolerant estimate had been caused primarily by the antics of Major William Jackson, who proceeded to Amsterdam after Laurens and Paine had returned to America. There Jackson attempted to persuade Adams and the other Americans that Laurens had "done more for the United States in the short time of his being in Europe, than all the rest of their Diplomatic Corps put together." He had also demanded that Franklin turn over to him one and a half millions for transfer to America and had backed up his demands by affirming that Franklin had no right to dispose of the money since Laurens had obtained it without his knowledge or concurrence. This affirmation Franklin could not let pass, even though he would "rather lend a little Credit to a Friend, than take away from him." Jackson's impertinent reproaches made it necessary for Franklin to insist that the truth be on record. He absolutely refused to surrender any of the money in his keeping, since it was needed for unpaid bills and there was no indication that it would be replaced by the projected loan in Holland. Were he to let this money out of his hands, he maintained, the credit of America would be destroyed.

Perhaps to Jackson and Adams, whom Jackson kept fully informed, it may have appeared that Franklin had personal reasons for not relinquishing these funds. Years after Franklin's death, Adams actually raised the question whether Franklin had appropriated large sums of public money to his own use, and Jackson may have contributed to his suspicions. When Jackson continued to press his demands for the one and a half millions, now using the argument that Franklin's refusal was holding up a costly convoy for America, Franklin lost all patience. He derided the "young Gentleman" for his superior airs and reminded him that the "special Department and Employ in public Affairs, of which you are so vain, is but of yesterday, and would never have existed but by my Concurrence." Two months later Jackson discovered that the captain with whom he had been scheduled to sail with the money was actually in league with the British, and he then wrote Franklin a humble letter of apology, acknowledging that America was indebted to Franklin's prudence for the preservation of her property.

Although Franklin sought always to maintain an unruffled exterior, he was sensitive to the attacks of his enemies and naturally resented them. Lee and Izard, he considered his "open, and, so far, honourable Enemies; . . . the Adams, if Enemies, . . . more covered," and therefore more to be feared. He confided to Francis Hopkinson, 13 September 1781, that Lee and Izard "are unhappy, that they cannot make everybody hate me as much as they do; and I should be so, if my Friends did not love me much more than those Gentlemen can possibly love one another." Franklin even converted his enemies to some practical purpose, admitting in the spirit of La Rochefoucauld that they had probably been of some advantage to him. "They serve to put us upon correcting the Faults we have, and avoiding those we are in danger of having. They counteract the Mischief Flattery might do us, and their Malicious Attacks make our Friends more zealous in serving us and promoting our Interest." Yet Franklin was not always philosophical on the subject. He confided to Samuel Cooper, 15 May 1781, that "I know not whether a *Belly-full* has been given to anybody by the Picking of *my Bones,* but picked they now are, and I think it time that they should be *at rest.*" In weighing the rewards of public service in a letter to Robert Morris, 26 July, he pointed out that the Publick is often niggardly, even of its Thanks, while you are sure of being censured by malevolent Criticks and Bug-writers, who will abuse you while you are serving them, and wound your Character in nameless Pamphlets; thereby resembling these dirty stinking insects that attack us only in the dark, disturb our Repose, molesting and wounding us, while our Sweat and Blood are contributing to their Subsistence.

In this rhetoric, Franklin was going all the way back to an essay in the *Pennsylvania Gazette* in which he had chastised those ill-natured people who "delight (to use their own Phrase) in *touching gall'd Horses* that they may see 'em winch." These disagreeable wretches he had compared to "the meanest Insect, the trifling Musketoe, the filthy Bugg," in their "Power of giving Pain to Men."

The envy displayed by Franklin's political associates reminded him of the similar petty behavior of his scientific rivals, a subject which had been out of his mind for many years. Now he contemplated the irrationality of a system of moral relationships in which a man makes enemies by "labouring disinterestedly for the Good of his Fellow Creatures," observing to Jan Ingenhousz that

there are Minds who cannot bear that another should distinguish himself even by greater Usefulness; and tho' he demands no Profit, nor any thing in Return but the Good Will of those he is serving, they . . . would give the Credit . . . to a Man that liv'd 3000 years ago, or at 3000 Leagues distance, rather than to a Neighbour or even a Friend.

The disillusioned public servant's morale took a decided turn for the better, however, when he learned late in August that Congress had done him the honor of refusing his resignation. It would be, he fancied, a double mortification to his enemies "that I should ask as a Favour what they hop'd to vex me by taking from me; and that I should nevertheless be continued." Now he was prepared to "buckle again to Business, and thank God that my Health & Spirits are of late improved." Probably the improvement was a direct result of his vindication in Congress rather than merely coincidental.

Early the next month Franklin received overwhelming public testimony of his vindication as a diplomat—news that he had been appointed joint peace commissioner. He immediately presented his credentials at court together with his instructions to confide entirely and implicitly in Vergennes. Vergennes was naturally delighted since, through his henchman La Luzerne, minister plenipotentiary in Philadelphia, he had arranged in Congress both the appointment and the instructions. La Luzerne had craftily pointed to the continued need for French aid to persuade Congress to add Franklin, Jay, Laurens and Jefferson to the ranks of the peace commissioners and to instruct them to undertake nothing without the knowledge and concurrence of Vergennes. The latter's manipulation of Congress might appear to support John Adams's later charge that Franklin was subservient to French policy makers rather than the exponent of an independent American policy. It would be more exact to say that Franklin's views usually coincided with those of the French. When they eventually came into conflict, Franklin had no hesitation about taking an independent road.

When writing about his joint appointment to Adams, who was still in Holland (12 October), Franklin cleverly played down the importance of his role in order to make it more palatable to his usually disgruntled countryman. He had never known any peace, he affirmed, even the most advantageous, "that was not censured as inadequate, and the makers condemned as injudicious or corrupt." The peacemakers may be blessed in heaven, he added, but in this world "they are frequently *cursed.*"

Soon Franklin had cause to exult over the most exciting and welcome news of the year, the rout of the British and surrender of Cornwallis at Yorktown. The tidings reached Franklin during the night of November 19–20, 1781, and he joyfully sent out announcements before daybreak, expressing the victory in symbolic terms: "The infant Hercules in his Cradle has now strangled his second Serpent, and gives Hopes that his future History will be answerable."

Even the weather seemed to bring the year to a joyful close in keeping with Franklin's improved health and high spirits. By

Christmas there had not been the slightest appearance of winter, and on that day he dined with the doors and windows open as in summer. Yet he was careful not to let the military victory overcome his sense of reality. Knowing that war is filled with a variety of uncertainties, he adopted the same attitude of imperturbability toward "this game" of war which he customarily showed in his chess games. In bad fortune, he hoped for good; and in good, he feared the bad.

❖❖*❖*❖*❖*❖*❖*❖*❖*❖*❖*

29. *Political and Private Gratitude*

IN THE midst of his multitudinous functions—ranging from those of ambassador to purchasing agent—Franklin still had time for writing journalistic propaganda, which he felt was vital for ultimate victory.

In the summer of 1782 he circulated another of his political hoaxes—a supposed "Supplement" to a Boston newspaper containing two presumed letters: one to the governor of Canada accompanying a grisly collection of scalps taken by the Indians from the frontier inhabitants of the middle colonies; and the other from John Paul Jones, rejecting the title of pirate which the English had given him and applying it to the King of England for the "horrible wickedness and barbarity" he had practised toward the Americans. In the ironical vein of Swift, Franklin gave a circumstantial account of the arrival of the wagonload of scalps in Boston:

Thousands of People are flocking to see them this Morning, and all Mouths are full of Execrations. Fixing them to the Trees is not approved. It is now proposed to make them up in decent little Packets, seal and direct them; one to the King, containing a Sample of every Sort for his Museum; one to the Queen, with some of Women and little Children; the rest to be distributed among both Houses of Parliament; a double Quantity to the Bishops.

At the same time, Franklin reacted with horror to reports from home that frontier Americans had slaughtered an entire community of peaceful Moravian Indians. These abominable murders even challenged his belief in the orderly dispensation of providence in this world. "Some of the Indians may be suppos'd to have committed Sins," he mused, 7 July 1782, "but one cannot think the little Children had committed any worthy of Death." Franklin laid even these frontier murders at the door of George III. Since the wicked King had furnished some savages with hatchets and knives and promised them a bounty for the scalps of defender-farmers, Franklin reasoned, the exasperated frontiersmen had retaliated against all Indians without discrimination. The extent of the British Monarch's crimes made Franklin see the impossibility of "giving equivalent Punishment to a wicked Man in this Life," and he was therefore the more convinced "of a future State, in which all that here appears to be wrong shall be set right, all that is crooked made straight."

Accounts of British atrocities and the horrors of a naval engagement between the fleets of Rodney and De Grasse, "the Decks covered with mangled Limbs, and Bodies dead or dying," seem to have immersed Franklin into a mood of deep gloom during which he expressed his most pessimistic view of humanity. He confided to Joseph Priestley, 7 June 1782, that he was filled with admiration the more he discovered about inanimate nature, but the more he learned of animate or moral nature the more he became disgusted. Men seemed to take

more Pride and even Pleasure in killing than in begetting one another; for without a Blush they assemble in great armies at Noon Day to destroy, and when they have kill'd as many as they can, they exaggerate the Number to augment the fancied Glory; but they creep into Corners, or cover themselves with the Darkness of night, when they mean to beget, as being asham'd of a virtuous Action.

Franklin had even begun to wonder "whether the Species were really worth producing or preserving." We might therefore conclude that at this moment he was ready to abandon his lifelong advocacy of an augmented population, were it not for the recent discovery of Robert Newcomb that Franklin in these somber lines was only paraphrasing a passage from Montaigne. His bitterness was merely temporary and histrionic.

Three months later, in a mellow mood engendered by the progress of peace negotiations, Franklin affirmed the superior importance of moral attainments over scientific discoveries to Sir Joseph Banks, president of the Royal Society (9 September) .

Now he longed to be occupied once more with philosophic discussions of projects "to extend the Power of Man over Matter, avert or diminish the Evils he is subject to, or augment the Number of his Enjoyments." But much as he praised scientific investigation in theory, he never repudiated his youthful maxim that political responsibilities supersede the pleasures of scientific research. In a letter to the Abbé Soulavie in the same month he revealed a quizzical scepticism concerning the relationship of science to absolute truth: "Superior beings smile at our theories, and at our presumption in making them."

This is the period when Franklin wrote a mildly scatological satire on the Royal Academy of Belgium, one of the ubiquitous eighteenth-century scientific and literary establishments parallel to Franklin's own American Philosophical Society. It reveals that Franklin did not consider sacred all projects alleged to be "scientific," that his native good humor helped to carry him through periods of depression, and that his youthful zest for punning had not in the least diminished. According to the custom of the time, the Academy offered a prize for the best answers to some academic problem or query, and Franklin found the one supposedly current both trivial and ridiculous—"on some given figure inscribe the maximum number of times some smaller figure, also given, may be inscribed." In a mock-serious letter addressed to the Academy, Franklin proposed an alternate question, "To discover some Drug wholesome & not disagreeable, to be mix'd with our common Food, or Sauces, that shall render the Natural Discharges, of Wind from our Bodies, not only inoffensive, but agreeable as Perfumes." The rest of the letter extols the advantages of Franklin's proposal in measured phrases graced with such ingenious puns as "avoid the Report," "give Vent to his griefs," and "one's Scent-iments." Quoting Bacon, Franklin claimed that the desired invention would bring philosophy home to men's business and bosoms.

In dispatching a copy to William Carmichael in Spain (23 January 1782), Franklin recognized that his puns could not be translated and that they had too much "*grossièreté* to be enjoyed by polite Spaniards." And in the next year, reminded of his hoax by the first balloon experiments with "inflammable Air," Franklin sent a copy to Richard Price, remarking that their mutual friend Priestley, "who is apt to give himself *Airs,* [!] and has a kind of Right to every thing his Friends *produce* upon that Subject" might like to see it as well.

In a similar jocular mood, Franklin congratulated Lafayette, whose wife after a seven-months' pregnancy had given birth to a daughter named Virginia after the American state (17 September 1782). Still dominated by his philoprogenitive sentiments, the indulgent patriarch hoped that Mme. de Lafayette would produce a child for each of the thirteen states, "but as that may be in the common Way too severe a Task for her delicate Frame, and Children of Seven Months may become as Strong as those of Nine," he consented to an abridgement of two months for each and wished her "perfect Ease, Health & Pleasure" for the twenty-six months thus gained.

In the sensitive political matter of pressing France for more aid and soliciting new loans in other quarters, Franklin consistently applied a policy of caution and reserve. He communicated to Robert Morris, 9 January 1782, his long-standing fear that America would eventually exhaust French patience, by "successive afterclap Demands for more and more money," and recommended in Poor Richard's fashion that America should begin to rely on its own strength. The funds which had been already obtained from France were constantly being drained by requests from America and from the other commissioners, and Franklin told Adams, 12 February 1782, that this harassment "among other things made me quite sick of my Gibeonite office—that of drawing water for the whole congregation of Israel." To make matters worse, French creditors were incessantly clamoring for payments. Beaumarchais, for example, at one time beseeched Franklin with tears in his eyes to give up an American cargo as part payment of the debt to his company.

France continued to be the only reliable source of funds, neither Spain nor Holland, where American agents had long been soliciting, producing anything but prospects. Aware that these fruitless supplications put America in a bad light from the outside, Franklin advised Jay, who had been in Madrid since

April 1780, to notify the Spanish court that unless a treaty could speedily be negotiated he would ask Congress to be recalled. Franklin sent the letter under cover to a Spaniard in Madrid who would inevitably open the letter, read it, and communicate its contents to the court. Ever since his early years as a Philadelphia printer, Franklin recognized the value of prestige on both the personal and political level, and he warned Jay that the slight Spain had "put upon our offer'd Friendship is very disreputable to us." Since victory and independence were virtually assured, Franklin could afford to show his resentment to Spain.

When in the autumn of 1782 it became absolutely indispensable for America to secure more funds, Franklin approached Vergennes with the reminder that Congress had repudiated some peace overtures proposed by Sir Guy Carleton and had determined to continue the war until a peace satisfactory to Louis XVI as well as to itself could be concluded. Vergennes replied that some additional aid could be extended but not as much as Congress had declared to be essential. Thereupon Franklin in his dispatches continued to defend French generosity and good will. With some exasperation he reminded Livingston, in charge of the office of foreign affairs, 5 December 1782, that there were bounds to everything, including French resources, and that Americans had no reason to assume that "France has money enough for all her occasions, and all ours besides; and that, if she does not supply us, it is owing to her want of will, or to my negligence."

In the same month, he repeated to Robert Morris his conviction that Americans ought to do more for themselves. "It is absurd, the pretending to be lovers of liberty while they grudge paying for the defense of it." Self-help and self-reliance had been the theme of Franklin's whole life. Now all of America was behaving as though it had never heard of Poor Richard, and Franklin was not pleased.

30. *Negotiations for Peace*

A S WE have already seen, Adams had been appointed sole commissioner to negotiate peace as far back as the fall of 1779, and Franklin, after being appointed joint commissioner, had no desire to take over Adams's duties or prerogatives. Yet English emissaries persisted in making direct contact with Franklin as they had been doing virtually from the moment of his arrival in France.

His steadfast policy of grateful reliance on the generosity of France was put to the test in the first weeks of 1782, when David Hartley wrote that he had heard reports that Franklin now believed the time to be ripe for America to enter into a separate treaty with Great Britain. Franklin did not rise to the bait. He replied, 15 January, that he was "concerned to find, that one cannot give Vent to a simple Wish for Peace, a mere Sentiment of Humanity, without having it interpreted as a *Disposition to submit to any base Conditions* that may be offered us, rather than continue the War." In the early days of the struggle, England had sought to make peace without recognizing American independence; now she sought to make peace without respecting America's treaty obligations to France. These were the base conditions to which America would never submit. Franklin roundly declared that "there is not a Man in America, a few *English Tories* excepted, that would not spurn at the Thought of deserting a noble and generous Friend, for the sake of a Truce with an unjust and cruel Enemy." Hartley had proposed a truce of ten years during which America would remain passive while England continued the war against France. Franklin replied that by such an arrangement "We should have so covered ourselves with Infamy, by our Treachery to our first friend, as that no other Nation can ever after be disposed to assist us, however cruelly you might think fit to treat us." Here both gratitude and interest demanded the same policy of loyalty. America was "too sensible of the Value of the World's good Opinion," to forfeit it all by a perfidious truce.

Possibilities of serious proposals for peace became more realistic after the fall of the ministry of Lord North in March 1782, following on the heels of Cornwallis's surrender at York-town. The Whig ministry which succeeded had embraced a policy of reconciliation, and Franklin's old friend Lord Shel-burne had been appointed secretary of state for the Southern Department in charge of colonies, while the leader of the pro-American forces in Parliament, Charles Fox, had been made foreign secretary. Both ministers sent emissaries to Paris for informal peace talks with the American representatives, and Franklin dealt with them singlehanded until the arrival of John Jay late in June and Adams late in October.

The story of these negotiations has been told many times, although never fully, and it would require a whole book to depict Franklin's part. Here there is space only for the high-lights. Fox, who favored American independence, was respon-sible for negotiations with France, Spain and Holland. Shel-burne, as colonial secretary, had America as his charge. Al-though a friend of Franklin, he would have preferred to retain America under some form of connection with the empire. Inevitably, Fox and Shelburne became distrustful rivals.

"Great Affairs," Franklin remarked in his own account of the negotiations, "sometimes take their rise from small Circum-stances." Shelburne sent as his emissary Richard Oswald, an amateur diplomat one year older than Franklin, with a practical rather than a speculative mind. He appeared abruptly in Passy early in April in the company of Franklin's old friend Caleb Whitefoord, who made the introductions. In England, Henry Laurens had told Oswald that "Dr. Franklin knows very well how to manage a Cunning Man; but, when the Doctor converses or treats with a man of candour, there is no man more candid than himself." Deciding on a policy of candor, therefore, Oswald admitted in the preliminary round that the ministry had once wanted to make a separate peace with America and continue the war with France and Spain, but he affirmed that it now sincerely desired a "General Peace." Franklin on his side let Oswald know America's determination not to treat "but in Concert with France." Then he arranged for Oswald to see Vergennes, who made the obvious point that, since England was the only party without allies and as such needed to consult no other power, it should be the one to make the first proposals. Later Franklin observed that since he and the other American commissioners —at that moment on their way to Paris—had full powers from Congress to treat for peace, Oswald should inform Shelburne that nothing more could be done until the British could send agents with equal powers. Vergennes refused to discuss conditions with Oswald on the grounds that he could not bargain alone—that all the allies must concur in the treaty. He even refused to give or receive general propositions or indicate French demands.

On the next day Franklin freely discussed with Oswald the American demands, including the cession of Canada and Nova Scotia, while consulting a paper in his hand. Oswald asked Franklin if he could take this paper back to England with him, and Franklin in a weak moment agreed. By so doing he was guilty of the unilateralism which Vergennes had repudiated. Since he did not later inform Vergennes of the paper, Franklin was the first to break the solidarity of the allies.

Oswald returned to Paris in May, but with nothing more substantial to offer than the news that Fox was preparing to send another agent, Thomas Grenville, son of the former Chancellor of the Exchequer whose Stamp Tax policies had harassed the colonies before the war.

A few days later, Grenville arrived, bearing a highly complimentary letter to Franklin from Fox. In their first conversation, Grenville affirmed that "England was willing to treat of a general Peace with all the Powers at War against her, and that the Treaty should be at Paris." Early in the morning on the day after Grenville's arrival in Paris, he and Franklin were received by Vergennes at Versailles. Grenville got down to business by intimating that if England "gave" America independence, France in return should restore some of the islands she had conquered from England. Both Vergennes and Franklin smiled at the proposed offer of independence, Franklin curtly remarking that "we do not consider ourselves as under any Necessity of bargaining for a Thing that is our own and which we have bought at the Expence of much Blood and Treasure." When Vergennes and Franklin affirmed that England, having provoked an unsuccessful war upon its neighbors, could not reasonably expect "to sit down whole, and have every thing restor'd, which she had lost in such a War," Grenville argued that the war had been provoked by the encouragement which the French gave to the Americans to revolt.

On which M. de Vergennes grew a little warm, and declar'd firmly, that the Breach was made, and our Independence declar'd, long before we receiv'd the least Encouragement from France; and he defy'd the World to give the smallest Proof of the contrary. "There sits," says he, "Mr. Franklin, who knows the Fact, and can contradict me if I do not speak the Truth."

Vergennes did not speak the truth at all, and Franklin knew it full well since he had himself been in contact with the French agent Bonvouloir in Philadelphia months before the Declaration of Independence. Yet Franklin did not contradict his ally—using his taciturnity in the service of his diplomacy. He felt that the interests of his country justified his silence.

Late in May, he received a letter from Henry Laurens containing the prediction that Franklin should "be called blessed" for his peacemaking. Franklin replied with his frequently expressed sentiment that the blessing promised to peacemakers in the New Testament "relates to the next World, for in this they seem to have a greater Chance of being curst." He also cited another text, "that in '*the Multitude of Counselors there is Safety*,'" which, he observed, promises safety to the counselors as well as to the counseled because the responsibility for errors would be shared on a wider base. Franklin wanted Laurens and the other negotiators to join him as soon as possible—a different attitude from his feelings when he had advocated that the commission for European alliances be reduced to one man.

At a private session on June 1, Grenville assured Franklin of the great esteem in which the latter was held by the British ministry and of the firm and general belief that no other man was as capable of proposing the proper means of bringing about a reconciliation. Franklin remarked in his journal that at one time such flattering language might have made him vainer and have worked a greater effect on his conduct than at present, when he found himself so near the end of life "as to esteem lightly all personal Interests and Concerns." Nevertheless, some days later when the Swedish ambassador asked Franklin whether he had powers for making a treaty with Sweden, the King of that nation having particularly expressed a desire to conclude such a transaction with him, Franklin reported the conversation to Congress, admitting that he had perhaps "some vanity" in doing so. By this time, it is apparent that vanity was to Franklin a subconscious obsession, one of the most persistent themes in his personal writings. Adams once said that Franklin was the only man he ever knew who claimed to be free from vanity but was, in fact, "the vainest man and the falsest character I have ever met with in life." Although we need not accept this estimate of Franklin's character, it is nevertheless solid evidence that the theme of being exempt from vanity played as large a role in his conversation as in his writing.

Although Franklin got along well enough with Grenville, he preferred Oswald as a negotiator since the older man seemed "to have nothing at heart but the Good of Mankind, and putting a Stop to Mischief." Grenville, as a young statesman, could "be suppos'd to have naturally a little Ambition of recommending himself as an able Negotiator." Franklin used his influence to have the older man established over the younger, and internal political events in England fostered his wishes. On 1 July, Shelburne succeeded Rockingham as prime minister, Fox resigned, and Grenville's place was given to Alleyne Fitzherbert, a nonentity. Oswald remained in Paris as the dominant voice. He was later joined by Franklin's young friend Benjamin Vaughan, as an aide and courier.

In the meantime Jay arrived in Paris (23 June) and exchanged notes with Franklin on the British negotiations and the reserve of the Spanish court. On 9 July Franklin communicated orally to Oswald four points which he felt were "indispensable" for peace between America and England and an additional four which he considered "advisable." Even though America and France were committed to a joint peace, Vergennes had agreed to a *modus operandi* by which each state would make its own treaty with England. "All that is necessary to be observ'd for our Common Security is that the Treaties go on hand in hand and are sign'd all on the same day." In actual fact, Franklin and Vergennes kept secrets from each other in the preliminary stages of talks with England, and each made greater concessions than the other would have approved.

In August, Jay met Oswald for the first time and put somewhat of a damper on the amiable relations which Franklin had established. Oswald's commission had called for him to negotiate with representatives of the former "colonies or plantations," but Jay flatly insisted that the bargaining authority was vested in the independent United States of America. Vergennes made light of Jay's scruple, pointing out that "names signified little; that the King of Great Britain's styling himself the King of France was no obstacle to the King of France's treating with him." Franklin was inclined to accept this reasoning, particularly since he had used it himself in 1769 in viewing England's claim to legislate for the colonies. "We shall," he had written, "consider it in the same Light with the Claim of the Spanish Monarch to the Title of King of Jerusalem." After the interview, Franklin advised Jay to acquiesce in Vergennes's opinion on the grounds that "this court had hitherto treated us very fairly and that suspicions to their disadvantage should not be readily entertained." Jay, however, was as cautious in his dealings with Vergennes as with the British. On returning from the conference, he wrote to Robert Livingston:

I could not forbear observing to Dr. Franklin that it was evident the Count did not wish to see our independence acknowledged by Britain until they had made all their uses of us. . . . If we once found ourselves standing on our own legs, our independence acknowledged, and all our other terms ready to be granted, we might not think it our duty to continue in the war for the attainment of Spanish objects.

Several months later, Jay similarly declared that the French "are interested in separating us from Great Britain, and . . . it is not their interest that we should become a great and formidable people."

Jay's suspicions of French and Spanish complicity had a great deal to do with the manner in which the preliminary articles were eventually signed. Vergennes's confidential secretary, Gérard de Rayneval, had shown Jay a memoir on 6 September, incorporating discussions between Rayneval and the Spanish ambassador, Aranda, on the western boundary of the United States. They proposed to keep the new nation east of the Mississippi, turning over the Ohio country to England and organizing the southwest as a Spanish Indian protectorate. Franklin, as a perennial spokesman for westward expansion and rising population, was no more likely than Jay to accept such restrictions. Nearly two years previously, 2 October 1780, Franklin had written to Jay that he would rather agree with the Spanish "to buy at a great Price the whole of their Right on the Mississippi, than sell a Drop of its Waters. A Neighbour might as well ask me to sell my Street Door." Now that military victory was assured, Franklin was in no mind to surrender the Mississippi through the peace terms. On 12 August 1782 he wrote to Livingston, denouncing Spain's "design to coop us up within the Allegheny Mountains" and advising Congress to "insist on the Mississippi as the boundary and the free navigation of the river."

Rayneval, on the day after showing Jay his memoir, mysteriously left for London. Then on 10 September Jay received a copy of an intercepted letter from Barbé-Marbois, French chargé d'affaires in America, advising Vergennes against granting the United States rights to the Newfoundland fisheries. These events convinced Jay that Vergennes was planning a gigantic doublecross—particularly to abandon insistence upon British recognition of American independence as a preliminary to the peace treaty. Without consulting Franklin, he thereupon sent Benjamin Vaughan to inform Shelburne that England could at that moment "cut the cords which tied us to France, for that, though we were determined faithfully to fulfill our treaty and engagements with this court, *yet it was a different thing to be guided by their or our construction of it.*" The concessions Jay wanted were immediate acknowledgment of independence, a share in the fisheries, and access to the Mississippi—virtually the same conditions which Franklin had labeled as "indispensable." Jay had completely transferred his suspicions from England to France. He explained to Livingston that he was obliged to send Vaughan in secret without Franklin's knowledge because "Dr. Franklin does not see the conduct of this court in the light I do . . . he believes they mean nothing but what is friendly, fair and honorable." As Jay viewed his own position, he wanted to be honest and grateful toward France but was not willing to give up his own personal independent judgment or surrender the autonomy of the United States to Vergennes.

Before coming to a decision on Jay's proposal, Shelburne sent Vaughan back to Paris with instructions to pay particular attention to Franklin. Vaughan sounded him out on Shelburne's still-cherished project of a "Federal union," to which Franklin responded coolly. He learned, however, that Franklin had not been apprised of anything passing between Jay and Oswald beyond the exchange of powers.

Vaughan wrote back to Shelburne, impressing him with the need of preventing delays in London, not only "to get out of the reach of Interruption from the French" but also "to get out of the reach of interruption from Mr. Adams." The latter was awaited momentarily, and Vaughan, who did not know him personally, expected him to be a hard opponent, easily heated and ambitious, with strong anti-British feelings.

On 8 October 1782, Oswald agreed with Jay and Franklin upon preliminary articles for a treaty, and three days later Vaughan supplied Shelburne with extensive arguments why it would be "wise and fit" for Britain to accede to them. The British cabinet, meeting 17 October, however, found Jay's articles too favorable for the Americans and sent a new "tough" commissioner, Sir Henry Strachey, to counteract Oswald's accommodating, pro-American attitude.

Strachey's American counterpart, Adams, also rumored to be a hard bargainer, arrived in Paris 26 October. He had hitherto not thought it proper for him to come to Paris until the British diplomats had full powers to treat with "the United States of America." Franklin, of course, had no reason to believe that Adams would be any more amiable in dealing with his fellow Americans than with the British. Adams had always criticized Franklin's love of pleasure, his extravagance, and his dinner-table diplomacy. On Adams's arrival in Paris, an American friend, Matthew Ridley of Maryland, told him that Franklin's health had forced him to give up his Sunday dinners temporarily, but that he was now improving. Ridley, who had no official status but was in the confidence of the negotiators, told Adams that Jay stood firm and independent in looking after his country's interest, even to the point of ignoring the instructions of Congress to confide in Vergennes, but that Franklin seemed more pliable.

Adams wrote in his diary that he foresaw acting "a delicate, a nice, a critical part" between "two as subtle spirits as any in the world." Although willing to grant Jay the same level of honesty as he possessed himself, Adams predicted that Franklin's "cunning will be to divide us; to this End he will provoke, he will insinuate, he will intrigue, he will maneuver." On his first visit to Jay, Adams discovered that they saw eye to eye on every problem confronting them—and then he "spoke freely" his unflattering opinion of Franklin.

According to Ridley, Adams at first had no intention of visiting Franklin. He thought it unnecessary, and "after the usage he had received from him he could not bear to go near him." But after much persuasion from Ridley, Adams overcame his aversion and sought out Franklin in Passy. Rather agreeably, he discovered that the patriarch had no inclination to quarrel. Adams, nevertheless, made no secret of his preference of Jay, praising his "Principles, Wisdom, and Firmness."

Since Franklin was clearly in the minority, he probably

decided that he would either have to go along with Jay and Adams in acting independently of Vergennes or still further delay the negotiations. The next day, 30 October, when the three Americans met with Oswald and Strachey, therefore, Franklin remarked to his countrymen, "I am of your opinion, and will go on with these Gentlemen in the Business without consulting this Court."

Strachey unsettled the negotiations, however, by asserting British claims to the western lands, a note which Vaughan felt was ill-advised. He informed Shelburne of his opinion, 29 October, that this territory would be of no benefit to England even if granted—and that the American commissioners were bound by their instructions from Congress to insist upon it. For England to press the point might lead to the breaking off of negotiations and an even closer accord between America and France. "Mr. Adams is sufficiently well disposed to us at present," he concluded, "but God Almighty defend us from delay." Three days later, Vaughan strengthened his warning with the report that the Americans "would have been better pleased with a style of confidence, than with a style of bargain."

Moderation prevailed, and on 29 November 1782 Oswald and the American commissioners signed preliminary articles, granting to America the western lands as well as rights to the Newfoundland fisheries. Franklin confided to his friend La Rochefoucauld that the events of the day had made him happier than he had ever hoped to be at his age. At the conclusion of the agreement, Franklin and Oswald exchanged portraits. The happy ending of the negotiations must have softened Adams's feelings toward Franklin. In his diary for 30 November after the signing, he remarked about Franklin, "He has accordingly met Us in most of our Conferences, and has gone on with Us, in entire Harmony and Unanimity, throughout, and has been able and useful, both by his Sagacity and his Reputation in the whole Negotiation."

Discussions still went forward, however, concerning the general peace, and Vaughan reported, 4 December, Franklin's opinion that the English could mollify the European powers by offering to exchange Gibraltar (always a sore point with Spain) for territory in the Caribbean. At the same time Vaughan tried to assure Shelburne that he had protected himself from coming under Franklin's domination. "Dr. Franklin's behavior is such as indeed flatters me," he admitted; "but I am very sorry to hear him talk of our spending evenings together at Passy. It looks as if he had more steps in his business than your Lordship would like." Strachey's ill-mannered behavior, Vaughan felt, was a greater danger to British diplomacy than Franklin's charm.

Three days later, Vaughan repeated Franklin's opinion, which he obviously shared, that the commissioners had missed an opportunity for mutual benefit by omitting an article for the reciprocity of commerce between America and Britain. The Spanish and French courts, therefore, should be pleased with the preliminary articles—even though "formed without their privity"—since "we have stopped short of the mischief we might have done them by not proceeding to reunion and reciprocal commerce." Franklin had assured Vaughan that the Americans had exceeded their instructions and expected to be reprimanded by Congress, and he repeated his often-used sentiment that "peacemakers in this world usually get abused." Franklin, as usual, was right in his prediction. Vergennes immediately wrote to the French ambassador in Philadelphia, Barbé-Marbois, suggesting that Congress be informed of the lack of politeness shown by the commissioners—even Franklin.

At the same time, Franklin undoubtedly realized, as Vaughan expressed it, that even if the French court felt a disposition to complain about the American unilateral action, "they would suppress it, from the consciousness of the tricks they have played America." France and Spain had been playing the same game. Still Vergennes could not help feeling that the Americans were slipping away from the French orbit, and he sent Franklin an aggrieved note, 15 December, seizing as the pretext for his reproaches a relatively trivial matter—Franklin's requesting a British passport for the sailing of the vessel *Washington,* which was to carry news of the preliminary articles to Congress. Vergennes deliberately chose cold and artificially polite language:

I am at a loss, Sir, to explain your conduct, and that of your colleagues on this occasion. You have concluded your preliminary articles without any communication between us, although the instructions from Congress prescribe, that nothing shall be done without the participation of the King.

Franklin's reply, 17 December, has been called another of his diplomatic masterpieces. Frankly admitting Vergennes's grievance, he partially justified himself on the grounds that he had given Vergennes notice of the despatching of the ship. In regard to the hidden but fundamental point at issue, the separate negotiations, he affirmed unequivocally that "nothing has been agreed in the preliminaries contrary to the interests of France; and no peace is to take place between us and England, till you have concluded yours." In the next sentence, however, Franklin admitted his fault in not consulting Vergennes before signing: "we have been guilty of neglecting a point of bienséance." But having made the admission, he exhorted Vergennes not to allow this "single indiscretion" to ruin the great work which had already been accomplished. Indeed he used Vergennes's chagrin as a means of pressing for more funds: "the whole edifice sinks to the ground immediately, if you refuse on that account to give us any further assistance." Returning to his theme of sincere gratitude to the French court, Franklin affirmed that "no Prince was ever more beloved and respected by his own subjects, than the King is by the people of the United States." Then he closed on the note of French national interest. *"The English, I just now learn, flatter themselves they have already divided us.* I hope this little misunderstanding will therefore be kept a secret, and that they will find themselves totally mistaken."

This letter magically rectified the "little misunderstanding." Not only did Vergennes accept the sailing of the *Washington* with a British passport, but he gave Franklin an order for six thousand livres to be sent in the ship. To make Franklin's pleasure complete, the passport had been signed by the English King's own hand and had acknowledged the Americans by their title of the United States of America.

Having himself apparently slipped from under the dominating influence of Vergennes, Franklin made clear in a letter to Samuel Cooper, 26 December, that his greatest fear now was that anti-French sentiment in the United States might destroy the good understanding existing between France and America and do the Americans "irreparable injury." He insisted that it was the French connection which gave them "weight with England, and respect throughout Europe" and that if they were to break their faith with France "England would again trample on us, and every other nation despise us." Now and during the rest of his public life, Franklin followed the firm policy that "the true political interest of America consists in observing and fulfilling, with the greatest exactitude, the engagements of our alliance with France, and behaving at the same time towards England, so as not entirely to extinguish her hopes of reconciliation."

Perhaps Franklin so strongly stressed the Franco-American alliance because he realized that the articles he had signed favored the English and would on that account be unpopular at home. Even Benjamin Vaughan recognized that "besides secretly signing a very offensive treaty," the commissioners had "tried to restore English and eradicate French connections, by giving the leaders of Congress a history of French intrigues, and a recommendation of the English system." It is well known that, of the American commissioners, Adams was considered to be pro-British and Franklin pro-French. Indeed Adams, who originally had been appointed the sole commissioner, affirmed quite correctly, as we now know, that Vergennes had intrigued to have his appointment revoked and Franklin named in a new five-member board. According to Vaughan, Adams in all his speeches in Congress "had maintained that G. Britain was not to be distressed to a greater degree than was necessary to enable America to preserve her liberties and her engagements." Vaughan had no doubts whatsoever that Congress had picked negotiators who were friendly to England. In his words, "Messrs. Jay, Adams, and Laurens were avowed Englishmen, and I think they say Mr. Jefferson likewise; and all who understood Dr. Franklin know that Dr. Franklin is an Englishman upon the broadest principles." Vaughan was vague about Jefferson, who was not present during the negotiations, and Laurens had come to detest England because of his imprisonment in the Tower of

London. But Franklin was at least as much of an Englishman as he was a tool of Vergennes. Vaughan had moreover wisely read the character of John Adams, whom he described as "no less a decided enemy to Dr. Franklin, than to M. de Vergennes." According to Vaughan, Adams attributed to these two jointly "every hostile measure" ever conceived against him, including "every pasquinade in the newspapers."

Despite the signing of preliminary articles between the United States and England, the war continued, and the French, Spanish and Dutch interests were still unresolved. Vergennes, who was earlier disposed to a general peace, had come to think that England was merely trifling in signing preliminary articles, and Benjamin Vaughan feared that he would take an intransigent position in regard to negotiations with the Dutch. In the middle of January he suggested to Franklin that he advise Vergennes to adopt a more moderate tone so that Shelburne could propose a peace which would be acceptable to his critics in Parliament. Careful not to suggest that Franklin owed a helping hand to the English on account of their having complied with American desires in their own negotiations, Vaughan introduced "the topic of humanity" and Franklin's duty to America in working for a general peace. Franklin was not difficult to persuade, not only on philosophic grounds but out of his friendship for Vaughan and Shelburne. As Vaughan remembered their conversation, Franklin said that the English ministers

were indeed in a hard case, because they acted for an ignorant or misinformed public, and the great reason of all which seemed to be that the nation's strength was misrepresented to them. War, he said, was made according to the mistaken imaginations of the people, and peace according to their real necessities as seen by the peace makers; and hence the frequent idea that they were bribed.

On the day Vaughan reported this conversation to Shelburne, 18 January 1783, Vergennes wrote an urgent note to Franklin asking him and the commissioners to meet with him on the next morning and to bring William Temple Franklin as a scribe and translator. Franklin sent a note to Adams and both appeared as desired (Laurens and Jay being absent from Paris) and learned that the occasion was to be the signing of preliminary articles of peace between France, Spain and England. Possibly Vergennes had invited the Americans less as an overture of politeness than as a subtle rebuke for their failure to make the same gesture when concluding their own treaty. The European commissioners formally signed their articles along with an agreement for the cessation of hostilities, which Franklin and Adams signed with the others. For the world at large, this was merely the bringing to a close of another war, but for the two Americans the signing represented official recognition of their country not only as an independent nation but as an international power to be reckoned with.

❖❖*❖*❖*❖*❖*❖*❖*❖*❖*❖*❖*

31. Tidying Loose Ends

T HE end of the war meant for Franklin relief from his most pressing public business, even though there remained minor tensions and irritations and above all the need to combat English propaganda implying that internal strife was tearing America apart. Nevertheless, Franklin felt free to devote more of his attention to personal affairs.

After a total silence of three years, he wrote again to his sister, promising her the means by which she might finally be enabled to live at ease in her old age. Jane in reply expressed the fervent wish that he would now realize that he had devoted himself sufficiently to the public and would put into execution his often-expressed desire of sitting down to spend the evening with his friends. With this in view, she had begun looking around Cambridge for a "commodious seat" to receive him on his return.

Franklin, however, discouraged this house-hunting, 13 September 1783, as "a Project of the Heart rather than of the Head" and reminded Jane that "we are grown old, and that before we can have furnish'd our House, & put things in order, we shall probably be call'd away from it, to a Home more lasting, and I hope more agreeable than any this World can afford us."

Even though Jane's main contact with her brother recently had been through the newspapers, he had regularly been receiving letters from Caty Ray Greene about Jane's unhappiness in not hearing from him. In October 1781, Jane had gone to Boston for "a little comfort," thinking that Jonathan Williams may have had some news. In May 1782, Caty wrote that Jane had not had a line from her brother for such a long time that she could scarcely speak of him without crying—even though she had received a very handsome gift of money through Williams.

Franklin was considerate, even generous, to most people,

including Jane, when their needs and sorrows aroused his compassion, but he needed reminders. Of course, he had many other affairs on his mind—whereas for Jane, her illustrious brother was life's most important concern. Even Mme. Helvétius often complained in Franklin's Passy circle that he loved people only when they were within his range of vision.

As Franklin entered the seventy-eighth year of his life, he looked back on his past with mingled sadness and satisfaction. The previous year had carried off his friends Dr. Pringle, Dr. Fothergill, Lord Kames, Lord Le Despencer, and his English "wife" Mrs. Stevenson. To her daughter Polly, now the widowed Mrs. Hewson, Franklin repeated a sentiment which he now applied frequently to his remaining old friends, "The fewer we become, the more let us love one another." In recalling the period of nearly a quarter of a century during which he had lived in the same house with the Stevensons, Franklin remarked that in all that time they had never had the smallest misunderstanding and that their friendship had been "all clear Sunshine, without the least Cloud in its Hemisphere."

In the same mellow mood, Franklin confided to an English friend, John Sargent, his satisfaction in a long life passed

without any uncommon Misfortune, the greater part of it in Health and Vigor of Mind and Body, near Fifty Years of it in continu'd Possession of the Confidence of my Country, in public Employments, and enjoying the Esteem and affectionate, friendly Regard of many wise and good Men and Women, in every Country where I have resided.

At the same time, however, he began to feel his physical infirmities more acutely and wrote a private letter to Thomas Mifflin, wealthy Philadelphia merchant and political leader, urging him to press Congress to act on his request to be relieved of his duties. In congratulating Elias Boudinot on retiring into private life from the presidency of Congress, he remarked enviously that he could "scarcely conceive a happier Being than the Man, who, having been long laden with public Cares and fatigu'd by every-body's Business, is allow'd to retire into the Bosom of his Family, and enjoy Otium cum dignitate."

With the dashing of his hopes to have his grandson marry Cunégonde Brillon and his own of marrying Mme. Helvétius, Franklin abandoned his project of ending his days in France and began dreaming of returning to America after a possible final trip throughout Europe. He still felt that the French were "an amiable People to live with." They loved him and he loved them. Yet, he confessed that he nevertheless did not feel at home with them, and he admitted that he wished to die in his own country. When he received the news of Mrs. Stevenson's death, he revealed that he had once thought of returning to England for a protracted sojourn before returning to America, but since most of his dear English friends had passed away and he would not wish to seem to be "braving and insulting" the English government, he decided to spend only a few days in England on his way back to America. In the meantime, he invited Polly Hewson to visit him in the spring of 1783.

But when this season arrived, he was uncertain whether he would be able to carry out his intention of visiting Italy and Austria. By September 1783, when Benny Bache, now fourteen years old, had returned from Geneva because of internal turmoil in that city, and Franklin still saw no prospect of being relieved of his duties, he wondered whether Polly would oversee Benny's subsequent schooling in England. At the same time he strongly advised her to take her own children to America, where the means of good education were better than in England.

Franklin persuaded Jay to agree to take Benny Bache with him in September on a visit to England, where Jay was to take the waters at Bath, but at the last minute Benny and his cousin showed such fondness for each other's company that Franklin decided both grandsons should remain in Passy until Franklin himself should go to England. In the meantime, he engaged one of the most celebrated printers of France, Philippe-Denis Pierres, to instruct Benny in the principles of the printing art. Benny wrote to his father in December than he was delighted with this training but that Franklin himself longed to return to America.

During these months, the growth of a stone in the bladder joined forces with gout in giving Franklin acute physical discomfort. In both May and December 1783, he begged Vergennes to excuse him for failing to attend court functions at Versailles, explaining that even in the easiest carriage the stone "gives me Pain, wounds my Bladder, and occasions me to make bloody Urine." Indeed because of the onslaughts of the stone, the ailing diplomat inclined more and more to his earlier belief that the gout was actually more of a benevolent remedy than a malady, since he always found his "Health and Vigour of Mind improv'd after the Fit is over." Vergennes had been transacting necessary business with William Temple Franklin since illness kept his grandfather from attending the court.

Although theoretically there were five American peace commissioners in Europe, three of whom signed the preliminary articles, Jefferson never arrived in time for the treaty and Franklin was the only one of the other four who remained constantly in Paris. Signing of the definitive treaty dragged on because of a series of changes in Parliament during the winter of 1783 and the following spring. Oswald was eventually replaced by Franklin's old friend and advocate of peace, David Hartley. The opposition party in Parliament clamored against Shelburne's concessions, but Franklin, like most observers, believed that "the Attack is rather against the Minister." He assured his friend Bishop Shipley, 17 March 1783, that "none of the opposition would have made a better Peace for England." In answer to the English critics who complained that the treaty lacked "reciprocity" of concessions, Franklin indignantly pointed out that America had refrained from demanding compensation for the burning of its coastal towns and predicted that he and his fellow commissioners would be blamed in America for not insisting on reparation. For Franklin, the great villain in the war, next to George III, had been Parliament, and he could not completely forgive even his old, friend Strahan, who as a Member of Parliament had "dipt his Hands in our Blood."

Not until July 1783 did Franklin hear how Congress had received the provisional treaty (with approval in the main, but with reservations concerning its being signed without French participation). In defending himself and his colleagues for their independent action, Franklin wrote to Livingston, 22 July, one of the most astringent public letters of his whole career. They had all done what appeared best at the time, he affirmed, and Congress, after giving them a hearing, could censure them if they had done wrong. Yet the Congress should consider that it had allowed them some independence of judgment by appointing five commissioners: otherwise "one alone could have made a Treaty by Direction of the French Ministry as well as Twenty."

As many historians have observed, when Congress in June 1781, at the urging of the French minister, Gérard, had enjoined the commissioners to undertake nothing in their negotiations without the knowledge and concurrence of Vergennes, it had made them tools rather than free agents. Although Franklin, more than anyone else, retained feelings of gratitude toward the French court, he, as well as Jay and Adams, cherished his own independence and that of his own country even more. They had violated their instructions but knew that they had served their country in so doing.

The English, after all their delays and maneuvers, finally proposed that the preliminary articles be accepted as the definitive treaty with no alteration except the addition of a formal preamble and conclusion. They were naturally even more sensitive than Franklin to the negotiations being "carried on under the Eye of the French Court," and at the last minute Hartley refused to go to Versailles for the signing but insisted that it be done at Paris. Although this Treaty of Paris, 3 September 1783, has been depicted in history and art as a major historical event, it was actually somewhat of an anticlimax and by no means an occasion of glittering solemnity. Opinion is divided as to which of the two, Jay or Franklin, should be given credit for the favorable peace terms—or indeed whether either might have obtained greater advantages for the United States by himself. Probably each made a unique contribution: Franklin, the climate of opinion which made negotiation possible; Jay, the boldness and firmness which secured maximum concessions. Nor should we forget that Adams had given firm support to Jay and, in Holland, had previously not only kept the United Provinces from joining England but had also negotiated a sizable loan.

Three days after the actual signing, Franklin warned Hartley that the English were deceiving themselves by entertaining hopes that the new American nation was in danger of falling apart. Although modest about his personal achievements, Franklin made no attempt to check the warmth of his patriotic pride. His countrymen, he affirmed, were "more thoroughly an enlightened people, with respect to . . . political interests, than perhaps any other under heaven," and their minor domestic misunderstandings were being "monstrously magnified" by the British "microscopic newspapers." The best interest of England as well as America would be a "thorough reconciliation," not the vain hope of a new pro-British revolution. Hartley had expressed an apprehension that "the cement" of the new confederation might be annihilated, but Franklin, reverting to his famous analogy concerning the empire, assured him that "There is sense enough in America to take care of their own *china vase.*"

The cynical doubts of such friends as Hartley and the absolute fictions of many London newspapers led Franklin to warn Thomas Mifflin that the English who represented the American states as so many anarchies "bear us no good Will, and . . . wish the reality of what they are pleas'd to imagine." For this reason, he felt that America could not be too careful to preserve its political friendships in Europe and secure its credit by punctually discharging its debts. "We know not how soon we may have a fresh Occasion for Friends, for Credit, and for Reputation." America as a "Virgin State" should not only avoid committing any act of injustice but also guard against any suspicion of it.

32. Personal and Public Vindication

ONE important means Franklin used to advance the reputation of his country abroad was to circulate copies of the constitutions of the thirteen American states, documents which he viewed with great pride. Franklin provided the texts, persuaded his friend La Rochefoucauld to translate them, petitioned Vergennes to use his influence with the Keeper of the Seals to grant permission for publication, and arranged with Benny's tutor, Philippe-Denis Pierres, for the printing. Franklin prevailed upon Vergennes in March 1783, but approbation was not granted until June, and even then the Keeper of the Seals made the marginal proviso that Vergennes subject the printed text to a final scrutiny. The harassed printer Pierres, in explaining these delays to Franklin, remarked, "You see, Sir, that Paris does not at all resemble Philadelphia, and we need here a second Franklin—if it were possible for two to exist—in order to deliver us from these fetters."

While the state constitutions were circulating in Paris, Franklin first revealed that his social opinions had veered to the left, perhaps under the influence of the tensions and turmoil of French court life and the intellectual ferment of the *philosophes.* Now he openly doubted that the European class system greatly promoted civic good or the service of one's country. Taking a well-known English philanthropist, Thomas Hollis, as an example of the prodigious "quantity of Good that may be done by one Man, *if he will make a Business of it,*" Franklin contrasted Hollis's achievement with "the general Frivolity of the Employments and Amusements of the rank we call Gentlemen." Every European kingdom in every century, Franklin affirmed, "may have seen three successions of a set of a thousand each" of these gentlemen, and no one set have done as much good as that effected by Hollis alone.

Franklin elaborated this manner of thinking to condemn hereditary aristocracy in a famous letter to his daughter Sally, 26 January 1784. Here he outlined his opposition to the recently formed Society of the Cincinnati and to all forms of hereditary aristocracy. On moral grounds, he argued that honor is a personal thing and cannot be communicated to those who had no share in obtaining it. Not only is the concept of hereditary honor groundless and absurd, he maintained, but also it is harmful to the posterity considered inheritors since they are likely to become proud and disdainful of useful labor and, like much of the European *noblesse,* descend into poverty. On mathematical grounds as well, Franklin proved hereditary honors to be absurd. After nine generations—a period of only 300 years—a descendant of an honored ancestor would have so much blood from other sources mingled in his veins that only the 512th part would stem from the man whose title had descended to him. Later, Franklin regretfully observed that both Washington and Lafayette had "missed a *beau moment*" when they accepted membership in the Cincinnati. Yet he himself missed the same noble opportunity of making a stand against privilege, for after returning to America he inconsistently accepted honorary membership in the Cincinnati, perhaps allowing his vanity to overcome his principles.

Franklin asked the Abbé Morellet to translate his remarks on the Cincinnati, apparently hoping that they could be used to modify the French social order. Morellet did as requested, but strongly advised against publication, lest some of Franklin's aristocratic friends turn against him. Later in the year, two rising authors, Mirabeau and Chamfort, apparently on their own initiative, called on Franklin to discuss using their own translation of his letter in a printed satire against the French system of hereditary rank. Franklin willingly cooperated, and their work, *Considérations sur l'ordre de Cincinnatus,* soon appeared in both French and English editions, a text, according to Chamfort, which delivered "the most forceful blows against the French aristocracy in public opinion."

Even in some quarters in America, Franklin's opinions on aristocracy would probably have seemed extreme at the time. His strong self-identification with the political fortunes of his country had developed in him a social concept which he had never before expressed—the notion that the state is an all-important entity, superseding the private interests and desires of any and all of its individual members. Now he even modified his earlier individualistic economic views, which were, as we remember, harshly opposed to schemes of social welfare. In condemning the remissness of his countrymen in paying their taxes, he expressed a theory of property almost socialistic. With the exception of the savage's temporary shelter and necessary minor articles for subsistence, Franklin described all property as "the Creature of public Convention." Natural right, he argued, gives each man title to all the property necessary for "the Conservation of the Individual and the Propagation of the Species," but all other property "is the Property of the Publick, who, by their Laws, have created it, and who may therefore by other Laws dispose of it, whenever the Welfare of the Publick shall demand such Disposition." This comprehensive claim of property as the creation and appurtenance of the public foreshadows the wave of utilitarian and socialistic theories which grew up in the nineteenth century. Franklin advised those people who would not accept civil society on these terms to "retire and live among Savages." Undoubtedly he was motivated by his new social consciousness when he assured Thomas Mifflin, 26 December 1783, that "if the Congress should think my continuing here necessary for the public Service, I ought, as a good Citizen, to submit to their Judgment and Pleasure."

He had heard grim reports from his daughter a few weeks earlier, 5 November, about Congress having "lost much of the confidence of the people" by its wandering from city to city instead of deciding on a permanent capital, but he was undoubtedly pleased by the comment of his old friend General Gates that "they were all splitting and separating, that no man could hoop the barrel but you, and that you were much wanted here."

Franklin was just as concerned about the reputation of his

country in cultural as well as in political achievements, although he had not changed his early opinion that Europe offered greater encouragements to learning. He told Ingenhousz in May 1783 that "our Geniuses all go to Europe." With obvious partiality, he affirmed that "in England at present, the best History Painter, West; the best Portrait Painter, Copley; and the best Landscape Painter, Taylor, at Bath, are all Americans."

Whenever the question of commercial relations with the United States was broached, whether on a large scale or small, Franklin insisted that he had neither the knowledge nor the authority to give advice or make agreements. Indeed, because of his absence of twenty-five years, he once affirmed that it would be "an invidious & dangerous Thing" for him to suggest mercantile connections.

He continued, however, in his efforts to persuade England to agree to a principle to be established as a "future Law of Nations" that all privateering be abolished in war and that no coercion be used against civilians, in other words, that even in war all commerce should be free. During the preliminary peace talks, he had submitted these proposals to Oswald, who had declined to accept them. Once again in the subsequent January he tried to interest Oswald in his scheme but commented realistically, "I rather wish than expect, that it will be adopted." In May he succeeded in pressing his papers upon Hartley, who did nothing but transmit them to London, where they were buried. Eventually, however, his proposal was embodied in a treaty between the United States and Prussia, proudly signed by Franklin 9 July 1785, his last public act before leaving France. Franklin later told Thomas Paine that he had shown the article to Vergennes, who approved it and said he would make such an agreement even with England although he knew the English would never consent—"they were so fond of robbing and plundering."

As one of the results of the peace treaty, the hostility between Franklin and Adams, which had been building up since their first acquaintance, flared out in the open. As we have seen, even from the moment of their first collaboration, their opposing personalities clashed. At first, the easygoing Franklin paid little attention to Adams's stiffness, but the strait-laced Adams could not abide Franklin's urbanity, zest for life, and universal popularity. From the start, Adams sensed that he was overshadowed in public esteem by someone whom he considered no more deserving than himself. He bridled at what he considered Franklin's ingratiating manners, dissembling, and popularity seeking, and he was easily infuriated by lax morality.

Almost as soon as Adams arrived in Paris, Turgot observed that he was "ulcerated and extremely jealous of Franklin." Indeed Adams was so envious of the older man's glittering reputation that he accused him of promoting it through self-serving publicity. In reference to Franklin, he charged, in December 1778:

A Man must be his own Trumpeter, he must write or dictate Paragraphs of Praise in the News Papers, he must dress, have a Retinue, and Equipage, he must ostentatiously publish to the World his own Writings with his Name, and must write even some Panegyrics upon them, he must get his Picture drawn, his Statue made, and must hire all the Artists in his Turn, to set about Works to spread his Name, make the Mob stare and gape, and perpetuate his fame.

On the whole Admas was right about the fact, if not the intention.

Even more rankling to Adams than Franklin's prestige with all Frenchmen, and particularly with Vergennes, was the jealous suspicion that Franklin would become the first ambassador from the United States to the Court of St. James's, a position which Adams, like many others, regarded as "the apple of paradise." Vaughan had actually proposed to Franklin in December 1782 that he would be the logical choice. At first the elder statesman seemed receptive to the notion but then returned to the plan he had consistently expressed to his family, as Vaughan expressed it, of "giving up all public business and merely *visiting* England before he went to America." Adams must have learned of Vaughan's proposal, for in the next month when William Temple Franklin asked him to sign a letter authorizing Temple to serve as secretary for the Commission for Peace, Adams not only refused his signature but went into a harangue on the ill treatment he had met with from Vergennes. In his diary he concluded that "this Letter and other Circumstances convince me that the Plan is laid between the C. de Vergennes and the Dr., to get Billy made Minister to this Court and not improbably the Dr. to London."

As early as March 1783, Franklin had begun to call Adams a "certain malicious madman" because of his ungrateful ravings against France and its ministers. And in writing to Livingston in July about the divergence of his opinions from Adams's on the good will of France, he admitted that he was risking the creating of "a mortal Enmity," probably not aware that this enmity had already developed. He warned Livingston against believing Adams's insinuations against the French court and assured him that the examples of alleged ill will were as imaginary as Adams's fancies that Franklin and Vergennes were "continually plotting against him, and employing the News-Writers of Europe to depreciate his Character."

In the fall of 1783, Franklin received warning from Samuel Cooper that the report was being generally circulated in America that the French court had opposed America's receiving much of the territory and fishing rights which had been granted by the treaty and that Franklin "favoured, or did not oppose, this design against us; and that it was entirely owing to the firmness, sagacity, and disinterestedness of Mr. Adams, with whom Mr. Jay united, that we have obtained these important advantages." This evidence finally awakened Franklin from the apathy with which he had regarded the attacks of his colleagues. He immediately wrote to Jay and Adams, stating that he "ought not to suffer an accusation, which falls little short of treason . . . to pass without notice" and politely asked them to furnish certificates refuting it. Jay immediately provided an unequivocal affirmation of his absolute and wholehearted patriotism, and Adams sent a cold and grudging admission of the same thing.

The other major accusation of Franklin's "miserable

Calumniators" was that he had profited from public funds, an obvious untruth. "As to the two Charges of Age and Weakness," he wrote to Josiah Quincy, "I must confess the first, but I am not quite so clear in the latter; and perhaps my Adversaries may find that they presum'd a little too much upon it, when they ventur'd to attack me." Although Franklin disliked "these petty Personalities," he was still resentful of "Mr. A's Calumnies," which, he affirmed, were in Paris generally "imputed to the true cause, a Disorder in the Brain."

As a diplomat, Franklin certainly had exposed himself to legitimate criticism. As Adams maintained, he was more under Vergennes's influence than were any of his colleagues and perhaps more than the good of his country would allow. But, on the other side, he was the first to break the pledge which he and Vergennes had mutually made not to negotiate with the British without consulting the other. If this is a fault, it was just the opposite fault from that which Adams condemned. Also the dinner-table activities which Adams branded as dissipation were designed to improve contacts and smooth negotiations as much as to gratify Franklin's social inclinations.

Franklin as much as Adams had the welfare of his country at heart, and since at the time there was no established pattern of American diplomatic practice, each man was forced to interpret and improvise methods which would best achieve national interest. Beyond this, Franklin's personal prestige and urbanity gave him advantages in negotiation far beyond Adams's reach and enabled him to wrest concessions from both England and France which probably no other American could have obtained.

✳✿✳✿✳✿✳✿✳✿✳✿✳✿✳✿✳✿✳✿✳

33. *Aftermath of the Peace*

FRANKLIN had served his country well, and he was sure that its future would be bright. Yet little of the luster of victory would brighten his personal life. As he had predicted, nobody blessed him for his peacemaking; Adams to the contrary spread charges that his conduct had bordered on treason, and Congress stubbornly refused to grant William Temple Franklin any reward or recognition for his services. Franklin could not decide whether he should remain in France, take up a new residence in England, or return to Philadelphia.

While trying to come to a decision, he found pleasure in the most spectacular scientific discovery of the late eighteenth century, that of flying by means of lighter-than-air balloons. Franklin was one of the most enthusiastic witnesses of the first human flight, 20 November 1783. Hot air was produced in the balloon, open at the bottom, by burning straw in a basket beneath. One of the courageous passengers on this flight, the Marquis d'Arlandes, called at Franklin's house that same evening together with the inventor of the method, Montgolfier. When Franklin later described the passage over Paris to Joseph Banks, President of the Royal Society, he expressed his regret that the English did not keep pace with the French in scientific investigation—even when success or useful results were not guaranteed. Identifying himself with the French, Franklin observed that "if we do a foolish thing, we are the first to laugh at it ourselves, and are almost as pleased with a bon mot or a good chanson, that ridicules well the disappointment of a project, as we might have been with its success."

On the first day of December, Franklin along with most of the population of Paris witnessed the next important step in aerostatics, the flight of a closed inflated balloon. Franklin, watching from his carriage, reported that "Never before was a philosophical experiment so magnificently attended." The popular press reported his remark that the earliest balloon had been an infant, this one a giant. He did not expect the balloon to become a common carriage in his own time but ruefully admitted that, if it were, it would be extremely convenient for sufferers from the stone like himself, who could not use conventional transportation over rough pavements.

Franklin also kept up his own scientific experiments, devising, for example, some improvements in his famous stove. The French government at the time was seeking a method of substituting coal for wood as a domestic fuel, and one of Franklin's friends, Antoine Alexis-François Cadet de Vaux, a philanthropic pharmacist and chemist, was conducting experiments in baking bread with the new fuel. He prevailed upon the Philadelphia inventor to design an adaptation of his stove for this purpose and then wrote to Vergennes, 28 March 1783, asking him to urge Franklin to write out detailed observations on the construction of the stove and the experiments he had conducted. A year later Franklin sent samples of bread baked on his stove but remarked that he could not use it regularly since he lacked a sufficient supply of coal.

Cadet de Vaux was also editor of a daily periodical, the *Journal de Paris,* where Franklin published a bagatelle he had originally presented to Mme. Brillon as one of his "serious pleasantries." This was a gentle parody of a class of articles regularly appearing in the *Journal de Paris,* those on practical usefulness and household hints, printed under the heading of "Economie." The title which has been given to it in English, *An Economical Project,* is not really a title at all but merely the feature heading from the *Journal.* In keeping with the tone of articles on such inventions as his stove, Franklin described a gathering at which had been demonstrated an oil lamp newly invented by two well-known scientists, Quinquet and Lange. The lamp shed a brilliant light, but some spectators wondered whether the expense of the oil might not offset the advantage of the increased light. Franklin went home to bed, pleasantly contemplating this concern for economy. At six in the morning, he was awakened by an unexpected noise and discovered to his amazement that the room was filled with light. Thinking at first that several of the new lamps were in the room, he gradually realized that the light actually came from the sun. As a major economic reform, therefore, he suggested that the municipality ring bells and set off cannon at sunrise daily to awaken the citizenry. To silence jealous minds who might try to depreciate his discovery, Franklin admitted that the almanacs of the ancients may have indicated the early rising of the sun, but he added that there is no evidence "that they knew *he gave light as soon as he rose.*" In this parody, Franklin was making fun of his own addiction to thrift, of his scientific papers, and of his own habit of staying up until dawn to play chess or enjoy himself in other ways when the temptation was too great to be resisted.

Cadet de Vaux published the squib in the *Journal de Paris,* 26 April 1784, and it was reprinted there 30 November 1795, where Quinquet, the inventor of the lamp, noticed it and thereupon revealed that he had himself seriously communicated views similar to Franklin's to several official bodies.

Another of Franklin's bagatelles, signed by the same pseudonym as the letter on daylight-saving, "Une Abonnée" (a subscriber), was presumably also designed for the *Journal de Paris* but was never published there. Resembling his earlier unprintable satire on the Royal Academy of Belgium, Franklin's squib describes an air "lighter and more expansive than the inflammable gas" used to inflate balloons. He had discovered "a material ten times lighter than inflammable air . . . in the Promises of Lovers and Courtiers; in the sighs of widowers, in the good resolutions made in a storm at sea, and in sickness on land, and above all, in the compliments contained in Letters of Recommendation."

For the benefit of his friends in England, Franklin wrote another hoax in the vein of his William Henry narrative, this time an alleged *Letter from China* by a former sailor with Captain Cook, who, after a series of incredible adventures, finds himself in a Chinese prison. Franklin sent the piece to Benjamin Vaughan, who eventually had it printed in a monthly periodical, *The Repository.* The work is as close to pure narrative for the sake of entertainment as anything Franklin ever wrote. His sailor, like a European *picaro,* travels over China, associating with all classes of society. Franklin's satire is mild and the targets obscure. He reflects, for example, on the English fondness for tea, revealing that much of it sent to European countries is merely counterfeit tea, made "of the leaves of sweet potatoes," which the Chinese themselves never drank.

Among the political notions which Franklin incorporated in his hoax were his convictions that the Quakers were right in dispensing with a paid clergy and his related belief that legislators should serve for little or no pay.

News from Congress of its acceptance of the peace treaty finally arrived on the last day of March 1784, and Franklin wrote to Hartley announcing his readiness to exchange ratifications. When these formalities were at last carried out, he admitted to Charles Thomson, 13 May, that this was a happy event he had hardly expected to live to see. But he was more inclined to worry over the future of his country than to rejoice in its victory. Without absolute fidelity to its treaties and financial obligations, he warned, the reputation of America would be tarnished and the nation would become subject to fresh attacks.

Franklin's work in Europe was still not at an end, for he was under orders to negotiate treaties of commerce with any powers which presented themselves for the purpose, including England. Franklin confided to Laurens in April that he was none too optimistic about the results of commercial agreements which would combine his "ignorance" with Adams's "positiveness."

His primary concern—apart from securing permission to return home—remained the future welfare of William Temple Franklin, and he wrote tirelessly in his grandson's behalf to anyone whose influence he believed would be instrumental in providing Temple a diplomatic appointment, preferably as secretary to Franklin's successor or chargé d'affaires in the interim. Privately, however, he resigned himself to having his request ignored. In some measure, the indifference of Congress was Franklin's own fault. When he had first begun to petition in Billy's behalf, Henry Laurens advised him to send his grandson back to Congress with a shipment of money so that a personal introduction could help remove "prejudices" which had been entertained against him. Franklin replied, however, that he could not spare his grandson for the voyage. William Temple's plight was the main reason Franklin had initiated his other grandson into the printing trade. Although he had originally thought of having Temple train his cousin for public business, he had become convinced that "Service is no Inheritance" and had determined instead "to give him a Trade that he may have something to depend on, and not be oblig'd to ask Favours or Offices of anybody."

In one sense the studied refusal of Congress to reward William Temple Franklin was a foretaste of the callousness which that body was soon to reveal at the death of Franklin. Also, certain members may have interpreted Franklin's intercession for Temple as a type of nepotism, which, of course, it was in part, even though Franklin habitually extended his family wings so broadly that he could very well have spread them to embrace almost any promising young man.

Congress, apparently having heard rumors that the commissioners in Paris enjoyed an opulent standard of living and entertained lavishly, thereupon reduced their living allowance. Franklin ironically commended this economy drive to Adams, whom he may have held partly responsible. Visiting Americans, he promised, "must be contented for the future, as I am, with plain beef and pudding. The readers of Connecticut newspapers ought not to be troubled for any more accounts of our extravagance."

By the time that Adams again took up residence in Paris, late in August 1784, however, he and Franklin once more lived in terms of open cordiality and frequently dined together. Perhaps harmony prevailed because the task of negotiating commercial treaties was easier on the nerves than the manifold cares of wartime or because Jefferson, who had finally joined his fellow commissioners, exercised a moderating influence. Adams acknowledged with surprise that "The Dr. is very gracious, never so much so since he was born, at least since I knew him."

Earlier in the year, Franklin's retrospective view of his own private character had led him to generalize about his enemies, both in England and America. He recognized that, as a public official, he had implacable foes but felt that he could "thank God there are not in the whole world any who are my Enemies as a Man." He found it a "comfortable Reflection" in his old age that no human being could justly say "Ben. Franklin has wrong'd me." Unfortunately this easy assurance did not mean that Franklin's enemies shared his comfortable reflection.

Although at the time he was conscious only of the calumnies which he believed Adams and others had been circulating in America, a malevolent animosity still tormented the mind of Franklin's old antagonist, William Smith. Franklin wrote to Laurens, 13 March 1784, asking his aid in refuting aspersions on his character and admitting that the only ambition he still possessed was "that of dying with the fair Character he had long endeavoured to deserve." To give these serious thoughts a less somber note, Franklin added that he was too modest to claim infallibility for himself in general but that he was like most people in claiming it in particular instances. After quoting Steele to the effect that the difference between the Church of Rome and the Church of England is "that the one pretends to be *infallible,* and the other to be *never in the wrong,*" he affirmed that "in this latter Sense, we are most of us Church of England men, though few of us confess it, and express it so naturally and frankly, as a certain great Lady here, who said, 'I don't know how it happens, but I meet with nobody, except myself, that is *always* in the right.' " In the last speech Franklin ever made—one in the Constitutional Convention—he quoted these humorous words almost verbatim, another example of his extraordinary power of memory.

Franklin's retrospective mood was encouraged by Benjamin Vaughan and two French friends, Le Veillard, future mayor of Passy, and La Rochefoucauld, who urged him to continue the writing of his autobiography. Some time during the year 1784, he wrote the second part, which is devoted primarily to his scheme for obtaining moral perfection. The large amount of moral retrospection in his correspondence at this time may have been in part an outgrowth of this literary endeavor.

In one of his letters to Samuel Mather, 12 May, he testified to the salutary influence on his life of reading a book by the clergyman's father, the great Cotton Mather, *Essays to Do Good*. He revealed as well an unusual mental characteristic apparent also in his memoirs, an almost superstitious preoccupation with odd relations and coincidences in numbers and events. Recalling that he had left Boston in 1723 and revisited the city every tenth year thereafter until 1773, when he was residing in England, he added that he had hoped to be there also in 1783 but had not been able to prevail upon Congress to relieve him of his duties in Paris. In 1770, he had presented the same numerical patterns in a letter to a distant cousin, evincing a pleasure akin to that which he found in working out his magic mathematical circles.

During the summer of 1784, Franklin received a conciliatory letter from his son, regretting their estrangement and inquiring about his own son, William Temple. Apparently Franklin felt more pain than paternal satisfaction, for his reply revealed stronger patriotic feelings than tender ones. Nothing had ever hurt him so much, he wrote, "as to find myself deserted in my old Age by my only Son; and not only deserted, but to find him taking up Arms against me, in a Cause, where my good Fame, Fortune and Life were all at Stake." Then, perhaps realizing that he had gone a little too far in playing the aggrieved father (and documents from 1776 do not indicate that Franklin's suffering at that time was so great as he now pretended) , he admitted that he had no right to blame his son for his political views since all opinions are not in our own power. "They are form'd and govern'd much by Circumstances, that are often as inexplicable as they are irresistible." Yet immediately after this highly rational principle and the admission that few would have censured William for remaining neutral, Franklin added the very debatable concept, which he underlined, that *there are Natural Duties which precede political ones, and cannot be extinguish'd by them.*

Franklin admitted rather coldly that he would like to see his son when convenient but added that he would not like him to come to France at present. William would have to be content with seeing Temple, whom Franklin was then sending to London, carrying his letter. Franklin intended Temple to study law eventually, "as a necessary Part of Knowledge for a public Man," and to this purpose he asked William to turn over his lawbooks to his son. Poignantly he cautioned William against introducing his son "to Company, that it may be improper for him to be seen with."

William Temple set out immediately on his journey, and Franklin, requiring him to write by every post, felt all the concern of a parent during his child's first absence from home, particularly when he heard that Temple had contracted and been cured of a fever. In September he gave his consent to the young man's making a holiday trip with his father, which would require him to stay in England until the middle of October. For almost a month thereafter, Franklin received no letters from his grandson and was hurt and angry, particularly when his acquaintances asked for tidings. "Judge what I must feel, what they must think," he complained, "and tell me what I am to think of such neglect." He was sure it must have been neglect, for even if Temple's fever had returned William could have sent some word of explanation. Franklin's letter crossed one from Temple, however, and he was mollified, even consenting to Temple's staying away until the end of October.

Franklin probably worried that William might try to wean Temple away from his grandfather's influence—and Franklin had reason for his suspicion. In the summer of 1782, Temple had approached Benjamin Vaughan secretly, proposing that he ask Shelburne to reward the New Jersey governor with a post in the British diplomatic service. Temple urged Vaughan to report that William had been "the only Governor that gave to his Court plain and wholesome advice before the war." This was at the very moment that Franklin was holding out as the most intransigent of the American commissioners against any form of recompensing loyalists. Adams wrote in his diary at the time (26 November 1782), Dr. Franklin "is very staunch against the Tories; more decided a great deal on this Point than Mr. Jay or my self." To say the least, Temple, in his solicitude for his father, was showing marked disloyalty to his grandfather, no matter how exemplary his filial concern may have been.

During the entire year Franklin continued to suffer from the stone, but he had no thoughts of undergoing an operation. He experienced acute pain only when traveling by carriage or making sudden movement, and he hoped by "abstemious living and gentle exercise" to keep the stone from growing larger. Once in the company of a learned audience, composed of a physician, René des Genettes, the scientists Bailly and J.-B. Le Roy, and the future mayor of Passy, Le Veillard, Franklin deserted his customary taciturnity to discuss the nature and cure of his malady. He observed that the erudite d'Alembert, well documented on the probabilities, had constantly refused to undergo an operation because of its accompanying dangers and his advanced age and that Buffon for the same reason endured his suffering with patience. Later Franklin learned that Buffon suffered pains exactly like his own.

He explained to Jay, 6 January 1784, that he could get around quite well as long as he traveled by foot, adding, "I am chearful, enjoy the company of my Friends, sleep well, have sufficient appetite, and my Stomach performs well its Functions." Lest the latter happy condition change, he refused to take drugs, having a greater fear of "the Medicines than of the Malady." He believed, as he wrote to a French physician, that every rich city contains "a Number of Persons who are never in health, because they are fond of Medicines and always taking them, whereby they derange the natural Functions, and hurt their Constitutions." Franklin was certainly no hypochondriac, although he recognized psychological influences upon health. In regard to the reputed magical cures of Mesmer, which Franklin looked upon sceptically, he admitted that if the wizard's disciples could "be persuaded to forbear their Drugs in Expectation of being cured by only the Physician's Finger or an Iron Rod pointing at them, they may possibly find good Effects tho they mistake the Cause."

Another of Franklin's ailments was that of failing eyesight, which he remedied by his own invention of bifocal glasses. "If all the other Defects and Infirmities were as easily and cheaply remedied," he remarked to his old friend George Whatley (21 August, 1784), "it would be worth while for Friends to live a good deal longer, but I look upon Death to be as necessary to our Constitution as Sleep. We shall rise refreshed in the Morning."

Franklin found the pain of the gout and stone easier to bear throughout the next winter of 1785 because Polly Hewson, now a comfortable matron in her forties, had finally made the plunge and come to Passy with her three children to stay with her old friend, breakfasting with him most mornings, taking tea in the evening, and playing cards at night. Because of her company, Franklin "pass'd a long Winter, in a manner that made it appear the shortest" of any he had ever known. Polly did not return to England until April 1785, when Franklin was making his own preparations for his homeward journey to America. No evidence has so far come to light as to whether Polly ever came into contact with Mmes. Brillon and Helvétius or whether she knew of Franklin's local amours. Significantly, however, his correspondence with these French ladies dropped off sharply after Polly's arrival.

Franklin's major political concern remained the false reports emanating from England concerning the alleged internal dissensions in America, which had abated the desires of other European powers for commercial treaties. Although he stubbornly attacked these rumors vis-à-vis all Europeans, he admitted to Jay (3 February 1785) that he was disturbed by his country's failure to meet the first year's interest due to France as well as by the constant moving of Congress from place to place. But he pretended to Hartley (3 January) that Congress was in no hurry to negotiate a commercial treaty and shrewdly painted a very prosperous picture of the American economy. To Vaughan, he expressed the theory, 5 March, that the British fabricated accounts of political confusion and oppression in America as "necessary Bugbears to keep your People from Emigrating and make them more content with their Brothers at home." Franklin even professed to be glad of the British tales, since they might "keep Fools from us, whom we do not want."

In a letter to a British publicist, Francis Baron Maseres, a financier with whom Franklin and Richard Jackson had been associated in the days of the Canada pamphlet, Franklin pre-

sented a retrospective view of the Revolution in a virtual formal
letter of farewell to his former English associates. Even for
England, he maintained, American independence would prove
to be more favorable than the old system of keeping the colonies
in subjection. Once more using his symbol of the porcelain vase,
he remarked that the parts of the empire "must now do as well as
they can for themselves," but he had great hopes for the western
part and offered good wishes for the other. Perhaps with his son
William in mind, he grimly stated the case against the Loyalists
and, with precedents drawn from British history, vindicated the
confiscation of their estates. Harking back to the political
platform of the *Pennsylvania Gazette* in its opposition to the
arbitrary policies of proprietor and governor, Franklin passion-
ately described the philosophy and sentiment of his countrymen
as "resisting arbitrary impositions, that were contrary to common right and to their fundamental constitutions, and to constant ancient usage." In a sense, this doctrine epitomizes the
basic policies which Franklin had supported during his whole
political career from assemblyman to plenipotentiary.

Some time during the previous year, a township in Massachusetts had taken the name Franklin in his honor and had
proposed building a steeple for its church if Franklin would
provide the bell. Franklin felt that the townspeople would do
better to defer construction for the present and accept instead
his gift of the nucleus of a parish library, "Sense being preferable to Sound." His sister Jane, learning about her brother's
proposal through Jonathan Williams, repeated the wordplay
approvingly and recommended Samuel Stennett's *Discourses on
Personal Religion* as a good book to be included. At the
dedication of Franklin's library, the minister preached from the
significant text, "Show thyself a Man."

In June 1785, Hugh Roberts, the only surviving member of
the Junto except Franklin and Philip Syng, wrote to remind
Franklin of the melancholy aspects of their longevity, adding
that "few, if any, are capable of judging of the imbecility of an
old man, but an old man." Franklin undoubtedly left Paris
before this letter could be delivered, but he wrote on the same
subject himself to another old crony, George Whatley. The

latter, less optimistic and more materialistic than Franklin about death, could not understand Franklin's doctrine of "our rising from it, or after it, refreshed in the morning." Also he professed to feel complete indifference about his reputation after death, paraphrasing Alexander Pope:

> . . . he ne'er cared a pin
> What they said or may say of the Mortal within.

Franklin, for his part, felt that it is "natural to wish to be well spoken of, whether alive or dead" and preferred the sentiment of a song by a different Pope, Walter:

> May I govern my Passions with an absolute sway
> Grow wiser and better as my Strength wears away,
> Without Gout or Stone, by a gentle Decay.

In his youth Franklin had sung this refrain a thousand times, but he now ruefully admitted at fourscore that the three contraries had befallen him, "being subject to the Gout and the Stone, and not being yet Master of all my Passions." He based his faith in a future life on his observation that God exhibits frugality as well as wisdom in his works. Finding himself existing, Franklin therefore believed that he would always exist in some shape or another.

He reflected an even more complacent view of old age one day on a visit to Mme. Helvétius, when she expressed the hope that he was happy.

I become more so every day [he replied]. I have never had the misfortune of finding myself ill. First poor, then rich, I have always been content with what I have, without thinking about what I have not; but since I have begun to age, since my passions have diminished, I feel a well-being of mind and heart that I never knew before and which is impossible to know at the age of . . . young people. . . . At that age, the spirit is *exterior;* at mine, it is *interior;* it looks out the window at the stir of those who pass by without taking part in their disputes.

34. Home Again

AFTER months of waiting, Franklin finally received permission from Congress for his home-coming, 2 May 1785, while in the midst of a long letter of scientific recollection to Jan Ingenhousz. He was so carried away that he unrealistically invited his fellow scientist to accompany him to America to cooperate in scientific experiments. "I shall now be free of Politicks for the rest of my Life," he exulted. "Welcome again my dear Philosophical Amusements." Franklin was equally tired of office routine and the burden of being a celebrity, which exposed him "to numberless Visits, some of Kindness and Civility, many of mere idle Curiosity, from Strangers of America & of different Parts of Europe." Such attention, he admitted, "may for a while flatter one's Vanity, but its Effects are troublesome." His desire to return to scientific retirement was no pose but the same genuine concern for privacy he had expressed almost forty years previously when he had disposed of his printing business in Philadelphia.

His French friends at first attempted to dissuade him from leaving, three of them offering him a place of permanent residence. They argued that the French people universally loved and esteemed him, that his friends in America were constantly being diminished by death, and that at home he would encounter envy and enmity provided that he even survived the voyage. Presumably France and America would have been equally well suited for his philosophical pursuits, but he explained to his daughter that the desire to spend the remainder of his life with his family had decided him for America. Probably since he had been unable to establish a permanent family connection with either Mme. Helvétius or the Brillons, he succumbed to a natural nostalgia for his native land and pleasantly anticipated the plaudits of his countrymen.

He wrote immediately to Vergennes, 3 May, thanking him for his protection and countenance during the first uneasy weeks in Paris as well as for his continued favors. Because his malady still prevented attendance at Versailles, he asked the minister to convey to Louis XVI his deep sense of "all the inestimable Benefits his Goodness has conferr'd on my Country."

On the same day, Franklin prepared a memorandum for Barclay, the American fiscal agent in Paris, showing that the government owed him 263,818 livres for the period since April 1781. In the previous year Congress had reduced the salaries of plenipotentiaries from 2,500 livres to 2,000 livres annually, an action which Franklin knew about since he had ironically condoled with Adams over it. When Barclay queried Franklin's continuing to reckon the old figure as his salary, he shrewdly quoted the original resolution of Congress in 1779 and affirmed that he had received no official notice that it had been changed. Admitting that he had heard of the general salary cut, he argued that it must apply only to new appointees, since a minister appointed under the old system and encouraged "to engage in a Way of Living" for the honor of his country could not suddenly reduce his expenses by one fifth. Yet he expressed his willingness to rest the ultimate decision on the "Equity of Congress," from which he expected "some Consideration."

As late as 12 June 1785, Franklin was still undecided whether he could make the homeward journey in this year. His health would not permit his traveling overland to L'Orient on the west coast of Brittany, and there was no scheduled packet from Le Havre until 20 August, a date involving the risk of equinoctial storms. He even wrote to Mme. Chaumont, asking whether it would be convenient for him to spend the ensuing winter at the castle of Chaumont on the Loire, which he could reach by water.

One of Franklin's last personal duties before leaving Paris had been to put into practice his principle of a chain of benevolence by offering advice and assistance to a young American friend, the grandson of his former benefactor, Samuel Vernon of Newport, whose money Franklin had indiscreetly broken into as a young man. The grandson, William Henry Vernon, having resided in France for several years, had approached Franklin in September 1784 with the request that he certify a draft from London. Franklin not only did so but offered to lend the money himself if the draft were still not redeemable. Young Vernon accepted the offer but was unable to pay on the due date. Instead of causing the young man any embarrassment, Franklin lent him a further sum in the following February. About that time a masked lady approached William Temple at a ball to tell him that poor Vernon was wasting the prime of his life in Paris and implored him to intercede with Franklin to persuade the errant youth to return home. Otherwise, she predicted, he would be lost. Next Vernon's landlord sought out Franklin to complain that his lodger had not paid the rent for many months. Franklin then exhorted Vernon to go home immediately, promising, if necessary, to advance him further money to meet his debts. But the young man stubbornly refused to budge from Paris. He seemed to have all the qualities of a sober, useful citizen except for his inability to stay out of debt and his inexplicable attachment to Paris. "If a Lady is in the Case," Franklin mused, half reminiscently, "it is the less to be wonder'd at, the wisest Men being sometimes enslav'd by very improper Connections of that Sort." Young Vernon, however, failed to understand Franklin's good intentions. As Franklin expressed it, "I am afraid I disoblig'd . . . more by the Advice, than I oblig'd by the Money: tho' at the Time he was in great Need of both."

Franklin eventually asked the elder Vernon in America to pay his sister Jane Mecom the money he had advanced to the errant youth. Vernon did so reluctantly, insisting on deducting five dollars for exchange, after which Franklin told Jane composedly, "we must think it well that you got anything."

It was essential that Franklin be "better stow'd" on his return home than he had been on his eastward voyage, or he would not be able to last the trip. At last he arranged for an American ship, the *London Packet,* to pick him up with his goods at Cowes, off the Isle of Wight in the English Channel. Optimistically he wrote to Polly Hewson that the ship had "plenty of room for you and yours."

Under the supervision of Benny Bache and William Temple Franklin, who was recovering from a fever, the packing of Franklin's enormous collection of household effects began on 25 May. When the job was completed, sixty-seven cases—including Franklin's printing press, properly dismantled—lay ready for loading, all bearing lead discs to pass them through the French customs. Jefferson arranged that the English customs would similarly dispense with the usual inspection at Cowes. The boxes were to travel on mule-drawn barges on the meandering Seine to Le Havre, but the twisting of the river made the trip by road about half the distance and far more rapid and comfortable. Franklin, therefore, asked for and received permission to borrow the royal litter to take him as far as Rouen. This was an elaborate carriage drawn by three mules in which the passenger could either sit or recline. As a parting gift and further token of esteem, Louis XVI sent the retiring ambassador his miniature in a frame studded with 408 diamonds.

Franklin's last official act was the signing, 9 July, of the treaty of commerce with Prussia, the treaty containing Franklin's article abolishing privateering.

Departure had been scheduled for daybreak on 12 July, but last-minute farewells and financial settlements consumed nearly the whole day. Franklin stayed on for dinner with the Chaumont family and was not on the road until after five in the evening. The procession, headed by Franklin in his litter and followed by two carriages, one bearing Le Veillard, the two grandsons and a servant, the other holding Chaumont and his daughter, passed through the Bois de Boulogne to the Porte Maillot, accompanied on foot by a number of friends and curiosity seekers. As Jefferson later wrote, when Franklin left Passy, "It seemed as if the village had lost its patriarch." At the rear of the procession there followed a wagon holding twenty-seven pieces of baggage weighing altogether 1,700 pounds. The travelers made the first twelve of their more than 140 miles by eight o'clock. Before starting out the next morning, Franklin wrote to his sister, informing her of his last official act in France and his imminent arrival in Philadelphia. "I have continu'd to work till late in the Day," he wrote; " 'tis time I should go home, and go to Bed"—the same analogy between sleep and death which he had used many years previously in his parody of religious meditations in the *Pennsylvania Gazette.*

Recent letters from Jane had not been very cheerful concerning the infirmities of old age. Suffering attacks of dizziness, she had begun to fear that she would live out the rest of her life "in such Circumstances as Dean Swift was." Despite the anguish of mind she suffered from hearing of Franklin's grievous physical malady, she still found his circumstances to be preferred to her own, since retaining one's "Intlectual Faculties & such Fortitude to bear up under it must be Preferable to a Senslis Stupidetie." She lay awake nights, nevertheless, "thinking what Excruciating Pains you might then be Incountering while I a Poor Useles, & worthless worm was Premitted to be at Ease."

Presumably Franklin made another late start on the second day of travel, for the party then covered only twenty miles. On the fourth day, they reached the cathedral town of Rouen, where one of the directors of the Academy of Rouen presented him with a kind of magical square or acrostic, supposed to spell out FRANKLIN, but he could not comprehend it.

Before leaving Paris, Franklin had distributed presents and keepsakes to most of his friends, and on the way to Rouen he remembered that the Abbé Morellet had taken a great liking to his armchair or *fauteuil doctoral.* Going to bed early, Franklin asked William Temple to send a request to their former landlord Chaumont that he turn over the chair to Morellet. Chaumont complied, and Morellet proudly inscribed his gift, *Benjamin Franklin hic sedebat.*

On the fifth day of travel they reached the coastal town of Balbec and completed their journey on the sixth day, 18 July, entering Le Havre at five in the evening. Franklin had borne the jostling and strain with surprising ease. Indeed his strength and spirits seemed to improve with every step of the way, vindicating his theory that his annual vacation jaunts, which he had been obliged to forgo for the past eight years, had helped greatly to preserve his health and vigor throughout his life.

At Le Havre they were joined by the eminent sculptor Houdon, whose bust of Franklin had been the rage of Paris ever since its exhibition in 1779. The artist had not been presented to Franklin, however, until late in 1783, having worked from sketches and observations in public. Shortly afterwards Franklin and Jefferson engaged Houdon on behalf of the Assembly of Virginia to execute a statue of Washington, and the master and his three assistants were planning to sail on the same vessel with Franklin. By engaging Houdon, Franklin had aroused the professional jealousy of Houdon's chief rival Caffieri, whom Franklin had commissioned in 1776 to create for Congress a monument celebrating the heroic death of General Montgomery. Caffieri, a friend of Mme. Helvétius, then completed a bust of Franklin in the spring of 1777, which Charles Sellers, the authority on Franklin iconography, has called the "best reflection of Franklin's appearance, carefully and surely made by a competent artist, from life." Franklin's sister termed an engraving based upon it, "more to your Likeness than any I have heartofore seen." Although all evidence indicates that Franklin considered it to be undoubtedly superior to Houdon's, he still gave the latter the coveted Washington commission. When the aggrieved Caffieri complained bitterly of being supplanted, Franklin patiently explained that Congress and the State of Virginia were distinct governments and that Virginia, in selecting his rival, may perhaps "not have made a better Choice" but certainly had done Caffieri no injustice. Houdon and his workers had traveled from Paris by diligence, or stagecoach, and had sent all their effects by barge.

At Le Havre, Franklin received a letter of farewell from Mme. Helvétius, who predicted mutual happiness if he would return to her little retreat. Earlier Mme. Brillon had written in a warmer strain: "All the days of my existence I shall remember that a great man, a sage, wanted to be my friend. My best wishes will follow him everywhere; my heart will miss him eternally."

Several vessels offered to take Franklin to Southampton, but he found them all too expensive and preferred to wait for the packet. The entire party embarked for the channel crossing at ten in the morning of 22 July and, owing to the rough weather, were at sea for forty-six hours before docking at Southampton. At the last moment, Le Veillard decided to continue as far as England with his friend, in order, as he later confided to Condorcet, "to defer the melancholy instant of an eternal separation." All of the passengers were deathly sick except Franklin, who proved to be as good a sailor as he had been in his teens. He later admitted, nevertheless, that after every one of his sea voyages he had solemnly resolved never to take another.

The party remained in Southampton for three days, during which Franklin was reunited with his estranged son, apparently with no great display of emotion on either side. Also on hand were Bishop Shipley, his wife, and his daughter Catherine, the nymphet of the carriage ride many years before. All stayed with Franklin until the last moment.

After Franklin and his son had gone through the approved civilities, William sold his real estate holdings in New Jersey to William Temple for the sum of 48,000 livres, which Franklin advanced as a loan to be secured by a mortgage. Optimistically, Franklin gave William a power to recover any money from the British government which it still owed him.

Still an inveterate swimmer, Franklin went to bathe in Martin's Salt Water Hot Baths and performed the incredible feat of falling asleep while floating on his back and remaining for an hour in this position without sinking, turning or waking. Later he remarked, "Water is the easiest bed that can be."

For some reason Polly Hewson did not come to Southampton either to embark with her friend or to bid him farewell—a great mystery. Franklin took his leave by letter, but in a quite different vein from his calm allegory to Jane about going home to bed. He had not given up his vision of Polly's coming to Philadelphia and promised that she would always find an affectionate friend in him and, after his death, in his children.

On 27 July, Franklin learned that the *London Packet* was waiting at Cowes, off the Isle of Wight, and the voyagers with their friends set out by shallop to board her, arriving in time for tea with the captain, Thomas Truxtun. The vessel, built in

Philadelphia and returning on the westward leg of its maiden voyage, probably offered, as she advertised, about as "elegant and convenient accommodations" as were then available on the Atlantic. The escorting party stayed on board for a round of festivities until four o'clock the next morning, and the ship sailed an hour later, long before which Franklin had retired for his sleep. The heavy baggage, making its way down the Seine, did not reach the *London Packet* in time and had to be left for another vessel.

Since the baggage of the Houdon party also was left behind, the hapless artists were obliged to depend on the other passengers for an occasional change of linen. In addition to those already named, Franklin's fellow voyagers consisted of his grandnephew, Jonathan Williams, Jr., and thirteen German redemptioners, i.e., emigrants who would be obliged to redeem the cost of their passage by working upon arrival. So that Franklin would not be disturbed by disagreeable company, he had engaged all the cabin space for his party.

The voyage was on the whole smooth except for one extremely violent wind, the like of which Captain Truxtun had never before experienced, which sent the bowsprit sail crashing to the deck. To pass the time, Benny and Temple kept diaries, and Franklin resumed his observations of the Gulf Stream and wrote three scientific papers.

These he composed instead of continuing his autobiography, since the former could be written out of his head but the latter required documentation. Franklin dedicated one of his papers, *Maritime Observations,* to David Le Roy, who had earlier written on the navigation of the ancients. In his work, Franklin set forth many of his observations on the Gulf Stream, explained why some sinking ships which had been abandoned still remained afloat, and suggested a new manner of rigging sails for maximum speed. Finally, he presented various hints for preserving life in the event of shipwreck.

The most interesting passage for modern readers in Franklin's second piece, *On the Causes and Cure of Smoky Chimneys,* concerns his annoyance with human perversity in divorcing esthetics from nature.

In time [he complained], perhaps, that which is fittest in the nature of things may come to be thought handsomest. But at present when Men and Women in different Countries show themselves dissatisfied with the Forms God has given to their Heads, Waists, and Feet, and pretend to shape them more perfectly, it is hardly to be expected that they will be content always with the best Form of a Chimney.

Before leaving France, Franklin had expressed to the Abbé de La Roche the same preference for humble yet useful objects over incommodious luxury. He ridiculed the quantities of "marble, porcelain and gilt squandered without utility, elegant fireplaces which smoke without heating; tables on which one cannot write without freezing . . . ; beds and alcoves where one may sleep in good health, but where in sickness it is impossible to be cared for or to read or to write comfortably." In his shipboard tract he also elaborated on his theory of fresh air, admitting that at one time he, like most of his contemporaries, had suffered from aerophobia. But now he hoped that the research of a century or two might convince mankind that fresh and cool air "is not bad even for People in Health."

Franklin's third treatise, *Description of a New Stove for Burning of Pitcoal,* consisted of the observations which, two years previously, Cadet de Vaux had implored him to put into writing.

The *London Packet* sighted land on 11 September and docked at Franklin's "dear Philadelphia" early in the morning three days later. Franklin concluded his travel diary: "God be praised and thanked for all his mercies."

Richard Bache sailed out to greet his relatives in a small boat, and they were welcomed by a salvo of cannon shots, the ringing of bells, and "a crowd of people with huzzas," a crowd so large that it seemed to be the whole population of the city. The houses were decorated with the flags of all nations, including England. Temple "cried for joy all through the streets," and his tears were doubled when he saw that he "was not the only one thus moved." Franklin's daughter Sally, who was working in her garden when she heard news of her father's landing, collapsed on a wheelbarrow and wept. The crowd followed Franklin to his very door and watched the touching scene of the meeting of father and daughter.

As could be expected, almost as soon as Franklin crossed the threshold of his house, friends and dignitaries came pouring in to bid him welcome. These included, 15 September, a delegation from the Pennsylvania Assembly, headed by its speaker, John Bayard; on the next day, the faculty of the University of Pennsylvania, headed by its Presbyterian provost, John Ewing; and, on 17 September, fifteen members of a political organization, the Constitutional Society.

Violent party conflicts had broken out in Pennsylvania during Franklin's absence, involving interests as irreconcilable and clashes of personality as discordant as any Franklin had experienced in the sordid campaign of 1764. The chief issue now was the state constitution, drawn up in 1776 when Franklin had been president of the convention. Since Franklin was generally believed to have inspired most of its fundamental philosophy, the Constitutional Society looked upon him as its patron and sought to trade on the prestige of his name. The wary Franklin, however, in addressing the Constitutionalists, limited his remarks to the past without making any commitment for the future. "My principal merit, if I may claim any, in public affairs," he said, "is that of having been always ready and willing to receive and follow good advice."

On the next day, the Anti-Constitutionalist party announced that Franklin would run with its backing for a seat on the Supreme Executive Council of Pennsylvania, and eventually the Constitutional Society and the Mechanical Society (skilled workers) also nominated him. Franklin felt that his influence would help in reconciling the antagonisms of the various factions. Jay, however, feared that "if he gives himself up to one, he must expect hostility from the other."

In the meantime, Franklin's "adopted political son," Thomas Paine, sent a letter of felicitation from New York, expressing the wish that Franklin would never have cause to regret having been the one to introduce him to America. After congratulating Franklin on his retirement, he explained that he would have delivered his message in person were it not for his pursuing an "affair" with Congress, the seeking of reimbursement for his services during the Revolution, an activity which Franklin himself would soon be forced to engage in on his own behalf.

Franklin found it almost embarrassing to reply that he would not be devoting himself to ease and rest as Paine and everyone else expected, but that he had acceded to the demands of his fellow citizens to present himself for the office of councilor at the next election. Modestly he predicted that "without doing the good propos'd, I shall find myself engag'd again in Business more troublesome than I have lately quitted."

It was easier for Franklin to write to George Washington, informing him of the arrival of Houdon to sculpt his bust. Washington enjoyed such a great reputation among the French people, Franklin wrote, that they universally hoped to see him in their midst, but, when told that this was extremely improbable, they could be satisfied only by "a Sight of his perfect Resemblance" by means of their best sculptor.

As was expected, Franklin was elected to the Executive Council of Pennsylvania by acclaim, 11 October, and, as might also have been predicted, he was chosen Council president a week later, on the day after taking his seat. The General Assembly then came together with the Council to elect Franklin as president of the state, 26 October, only one voice in seventy-seven voting against him. He assumed office on the last day of the month.

His private letters indicate an ambivalent attitude toward the new honor and responsibility. For Mme. Helvétius, to whom political office was less important than a close circle of congenial friends, he described his re-entry into political life as a "weakness" predicated on the hope of doing good for his people. Without this expectation, he would have preferred accepting her invitation to finish his days in her company. In even stronger language to Dr. and Mrs. John Bard, a physician and intimate friend since the earliest days of Franklin's electrical experiments, he condemned himself for lacking "firmness enough to resist" the desires of his fellow citizens to harness him again in their service. "They engross the prime of my life. They have eaten my flesh, and seem resolved now to pick my bones." And he suggested to Bishop Shipley that he might retire after one year. But to the politically oriented David Hartley, Franklin proudly reported the addresses from all ranks by which he was welcomed home as well as the nearly unanimous vote by which he was elected president. And with equal pride he announced to Jan Ingenhousz that he had been "plac'd at the Head of my Country by its unanimous Voice."

The Pennsylvania constitution then in force had gone through some changes during Franklin's absence in France, one of which—a provision requiring an oath of allegiance to the constitution itself as a requisite for voting or office-holding—he felt compelled to speak out against (11 November) in his first message to the Assembly. These test laws, he affirmed, "are at present, on various accounts, the cause of much uneasiness in the State. We are, therefore, of opinion that it is now expedient to revise them." Previously, while the constitution was being framed, Franklin had opposed a similar clause requiring Assembly members to declare their belief that the whole of the Old Testament was given by divine inspiration, but, fearing that an even more compromising declaration might be proposed, he had accepted the clause after first prevailing upon his colleagues to agree that no further or extended profession should ever be required.

Apparently Franklin did not write to his sister until he had been at home for over a fortnight, although other members of the family undoubtedly sent her the good news of his arrival. Jane had expressed a strong desire to see her brother again, but he dissuaded her from making the arduous trip to Philadelphia since he hoped to visit Boston in the coming spring. Franklin's grandnephew Jonathan Williams, Jr., through an unfortunate investment, had lost all the capital he had put aside in Europe, and Franklin thereupon thought of the family crown soap as a potential money-maker for him—as he had earlier suggested it to other members of his family. He asked Jane, therefore, to furnish Jonathan the recipe and also to make up for himself a parcel of the soap to the weight of forty or fifty pounds to be used as presents for his friends in France. Franklin apparently felt that the occupation would be good for his sister as well as offering Jonathan guidance in the manufacturing process. Jane accepted the task with alacrity, suggesting that an emblem of thirteen stars for the states be stamped on each cake.

When Jane chided her brother for accepting the burden and responsibility of the presidency of Pennsylvania, he characteristically replied that all of us have wisdom enough to judge how other people should manage their affairs, "and 'tis possible I might blame you as much if you were to accept the Offer of a young Husband." He was teasing both himself and Jane.

On 1 January 1786, Franklin wrote to his sister that God had brought them, "the last Survivors of 17 Brothers & Sisters to the Beginning of a new Year," and that the "Health & Strength we enjoy at so advanc'd an Age, now near Fourscore [nearly eighty-one for Franklin], is a great Blessing." Many times during the year he confided to various friends that the pain of the stone had not augmented since leaving France, and in October he even said, according to Benjamin Rush, "that in the last 30 years of his life, he had never enjoyed better health, than at present." A few weeks earlier he had discussed the subject of tobacco with Rush and expressed his opinion that in a few years it would go out of use. After discoursing on the decrease of smoking in England and snuff-taking in France, he concluded that no form of tobacco was advantageous. He had associated with many persons who used it, but none had ever advised him to follow their example. He had never snuffed, chewed or smoked.

On New Year's Day, Franklin briefly realized his retirement goal of returning to scientific pursuits. He and Thomas Paine, now returned from New York, spent the entire day from noon dinner until after tea experimenting with a smokeless candle of Paine's invention. Paine at this time had already embarked upon a much vaster project, the designing of the first iron bridge in America. By the end of the year he had erected a model, thirteen feet long on a scale of 1 to 24, which he stored temporarily at Franklin's house. On one occasion, the two scientists along with David Rittenhouse put the bridge model through the test of standing on it all at one time, and eventually Paine transferred it to the committee room of the State House.

Franklin became for Paine the model of an ideal and happy old age: "His mind was ever young, his temper ever serene; science, that never grows grey, was always his mistress."

Although encouraging and helpful toward Paine, Franklin in these days failed to live up to his much publicized principle of supporting young talent and hailing scientific enterprise. When John Fitch, who preceded Fulton as the inventor of the steamboat, solicited Franklin's approval of his drawings and models, Franklin refused to give him a statement that his project had any value or help him in obtaining subscriptions to build a steamboat. He merely went to his desk and took out a small sum of money which he held out, apparently to rid himself of a troublesome visitor. Fitch refused to accept the money unless Franklin would acknowledge it as a subscription to the steamboat. "I esteem it," Fitch later wrote, "one of the most imprudent acts of my life, that I had not treated the insult with the indignity which he merited, and stomped the poltry [sic] Ore under my feet." Paine, however, behaved in a quite different fashion, showing the eager entrepreneur a method of simplifying his apparatus and giving him five shillings for one of his maps of the Northwest. Franklin's behavior toward Fitch exhibited the same chill disregard he had earlier shown toward the Chevalier de Berny in France.

Samuel Vaughan, brother of Benjamin, visited Franklin frequently and once reported his prodigious memory—a characteristic confirmed in Franklin's writings by his extraordinary capacity to repeat his own phraseology of many years past. Vaughan knew of "few transactions, subjects or publications, ancient or modern, that are of any note but what he retains and when necessary in conversation will repeat and retain with wonderful facility." Franklin bathed "twice a week statedly (for hours) in a hot bath," contentedly sitting in a copper shoe-shaped vessel and reading with his book comfortably placed on a support across the top. Andrew Ellicott, the surveyor of

Washington, D. C., who spent a day in Franklin's company, expressed surprise that he continued to shave himself at his advanced age. The practical philosopher replied, "I think happiness does not consist so much in particular pieces of good fortune that perhaps accidentally fall to a man's lot, as to be able in his old age to do these little things which, was he unable to perform himself, would be done by others with a sparing hand."

From his sister Jane, Franklin received a request for a copy of the phonetic alphabet which he had originally devised in the Stevenson household. Although he and the brilliant Polly had heretofore been the chief experimenters to use it, he had conceived it for humbler minds such as Jane, who was in her own words one "of the Thousand, & thousands, that write on to old Age and cant Learn" traditional spelling. Like Franklin's revision of the Book of Common Prayer, Franklin's alphabet is a further example of his concern for the ordinary human being. Jane and her daughter succeeded in mastering the art of writing it in three days. When Noah Webster in this same year acquainted Franklin with a scheme of his own for reforming the alphabet, Franklin enthusiastically welcomed the young linguist as an exponent of similar ideas and promised his best support.

Franklin consoled Jane for her bad spelling (4 July 1786) with the assurance that "as our Alphabet now Stands, the bad Spelling, or what is call'd so, is generally the best, as conforming to the Sound of the Letters and of the Words." Relating an anecdote of a chambermaid's ability to understand phonetic spelling better than the traditional spelling of her employers, he led Jane to speculate on the theory that environment produces genius, that thousands of eminent scientists and philosophers "have Probably been lost to the world, and lived and died in Ignorance and meanness, mearly for want of being Placed in favourable Situations, and Injoying Proper Advantages." Since Jane had before her the example of her eminent brother—whose advantages had not been much greater than her own—she could not quite accept this romantic theory. She soberly remarked, therefore, that "very few we know is Able to beat thro all Impediments and Arive to any Grat Degre of superiority in Understanding."

Jane, with the aid of Jonathan Williams, Jr., had made the soap which Franklin wanted for gifts to be sent to France, but when it arrived in Philadelphia he discovered that it had been affected by frost and would crumble. He, nevertheless, sent twenty-two cakes to be distributed to eighteen of his French friends, identifying it merely as "not made for Sale in this Country at present." His daughter also experimented with dissolving and reshaping some of the remaining cakes. In the eighteenth century, good soap was a valuable commodity, no matter where produced.

In his concern for Jane's welfare, Franklin did not rely exclusively on her own letters, as an index of her needs, but asked Jonathan Williams, Jr., to tell him frankly whether "she lives comfortably, or is pinched" since she may have been "too cautious" in mentioning her difficulties.

The rest of Franklin's family was presenting no problems. Sally, her husband and their children went about their daily routine, delighted with Franklin's genial presence and the prestige of his great name. Benny Bache was studying diligently at the University of Pennsylvania as further preparation for his career as a printer, and William Temple, on the surface "seriously intent upon a Country Life," had begun cultivating the farm he had taken over from his father. Although Franklin was a city man himself, he adhered to the theory that agriculture is "the most independent, the most useful & therefore the most honourable of all our Employments." Franklin had pushed both his son and his grandson into country life, but neither took to it. William was always more of a politician than a gentleman farmer, and after Franklin's death William Temple made his way back to the more congenial atmosphere of London and Paris.

Franklin's dominating principle in rearing both his son and his grandsons was that they should stand on their own feet and not depend upon him for a livelihood. He had frequently remarked to Cabanis that his heirs would find it difficult to appreciate the values of life unless the need of establishing themselves spurred their activity. "I would hold myself culpable toward them," he said, "if I sought to shower upon them the advantages which ordinarily one enjoys heartily only when one has conquered them by his own efforts." Agreeing with the religious writer Isaac Watts that the man who raises a large family stands "a broader Mark for sorrow," Franklin argued that he stands a broader mark for pleasure as well.

His own domestic situation was ideal, his offspring waiting on him in a house he had built twenty-three years before to his own specifications. It stood near the public market in Market Street. He began an addition to the house, a long room to be used as a library and repository for his instruments. "I hardly know how to justify building a Library at an Age that will soon oblige me to quit it," he confided to his sister; "but we are apt to forget that we are grown old, and Building is an Amusement." He gave another explanation to Thomas Paine after the building was completed and he was putting his books on the shelves:

It has always been my maxim to live on as if I was to live always. It is with such feeling only that we can be stimulated to the exertion necessary to effect any useful purpose. Death will one day lay hold of me, and put an end to all my labours; but, till then, it is my maxim to go on in the old way. I will not anticipate his coming.

Franklin at this time invented a "Long Arm" or instrument for taking books down from high shelves since "old men find it inconvenient to mount a ladder or steps for that purpose, their heads being sometimes subject to giddiness, and their activity, with the steadiness of their joints, being abated by age."

Franklin also spent many pleasant hours in his garden, sometimes sleeping, sometimes taking his nude air baths, and sometimes both. One day he espied a friend's maidservant tripping across the green with a letter which he was extremely anxious to receive. His long habit of going without clothes, coupled with his desire for the letter, led him to forget his nakedness and run out to meet her. She fled in terror, screaming to her master that the poor old gentleman had been murdered.

"The Indians got possession of the farther end of the village in the night; the chief is in the poor Doctor's house, and as soon as he saw me he ran out, tomahawk in hand, to scalp me." Considering that the well-furnished Philadelphia market constituted the best of vegetable gardens, Franklin turned the land on which his house stood "into grass plots and gravel walks, with trees and flowering shrubs."

Since the entire winter passed without Franklin's receiving any word from Polly Hewson about her welfare or plans, he wrote to her in May 1786, reminiscing over old times and extolling the pleasures and comforts of his situation in Philadelphia. The only advantage of London, he maintained, was the theatre. By the end of the month a letter had come from Polly with the welcome news that she had almost made up her mind to come to America if she could find a ship suitable to make the hazardous and oppressive voyage. Franklin immediately wrote back recommending an agent in London who would help with her travel plans. To taunt her and strengthen her resolve, he added that Temple despaired of her ever coming because she had formerly been so irresolute about her earlier journey to Paris.

The next thing Franklin knew, Temple received a letter in September from John Wilkes, announcing that Polly and her family were already en route to the United States. On 17 October, Polly wrote to Franklin from her ship already in sight of the American shore, asking for his aid in procuring lodging.

Although enshrined as president of his state, Franklin still had doubts concerning the extent of his personal popularity elsewhere in the Union, particularly in New England, where the Adams influence was paramount. On 1 January 1786, he wrote to his old scientific colleague, Bowdoin, thanking him for a letter of congratulation, which had assured him that all his old Boston friends had not been estranged by the "malevolent Representations" of his conduct which had been circulated there. In the next month he inquired of Jonathan Williams, Jr., in what light he now stood among the New England "Country folks," after the calumnies propagated against him apparently emanating from "the Brantry [Braintree] focus," i.e., the Adams clique.

Even though Franklin's reception in Philadelphia had been warmer and more enthusiastic than he had expected and his popularity had continued to stand up, he was prepared for it to diminish and even for his political career to end in disaster. As he later explained to the Abbé de La Roche, "a Man in high Place has so many Occasions, which he cannot avoid of disobliging, if he does his Duty; and those he disobliges have so much more Resentment, than those he obliges have Gratitude, that it often happens when he is strongly attack'd he is weakly defended."

There is some evidence to indicate that Franklin's elevation to the presidency of Pennsylvania gave a deceptive illusion of universal esteem. Even though his great achievements rendered him virtually invulnerable to open criticism, there existed an undercurrent of hostility and resentment among the conservative elements in the state. In retrospect, Deborah Norris Logan, wife of Senator George Logan, "often thought that Dr. Franklin must have sensibly felt the difference between the *éclat* which he enjoyed at the Court of France and the reception which he met with upon his final return to his native country." Although the mass of people in Pennsylvania was "decidedly democratic," Mrs. Logan discerned "a contrary spirit then dominant and thinly diffused over the surface of society which rejected the philosopher because they thought he was too much of that popular stamp." William Smith, despite his temporary disgrace during the Revolution, still wielded great influence among the literati of Pennsylvania, and the conservative political forces of the state had more in common with Smith's aristocratic pretensions than with Franklin's theories of political democracy. According to Mrs. Logan, Franklin's visitors consisted chiefly of foreigners of the first distinction and a few of his old and tried friends.

Franklin, with his usual openness concerning motivations and sentiments, admitted that he sometimes indulged his own vanity by contemplating the esteem in which he was held and by recounting the near unanimity of his election to the presidency. At the same time he was embarrassed at receiving lavish compliments in public. At a meeting of the American Philosophical Society in February 1786, Benjamin Rush caused him acute discomfort by delivering a "most extravagant encomium" which Franklin prevailed upon him to omit in the published version of his discourse.

Perhaps Franklin thought that it would be more fitting for Rush to save his panegyric for a funeral elegy. He had no way of knowing that his Philosophical Society would have the incredible bad taste of appointing as official eulogist his most bitter enemy, Parson Smith.

✳❖✳❖✳❖✳❖✳❖✳❖✳❖✳❖✳❖✳❖✳❖✳

35. The Rising Sun

THE winter began auspiciously for Franklin following upon his election to a second one-year term as president of Pennsylvania in October 1786–this time with no dissenting voice but his own. He predicted to Jane in December that the season would be severe, and she replied in the following March that his prediction had "held Invariable." In April 1787 he received notification that he had been chosen a delegate to the Federal Constitutional Convention, and for the rest of the year the Constitution was to be his primary concern, along with his health, his house, and his business affairs.

In April, because of the illness of the vice president of Pennsylvania, Franklin was extremely busy with state business, but he nevertheless took time out to write a dozen letters to his friends in France, introducing Thomas Paine, who was going to Paris to promote his iron bridge.

He assured Le Veillard that the stone, although grown heavier, did not give him any more pain than when at Passy, ascribing his good fortune to his temperate life, abstinence from wine, and daily exercise with dumbbells. With resignation he affirmed, "people who live long, who will drink of the cup of life to the very bottom, must expect to meet with some of the usual dregs." In addition to the maladies of the stone and the gout, he now counted old age as a third. He confided to George Whatley, "I am grown so old as to have buried most of the friends of my youth, and I now often hear persons whom I knew when children, called *old* Mr. such-a-one, to distinguish them from their sons now men grown and in business." Reverting to a favorite metaphor, he added, "I seem to have intruded myself into the company of posterity, when I ought to have been abed and asleep." Yet, he continued, if he had departed at seventy, he would have lost some of the most active years of his life, those occupied with "matters of the greatest importance," including the Constitutional Convention.

His scientific friend, Buffon, who was also afflicted with the stone, wrote to ask about Franklin's methods of treatment. Franklin recommended taking blackberry jelly before retiring at night, a remedy, he surmised, efficacious primarily because of the boiled sugar it contained.

When Franklin began construction of the library attachment to his house, he also built two houses on adjoining property for rental purposes, one intended as a printing office for Benny Bache. "Building," he explained, "is an old Man's Amusement. The Advantage is for his Posterity." The library was on the second floor of the addition, the first floor being devoted to a dining room large enough to seat twenty-four persons. Each room had windows at the north and south sides, the dining room boasting a handsome fireplace in the middle decorated with marble slabs. One of Franklin's household appliances greatly impressed George Washington—a mangle or machine for pressing flat laundry instead of ironing. Other unusual devices included a glass machine for illustrating the circulation of the blood and a rolling press of Franklin's own invention to make copies of letters in two minutes. He had also invented for his comfort a large armchair with a fan attached to a lever at its base, which he could move with his foot. In summer he sat in his garden, rocking and fanning.

Franklin used his house as the meeting place for a number of discussion groups, including the Society for Political Inquiries, founded in February 1787 with Franklin himself as president. Although the society had forty-two members, its meetings were only sparsely attended, since one of their number monopolized the proceedings with his incessant talking. Franklin as usual "said but little" after a subject was broached. The society, nevertheless, provides the clue to his whole political philosophy, its name suggesting that his pragmatic approach to politics represented, instead of mere expediency, the application of common sense and disciplined thought to individual problems.

Since the society was organized only a few months prior to

the Federal Constitutional Convention and some of its members were delegates, its deliberations probably foreshadowed those of the larger body. Franklin, as an elder statesman, elected to the convention primarily for his great prestige, looked upon it as parallel to the Assembly of Notables then being convened in France and considered himself and La Rochefoucauld, named to the French assemblage, as fulfilling similar destinies. Franklin had nothing to do with the skirmishes between economic radicals and conservatives which led up to the American gathering.

In some ways his attendance at the convention was a repetition of the days of the Continental Congress of 1775–1776. Many of his colleagues in the earlier congress were back with him, and they met in the same surroundings—the "long room" of the State House in Philadelphia, or Independence Hall. Hours of meeting were irregular, but usually between ten and four. Although Franklin was not present at all the sessions, he claimed at the end of the convention that he "attended the Business of it 5 Hours in every Day from the Beginning, which is something more than four Months." He had been the oldest member of the Continental Congress; now twelve years later he was again the oldest and, with the possible exception of Washington, the most eminent and respected.

On 16 May 1787, Franklin gave a dinner for the delegates who had arrived by then, a number, because of the bad weather, probably below the twenty-four-seat capacity of his dining room. For the occasion, he opened a cask of porter which had been sent him by Thomas Jordan, a London brewer. The company accorded the beverage "the most cordial reception and universal approbation," and Franklin characterized his fellow delegates as "Men of Character for Prudence and Ability." If good were not to come from the convention, he predicted, then it must produce harm, "as it will show that we have not Wisdom enough among us to govern ourselves" and strengthen the opinion "that popular Governments cannot long support themselves."

Because of his re-emergence as a national political figure, the newspapers burst out with lively new panegyrics on Franklin, which made him seem to his sister Jane "like a young man of Twenty-five." By an odd coincidence, this is exactly what William Pierce, delegate from Georgia, wrote about Franklin after viewing his performance in the convention. "He is 82 years old, and possesses an activity of mind equal to a youth of 25 years of age." In the rest of his sketch, Pierce had no doubt that Franklin was "the greatest phylosopher of the present age," but he left it to posterity to determine what claim he had as a politician. "It is certain that he does not shine much in public Council—he is no Speaker, nor does he seem to let politics engage his attention. He is, however, a most extraordinary Man, and tells a story in a style more engaging than anything I ever heard."

One of the stories which Franklin told outside the convention—and which he had told many times previously in France—concerned the volubility of the French nation. He had already remarked in print that in many polite companies "if you do not deliver your Sentence with great Rapidity, you are cut off in the middle of it by the Impatient Loquacity of those you converse with, and never suffer'd to finish it." In his story, a French bishop, coming into a company where another ecclesiastic was talking so long and incessantly that the newcomer could not get in a word of his own, finally cried out, "He is lost, if he spits."

At the opening session, Friday, 25 May, Washington was unanimously elected president of the convention. Franklin was supposed to make the nomination but was kept from attending by the bad weather. James Wilson moved that a secretary be appointed and nominated William Temple Franklin; while Alexander Hamilton nominated Major William Jackson (the young man who as Laurens's secretary in 1781 had annoyed Franklin by his blustering). Jackson was elected, perhaps in part because Temple's grandfather was absent.

Franklin was present at the next session, on the following Monday, but had little to say until 2 June, when he intervened to ask for debate on the subject of a single executive, stating that it was a point of great importance. Later in the day, Franklin made his first speech—a proposal that the executive receive no salary or reward whatsoever. Franklin had his remarks already written out and had them read by a colleague, his practice for all long speeches. "Occasionally, however, he would make short extemporaneous speeches with great pertinacity and effect." Franklin's notion that the executive should serve without salary goes back at least as far as his days as a London agent, and he even incorporated it in a codicil to his last will. In his speech in the convention he used arguments drawn from a letter to Strahan, 16 February 1784, some of them expressed verbatim. As before, his main point was that posts of honor should be kept separate from places of profit. Otherwise, he was fearful that the government would eventually turn into a monarchy. Franklin may have been thinking along these lines when a lady asked him after one of the sessions, "Well, Doctor, what have we got, a republic or a monarchy?" "A republic," he replied, "if you can keep it." In April, he had observed to some Europeans, "only a virtuous people are capable of freedom. As nations become corrupt and vicious, they have more need of masters." Franklin's motion against salaries was postponed for later consideration, less from conviction of its expediency than out of respect for its author, and it was never recalled.

On this same day, Benjamin Rush reported to Richard Price:

Dr. Franklin exhibits daily a spectacle of transcendent benevolence by attending the Convention punctually and even taking part in its business and deliberations. He says it is the most august and respectable Assembly he ever was in in his life, and adds, that he thinks they will soon finish their business, as there are no prejudices to oppose, nor errors to refute in any of the body.

Later in the convention, Franklin advocated moderate salaries for members of Congress and judges, although allowing for increases to judges as the country became more populous. He preferred a plural rather than a single executive and a single rather than double legislature and opposed granting the power of veto to the executive. All three measures placed greater control in the hands of the people and represented Franklin's further reaction away from the monarchical concentration of power in Great Britain.

Although the records of the convention are silent on the point, it is probable that he introduced in the sessions a parable against a plural legislature which he is known to have used as an argument two years later in regard to the Pennsylvania constitution. A snake with two heads and one body

was going to a Brook to drink, and in her Way was to pass thro' a Hedge, a Twig of which opposed her direct Course; one Head chose to go on the right side of the Twig, the other on the left; so that time was spent in the Contest, and, before the Decision was completed, the poor Snake died with thirst.

Franklin told a version of this parable to a clergyman with biological training, Manasseh Cutler, who visited him in his garden, 13 July, after the convention had adjourned for the day. Franklin showed him a zoological curiosity he had received not long before, "a snake with two heads, preserved in a large vial," which he thought was not a freak but a distinct genus. Franklin speculated on the plight of the snake if the heads should choose to go on opposite sides of the stem of a bush and was "going to mention a humorous matter that had that day taken place in Convention, in consequence of his comparing the snake to America," when some other delegates who were present reminded him that everything in the convention was to be kept a profound secret.

Yet it was Franklin's common humanity which chiefly impressed his visitor. Cutler had expected him to exude grandeur and majesty and felt in entering Franklin's house as though he were "to be introduced to the presence of an European Monarch." But his ideas were changed when he saw "a short, fat, trunched old man in a plain Quaker dress, bald pate, and short white locks, sitting without his hat under the tree." Franklin rose and welcomed Cutler with warm affability. Subsequently he showed his guest a huge volume on botany in his library, and they spent two hours examining it, Franklin all the time lamenting that he had not studied this science in early life and encouraging Cutler in the research the latter had planned for the future. Cutler was delighted with Franklin's extensive knowledge as well as his "incessant vein of humor, accompanied with an uncommon vivacity, . . . as natural and involuntary as his breathing." Franklin's gracious reception of Cutler illustrates another facet of his natural feeling for other people. In the company of a botanist, he showed greatest interest in botany; in discourse with a theologian, it was always theology which came to the fore.

Debates in the convention proceeded with harmony and evenness until the question of the proportion of representation for the various states arose, and then some tempers flared up. Franklin gently chided the delegates, 11 June, warning that "positiveness and warmth on one side, naturally beget their like on the other." Then he proposed a compromise that the states be equal in representation but that the larger ones bear a larger proportion of the expense of government.

In the spirit of his plea for coolness and even temper, Franklin made his more famous proposal, 28 June, that the convention be opened every morning with prayers. Gloomily interpreting the continual conflicts and discord, particularly between small states and large ones, as "a melancholy proof of the imperfection of the Human Understanding," Franklin wondered why the assembly had never called in the aid of "the Father of lights to illuminate our understandings." Remembering the daily prayers he had heard in the same room at the outset of the Revolution, he attributed America's success in that contest to the gracious intervention of a superintending providence and moved that henceforth one or more of the clergy of the city be requested to implore the assistance and blessing of heaven each morning before the regular business. But as Franklin tersely noted on the manuscript copy of his speech, "The Convention, except three or four persons, thought Prayers unnecessary," and the motion was allowed to drop by adjournment. Despite the refusal of the convention to ask for divine intercession, Franklin nevertheless affirmed in print a year later his belief that the convention had been to some degree "influenc'd, guided and governed" by Providence. In philosophy, Franklin's proposal conformed with the fundamental deism he had upheld throughout most of his life.

In later debates, Franklin revealed his international point of view by opposing the requirement of fourteen years' American citizenship for eligibility to Congress. Citing the past friendship of Europeans to America, Franklin preferred four years. "When," he argued, "foreigners after looking about for some other Country in which they can obtain more happiness, give a preference to ours, it is a proof of attachment which ought to excite our confidence & affection." In the more important issue of property qualifications for holding office, he observed that the Constitution would be much read and discussed in Europe and that if it should greatly favor the rich it would damage America "in the esteem of the most liberal and enlightened men" and discourage the common people from emigrating. He had previously advocated a broad suffrage without property restrictions. Despite the sternness of his economic opinions, Franklin now showed a new sympathy with the masses. In the words of an eyewitness, he "expressed his dislike of every thing that tended to debase the spirit of the common people."

When the work of the convention was finished, but doubt existed as to whether the delegates would agree to accept as a whole the document which they had constructed point by point, Franklin made a speech, 17 September, which succeeded in uniting the dissident elements. Beginning with the admission that he had many times changed his own opinion on important subjects as a result of more information or fuller consideration, he declared that increasing age had convinced him of the wisdom of doubting his own judgment and considering that of other people. Admitting that the Constitution as devised was not perfect and that it contained some provisions which he did not at present approve, he still doubted whether any other available group of men could make a better one. Any assembly of wise men, he affirmed, inevitably incorporates "all their prejudices, their passions, their errors of opinion, their local interests, and their selfish views." For this reason, he was amazed that the present assembly had devised a "system approaching so near to perfection as it does," and he consented to it "because I expect no better, and because I am not sure, that it is not the best." Since any objections to it on the part of the delegates if they became known on the outside might prevent its being generally adopted, he urged each of his colleagues to follow his example of doubting "a little of his own infallibility" and put his name to the document.

It had been concerted in advance that Franklin, as the most revered name in the assembly, should make this plea for unanimity and that, instead of having each member sign as giving his individual assent, the formula should run, "by the unanimous consent of *the States*." Despite this loophole for dissenting members to sign without committing their personal approval, two delegates from South Carolina still voted in the negative and kept the instrument from receiving unanimous approval.

While the delegates were signing, Franklin drew the attention of two of his colleagues to an image of the sun in a painting behind Washington's chair and observed (virtually his only venture into art criticism), "that Painters had found it difficult to distinguish in their art a rising from a setting sun." Throughout the sessions, he continued, he had frequently observed the sun behind the President and along with the vicissitude of his hopes and fears had not been able to tell whether it was rising or setting. "But now at length," he concluded, "I have the happiness to know that it is a rising and not a setting Sun."

When the convention was all over, Franklin wrote to his sister that the forming of a scheme to "accommodate all the different Interests and Views was a difficult Task." He had some doubts that the Constitution would be received by the states with as much unanimity as it had been accorded in the assembly, but he concluded philosophically, "We have . . . done our best, and it must take its chance."

After the Constitution had been printed, Franklin sent copies to his friends in Europe, including Le Veillard and La Rochefoucauld, the earlier translator of state constitutions. He suggested to Ferdinand Grand, a French banker, that, if the plan succeeded, it might serve as a model for a European Federal Union or single Grand Republic comparable to the historical dream of Henri IV.

On the last day of October (1787), Franklin was elected for the third time president of Pennsylvania, once again his own vote being the only negative one cast. Apparently this mark of loyalty and affection from his fellow citizens touched him more than the respectful attention of his colleagues in the convention. He confided to his sister that "this universal and unbounded confidence of a whole people flatters my vanity much more than a peerage could do."

36. The Setting Sun

THE sun which Franklin observed on the painting in Independence Hall may have symbolized a new day for America, but it represented a setting sun for Franklin himself. His public life had now virtually come to an end, even though his conduct in the convention had gained him "much credit within doors," and he had been re-elected president of Pennsylvania. He realized that henceforth he would be more of a figurehead than dynamic leader.

Physically Franklin's participation in the convention had been a last burst of energy, which carried over for the rest of the year. His friends attributed his more vigorous appearance to "the daily Exercise of going & returning from the Statehouse." But early in January 1788 he sprained his wrist and right arm up to the shoulder by a fall on the stone steps leading into his garden. For a time writing became extremely difficult, and he never again recovered his full strength. At the time of his fall, Franklin's scurvy or "cutaneous malady" was as bad as it had ever been in the past, though it practically disappeared a few months later concurrently with an acute swelling which came upon him as the consequence of a new seizure of gout. Franklin wondered whether there could be any connection between the appearance of one malady and the decline of the other.

By June 1789, the pain of the stone had become so extreme that he was forced to take opium to relieve it. The drug gave him temporary ease but took away his appetite and interfered with his digestion. In September he described himself as "totally emaciated" with little remaining "but a Skeleton covered with a Skin." He had completely abandoned faith in any remedy for the stone but had established himself in the "palliating system" which made life "at least tolerable." Even though he had spent the last two years in excruciating pain, he was pleased to have lived them through to see the origin of the new government.

On one occasion when he was particularly exhausted by pain, James Madison, paying him a visit, expressed the hope that he was using opium as sparingly as possible since frequent doses would undermine his constitutional strength. Franklin replied that he was well aware of the deleterious effects of opium, "but he had no other remedy; and thought the best terms he could make with his complaint was to give up a part of his remaining life, for the greater ease of the rest."

In July 1788, Franklin completed his will, adding a codicil in the following year. He identified himself first as printer, then as former minister to France, and last as incumbent president of Pennsylvania. By and large he listed his bequests in conventional order, according to consanguinity rather than the degree of affection in which he held his legators. His son William, therefore, headed the list, but his legacy was modest, comprising all of Franklin's books and papers already in his possession, all his outstanding debts to his father, and all his father's claims to land in Nova Scotia, the last very tenuous properties indeed. As a final display of displeasure toward his son, Franklin announced that "the part he acted against me in the late war, which is of public notoriety, will account for my leaving him no more of an estate he endeavoured to deprive me of." All was not forgiven, despite Franklin's precept to "forbear resenting injuries so much as you think they deserve."

To his daughter Sarah and her husband, Franklin left nearly all his real and personal property in Pennsylvania, together with Louis XVI's miniature, set with its 408 diamonds. Characteristically, Franklin requested that his daughter "would not form any of these diamonds into ornaments either for herself or daughters, and thereby introduce or countenance the expensive, vain and useless fashion of wearing jewels in this country; and those immediately connected with the picture may be preserved with the same." Perhaps Sally's strain of worldliness explains why Franklin seems never to have lavished the same affection upon her as upon some of his other relations. As though to vindicate her father as a prophet, Sally promptly sold all of the jewels after his death except "those immediately connected with the picture" and set off for Europe with her husband in 1792.

Realizing that his sister Jane would not be likely to survive him for long, Franklin left her only the house she occupied in Boston as well as fifty pounds a year for life. To William Temple, he left 3,000 acres of land which had been granted by the State of Georgia as well as the bond representing the money Franklin had lent him in Southampton. To Benny Bache, whose future was already assured by the bequest to his parents, Franklin left all his types and printing materials in Philadelphia, worth nearly one thousand pounds. Finally, Franklin requested that his body be "buried with as little expense or ceremony as may be." This last is not necessarily a reflection of the Poor Richard philosophy of thrift but an expression of modesty and simplicity, not unusual at the time.

In the codicil to his will, Franklin repeated his "fixed political opinion . . . that in a democratical state there ought to be no offices of profit" as a prologue to describing his project to turn over his salary as president of Pennsylvania to develop endowment funds for the cities of Boston and Philadelphia. The accumulated salaries were to be lent out at interest to "young beginners in business," and after the passing of a century the accumulated profits were to be spent in public works. Franklin attributed this scheme to the reading in France of a tract on the virtue of saving, *le Testament de Fortuné Ricard* by C. J. Mathon de la Cour, and he had written to the author, 18 November 1785, acknowledging the hint. The French work was itself an imitation of *The Way to Wealth,* and in both France and England it was thought to be from Franklin's pen. Before leaving France, Franklin had written to Vaughan, disclaiming authorship, as well as to Price, describing it as a vigorous and pleasant illustration of Price's doctrine "of the immense power of compound interest." "Projects that may be absurd in a Man to undertake for himself," he remarked to Vaughan, "may nevertheless be wise in States, they being long-liv'd Animals."

After filing his will, Franklin made a final attempt to obtain compensation from Congress for his expenses in France. Three years after submitting his accounts, he had still been paid only

BENJAMIN FRANKLIN

his bare salary. To make matters worse, some unfriendly newspapers were insinuating that he was indebted to the government
for large sums, and in Congress itself whispers were heard
associating him with the "lost million" of Beaumarchais. To stir
the memories and consciences of the members of Congress,
Franklin hopefully submitted a *Sketch of the Services of B.
Franklin to the United States of America*. Here he summarized
his duties as colonial agent in London, his journalistic propaganda at that time, his encouragement of the Revolution, his
official journeys to Boston in 1775 and to Canada in 1776, and,
most important, his services in France beyond the duties of
commissioner and plenipotentiary. He had served as consul, as
judge of admiralty, as merchant, as his own secretary (until
aided by William Temple Franklin), and, most fatiguing of all,
as comptroller for the entire European financial operation.
During this confining business, for eight years, he was deprived
of his annual vacation trip for exercise, a deprivation to which
he attributed his stone and gout.

Aware that Arthur Lee and John Jay had both been rewarded with appointments on their return from Europe, he
informed Charles Thomson, 29 December 1788, of his expectation that Congress would at least grant him some tract of
western land. The only favor he had officially asked of Congress
was the appointment of William Temple Franklin as secretary
of the Commission for Treaties, and this had been refused.
Despite the flag-waving on Franklin's return to the United
States, Congress certainly had not been unduly appreciative.
But since Arthur Lee was a member of the treasury board and
his brother, Richard Henry Lee, a member of Congress, perhaps nothing more could have been expected.

Thinking about his will probably reopened the wound
caused by Franklin's separation from his son, for at the time he
was making it out he congratulated an old Boston friend and
fellow punster, Mather Byles, only a few months younger than
Franklin himself, on having a daughter at hand to care for him
with filial attention. Franklin had a few words of praise for his
own daughter, "the Comfort of my declining Years," but many
bitter ones about his son, who "estrang'd from me by the Part

he took in the late War, . . . keeps aloof, residing in England, whose Cause he *espous'd;* whereby the old Proverb is exemplified:

> My Son is my Son till he take him a Wife;
> But my Daughter's my Daughter all Days of her Life."

Rarely did Franklin evince the same affection for his daughter that he had shown for his grandsons in France or for his infant son Francis. As his warmest tribute to Sally in the year before his death, he could remark merely, "I have seven promising grandchildren by my daughter, who play with and amuse me, and she is a kind attentive nurse to me when I am at any time indisposed."

In the last year of his life, he encouraged his little granddaughter to study her lessons at his bedside, sitting on a stool and writing out her words to learn spelling. He made her look in the dictionary for the meaning of all words she did not know, and when her attention lagged, he would say, "Debby, is not that line of spelling ready yet?" When she was diligent, he rewarded her with a spoonful of the fruit jelly which he kept constantly at his bedside for the relief of the stone.

Franklin still concerned himself about harmony in his family and was particularly anxious that his sister Jane keep on good relations with Jonathan Williams, their nephew, and Jonathan Williams, Jr., their grandnephew. If anything was amiss in their relations, he admonished his sister, 3 August 1789, "I should have concluded that it was your Fault: for I think our Family were always subject to being a little Miffy." Franklin added a little family homily concerning some of the Nantucket Folgers whom he had invited to dine in the preceding year when they were visiting Philadelphia. "Their Answer was that they would — if they could not do better." Franklin supposed they did better, as he wrote to Jane, "for I never saw them afterwards; and so had no Opportunity of showing my Miff if I had one."

Franklin felt constantly compelled to impress an optimistic philosophy upon his sister, especially in regard to the death which both were soon to face. "It may not be amiss to allow ourselves beforehand the enjoyment of some expected pleasure, the expectation being often the greatest part of it," he wrote 31 May 1788, "but it is not so well to afflict ourselves with apprehensions of misfortunes that may never arise." A year later, after hearing that Jane had suffered tearful apprehension concerning his health, Franklin gently rebuked her. "There are in life real evils enough, and it is time enough when the real ones arrive." In similar vein he told his stepniece that, in the comfortable intervals between his attacks of pain, he still amused himself as he had as a man of fifty, "Reading or Writing, or in Conversation with Friends, joking, laughing, and telling merry Stories."

Probably Franklin considered as his most important activity during these days the continuation of his memoirs, which he had been forced to delay for one exigency after another ever since 1771. Although in February 1788 he suggested to Le Veillard that he would be unable to resume work until he should give up the presidency in the fall, he actually took up his pen after completing his will and by 24 October had brought the story down to his fiftieth year, and he expected to complete it in a few months. The section covering his life after 1756, he told La Rochefoucauld, 22 October, would cover "more important Transactions" than the previous personal history, but he still felt that the earlier part "will be of more general Use to young Readers; as exemplifying strongly the Effects of prudent and imprudent Conduct in the Commencement of a Life of Business." He had in the interests of brevity, he told Benjamin Vaughan, 24 October, omitted all details not having "a tendency to benefit the young reader, by showing him from my example, and my success in emerging from poverty, and acquiring some degree of wealth, power and reputation, the advantages of certain modes of conduct which I observed, and of avoiding the errors which were prejudicial to me."

In December, when he had finally retired from all branches of public service and begun to feel a free man, he reported to the Abbé Morellet that the "calling past Transactions to Remembrance" in the writing of his life gave him the feeling of living his life over again.

It is to be noted that Franklin did not carry out his earlier thought of turning the last part of his autobiography into a vindication of his public career or use it as a device for gratifying his vanity. On 3 June 1789, he told Benjamin Vaughan that he found it "a difficult task to speak decently and properly of one's own conduct," and he felt the need of "a judicious friend to encourage me in scratching out." He even wondered whether it would be proper to publish his memoirs during his lifetime. In June he finally sent copies of his manuscript to the three European friends who had exhorted him to the task, Vaughan, Le Veillard and La Rochefoucauld, admitting that he had made no progress in the past six months. In his letter to Vaughan he gave advice on literary composition, particularly on method, paradoxically the one quality which in his memoirs he had accused himself of lacking in his own style.

Although Franklin deliberately kept from turning his memoirs into an *apologia pro vita sua* in any sense, he subsequently wrote a long narrative, *Observations Relative to the Intentions of the Original Founders of the Academy in Philadelphia,* which could be interpreted as self-vindication and could very well have fitted into his autobiography. Bearing the date June 1789, the work vindicated the philosophy of vernacular instruction in the English school, the educational philosophy which William Smith had ruthlessly defied during his control of the Academy. Because of Smith, Franklin had bitterly complained to Kinnersley in 1759 that the trustees had privately decided all the policies of the Academy without his knowledge or participation. Now thirty years later, after the Academy had evolved into the University of Pennsylvania, after the wrecker William Smith had been dismissed because of his Tory war record, and after all of the original trustees except Franklin were dead, he suddenly took up the battle once more. It is a mystery, never before even commented upon, that Franklin should take time to write about this apparently defunct issue at the very moment when his friends were imploring him to carry on his autobiography to encompass the great transactions of the latter part of his life. His *Observations* represent not only a statement of Franklin's personal recollections but a systematic search into the minutes of the Academy during the period when he had been out of the country. In other words, he had undertaken a laborious job of historical research. Why?

Could it be that Franklin realized that William Smith was attempting to regain his prestige as an educator and political leader and that Franklin took this final method to discredit his old enemy? Smith is not once mentioned by name in the *Observations,* although anyone familiar with the background of the Academy would have understood that he was being attacked by Franklin's charge that the history of the institution revealed "a constant Disposition to depress the English School in favour of the Latin." Yet on the surface, Franklin was writing merely to reinvigorate English instruction and to discredit Latin and Greek as useless adornments.

It is true that, in the summer of 1789, "some alterations in the System of Education pursued in the English school at the College were under consideration," and Franklin may have had no other motive than to communicate his experience and opinions. In his paper he assumed a degree of blame for "having too easily submitted to the Deviations from the Constitution, and not opposing them with sufficient Zeal and Earnestness" and characterized his observations as an attempt to make amends by "bearing Testimony against those Deviations."

Yet certain background developments in the University of Pennsylvania indicate that more was at stake than a debate over educational philosophy. In 1779 the old College of Pennsylvania (the descendant of Franklin's Academy) because of the Toryism of Smith and most of its trustees had been converted by an act of legislature into the University of Pennsylvania with John Ewing, a Presbyterian, replacing the disgraced Smith, and control being removed from the Anglican church. In September 1784 the former trustees of the College of Philadelphia launched a movement to have its charter restored under their control, and in March 1789 the legislature acceded to their wishes. Smith, ever since 1782, had been on the Eastern Shore of Maryland, serving as president of the newly created Washington College. In July 1789, the month after Franklin's *Observations,* he returned from exile to become once more Provost of the

University. It would seem quite plausible that Franklin had heard of Smith's imminent return and that he wrote his narrative either to head off his reappointment as Provost or at least to reduce his prestige. Despite the resumption of formal relations between Franklin and Smith early in the Revolution, Franklin's scrutiny of Academy records would have been enough to re-awaken Smith's consuming hatred. We shall see that it still existed after Franklin's death.

Although Franklin had retired from the political arena, he still retained a keen interest in the exciting events taking place in America and France. "We are making Experiments in Politicks," he told La Rochefoucauld approvingly, weighing the certainty of experimental knowledge against the dubiousness of theoretical, although he had some doubts concerning the risks involved in obtaining it. We remember that it had been Franklin's policy throughout his own political career to take advantage of situations as they arose rather than to attempt to enforce theoretical schemes. Reporting the gradual ratification of the Constitution to du Pont de Nemours, 9 June 1788, he observed that "we must not expect, that a new government may be formed, as a game of chess may be played, by a skilful hand, without a fault." The political game is based on chance rather than reason, or as Franklin put it, "the play is more like *tric-trac* with a box of dice."

For almost the first time in his adult life, Franklin now found himself remote from the printing world, the object of newspaper propaganda rather than an important force behind it. This may be the reason why, of the half-dozen pieces he wrote after the Constitutional Convention, two of them concerned abuses of the liberty of the press—personal accusation, detraction and calumny—abuses of which Franklin himself had recently been victim. One of his pieces, addressed to the *Pennsylvania Gazette,* complimented its editors on a fifty-year history of chaste conduct during which "scarce one libellous piece had ever appeared in it." Here Franklin went a little too far in self-commendation, for during the period of his editorship there had appeared many malicious pieces of personal accusation, although none from his own pen. The general impression now created by the press, he charged, is that "Pennsylvania is peopled by a Set of the most unprincipled, wicked, rascally, and quarrelsome Scoundrels upon the Face of the Globe." The great inconsistency in all of this, according to Franklin, was the abrupt change in public attitude as soon as a public figure died. "Tho' *living,* you give one another the characters of Devils, *dead,* you are all Angels!" Pennsylvania was "a good country *to dye in,* though a bad one to *live in."* Probably Franklin wrote this piece partly in retaliation to his own detractors.

In September 1789 Franklin addressed to the *Federal Gazette* a sardonic description of the "Supremest Court of Judicature in Pennsylvania, viz. the Court of the Press," condemning the reckless exercise of the journalistic power to "judge, sentence, and condemn to infamy, not only private individuals, but public bodies, &c. with or without inquiry or hearing." The only check he advocated for the power of the press or defense against abuse of its privileged position was "liberty of the cudgel" or physical retaliation—a remedy rather out of harmony with the Enlightenment philosophy of most of Franklin's pronouncements on public relations.

His caution against the press should not be interpreted as a conservative strain in his thought, however, any more than a series of remarks on the Pennsylvania constitution written a few weeks later, in which he expressed the hope that "our Representatives in the Convention will not hastily go into these Innovations, but take the Advice of the Prophet, *Stand in the old ways, view the ancient Paths, consider them well, and be not among those that are given to Change."* Those who quote this advice as an example of Franklin's distrust of "new and dangerous theories" quote it out of context, for it follows the most democratic statement Franklin ever made, a criticism of a proposal to establish property as a qualification for choosing members of one of the houses of the legislature, arrogantly denominated *upper.* This conception Franklin branded as an unwelcome "Disposition among some of our People to commence an Aristocracy, by giving the Rich a predominancy in Government."

Although Franklin's last public statements were critical of slavery, abolition sentiments in his career were never important. He took no stand whatsoever against slavery until relatively late in his life, and he never became a passionate opponent of the system. But he was president of the Pennsylvania Society for Promoting the Abolition of Slavery, which presented over his signature a memorial to the House of Representatives, 12 February 1789, Franklin's last public act. Also he signed a statement of the society, 9 November 1789, appealing for financial and moral support. Finally, he sent to the editor of the *Federal Gazette* a paper dated 23 March 1790, only twenty-four days before his death, ridiculing a speech in favor of the slave trade delivered in the House by James Jackson of Georgia.

In the same month, Franklin answered a direct question by the Reverend Ezra Stiles concerning his religious sentiments and his opinion of Jesus of Nazareth. Knowing that his statement would be given to the world, Franklin indicated that he believed "that the soul of Man is immortal, and will be treated with Justice in another Life respecting its Conduct in this." As to Jesus, he had doubts about his divinity but thought his "System of Morals" and religion "the best the World ever saw."

37. Death and Epilogue

SEVERAL of Franklin's contemporaries wrote accounts of his passage into the "sweet sleep of Death," but they are mutually contradictory. All we know for certain is that he died between ten and eleven at night on 17 April 1790. According to Richard Bache, his family was not prepared for the final moment since "he had not been long very ill." Polly Hewson was present but left no record of what took place, although she did describe in great detail a day during the previous summer in which she had read to Franklin Johnson's *Life of Isaac Watts*, while he was in great pain. Instead of lulling him to sleep, her reading stimulated him to recite several of Watts's poems, "a display of the powers of his memory and his reason."

Benjamin Rush circulated a similar account of Franklin's intellectual vigor.

A few days before he died, he rose from his bed and begged that it might be made up for him so that he might die "in a decent manner." His daughter told him that she hoped he would recover and live many years longer. He calmly replied, "He hoped not." Upon being advised to change his position in bed that he might breathe *easy*, he said, "A dying man can do nothing *easy*."

This account is apocryphal, since Rush added that Franklin asked in his will to have his printer's epitaph inscribed on his tombstone, a detail which is completely erroneous. Franklin's physician, Joseph Jones, reported that sixteen days before the end he was seized with "a feverish disposition" accompanied by an increasingly acute "pain in his left breast." Then five days before his death "the pain and difficulty of breathing entirely left him, and his family were flattering themselves with the hope of his recovery," when an impostume in his lungs suddenly burst. While he had power, he discharged the foreign matter, but as his power declined, he sank into a calm, lethargic state, immediately preceding the final moment.

Louis Otto, the French consul in New York, reported to his government that, a few minutes before his dissolution, Franklin "repeated these words founded on the religion that he had made for himself, *that a man is perfectly born only after his death.*" Possibly this quotation is based on a garbled version of Franklin's epitaph.

Franklin's funeral, "numerously and . . . respectably attended," took place on 21 April, but the formal eulogy was not delivered until 1 March of the following year. The man picked to prepare and deliver it was Franklin's deadliest and least-principled enemy, William Smith, chosen probably because he was both a clergyman and vice president of the American Philosophical Society. A worse choice could hardly have been made. It was particularly unfortunate since two of Franklin's real friends, who actually supplied Smith with biographical information for his lusterless speech, would themselves have been ideal for the task. One was Thomas Jefferson, very recently returned from France, a sincere admirer of Franklin's philosophy and political career; the other, Benjamin Rush, a lesser figure, but a practised and skilful orator.

Franklin's Philosophical Society, which was in charge of the ceremony, took "great efforts" to make the scene impressive. Virtually every notable in Philadelphia, including all the clergy and the entire national Congress, participated in the procession. But Smith's "eulogium" was exactly what one would expect from a mind balancing between indifference and animosity, an artificial, uninspired, rhetorical exercise, its insipidity the sole mitigation of its hypocrisy. Senator William Maclay considered it "trite and trifling." Yet it was the only public tribute to Franklin's memory which his countrymen could afford, even though such lesser contemporaries as James Bowdoin and Cotton Mather were each honored by at least a dozen printed funeral elegies. When Smith returned home after his empty oratory, his daughter remarked with great perception, "I don't think you believed more than one tenth part of what you said of old Ben Lightning-rod."

Franklin has been singularly unfortunate in some of the individuals destiny has appointed to be guardians of his reputation. When the House of Representatives met in New York on the day following Franklin's funeral, James Madison moved that its members wear mourning for a month, and the motion carried unanimously. On the next day, Charles Carroll made a similar motion in the Senate, and it was seconded by William Maclay of Pennsylvania. But to the latter's disgust, the coordinated efforts of the members who hated Franklin made it apparent that the motion would never carry, and his friends were forced to withdraw it. According to Maclay, a majority of the senators were hostile to Franklin for personal or political reasons.

Even George Washington refused to honor Franklin in death. Jefferson proposed to the President that "the executive department should wear mourning; he declined it, because he said he would not know where to draw the line if he once began that ceremony." Jefferson remonstrated "that the world had drawn so broad a line between him and Dr. Franklin, on the one side, and the residue of mankind on the other, that we might wear mourning for them, and the question still remain new and undecided as to all others. He thought it best, however, to avoid it."

As soon as the news of Franklin's death arrived in France, Mirabeau made a dramatic announcement in the National Assembly and proposed that the members wear mourning for three days. The gathering applauded with transport, wholeheartedly consenting to the tribute. Mirabeau's discourse, one of the most significant documents in the French Revolution, marks the first time in European history that the honor of state mourning had been accorded to a common citizen, one not a member of royalty. The gesture was actually and figuratively the precursor of the abolishment of aristocracy in France. The age of privilege in Europe had given way to the age of personal merit, and Franklin was the symbol of common humanity.

In the following weeks, a series of official eulogies was delivered in Paris, before the most eminent political and scientific bodies of the nation, each oration notable for its warmth and sincerity, in contrast to William Smith's pallid formality. The theme of these tributes was embodied in the decoration of a famous Parisian café which had been draped in black with the bust of Franklin placed under a pall between cypress branches and the single word VIR (man) inscribed at its base. One of the most eminent orators, Vicq-d'Azyr, secretary of the Royal Society of Medicine, opened his discourse 14 March 1791 with a pithy sentence which became almost immediately famous: "A man is dead, and two worlds are in mourning." Neither the orator nor his audience would have been able to comprehend the indifference of the American Senate or the American people.

In response to another motion in the French National Assembly a few weeks later, its president Sieyès addressed a long letter and a voluminous package to "The President of the American Congress" (a nonexistent title and position), transmitting the condolences of the Assembly as well as printed copies of the French funeral elegies. The arrival of the package in America created a delicate problem of protocol. Who was to receive and acknowledge it? Washington, President of the United States? Jefferson, Secretary of State? or Adams, Vice President of the United States (who also presided over the Senate but not the whole Congress)?

On 26 January 1791, the letter of Sieyès was communicated to the Senate, where it was received, according to Maclay, with an astonishing coolness and apathy. John Adams, still nurturing his jealous animosities, read the letter as presiding officer with ill-disguised distaste. Reflecting on both Franklin and the French Revolution, he read the official list of Franklin's distinctions, which "he chose to call 'titles,' and then said some sarcastic things against the National Assembly for abolishing titles." Maclay, as he listened, could not help picturing to himself the disappointment in store for the French patriots. Having warmly imagined the enthusiasm which should have been aroused in America by the reception of their letter and the announcement of the honors accorded to Franklin, they would be waiting impatiently for courteous and enthusiastic replies. But they would discover that the Congress, cold as stone, was embarrassed by their tribute, by Franklin, and by liberty itself.

Actually neither the Senate nor the House of Representatives acknowledged receiving the letter from the National Assembly. Washington answered as President of the United States and Jefferson wrote independently to express "the peculiar sensibility of Congress to the tribute paid to the memory of Benjamin Franklin," a phrase containing more politeness than truth.

Maclay's younger brother, a member of the Pennsylvania House of Representatives, introduced a motion in the state legislature, 14 February—no doubt at his brother's instigation—that a letter be sent to the president of the French National Assembly expressing "the high satisfaction" which the representatives derived "from the proceedings of that august body," the French Assembly, "who have paid so honorable a tribute to the memory of our late venerable president, Benjamin Franklin"—a reference to his three years as state leader. This motion passed, and the letter was sent.

Happily there were some Americans who regretted Franklin's death and responded to the sympathy of the French nation. But the majority of Franklin's countrymen seemed to share the apathy of the Senate if not the hostility of William Smith. Louis Otto reported, 12 December 1790, that "Franklin's memory has been infinitely more honored in France than in America. People are hardly susceptible to enthusiasm in this country—they praise and they blame coldly."

Probably even Franklin's greatest admirers, those such as Jefferson, Vaughan or La Rochefoucauld, failed to realize in detail the extent of his achievements. Even those who could appreciate his scientific and intellectual productions were not only incapable of estimating the value of his political and diplomatic services but for the most part completely unaware of them. Although Franklin's personal attachments were established originally by common intellectual or political interests, they developed into enduring friendships because of his individual charm—his manner of associating himself with the intimate concerns of those with whom he had contact.

When necessary, Franklin worked assiduously for his personal welfare as well as for his country, and he developed his intellect for practical ends as well as to satisfy his universal curiosity. At the same time, he revealed an almost childlike absorption in pleasure. Despite the impression created by his autobiography and prudential writings, few men of his time were more cognizant of convivial and fleshly delights. He found a Puckish joy in kicking over the traces and defying conventional Puritan ideals. Much as he praised the practical benevolence of such saints as Cotton Mather and Jonathan Edwards, he defied the moral rigor of Calvinism both in his writings and in his actions.

In society, he was shrewd, sophisticated and worldly, with little of the primitivism attributed to him in legend. As a man of letters, consistently displaying clarity and good sense, he virtually established an American style and an American literature.

The greatest intellectual puzzle of Franklin's life is found in his political philosophy—the contrast between some of his reactionary social concepts and his practical benevolent ethics. He opposed poor relief but worked to establish schools and hospitals. He emphasized thrift tirelessly and tiresomely in his writings yet refused to patent his own inventions. At issue was a conflict of values. He reflected the Puritan ethic of individual hard work for all classes of society and at the same time realized that widespread human comfort and dignity could not be obtained without joint action and social responsibility. Franklin probably did not realize the inconsistency in his political views, and, even if he had done so, he was devoted to the spirit of compromise rather than to formal consistency—a pragmatist in the best sense.

He believed, as he remarked in his autobiography, that "This is the age of experiments" and consequently that the new American nation was the result of experiments in government. In nearly every other area of thought, however, his theory preceded his practice.

In his general outlook on life, Franklin shared the philosophy of the Enlightenment, never better expressed than by his friend Abbé Morellet:

It is this ardor for knowledge, this mental activity which does not wish to leave an effect without seeking its cause, a phenomenon without explanation, an assertion without proof, an objection without a reply to it, an error without combatting it, an evil without seeking the remedy, a possible good without trying to attain it.

To succeeding generations, Franklin has been the symbol for many people of many different things: of the philosopher of the Enlightenment, of the universal genius of practical science, of the successful businessman, of the astute politician, and of the distinguished statesman. Admired by his own countrymen as an example of the rise from rags to riches, Franklin has been celebrated by the rest of the world for his moral and literary achievement, as the first man in American letters to acquire a genuinely international reputation.

Each one of Franklin's many careers represented only one phase of his rich and colorful personality. The secret of his success in each was his zest for life, his never-flagging curiosity, his easygoing disposition. He consistently preferred the simple to the ornate, the homely to the pretentious, the positive to the ethereal.

Despite his superior intellectual endowment, Franklin found his greatest enjoyment in the universal pleasures of life—home and fireside; friends and children; club and boudoir; drinking, joking, and love-making. In short, no matter how varied and successful his pursuits, he was in every sense a man above all. Or as du Pont de Nemours observed, there was not a feature of Franklin's "physiognomy or his life" which belied the inscription VIR under his portrait.

Acknowledgments

ALTHOUGH I have taken every advantage of the edition of Franklin's *Papers* now in progress at Yale University, most of the new materials which I present are not private letters but printed pieces in periodicals brought to light in Verner W. Crane's *Letters to the Press* and in my own articles.

The libraries in which I have done most of my work are the University of Maryland, Yale University, American Philosophical Society, Library of Congress, Bibliothèque Nationale and the British Museum. It is a pleasure as well as a duty to record my gratitude to these institutions and to the individuals serving them who have aided me in my research, particularly the present and past editors of the Franklin *Papers,* whose hospitality has been on the same high level as their learning. It is also a pleasure to acknowledge assistance, different in kind but equal in importance, extended to me through grants of the General Research Board of the University of Maryland.

My greatest personal debt is to the friends and scholars who have generously read parts of my work in manuscript and offered their advice and criticism. These include Adrienne Koch, Leonard W. Labaree, Helen Boatfield, Helene Fineman and Claude Lopez. Although these scholars have corrected errors and suggested additions, they do not by any means agree with all of my interpretations of events, and the view of Franklin's personality expressed in this book is entirely my own.

Notes

The chief printed collections of Franklin's writing are the following: *Papers,* Leonard W. Labaree *et al.,* eds. (New Haven, in progress) ; *Writings,* 10 vols., Albert Henry Smyth, ed. (New York, 1905–1907) ; *Franklin in France,* 2 vols., E. E. Hale and E. E. Hale, Jr., eds. (Boston, 1887–1888) ; *Benjamin Franklin's Letters to the Press, 1758–1775,* Verner W. Crane, ed. (Williamsburg, 1950) ; *Letters of Benjamin Franklin and Jane Mecom,* Carl Van Doren, ed. (Philadelphia, 1950) ; *Benjamin Franklin and Catharine Ray Greene,* William G. Roelker, ed. (Philadelphia, 1949) ; *Autobiographical Writings,* Carl Van Doren, ed. (New York, 1945) ; *Letters and Papers of Benjamin Franklin and Richard Jackson 1753–1785,* Carl Van Doren, ed. (Philadelphia, 1947) .

Any quotations from Franklin's writings not contained in one or another of these sources are identified either in the text or in the notes. Quotations from Adams, Jefferson and other major figures are from the standard editions of their works unless otherwise indicated.

The following abbreviations are used:

A.P.S.   American Philosophical Society
PAPS   *Proceedings of the American Philosophical Society*
PMHB   *Pennsylvania Magazine of History and Biography*

1

The material in this chapter is based on Franklin's autobiography supplemented by recollections of Pierre Cabanis, *OEuvres,* V, pp. 249 ff. The incident concerning family prayer is described in "Papers of Dr. Benjamin Rush," *PMHB* 29: 15–30. Information concerning Mather Byles appears in John Langdon Sibley, *Biographical Sketches of Graduates of Harvard University,* VII, p. 480. Franklin told the anecdote of his overeating to James Madison, who recorded it in his "Detached Memoranda," now in the Library of Congress and printed in *William & Mary Quarterly,* Series III, 1946, III, 536–540.

2

Franklin's physical appearance is described by Charles C. Sellers in *Benjamin Franklin in Portraiture,* pp. 3, 11. Daniel Fisher's account of Deborah's animosity toward William is printed in *PMHB,* 1893, XVII, 263–278. George Roberts's letter concerning Franklin's son is found in the

Charles Morton Smith mss (II, 32) of the Historical Society of Pennsylvania. Much new information on Franklin's family may be found in a University of Pennsylvania dissertation on microfilm by William Herbert Mariboe, *The Life of William Franklin,* 1962.

3

Paine's phrase describing Franklin's currency scheme appears in a manuscript "Plan for encouraging internal Prosperity," 31 July 1800, in the New York Public Library. Proof that the Junto discourse was intended to refute Franklin's necessitarian tract appears in a letter to Benjamin Vaughan, 9 November 1779, Jared Sparks, *Works of Benjamin Franklin,* I, p. 76. Franklin's visit to the Tuesday Club is described by Robert R. Hare in "Electro Vitrifico in Annapolis," *Maryland Historical Magazine,* 1963, LVIII, 62–66.

4

Franklin's burlesque of Smith's monologue is identified by A. O. Aldridge in "A Religious Hoax by Benjamin Franklin," *American Literature,* 1964, XXXVI, 204–209.

5

Franklin's philanthropic essays are identified by A. O. Aldridge in "Benjamin Franklin and the *Pennsylvania Gazette,*" *PAPS,* 1962, CVI, 77–81. See also the same author's "Franklin's 'Shaftesburian' Dialogues Not Franklin's," *American Literature,* 1949, XXI, 151–159. This article shows that a philosophical essay long thought to be Franklin's was taken from an English periodical, the *London Journal.*

6

The Leeds burlesque and the essay on paper currency are identified in *PAPS,* CVI, 77–81. Robert Newcomb's study "The Sources of Benjamin Franklin's Sayings of Poor Richard" (unpublished Maryland dissertation, 1957) is summarized in the Franklin *Papers,* I, 281–282. Franklin's doggerel poem is discussed by A. O. Aldridge, "A Humorous Poem by Benjamin Franklin," *PAPS,* 1954, XCVIII, 397–399.

7

The legend of Franklin's pudding-and-water meal appears in *PMHB,* 1924, XLVIII, 383. Logan's praise of Franklin appears in Franklin *Papers,* III, 185.

8

Franklin's observations on buttonhole making are described by Mrs. E. D. Gillespie, *A Book of Remembrance,* p. 17. Sally's list of weddings, 30 May 1765, is among the manuscripts of the A.P.S. Max Hall has included everything known about Polly Baker in his *Benjamin Franklin and Polly Baker.*

9

Collinson's letter to Colden on "the Polypus" is in the Colden *Papers,* III, 109, dated 30 March 1745, but internal evidence indicates that it should be dated a year later. Franklin's electrical discoveries are described by I. Bernard Cohen in *Benjamin Franklin's Experiments* and by J. A. Leo Lemay in *Ebenezer Kinnersley.* Franklin revealed his reaction to the compliments of Louis XV in a letter to Jared Eliot, 12 April 1753.

10

Jonathan Todd's remarks are printed in Franklin *Papers,* IV, 451. The significance of the essay on population is treated by A. O. Aldridge in "Franklin as Demographer," *Journal of Economic History,* 1949, IX, 25–44. Franklin's comparison of God to a mechanic appears in W. T. Franklin, *Memoirs* (London, 1818), I, 448.

11

Madison's praise of Franklin is reprinted in Max Farrand, ed., *Records of the Federal Convention,* III, p. 540. Franklin's relations with Caty Ray are sketched by William G. Roelker in *Benjamin Franklin and Catharine Ray Greene* (Philadelphia, 1949).

12

Braddock's letter praising Franklin, 5 June 1755, may be found in the London Public Records Office, America and West Indies, 82. C.O. 5.46. Sparks published a toned-down version in *Writings* of Washington, II, p. 78. Franklin's military career is traced by J. Bennett Nolan in *General Benjamin Franklin* (Philadelphia, 1936). The tribute of Franklin's officers appears in Jared Sparks, *Works of Benjamin Franklin,* VII, p. 111. Loudoun reported the conversation of Captain Kennedy, referring to Franklin's drinking, in his diary, 25 June 1757. I am quoting an extract from the original in the Huntington Library furnished by Mr. John R. Cuneo with the permission of the Library.

13

Franklin's scornful view of Thomas Penn is reported in T. Balch, *Letters . . . Provincial History,* pp. 100–111. Franklin's letter to Kinnersley is published in *PMHB,* 1889, XIII, 247–248. Whitfield J. Bell, Jr., gives full details concerning the Stevenson household in "All Clear Sunshine, New Letters of Franklin and Mary Stevenson Hewson," *PAPS,* 1956, XCX, 521–536. Strahan's letter to Deborah appears in Sparks, *Franklin,* VII, p. 157. Franklin's visit to Birmingham is described in *PMHB,* 1884, VIII, 403–406. Franklin's propaganda mill during his London sojourn is brilliantly described by Verner W. Crane in *Benjamin Franklin's Letters to the*

Press 1758–1775. Franklin's proposal to Pitt is described by A. O. Aldridge in "Franklin and Jackson on the French War," *PAPS*, 1950, XCIV, 396–397. Franklin's letter to Galloway, 17 February 1758, is in Yale University Library.

14

Thomas Penn's comment appears in Sparks, VII, p. 253. Franklin's travels are fully described by J. Bennett Nolan in *Benjamin Franklin in Scotland and Ireland* (Philadelphia, 1938). Strahan's comment on William Franklin appears in Sparks, VII, p. 158. Franklin's remark to Pitt about the proprietors was reported by William Franklin in a letter, now at Yale University, to Galloway, 26 August 1760. Maurice J. Quinlan describes "Dr. Franklin Meets Dr. Johnson" in *PMHB*, 1949, LXXIII, 34–44.

15

William described the trip to Holland in a letter to his sister printed in Carl Van Doren, *Franklin's Autobiographical Writings*, pp. 128–530. Whitehead's ironical verses on Smith are printed in Horace Wemyss Smith, *Life and Correspondence of the Rev. William Smith* (Philadelphia, 1880), I, p. 341. James Hamilton's caustic remarks are printed by Nolan, *op. cit.*, p. 103; those of John Penn in W. A. Duer, *Life of William Alexander*, p. 70. Cabanis indicated that Franklin applied his whistle parable to William. Franklin's feelings on returning to Philadelphia are described in Carl Van Doren, *Letters and Papers of Benjamin Franklin and Richard Jackson*, p. 92. William's letter on Deborah's aversion to the sea was printed by C. H. Hart, "Letters from William Franklin to William Strahan," *PMHB*, 1911, XXXV, 425–427. Franklin's western schemes are discussed in *Papers of . . . Jackson*, p. 207.

16

Franklin's letter to Strahan on the proprietary faction, 1 September 1764, is in the Yale University Library. John Dickinson's opposition to Franklin's nomination is printed in Sparks, VII, p. 269. Franklin's embarcation is described in an anonymous letter printed by J. Philip Gleason in "A Scurrilous Colonial Election," *William & Mary Quarterly*, 1961, XVIII, 83.

17

Franklin's currency scheme is printed in Crane, *Letters*, pp. 25–30. William's letter on wool, 10 May 1768, is in the A.P.S. Franklin's legendary bird is described in A. O. Aldridge, *Franklin and His French Contemporaries*, p. 204. Franklin wrote about honorary degrees for clergymen to Richard Price, 1 August 1767, Price Letters, *Proceedings of the Massachusetts Historical Society*, 1903, XVII, 263. Franklin's animosity toward Smith is described by H. W. Smith, *op. cit.*, I, p. 336. Deborah's letters to Franklin, 9, 13 October, 3, 7 November, 1765, are in the A.P.S. Her letter on standing firm in her own home, 22 September 1765, is printed in *Letters to Benjamin Franklin* (New York, 1859), p. 17. Edmund Burke compared Franklin to a schoolmaster, according to M. L. Weems, *Life of Benjamin Franklin* (Philadelphia, 1884), p. 197. Franklin's comments on the embellished version of his anecdote appear in Carl Van Doren, *The Letters of Benjamin Franklin and Jane Mecom,* p. 319. Michaelis described Franklin's visit in *Lebenbeschreibung von ihm selbst abgefasst* (Leipzig, 1793), pp. 102–111. William's letter denouncing Hall's defection is in the A.P.S. Polly's letter on William Temple's resemblance to his grandfather, 25 October 1784, is in the A.P.S.

18

Franklin's revamped currency scheme is described in Crane, *Letters,* pp. 25–30. Deborah's and William's letters to Franklin about Bache are in the A.P.S. Information about Margaret Ross appears in Mrs. E. D. Gillespie, *op. cit.,* p. 25. A bill for Franklin's beer exists in the A.P.S. receipted as paid 21 August 1770. Peale's account of Franklin in a compromising situation appears in Sellers, *op. cit.,* p. 81. Mazzei's account of Franklin's stove appears in *Memoirs of . . . Philip Mazzei,* H. R. Marraro trans., p. 165. Franklin's engineering activities are discussed by W. E. Lingelbach in "William Trent Calls on Franklin," *PMHB,* 1950, LXXIV, 43–50. Franklin's comment to Baskerville appears in Nichols, *Literary Anecdotes,* III, p. 455. Franklin's relations with the *Ephémérides* are described by A. O. Aldridge in "The Debut of American Letters in France," *French-American Review,* 1950, III, 1–23.

19

William Temple Franklin tells the same story of Franklin's visit with the printers, but gives no date and misprints *Hett's* for *Watts's, op. cit.,* I, p. 448. Proof that Franklin wrote *The Captivity of William Henry* is given by A. O. Aldridge in "Franklin's Deistical Indians," *PAPS,* 1950, XCIV, 398–410. Franklin repeated his cosmogonic myth of the Indian maiden in his later *Remarks Concerning the Savages of North America.* Franklin's letter to Richard Bache is in Gillespie, *op. cit.,* p. 20. He described his visit with Bache's sister in a letter to Deborah, 1 March 1769 in A.P.S. His letter to William about William Temple, 20 April 1771, is in A.P.S. Information about the memorial on silk culture is given by A. O. Aldridge in "Benjamin Franklin as Georgia Agent," *Georgia Review,* 1952, VI, 161–173. Franklin's court visit is described by W. E. Lingelbach, *PMHB,* 1950, LXXIV, 43–50.

20

Franklin's visit to a Negro school is described by Maurice J. Quinlan in "Dr. Franklin Meets Dr. Johnson," *PMHB,* 1949, LXXIII, 39. Sally's self-abnegating letter, May, 1770, is in A.P.S.

21

Franklin's journey is described by Jonathan Williams, Jr., in a manuscript in the Indiana University Library. Abbé Morellet tells the story of Franklin in the clothing factories and at Wycombe: Aldridge, *French Contemporaries,* p. 191. Franklin's trip to Ireland is described by J. Bennett Nolan in the work cited under Chapter XIV. King Frederick's orange-skin metaphor is quoted by Voltaire in a letter to Mme. Denis, 2 September 1751, Theodore Besterman, ed., *Correspondence,* XX, p. 43. Arthur Lee's charge against Franklin appears in Sparks, VIII, p. 58. Polly's letter on air baths, 2 November 1771, is in A.P.S. Strahan mentioned Franklin's proposal to Wharton in a letter to William Franklin, 3 April 1771, in A.P.S. Franklin's early relations with Priestley are described by Nolan, in the work cited above, p. 125.

22

The best contemporary description of Franklin's Cockpit ordeal is that of Jeremy Bentham in John Bowring, ed., *Works,* X, 59–60. Franklin's comments on leaving the Cockpit are recorded in *London Chronicle,* 8 May 1783, and Aldridge, *French Contemporaries,* p. 190.

23

Franklin's letter to Jonathan Williams, 28 September 1774, is in the Lilly Library of Indiana University. Quincy's impressions of Franklin are printed in *Memoirs of the Life of Josiah Quincy* (Boston, 1850), p. 250, along with Hillsborough's denunciation, p. 258, the record of Mrs. Stevenson's dinner, p. 317, and Franklin's advice against seeking French and Spanish aid, pp. 341–342. Richard Price reported Franklin's intention of returning to England in a letter to Josiah Quincy, Jr., April or May 1775, *Proceedings of the Massachusetts Historical Society,* 1903, XVII, 287. Franklin's opinion of Pitt is indicated in Aldridge, *French Contemporaries,* p. 203. M. L. Weems quotes Franklin's words on liberty in his *op. cit.,* p. 204. Priestley's account of Franklin's last day in England is quoted in Delaplaine's *Repository of the Lives and Portraits of Distinguished Americans,* II, p. 92.

24

Franklin's drinking bout with William and Galloway is described in P. O. Hutchinson, *The Diary and Letters of His Excellency Thomas Hutchinson,* II, pp. 237 ff. Franklin's activities in the Continental Congress are listed in Worthington Chauncey Ford, ed., *Journals of the Continental Congress,* VII, 79–80. His uninscribed bill is mentioned in *Affaires de l'Angleterre,* IX, cxxx. His opposition to army medical service is related in Madison's "Detached Memoranda" (see notes to Chapter 1) Nathanael Greene's comment appears in Bernhard Knollenberg, ed., *Correspondence of Governor Samuel Ward,* p. 105. That of Betty Greene appears in Louise

Brownell Clarke, *The Greenes of Rhode Island,* pp. 168–170. Franklin's homeward journey is described in Roelker, *op. cit.,* pp. 59–61. Mazzei's comment appears in his *Memoirs,* p. 224. The interview with Bonvouloir is described by Francis Wharton in *Revolutionary Diplomatic Correspondence of the United States,* I, pp. 333–334. Franklin's verbal changes are indicated by Carl Becker in *The Declaration of Independence,* pp. 100–104. Franklin's experience with the carpenter is described by Benjamin Vaughan in a document dated 6 May 1811 in the A.P.S. Franklin's opinion of bicameralism comes from *Thomas Paine to the Citizens of Pennsylvania on the Proposal for Calling a Convention* (Philadelphia, 1805), p. 23. Abbé Morellet's anecdote is repeated in Aldridge, *French Contemporaries,* p. 191. The meeting concerning the College of Philadelphia is described in Bird Watson, *Memoir of the Life of William White,* p. 69. The rejoinders of Adams and Franklin to Howe appear in Adams's *Diary* and in Howe's minutes of the conference in the New York Public Library, the latter of which is quoted in Carl Van Doren's *Benjamin Franklin,* p. 561.

25

A. O. Aldridge discusses Dubourg's part in the American Revolution in "Jacques Barbeu-Dubourg, A French Disciple of Benjamin Franklin," *PAPS,* 1951, XCV, 332–392. Franklin's comment to Rush on his appointment as commissioner appears in "Papers of Dr. Benjamin Rush," *PMHB,* 1905, XXIX, 15–30. Franklin's letter to William Temple, 28 September 1776, is in A.P.S. Vergennes's report of his interview with Franklin, 4 January 1777, is in Henri Doniol, *Histoire de la participation de la France à l'Établissement des États-Unis,* II, p. 114. Bailly's visit to Franklin is described in A. O. Aldridge, *Benjamin Franklin et ses contemporains français* p. 184. Franklin's physical appearance is described in Aldridge, *French Contemporaries,* pp. 43, 61; his joke with Turgot, *op. cit.,* p. 189; his joke about men and wigs in Philadelphia, in *Affaires de l'Angleterre,* III, clvi. Both William Temple Franklin and the Marquis de Chastellux told the story of Franklin's set speech in taverns: Howard C. Rice, ed., *Travels . . . by the Marquis de Chastellux,* 1963, II, p. 586. The manuscripts of the Chevalier de Berny are in the A.P.S. Franklin's joke on Stormont is told in *French Contemporaries,* p. 196. The fortunes of Ruault's dedication are portrayed *ibid.,* p. 64. The Comte de Lauraguais described Franklin in his cups in a letter to Vergennes, 20 September 1777, Stevens *Facsimiles,* XVIII, no. 1691. Franklin's theatrical expedition is described in *Courrier de l'Europe,* II, 162. His wearing of the symbolic coat is treated in *PMHB,* 1899, XXIII, 446, and 1905, XXIX, 27–28.

26

Franklin's opinion of the utility of elderly Frenchwomen appears in William Seward's *Anecdotes of Distinguished Persons* (London, 1798),

IV, p. 223. The manuscripts of Mme. Brillon are in the A.P.S. Background information is found in Aldridge, *French Contemporaries, passim.* Adams's warning against women-chasing ministers is in a letter to Elbridge Gerry, 3 September 1783, printed in Francis Wharton, ed., *Revolutionary Diplomatic Correspondence of the United States,* VI, p. 669. Adams's comment on French ladies is in a letter of 18 December 1778, quoted by Page Smith, *John Adams,* I, p. 415.

27

More details concerning Franklin and Voltaire are found in A. O. Aldridge, "Franklin and the Philosophes," *Trans. of First International Congress on Enlightenment* (Geneva, 1963), I, pp. 43–65. The remark of Mme. d'Épinay appears in Abbé Galiani, *Correspondance,* II, pp. 545–548. Documents concerning William Temple's brief service as aide-de-camp are found in the Paris Ministère des Affaires Etrangères: EU 9: 362–3; 10; 4–5. Sally expressed her desire for finery in a letter to her father, 14 September 1779, *Letters to Benjamin Franklin from His Family and Friends, 1751–1790* (William Duane, ed.; New York, 1859), p. 106.

28

Izard demanded Franklin's recall in a letter to Richard Henry Lee, 15 October 1780, quoted by Gerald Stourzh, *Benjamin Franklin and American Foreign Policy* (Chicago, 1954), p. 151. Gérard and Vergennes on Franklin's silence are also quoted by Stourzh, p. 153. Laurens's mission is discussed by A. O. Aldridge in *Man of Reason, The Life of Thomas Paine,* pp. 85–89. Jay's letter opposing Franklin's resignation is in Sparks, IX, p. 43.

29

Newcomb's study of "Benjamin Franklin and Montaigne" is in *Modern Language Notes,* 1957, LXXII, 489–491.

30

Sources for the peace negotiations are indicated in Stourzh, *op. cit.,* pp. 186–213. Vaughan's letters to Shelburne are printed in *Proceedings of the Massachusetts Historical Society,* 1903, XVIII, 406–438. His description of Adams's implacable hatred of Franklin and Vergennes is deleted in the printed version but may be seen in photostat at the William L. Clements Library of the University of Michigan.

31

The Chevalier de Keralio reported to Franklin, 21 March 1779, the complaint of Mme. Helvétius concerning his lack of consideration. The letter is in the A.P.S.

32

Franklin's circulating of the state constitutions is discussed in Aldridge,

French Contemporaries, pp. 67 and 244. The remark of Pierres is printed in Smyth, IX, p. 48. Franklin's membership in the Cincinnati is revealed by a notice in the *Pennsylvania Gazette,* 21 April 1790, requesting the members of the Cincinnati to assemble "with their order, and a black crape round the arm" and then proceed to the funeral of Dr. Franklin, "late of their Society." The comment of General Gates is reported in Gillespie, *op. cit.,* p. 21. Paine's report concerning Vergennes and the abolishing of privateering is in John Hall's diary, Moncure D. Conway, *Life of Thomas Paine,* II, p. 468. Turgot remarked on Adams's jealousy of Franklin in a letter to du Pont de Nemours, 18 March 1779; Gustav Schelle, ed., *OEuvres de Turgot,* V, p. 588. Adams commented on Franklin's publicity-seeking in a letter to James Warren, 2 December 1778, in *Warren–Adams Letters* (Massachusetts Historical Society, 1925), II, p. 72.

33

Franklin's relations with Cadet de Vaux are described in Aldridge, *French Contemporaries,* pp. 175–177. Adams remarked on Franklin's graciousness in a letter to Francis Dana, 4 November 1784, cited by Page Smith, *John Adams,* p. 616. Vaughan's correspondence reveals William Temple's intercession in his father's behalf: *Proceedings of the Massachusetts Historical Society,* 1903, XVII, 414. René des Genettes reported Franklin's medical discourse in *Souvenirs de la fin du XVIIIᵉ siècle,* I, p. 185. Franklin's letter to Vaughan on British anti-American propaganda, 3 January 1785, is in the A.P.S. Hugh Roberts's letter to Franklin is in the A.P.S.; Whatley's is in Sparks, X, p. 148. Franklin's view of his old age appears in Aldridge, *French Contemporaries,* p. 210.

34

Charles F. Jenkins tells the story "Franklin Returns from France—1785" in *PAPS,* 1948, XCII, 416–432. Jefferson's remark about Franklin's departure is in W. T. Franklin, *Memoirs,* I, p. 426. Sellers discusses the rivalry between Caffieri and Houdon, *op. cit.,* pp. 116–117. The farewell letter of Mme. Helvétius, directed to Le Havre, and that of Mme. Brillon, dated simply "10 juillet," are in the A.P.S. Franklin's remarks against incommodious luxury appear in Aldridge, *French Contemporaries,* p. 199. His comments on test acts appear in *Minutes of the Supreme Executive Council of Pennsylvania,* XIV, p. 576. His remarks on tobacco appear in "Papers of Dr. Benjamin Rush," *PMHB,* 1905, XXIX, 15–30. Paine's experiments are described in Hall's diary, Conway, *op. cit.,* II, p. 461. His remarks on Franklin's old age appear in *The Age of Reason,* Foner, ed., *Complete Writings,* I, 551. Franklin's rebuff of Fitch is described in Thompson Westcott, *Life of John Fitch* (Philadelphia, 1857), p. 147. Samuel Vaughan commented on Franklin's memory in a letter to Richard Price, 4 November 1786, *Proceedings of the Massachusetts Historical Society,* 1903, XVII, 355. Ellicott's remembrance of Franklin's shaving is quoted by Anne H. Wharton, *Social Life in the Early Republic,* pp. 54–55. Franklin's explanation to Paine of his library building appears in John Epps, *Life of John Walker* (London, 1840), p. 145. Franklin's garden air bath is described in T. J. Hogg, *Life of . . . Shelley,* 1906, p. 435. Temple's letter from Wilkes, 18 September 1785, is in the A.P.S. Deborah Logan included her reminiscences of Franklin in *Memoirs of Dr. George Logan . . .* (Philadelphia, 1901), pp. 38–39.

35

Washington described his impression of Franklin's mangle in his diary, 3 September 1787, *PMHB,* 1895, XIX, 189. Manasseh Cutler described some of Franklin's other inventions, *Life, Journals and Correspondence,* I, p. 268. Franklin's role in the convention is described in Max Farrand, ed., *Records of the Federal Convention,* 4 vols. Both Benjamin Rush and the Abbé Morellet record Franklin's story of the loquacious ecclesiastic. Cutler repeated the anecdote of the double-headed snake, *op. cit.,* I, p. 268.

36

Franklin's comment on opium appears in Madison's "Detached Memoranda" (see notes to Chapter 1). Franklin's letter to Vaughan on Fortuné Ricard, 5 March 1785, is in A.P.S. Franklin's attentions to his granddaughter are reported in Gillespie, *op. cit.,* p. 23.

37

Joseph Jones's report of Franklin's final illness is quoted by Whitfield J. Bell, Jr., in "Benjamin Franklin and the Practice of Medicine," *Bulletin of the Cleveland Medical Library,* 1962, IX, 62. Louis Otto's comment is quoted in Aldridge, *French Contemporaries,* p. 233. The remark of Smith's daughter appears in H. W. Smith, *Life . . . of the Rev. William Smith,* II, p. 344. The indifference of the United States Senate is recounted by William Maclay in his *Journal,* ed., Charles A. Beard, pp. 232–241, 340, 368. The French tributes are described in Aldridge, *French Contemporaries,* pp. 212–234, and Gilbert Chinard, *L'apothéose de Franklin.*

Index